EVOLUTION OF THE GREAT LAKES WATER QUALITY AGREEMENT

EVOLUTION OF THE GREAT LAKES WATER QUALITY AGREEMENT

Lee Botts *and* **Paul Muldoon**

Michigan State University Press • *East Lansing*

⊗ The paper used in this publication meets the minimum requirements of
ANSI/NISO Z39.48-1992 (R 1997) (Permanence of Paper).

Michigan State University Press
East Lansing, Michigan 48823-5245

Printed and bound in the United States of America.

11 10 09 08 07 06 05   1 2 3 4 5 6 7 8 9 10

LIBRARY OF CONGRESS CATALOGING-IN-PUBLICATION DATA
Botts, Lee.
Evolution of the Great Lakes water quality agreement / Lee Botts and
Paul Muldoon.
p. cm.— (The Dave Dempsey environmental studies series)
Includes bibliographical references and index.
ISBN 0-87013-752-2 (pbk. : alk. paper)
1. Water quality—Great Lakes (North America) 2. Water quality management—Great Lakes (North America) I. Muldoon, Paul R. (Paul Robert),
1956– II. Title. III. Series.
TD223.3.B68 2005
363.739'45260977—dc22
2005027197

The Dave Dempsey Environmental Studies Series
Cover design by Erin Kirk New
Book design by Sharp Des!gns, Lansing, MI
COVER ART: Satellite image of the Great Lakes from space. A protest banner
hoisted at the 1989 International Joint Commission biennial meeting in Hamilton, Ontario (used courtesy of Great Lakes United). Signing of the 1987 Protocol in Toledo, Ohio (used courtesy of the International Joint Commission).

🅖 green
press
INITIATIVE Michigan State University Press is a member of the Green
Press Initiative and is committed to developing and encouraging ecologically responsible publishing practices. For more information
about the Green Press Initiative and the use of recycled paper in book publishing, please visit *www.greenpressinitiative.org*

Visit Michigan State University Press on the World Wide Web at
www.msupress.edu

For Matthew, Benjamin, and Alex

... we humans who live in the Great Lakes Basin Ecosystem have been developing the basis for a viable Great Lakes Community ... by which I mean an identifiable bioregionally based society which can be defined in terms of shared values, interests, attitudes and behavior reflected in a set of social institutions.

Ron Shimizu, formerly with Environment Canada and an Associate
at the Institute of Environmental Studies at the University of Toronto

CONTENTS

FIGURES

PREFACE

THIS BOOK HAS BEEN WRITTEN IN THE SPIRIT OF BINATIONALISM ON WHICH the Great Lakes Water Quality Agreement is based. One of us is Canadian and the other American. Between us, we have been involved in the Great Lakes community that has sought implementation of the agreement throughout its history. Together we have tried to explain why we believe that any possibility of restoring and preserving the ecological integrity of the Great Lakes depends on the agreement and the community it created. We could not have completed the task without help and support from a multitude of sources.

This version of the agreement's history is based on a project that was initially sponsored by the Institute for International Environmental Governance at Dartmouth College. Results were published as a report in 1997 under the title *The Great Lakes Water Quality Agreement: Its Past Successes and Uncertain Future.*

Sections of the original report are included verbatim here with permission, but the history and the interpretation of its significance have been updated to April 2005. Jean Hennessey, Oran Young, and Konrad von Moltke at Dartmouth helped produce the 1997 report, with funding support by the Joyce, George Gund, Charles Stewart Mott, and Laidlaw foundations. We remain indebted to Oran Young for his insight and guidance in helping us to assess the success of the agreement and to Jean Hennessey for her inspiration and support for the original project. She is missed since her death in 2004. Support for this updated account has been provided by the Joyce and Johnson foundations, and by the Great Lakes National Program Office of the U.S. Environmental Protection Agency and Environment Canada, as well as the Canadian Environmental Law Association and the Lake Michigan Federation.

Many members of the Great Lakes community have also contributed by reading and commenting on the entire manuscript on a very tight deadline; by giving time to be interviewed, to answer questions, to discuss issues and points of view, and to provide documents and research materials; or by attending special events, such as the conference at the Wingspread Conference Center of the Johnson Foundation in Racine, Wisconsin, in January 2004. It is impossible to acknowledge their individual contributions here, but their names can be found in appendix 1.

Special gratitude is owed to John Jackson, longtime friend and colleague, for his accounts of experience with Remedial Action and Lakewide Management plans and the Lake Superior Zero Discharge Demonstration Project, and for his always friendly criticism. Glenda Daniel and Paul Botts assisted with the original report, and the staffs of the Lake Michigan Federation and the Canadian Environmental Law Association with this expanded version. Any errors are ours alone.

CHAPTER 1

THE CANADA/UNITED STATES PARTNERSHIP FOR THE GREAT LAKES

IN ALL FIVE OF THE GREAT LAKES, THE WATERS ARE AS BLUE AND BEAUTIFUL today as when they were discovered one-by-one by French explorers in the 1600s. They thought each new huge body of water was a sea, a system so large that it might provide the elusive Northwest Passage to the Pacific Ocean.[1]

They could see the beauty, and they may have suspected the wealth and power, that their discoveries could provide for future inhabitants of the region. They could not have imagined, and most people today do not realize, the pollution and other environmental threats that would cause Canada and the United States to form a partnership with the Great Lakes Water Quality Agreement to keep the waters clear in these freshwater seas.

The first Great Lakes Agreement was signed in 1972.[2] It was reviewed and renewed in 1978 and 1987. Another review is beginning in 2005. The purpose of this book is to consider results of the more than 30-year history of the U.S.–Canada partnership, and to ask what lessons can be learned to further the protection and enhancement of the future of the world's largest freshwater system.

Almost every description of the Great Lakes begins with the fact that together, Lakes Superior, Huron, Michigan, Erie, and Ontario, and their connecting channels, make up the largest freshwater system on earth. It is more than 1,200 miles from the head of Lake Superior to the mouth of Lake Ontario to the St. Lawrence River. Ships must travel 2,000 miles from Duluth, Minnesota, through the lakes and the river to reach the Atlantic Ocean. The nearly 300,000-square-mile watershed covers more land than England, Scotland, and Wales combined.[3]

In this water-rich region, about a third of the drainage basin is covered by the Great Lakes, and the rest contains hundreds of tributaries and inland

Features of the Great Lakes

- The five Great Lakes include Lakes Superior, Huron, Michigan, Erie, and Ontario, and their connecting channels, with 5,500 cubic miles (22,700 kilometers) of water.
- The Great Lakes drainage basin covers more land than England, Scotland, and Wales combined.
- The Great Lakes states have about 25,000 square miles of small lakes in addition to the Great Lakes, plus hundreds of miles of navigable rivers. Ontario has over 200,000 inland lakes.
- The lake system has over 10,000 miles (over 17,000 kilometers) of shoreline.
- The Great Lakes were formed by melting of glaciers that retreated about 10,000 to 15,000 years ago, and only receive 1 percent of new water each year in rain and snow.
- About 60 percent of North American steel and one-fifth of all manufacturing goods are produced in the Great Lakes region.
- The Great Lake states have almost 4 million registered recreational boats, or about one-third of the U.S. total.
- Year round, nearly 50,000 cubic feet of water per second is withdrawn from the lakes to generate electricity, for a total of 44,000 cubic meters annually.
- About 7,500 cubic feet a second, or 6,700 cubic meters a year, is used for drinking water for about 25 million people.
- About 70 to 80 percent of original wetlands in southern Ontario, and about 42 percent in Minnesota and 92 percent in Ohio have been lost since European settlement.
- The 1972 Great Lakes Water Quality Agreement was the first international agreement to restore and protect a large ecosystem across an international border.

SOURCE: Lee Botts and Bruce Krushelnicki, *The Great Lakes: An Environmental Atlas and Resource Book*, 3rd ed. (Chicago: Great Lakes National Program Office, U.S. Environmental Protection Agency, 1995).

lakes. The nearly 5,500 cubic miles of water in the lakes is enough to cover all of North America three feet deep. The 8,000 miles of shoreline border forests, wilderness, and cities like Toronto, Chicago, Cleveland, and Buffalo, as well as hundreds of smaller cities and towns. Rocky cliffs, miles and miles of sandy beaches, and what many consider the world's most beautiful sand dunes add their own beauty.

About 35 million people live within the Great Lakes basin, and 23 million depend on the lakes for water supply. The lakes generate wealth for the region through the concentration of industry, with one-fourth of the manufacturing capacity of the United States and massive production of electricity. Most use of the lakes for transportation is for distribution of bulk commodities and raw materials within the region, but the St. Lawrence Seaway provides access to ocean shipping. The estimated annual value of recreational boating, sport fishing, and tourism is up to $12 billion.

The Great Lakes are a unique natural resource, not just for North America but for the world. With the Great Lakes Water Quality Agreement and the Boundary Waters Treaty that preceded it, the United States and Canada are contributing a unique experience in environmental management that is derived from the character of the Great Lakes ecosystem and the special relationship that exists between these two countries.

Huge as they are, the Great Lakes are an essentially closed but interconnected system. They were formed by the melting of glaciers, and only one percent of their water is renewed each year by rain and snow. Only about the same amount flows out to sea. This means that pollution from the concentration of industries and people that live within the drainage basin mainly stays in the lakes.

Formerly it was thought that the pollutants to the lakes came mainly from point sources such as industrial discharges and sewage-treatment effluents. Then it was realized that they also come from nonpoint sources such as land runoff or the atmosphere.

The large surface area of the lakes makes them especially vulnerable to deposition of chemical contaminants such as polychlorinated biphenyls (PCBS) and heavy metals such as mercury. Many of the chemical contaminants come from within the region from incinerators, the burning of coal, and evaporation from landfills. Others arrive on air currents from as far away as Central America, and perhaps even farther, to be deposited into the waters of the lakes.

The lakes have also proved vulnerable to what is now called "biological pollution" by species that are not native to this region. The Europeans who settled the region deliberately introduced species such as brown trout, carp, and smelt. Construction of the Welland Canal to bypass the barrier of Niagara Falls in the nineteenth century made it possible for ocean species such as the alewife and the lamprey to spread from Lake Ontario into the rest of the lakes. In the twentieth century, ships began to bring species such as the zebra mussel—and to date, more than 150 other non-native species—from around the world in their ballast water. Scientists now fear that certain Asian carp may bring the worst threat of all to the natural ecosystem from the Mississippi River through the Sanitary and Ship Canal at Chicago.

The closed nature and the vulnerability of the Great Lakes, together with the joint U.S. and Canadian research and efforts to restore and preserve this system, are the reasons for the contributions of the Great Lakes Agreement to environmental management. It turns out that a systemic problem in the huge

---

Comparison of Characteristics of Canada and the United States

Population and Size: The United States has about 292 million people and Canada has about 30 million but both countries have nearly 4 million square miles of territory.

Origin: The two countries share a common history of discovery by European explorers. The United States was formed following rebellion against England and later acquisition of more land from Spain, Mexico, France, and Russia. Canada remained an English colony until becoming an independent commonwealth in 1867, after agreement was reached on location of the boundary with the United States

Economy: The diverse economies of both countries are based mainly on agriculture and manufacturing plus mining, timber production, and fisheries. The Canadian Gross Domestic Product (GDP) was approximately $934 billion and the U.S. GDP was approximately $10.45 trillion in 2002.

Relationship: Canada and the United States are each other's largest trading partner. Several treaties, including the 1909 Boundary Waters Treaty, intend to maintain the world's longest peaceful international border with 2 million border crossings in both directions each year prior to September 11, 2001. Canadians resent U.S. economic and political dominance, but tend to adopt U.S. culture. Most Americans are indifferent to Canada and tend to assume that Canadians share U.S. views and interests.

Similarities and Differences: Most Americans do not appreciate the two different systems of government and cultures of the two countries. Yet both are democracies with large natural resources and territories in relation to population and diverse populations with many recent

---

Great Lakes is nearly always a global problem. Not only has the agreement helped to identify and provide understanding of the causes of environmental problems, it is also helping to demonstrate solutions.

As explained in the history recounted here, the effort under the Great Lakes Agreement to control the excessive loadings of phosphorus that threatened Lake Erie and the other lakes was the first success in dealing with a major environmental problem across an international boundary. The agreement has also both identified the dangers of the presence of persistent organic chemicals to wildlife and human health, and continued to contribute to management concepts for preventing and controlling such environmental consequences. The ecosystem approach to environmental management and research that the U.S. Commission for Ocean Policy recommended for the oceans and coasts in April 2004 was first articulated in the Great Lakes Agreement in 1978.[4]

Behind the agreement and its results is the special relationship between

immigrants. English is the principal language of both, although Canada conducts official business in both English and French because of major concentrations of French culture.

Canada has a parliament, multiple political parties and a prime minister who serves only while he has the confidence of the parliament. Canada is a confederation where the provinces have more individual authority than the states in the United States, causing ongoing tension that is exacerbated by Quebec's repeated threats to seek independence. The provinces own most natural resources and about one-quarter of all Canadians live in Ontario, within the Great Lakes basin. Canadians generally accept authority, have a lower crime rate, and do not resort to litigation in the courts as much as Americans.

The United States is a federation with a constitution that sets up checks and balances between the executive, legislative, and judicial branches of government. The president is elected to head the executive branch for a set term of four years and a two term limit. The legislature has a Senate with two senators from each state and a House of Representatives with members in proportion to each state's population. The judicial branch can overrule both other branches. Essentially only two political parties can elect officials at any level of government. The presence of a stronger federal authority leads to ongoing tension over "states' rights". About 10 percent of the U.S. population lives within the Great Lakes watershed. Americans tend to challenge authority more in the name of individual rights, have a much higher crime rate, and are comparatively very litigious.

SOURCES: *http://www.cia.gov/cia/publications/factbook/rankorder/2001rank.html*; ; ; Lee Botts and Bruce Krushelnicki, *The Great Lakes: An Environmental Atlas and Resource Book*, 3rd ed. (Chicago: Great Lakes National Program Office, U.S. Environmental Protection Agency, 1995).

Canada and the United States. Understanding of this relationship is essential to understanding the history of the Great Lakes Agreement.

Canada and the United States have much in common, but also significant differences. Both are democracies with diverse populations, including many former and recent immigrants from around the world. Both have abundant natural resources and standards of living that are envied almost everywhere else. They share English as a language, though Canada is officially bilingual and nearly all official business in Canada is undertaken in both languages.

Their shared history was not always peaceful. Their foundations as nations began with exploration by European explorers—mainly French and English for Canada, but including Spain for the United States—and periods of colonialism. What is now Canada did not join in the American Revolution that led to organization of the United States as an independent country. Later, the original U.S. colonies acquired additional land from France, Russia, Mexico, and Spain, while Canada remained in English hands.

Even after Canada became a commonwealth rather than a colony, some American interests (including President Theodore Roosevelt) still thought that the "manifest destiny" of the United States ought to include the territory to the north. Finally, the United States accepted that Canada would remain independent, and the two countries resolved to be peaceful neighbors, leading to what is known in diplomacy as the "special relationship."

The relationship exists in spite of major differences. Canada has more total land, but the U.S. population is nearly ten times as large. Half of Canada's population lives in Ontario within the Great Lakes watershed, while the U.S. population is spread coast to coast with the center of the total in Kansas. Both countries are prosperous, but the United States has by far the largest economy in the world and is considered the last great power.

The political systems and the cultures are more different than most Americans realize. Canada has ten different provinces and three territories, with greater differences among them than exist for many of the 50 U.S. states. They are organized as a confederation, with the provinces having more independent autonomy than the states do in the United States. Both French and English are the official languages of Canada. It has several major political parties, while the United States has essentially only two.

The Canadian government is a parliamentary system, where the parliament has strong executive power. The federal parliament has an elected House of Commons, with elections every four to five years, and a Senate (which carries only nominal powers in practice) selected by appointment. The notion of "party discipline" means that members of the federal and provincial legislatures vote on party lines—implying that cabinet decisions, that is, executive decisions, normally are endorsed in the legislatures. The prime minister serves only as long as he or she has the confidence of Parliament.

The unique U.S. government is based on a system of "checks and balances" between the executive, legislative, and judicial branches of the federal government, and between the federal government and the states. The United States has been governed in accordance with the U.S. Constitution since 1789. The president is elected for a set term of four years and can serve only two terms. The U.S. Congress has two houses. Two members of the U.S. Senate are elected from each state every six years, and the members of the House of Representatives are elected every two years from districts that are proportional to the population.

In general, America has a deeper sense of individualism, while Canada is said to have a greater trust in government. While trite perhaps, the U.S. Constitution embeds "life, liberty, and the pursuit of happiness," while the Canadian Constitution allows the government to make laws for "Peace, Order and Good Government." It has been speculated that this difference accounts for the much lower crime rate in Canada than in the United States. Another reason is the Canadian tolerance for gun control, although this is not without controversy either.

Canada's multicultural approach accepts, if not promotes, ethnic diversity, making it one of the most ethnically rich countries in the world. While the United States also has many ethnic minorities, it is different in that it has large minority populations, such as the Hispanic and African American blocs.

The United States has ongoing tensions between "states' rights" and federal authority. The federal-provincial dynamic has historically dominated Canadian polity in part because the Canadian Constitution gives the provinces substantial legislative powers, particularly with respect to the environment. The western provinces have long pursued greater autonomy both within and outside the constitutional context. However, the greatest tension in Canada is with Quebec, with the separatist movement at times extremely powerful. In the mid 1990s, a referendum resulted in only 51 percent of Quebec voting to stay within the Canadian federation. Unlike the rest of Canada, Quebec's legal system is civil law (*droit civil*).

Canada fears the dominance of U.S. culture, and yet U.S. music, literature, and headlines are part of daily life. Most Americans are indifferent to Canadian affairs except near the border, and take for granted that Canadians and Canada are much like themselves and the United States. Both sides take for granted the sharing across the border that is the fundamental basis for the special relationship.

Each country is the other's largest trading partner, to the tune of $1 billion a day in goods, services, and investments across the border. Both depend on each other for defense systems in war and peace. Canada's defense policy remains focused on peacekeeping, and its military budget is a minute fraction of the United States'. Over the years, Canada generally was either silent about or endorsed U.S. military policy. However, Canadian refusal to participate in the recent Iraq War was an exception that illustrates some of the differences between the two countries.

From an environmental perspective, Canada and the United States share weather systems, the continental air shed, and many major transboundary waterways in addition to the Great Lakes. To date, no one on either side has been able to determine how to do anything about the weather, either alone or together, except to keep each other informed.

In response to recognition of "a seamless border" for air, an International Air Quality Advisory Board was established by the International Joint Commission of Canada and the United States in 1966.[5] Canadian concerns about acid rain led to many of the provisions in the 1990 U.S. Clean Air Act, and to the 1991 International Air Quality Agreement.

The Boundary Waters Treaty of 1909 was the result of joint desire for a system to share in decisions over use of waterways that cross the boundary. Later the Great Lakes Water Quality Agreement was developed as an executive compact under the treaty. The experience under the Great Lakes Agreement is the topic of the account that follows.

CHAPTER 2

ORIGIN OF THE GREAT LAKES WATER QUALITY AGREEMENT

T HE BOUNDARY WATERS TREATY OF 1909 REMAINS THE KEY COMPACT BE-
tween Canada and the United States that governs the use of boundary
and transboundary waters and provides the legal and institutional
foundation for the Great Lakes Water Quality Agreement. Together, these documents created a joint regime for environmental management of the largest
freshwater ecosystem in the world. This chapter provides an overview to the
Boundary Waters Treaty. It then describes the origins and content of the Great
Lakes Water Quality Agreement and the institutional framework it created.

The Boundary Waters Treaty

The Boundary Waters Treaty of 1909 originated primarily out of concern over
apportionment of water for producing hydropower near the end of the nineteenth century.[1] Beginning in 1783, a series of treaties and agreements had
dealt with uses and navigation rights in waterways that crossed the boundary.[2]
Now, public health was also a growing concern. Chicago had recently completed a canal system to divert its sewage effluents away from its drinking-
water source in Lake Michigan because of high rates of typhoid and cholera.[3]
One commentator noted that typhoid and cholera caused illness to the residents of most major Great Lakes cities, saying that "the filth and stench in the
waters of Great Lakes towns could be seen, tasted, and smelled, so the problem could not be ignored forever."[4]

In 1905 an International Waterways Commission was established between
the United States and Canada to investigate and report on the several new
issues that arose in this period. Protracted debate over water use in the St.
Mary's and Milk rivers, diversion of the Niagara River, and other situations
resulted in a call for a more permanent binational institution. The result was

the Boundary Waters Treaty, and establishment of the International Joint Commission (IJC) in Article VI.[5]

The International Joint Commission

The IJC was designed to resolve disputes and to avoid conflicts that "would inevitably arise between two sovereignties sharing both a continent and a frontier of continental dimensions."[6] The IJC has several functions.

First, using what is sometimes called its quasi-judicial power to apply governing principles for water use, the IJC decides whether to approve construction or other actions that will affect the levels and flows of boundary and transboundary waters. In Article VIII, the treaty sets out guiding principles for consideration of approvals, such as the fact that both countries have "equal and similar rights to the use of the water." An "order of precedence" is prescribed for various uses when there is conflict over competing uses. These governing principles are also used by the IJC for limited control of water levels in Lake Superior, Lake Ontario, and Lake Erie by operation of locks and control structures.

Second, when requested by both governments in what is called a "reference," the IJC investigates specific situations and makes recommendations to the governments on how to address problems. The investigation is carried out by a board of experts for each reference.

The third function of the IJC is its arbitral power to resolve disputes under Article X, although its relevance is limited since it has never been used.[7] On the other hand, the IJC is given credit for dispute avoidance.[8]

The emphasis on binational processes and equal sharing of responsibilities in the Boundary Waters Treaty reflects Canada's willingness to overcome its fear of domination enough to participate in a joint institution, and the United States' recognition of the need to cooperate in the management of a shared resource. By design, the IJC "has made equals of two very disparate nations . . . through the theory of equality on the Commission and equality on the boards in the field. . . . Size did not matter."[9]

Article IV of the treaty, the "anti-pollution provision," anticipated concern about water quality with a provision that neither party should cause pollution that would injure the health or property of the other side. Over three-fourths of the cases before 1944 concerned applications for "Orders of Approval" under Article VIII. The remainder were references, or requests from the governments to the IJC for investigations of issues, including pollution, under Article IX.[10] Prompted by the concern about waterborne disease, an investigation on water pollution began in 1912, but the governments did not act on the IJC's resulting recommendations, submitted in 1919.[11]

Former Canadian chairman Maxwell Cohen called the period from World War II to the early 1960s the "Great Works period," when locks and dams in the St. Lawrence Seaway and the Columbia River systems were developed.[12] Since the early 1960s, most attention has been given to air- and water-pollution problems in what is generally agreed to be "the environmental era," during which even issues of levels and flows have been addressed from new perspectives.[13] The fundamental operating principles of the IJC began under the treaty and continued under the Great Lakes Agreement until they appeared to be modified by individual commissioners in the 1990s.

IJC Operating Principles

To maintain the parity and equality that is the first operating principle of the IJC, the location of meetings is alternated on each side of the border, and the costs of joint activities are shared equally. Maxwell Cohen noted that "symmetry in the Commission offsets the political asymmetry resulting from differences in sheer size between Canada and the U.S."[14]

A second operating principle is that the IJC has been expected to work free from nationalistic considerations, and to seek the best solution to common problems based objectively on results of joint fact-finding studies. The traditional independence from consideration of national interest is not explicitly required in the treaty, which allows separate reports to the governments if the commission is unable to reach consensus.[15]

The tradition of binationalism dates from the first meeting of the IJC in 1911, when U.S. co-chair J. A. Tawney declared that, "as members of this Commission, we are therefore neither Canadians nor Americans, but we are each and all representatives of all the people on both sides of our International Boundary line."[16] A later U.S. commissioner, Charles Ross, echoed this sentiment after the Great Lakes Agreement was signed in 1972. He said that, with rare exceptions, the commission has acted "as members of a single body," with independence from United States or Canadian government interference, even though appointed by the heads of the governments of each country.[17]

According to Ross, the "singleness" in operation fostered development of an "esprit de corps" among the IJC members and their staffs, and the hundreds of public servants and other experts who serve in its institutions. This was why, he said, "to the greatest possible extent, national sovereignty gets lost in the shuffle."[18] In his 18 years on the commission under five U.S. presidents, Ross fiercely defended the tradition that no IJC commissioner met with another unless a representative of the other country was also present.[19]

A third operating principle has been reliance on common fact-finding as a viable and effective way to resolve disputes. Use of objective expert advice was cited in a 1975 Canadian Senate report as the basis for the governments' joint respect for the objectivity of ijc decisions. The report observed that "fundamental to the success of the ijc is the common fact-finding process which de-politicizes each problem and unites both technical staffs in the search for the basic facts of the situation."[20] Another commentator suggested that "without the use of the ijc's unique technical board procedures, neither side would have the confidence in each other's proposals."[21]

A fourth operating principle of detachment and distance from other interested parties is related to the reliance on expert advice. Before the Great Lakes Agreement, the ijc reported to the governments and, except for public hearings to gather information, generally did not consult with nongovernmental organizations or private parties. In the 1990s the basing of some recommendations in part on direct response to the views and wishes of the public and on consultation beyond the advisory boards would become a major change in the operations of the ijc.

The fifth operating principle requires that each commissioner operate "in his (or her) own professional capacity and expertise," rather than as a representative of the government or any other special interest. This principle is fundamental for the independence that the treaty prescribes for the commission as a whole, as well as its individual members. It has been perceived as creating conflicts of interest, especially for staff of government agencies and for commissioners who are given an appointment as a reward for political services. This principle also applies to members of temporary boards of experts, to the permanent control boards for levels and flow, and to the advisory boards called for in the Great Lakes Agreement.

Appointment of Commissioners

Members of the commission are nominally appointed by and serve at the pleasure of the prime minister in Canada and the president in the United States. Historically, the record shows that many commissioners have been appointed because of their special expertise, either technical or professional. It is also appears that a number of the appointments in the nearly 100-year history were made as rewards for past service in public office. Since 1980, however, most of the appointments seem to have been given to political allies of the party in power, with several in the United States as rewards for managing election campaigns.

The appointments are not made for a set term of office, and before 1980 there was never a total turnover in a panel of ijc commissioners at the same time. Since 1980 every president has dismissed the commissioners appointed by his predecessor and replaced them with his own appointees, but not necessarily immediately. In Canada, the current tradition is to appoint commissioners for a specific term of three years.

The consequence of this practice has been frequent gaps in membership and lack of institutional memory or experience that can be passed on to successors. Repeatedly in this period, all or nearly all of the commissioners have taken office at the same time, leaving a vacuum of leadership between appointments while new appointees become acquainted with the issues and their responsibilities.

Background to the Great Lakes Water Quality Agreement

Public and scientific concern about water pollution that began to grow in both countries following World War II appears to have helped motivate the U.S. and Canadian governments to negotiate a bilateral agreement. IJC activities that led to the agreement followed the traditional pattern for addressing levels and flow issues: use of binational boards of experts to make recommendations for actions to be taken based on results of fact-finding investigations requested by references from the governments.

A 1950 report to the IJC on a 1946 reference on growing pollution in the St. Clair, Detroit, St. Mary's, and Niagara rivers, and Lake St. Clair recommended "urgent action" to set "objectives for boundary water quality control," to establish boards to monitor and report on pollution problems in the connecting channels, and to propose reductions in the discharge of wastes.[22] The IJC noted that actions based on this recommendation were the first of their kind on an international basis, and led to major decreases in daily discharges of phenols, cyanides, oil, and suspended solids. Don Munton identified these first water quality standards as a policy innovation that anticipated what later became standard features of the pollution-abatement programs in both countries.[23]

In 1956, the United States proposed a new reference to investigate pollution of Lake Erie, Lake Ontario, and the St. Lawrence River. After Canada agreed, the United States suggested a broader study that would address both water quality and water quantity, because of the growing concern about fluctuations of lake levels. Levels that had been high in the early 1950s declined to historic lows by 1964, and the reference that led directly to the 1972 agreement was accompanied by a separate reference on levels.[24] The agreement grew directly out of a joint 1964 reference on pollution in Lake Erie and elsewhere in the lower lakes.[25]

As had been reported for large lakes in Europe, scientists carrying out research for the two advisory boards found that excessive phosphorus was the chief cause of accelerated eutrophication in Lake Erie and Lake Ontario.[26] Joseph DePinto and Thomas Young, two of the many scientists involved in the Great Lakes cleanup effort, defined eutrophication as "a process by which increases in the population of certain algae, encouraged by the presence of excess phosphorus in a lake, led to the depletion of oxygen in the water and the consequent deterioration of the lake."[27] Other results included changes in species of zooplankton and fish. Eutrophication was considered mainly to be an immediate threat to the lower lakes: Ontario, Erie, and Michigan.[28]

GROWTH OF PUBLIC CONCERN ABOUT POLLUTION

Within the Great Lakes, on both sides of the border, the citizen movement exploded with demonstrations and campaigns throughout the late 1960s and early 1970s, spawning new environmental groups and media profile for the issues.[29] Public demands for action increased as huge windrows of decaying algae piled up on Lake Ontario beaches, and a massive alewife die-off in Lake Michigan in 1967 not only interfered with swimming but threatened public water supplies and caused a secondary die-off due to botulism of shorebirds who fed on the dead fish.[30] Public agitation grew after a 1968 oil spill off Santa Barbara, California, coincided with rumors that oil drilling was to begin in Lake Erie.

As field work proceeded, public concern about water pollution was stimulated by the television spectacle of what appeared to be the Cuyahoga River on fire in late 1969, and a reporter's interpretation of the news about eutrophication as meaning that "Lake Erie is dying."[31] Earth Day, 22 April 1970, captured the emerging environmental conscience of the public.[32]

During 1970, both the U.S. Environmental Protection Agency and the Canadian Department of the Environment (now Environment Canada) were established. Both countries enacted new domestic legislation. Congress passed into law the National Environmental Policy Act and the Clean Air Act, while Parliament enacted the Canada Water Act.

FINAL REPORT ON THE 1964 LOWER LAKES REFERENCE

As the public demand increased for action, the IJC responded in 1969 with public hearings on a summary report, followed by the final report in 1970 for the 1964 reference.[33] Recommendations included new water quality objectives and control programs for the lakes themselves, with ongoing authority for the IJC to coordinate, evaluate, and verify the results. In 1968 dollars, it was estimated that the cleanup efforts would cost $1.3 billion for the United States and $211 million for Canada.[34]

The public and the leading limnologists who had served on the reference board were most alarmed about the visible results of accelerated eutrophication in Lake Erie, but the report also recommended attention to toxic contaminants.[35] Discovery of high levels of mercury in Lake St. Clair and Lake Erie in early 1970 and Canadian bans on commercial fishing added to the growing concern of both governments about the need for a possible new agreement for cooperative actions against pollution.[36]

Negotiation of the Agreement

In response to the scientific report and the growing public demand, a joint working group was formed to negotiate an agreement for Great Lakes cleanup. Relatively little has been written about the negotiation, although three issues seem to have dominated the discussions.[37] First, Canada took the position that each country should be allowed to pollute up to 50 percent of the lakes' assimilative capacity, that is, the amount of pollution the waters could take without significant adverse effects.

According to John Carroll, the United States "recognized that such an allocation would require a massive U.S. pollution control program (and only a small Canadian program). The United States thus rejected the fifty-fifty proposal and held that both countries were obligated to control pollution (with no proportion stated)."[38] This debate underscores the fact that conventional pollution was the chief concern in the negotiation of the original 1972 agreement, since there is no assimilative capacity by decomposition for the persistent organic chemicals that came to be the chief concern within a few years.

Second, Canada pushed hard for reduction of phosphates in detergents, as well as control of phosphorus in waste effluents. The United States was "unenthusiastic" about these proposals, but did accept the proposal for joint efforts to control phosphorus as a pollutant. Third, Canada took a more aggressive stance on upgrading publicly owned sewage-treatment systems because U.S. systems at the time were dramatically inadequate compared to Canada's. Again, a compromise was reached to upgrade the programs, or at least be in the process of upgrading sewage treatment by the end of 1975.[39]

After six years of study and two years of intense negotiations, the Great Lakes Water Quality Agreement was signed by Prime Minister Pierre Trudeau and President Richard Nixon on 15 April 1972. Later, the fact that the agreement was developed by a different process than the major new U.S. water-pollution control act that became law in the same year would create major issues as implementation proceeded.[40]

Nature of the Agreement

The 1972 agreement created a special regime, linked to the Boundary Waters Treaty, with the goal of cleanup and protection of all the lakes. The agreement is considered to be a standing reference under the Boundary Waters Treaty, but could be terminated by either side with one year's notice. One commentator views the agreement as an extension of the Boundary Waters Treaty, not as

---

Article I–Definitions

Article II–General Water Quality Objectives. These objectives provide narrative objectives agreed to by the two countries, such as committing to ensure that the waters are free from substances in concentrations that are toxic for human, animal, or aquatic life. Other objectives deal with putrescent sludge material, floating debris, materials that may cause a nuisance, and nutrients.

Article III–Specific Water Quality Objectives. These provisions commit to meeting specific numeric objectives for levels of reduction of pollutants as set out in Annex 1 to the agreement.

Article IV–Standards and Other Regulatory Requirements. This article commits the governments to have their domestic standards consistent with the agreement.

Article V–Programs and Other Measures. These provisions commit the governments to the development of programs directed toward the achievement of the water-quality objectives. These include programs for pollution controls from municipal and industrial sources and eutrophication from agricultural, forestry and other land-use activities; and pollution from shipping, dredging, and onshore and offshore facilities, among others.

Article VI–Powers, Responsibilities and Functions of the IJC. These provisions outline powers and responsibilities of the commission, including two references, one with respect to pollution from agricultural, forestry, and other land-use activities, and one pertaining to the quality of the waters of Lake Huron and Lake Superior.

Article VII–Joint Institutions. This provision mandates the establishment of a Water Quality Board and a Research Advisory Board, as well as a regional office located in the Great Lakes basin.

Article VIII–Submission and Exchange of Information. This article outlines requirements between the governments and the IJC concerning data and other information relating to water quality.

Article IX–Consultation and Review. This article requires consultation among the IJC and the governments. It commits to a comprehensive review of the agreement after five years.

Article X–Implementation. This article commits the governments to appropriating adequate funds to implement the agreement, and to enacting any necessary legislation to implement the agreement.

---

a separate compact. He suggests that the agreement "breathes life" into Article IV of the treaty, the anti-pollution provision.[41]

In effect, the scope and content of the agreement sets out what is meant by "pollution" for the Great Lakes. As the regime evolved and expanded, with substantial revision to the agreement in 1978 and a 1987 Protocol, new institutions were created to implement the agreement as the parties also developed new programs for implementation.

The Great Lakes Agreement is an "executive agreement" with somewhat ambiguous status. In other words, it is an agreement concluded by the heads of each country, and not a treaty or convention that would otherwise have to be ratified by Congress and Parliament. The U.S. Environmental Protection Agency (usepa) and some commentators suggest that it is not enforceable in and of itself unless its requirements are specifically incorporated into domestic legislation.[42]

Provisions of the Agreement

The 1972 agreement is a fairly straightforward document with two principal parts, the agreement and annexes. The body of the agreement contains a narrative description of fundamental goals, general objectives, and institutional arrangements, while the annexes list specific objectives and activities to be carried out. Important provisions are summarized in figure 1.

Article ii outlines the General Water Quality Objectives, which are broad and narrative in nature, while Article iii references the Specific Objectives that are spelled out in Annex 1. Commitments are also made in Article iv to develop specific programs for control of pollution from municipal, industrial, agricultural, and other sources. The principal objective of this initial version of the agreement was phosphorus reduction, with details in Annex 2.

The powers and responsibilities of the ijc are specifically described in Article vi. They include:

- Collation, analysis, and dissemination of data relating to water quality;
- Collection, analysis, and dissemination of data relating to the effectiveness of programs designed to achieve the objectives;
- Tendering advice to the parties and to state and provincial governments on water quality problems;
- Reporting annually on progress toward the achievement of the water quality objectives; and
- Authority to verify the data and information submitted by the parties and the state and provincial governments.

Two references, or requests for the ijc to investigate specific issues, were also incorporated into Article vi. One was a reference on Pollution from Land Use Activities that is generally referred to as pluarg, the acronym for the Pollution from Land Use Reference Group that ultimately produced more than 100 reports over several years.[43] The second called for investigation of pollution in the Upper Great Lakes (Superior and Huron), which was carried out by an Upper Great Lakes Reference Group.[44]

The agreement also empowered the ijc to establish a Water Quality Board and a Research Advisory Board. Members for these advisory boards are mostly recruited from governments, although other experts also were appointed to the Research Advisory Board. All board members are to act in their professional or expert capacities, rather than as representatives of their respective governments.

A Great Lakes Regional Office was also established under the 1972 agreement, located in Windsor, Ontario. Article IX mandated the parties to conduct a comprehensive review of the agreement five years after it came into force. This requirement led to renegotiation of the agreement and the development of a substantially different version in 1978, and a second revision in 1987. Another review is now underway.

Responsibilities of the Parties

The formal parties to the Great Lakes Agreement are the federal governments of Canada and the United States. State and provincial governments within the Great Lakes basin necessarily have an interest in the agreement and are specifically referred to in the agreement, but they consider the federal governments to have the ultimate responsibility for its implementation.[45]

With the signing of the agreement by the prime minister of Canada and the president of the United States, the federal governments, as the parties, accepted the primary responsibility for achieving the objectives of the agreement. This point has been the subject of confusion for many members of the public who think that the IJC has the primary authority for implementation.

In practice, the primary responsibility for programs to achieve the objectives of the agreement rests with the two principal federal environmental agencies for the governments, Environment Canada and the USEPA. This is why in day-to-day activities these two agencies are often referred to as "the parties" when they are really the lead agencies for the governments, who are the true parties to this historic agreement. As the lead agencies for the governments, the USEPA and Environment Canada are often deferred to by the foreign-relations agencies, even in the renegotiation that sometimes follows the required periodic reviews.[46]

The Role of the International Joint Commission after the GLWQA

The primary role of the IJC under the Great Lakes Agreement is to oversee the implementation process by the governments as an independent binational agency. The presence of such an agency is a unique feature of the Great Lakes Agreement. Much of the history of the agreement is concerned with how the role of the IJC strengthens the agreement and sometimes creates confusion and conflict.

THE INTERNATIONAL JOINT COMMISSION

The binational character that is the chief feature of all activity under the treaty extends to the ijc and all its institutions. The ijc itself has six members, three from each side, appointed by the prime minister and the president. Although each side or section has its own secretariat and a small permanent administrative staff in the national capitals of Washington and Ottawa, the Boundary Waters Treaty created the commission to be independent of the governments.

Each national section of the ijc consults formally with its own government through its respective foreign-policy agency, the Department of State in the United States and the Department of Foreign Affairs and Trade in Canada, but under the treaty the full commission is expected to make joint decisions independently. The secretariats communicate and work together directly on day-to-day matters.

ADVISORY BOARDS

For technical information and policy advice in conducting investigations, the ijc has depended mainly on boards or special committees with equal membership from each country. Board members are mainly staff of government agencies with appropriate authority and expertise who carry out their responsibilities for the ijc in addition to their regular duties in their home agencies. Under the Great Lakes Agreement, board membership has been extended to nongovernmental experts, including representatives of environmental organizations and industry.

The ijc has three types of advisory boards. One is permanent control boards for various parts of the Great Lakes hydrologic system that advise the ijc as needed on operation of the control structures that affect levels and flows. The second is special temporary study boards that are established for references to carry out fact-finding investigations and to advise the ijc about appropriate recommendations to the governments on specific subjects. The third type under the water quality agreement is ongoing advisory boards that are required to make periodic reports with recommendations to the ijc. These boards can also make special reports as needed and are more like the special investigative boards than the control boards.

Relations with the Governments

Under the treaty prior to the Great Lakes Agreement, most ijc decisions were reached by consensus, and the governments accepted and acted on most recommendations of the commission. Under the original 1972 water quality agreement, the governments generally accepted ijc proposals, as they had under the treaty. The lead agencies began to resist ijc recommendations after substantial change in goals in the 1978 version, and successfully set the stage for evading IJC oversight following renegotiation in 1987.

These withdrawals by the governments and the internal changes instituted in its operations by the IJC have been major factors in the history of the agreement in its third decade. Together, these major evolutions in the regime created by the agreement have led to significant uncertainties for the future of both the water quality agreement and the Great Lakes themselves. Figure 2 describes the institutional framework under the 1972 agreement.

The IJC in the Great Lakes Regime

The IJC has two roles in the Great Lakes regime. One role is formal and is required by the terms of the treaty and the agreement. The other role may be informal, is sometimes discretionary, and at times depends on the personality and initiative of IJC commissioners and staff. Changes in both kinds of roles have occurred since the agreement was adopted.

The formal role includes the specific functions and powers outlined in Article IV of the treaty, as well as the two references that led to the Great Lakes Agreement. Before the agreement, the IJC had advised the governments about specific problems and set orders for limited control by engineering works of levels and flows in Lake Superior, Lake Ontario, and Lake Erie. With the agreement, the IJC has been required to oversee management of a huge biological system, inhabited by 35 million people and affected by some of the largest concentrations of urban development in North America and the world.[47]

A requirement in the Great Lakes Agreement for joint monitoring of water quality gave the IJC a new evaluation role and provided accountability between the IJC and the governments, between the governments, and, increasingly over time, directly between the IJC and the citizens of both countries. Much of the debate about the effectiveness of the IJC and the Great Lakes Agreement over the years has concerned the fact that the binational agency has no powers to enforce its recommendations.[48] This is why nongovernmental representatives sought changes in the agreement in 1987 to increase accountability of the governments for their efforts.[49]

Great Lakes Regional Office

To help meet the new responsibilities imposed by the agreement, scientific experts were added to the expanded staffs of the IJC offices in Ottawa and Washington. Most of these activities, however, became the responsibility of the Great Lakes Regional Office called for in Article VII. The new jointly operated office was also directed to "provide a public information service for the programs."[50]

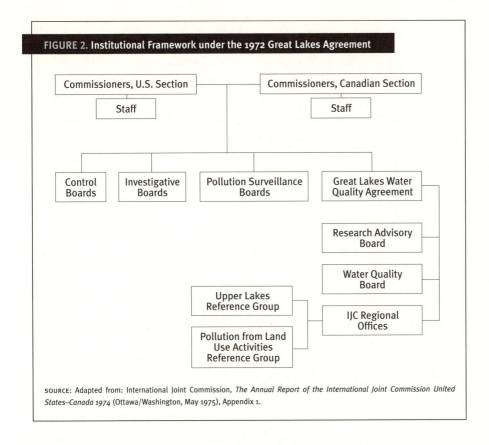

FIGURE 2. Institutional Framework under the 1972 Great Lakes Agreement

SOURCE: Adapted from: International Joint Commission, *The Annual Report of the International Joint Commission United States–Canada 1974* (Ottawa/Washington, May 1975), Appendix 1.

The office was established with a binational staff. The office also provides secretariat services to the IJC in its Great Lakes functions, and to the three advisory boards. In time, the office came to manage meetings, reports, and other arrangements for a multiplicity of committees, subcommittees, and task forces, as well as the two references. Placement of the office in Windsor, Ontario, across the river from Detroit, was meant to provide a central location within the watershed. The regional office also coordinates activities with other Great Lakes institutions such as the Great Lakes Fishery Commission and the International Association of Great Lakes Research.[51]

WATER QUALITY BOARD

The agreement directs that the Water Quality Board (WQB) be the principal advisor to the commission. The official members include heads of provincial and state environmental agencies. With some exceptions, the tradition has been for the director of the Ontario Regional Office of Environment Canada and the administrator of Region 5 of the USEPA to serve as co-chairs.

Before the 1990s, members of the WQB were generally the heads of agencies with policymaking authority. In recent years, however, actual participation on the WQB has increasingly consisted of operations-level staff members of the agencies represented.[52] Even more recently, membership on the board has evolved. For example, the membership includes a representative of the Conservation Authorities of Ontario who has since retired, but nevertheless still sits on the board. The Conservation Authorities have some limited role in local governments over such matters as flood control and watershed management planning. The board also has the executive director of the Great Lakes Cities Initiative, a former USEPA official who himself had formerly served as chair of the WQB. The Cities Initiatives operates as a nongovernmental, not-for-profit agency on behalf of local governments. This position was insisted upon by the IJC and opposed by the USEPA. The fact that the appointment stood demonstrates the continuing confusion of the role and nature of the board. The WQB has never had strictly nongovernmental members such as representatives of environmental organizations. Creation of a citizens advisory board was proposed in connection with the review of the agreement that led to the 1987 Protocol.

In the tradition of the IJC, under the Great Lakes Agreement members of the advisory boards are expected to serve "in their personal and professional capacity" as individuals, even when they are appointed because of their position with a specific government agency or research institution.[53] Nevertheless, possible conflicts between serving simultaneously as representative of an agency and as an impartial expert remain an issue. Most questions about conflict of interest have been raised about members of the WQB and persons who work for industry.[54]

SCIENCE ADVISORY BOARD

The Science Advisory Board (SAB) advises the IJC on science-related matters under the agreement. The SAB includes managers of Great Lakes research programs and other "recognized experts." The membership includes social scientists and representatives of industry and environmental organizations. The name of the board was changed from the Research Advisory Board (RAB) in 1978.

Initially the science board was an advisor to the Water Quality Board. Later it became a direct advisor to the commission itself.

COUNCIL OF GREAT LAKES RESEARCH MANAGERS

Although not called for as a separate board in the text of the agreement, a third advisory body, the Council of Great Lakes Research Managers, was formed by the IJC in 1984 and given full board status in 1994. The chief functions it performs formerly were carried out by the SAB.

Public Information

The agreement retained the binational character of the Boundary Waters Treaty in two ways: in the operation of joint institutions, and in allowing each country to achieve the common objectives under its own political system and laws. The agreement also fostered growth of a binational community concerned with its implementation by expanding the public-information services of the IJC.

The hearings held by the IJC on applications for construction of engineering works under the treaty had generally occurred near a particular location, with only local interests represented. The Great Lakes Agreement allowed the IJC to make information available about its progress at any time both to the governments and to the public at large.

Public-information services became a major activity and offered new opportunities for commission members to interact with the community that grew up around the agreement. Activities include production and distribution of the IJC newsletter, *Focus*, and organizing public meetings before the IJC makes its reports to the governments on progress in the Great Lakes. In recent years, commissioners have become more active in initiating new kinds of activities and means of consultation beyond the IJC institutions, often participating directly themselves.[55]

As implementation proceeded, this requirement helped increase direct involvement of citizens with the scientists, government personnel, and industry and other interests who came together in a large and diverse community committed to achieving the objectives of the agreement. Many participants believe that the political will of the governments to carry through on obligations under the agreement has been driven by the evolution of this community.

The Biennial Reports and Meetings

From 1972 to 1978, the IJC made annual reports on progress. From 1978 onward, the commission has, with some exceptions, reported every two years.[56] Since 1975, the IJC has held a public meeting to receive formal reports from the boards and to discuss the recommendations of the boards before developing its required progress report to the governments. Although members of the audience were initially allowed only to observe in the earliest meetings, in time presentation of the board reports to the IJC in public meetings became a mechanism for increased public understanding of Great Lakes problems, as well as for citizen activism.[57]

The reports of the IJC to the two governments include recommendations for actions needed to achieve the objectives of the agreement. In the 1980s, lack of response by the governments to the IJC reports came to be seen by the nongovernmental environmental organizations as a reason to demand more accountability of the parties, and was part of the reason they sought language for this end in the 1987 Protocol.[58]

The operations of the IJC had remained relatively stable during the decades between adoption of the treaty in 1909 and the signing of the Great Lakes Agreement in 1972. By contrast, over the more than three decades since the agreement was signed, the commission, new binational institutions, and the agreement itself have continued to evolve in a dynamic regime, just as environmental conditions in the Great Lakes themselves have continued to change dramatically.

OTHER ACTORS IN THE REGIME

Although the parties and the IJC are the entities formally recognized in the Great Lakes Agreement, many other institutions, agencies, and organizations play a role in the agreement processes. Participants include numerous academic as well as governmental research agencies that provide information, and nongovernmental organizations and institutions that bring attention and public awareness to the issues.[59]

Almost all either are binational by design, or seek communication and involvement with counterparts across the border. Some have missions independent of the water quality agreement, such as fisheries management, but increasingly over time have linked their goals or activities to its purposes and participated in the activities related to its implementation. This focus on the Great Lakes Water Quality Agreement is the foundation of the powerful sense of community that it has fostered.

It should be mentioned that First Nations and tribes have an obvious and important stake and growing influence in the Great Lakes. The clarification of treaty rights and land claims will further entrench the tribal and First Nations interests in virtually every aspect of Great Lakes governance. In some instances, First Nations saw the IJC and its processes as a means of manifesting its rights—such as ensuring appropriate membership, as nations within the Great Lakes community, on the various boards and committees. There are a number of specific institutions which are important, such as the Great Lakes Indian Fish and Wildlife Commission, which co-manages certain resources on behalf of 11 Ojibwa member tribes.

Evolution of Binational Efforts for the Great Lakes

The origins and content of the Boundary Waters Treaty are fundamental to understanding the evolution of the Great Lakes Agreement and its processes. The Boundary Waters Treaty is the foundation of the Great Lakes Agreement

FIGURE 3. Chronology of Major Events Leading to the 1972 Great Lakes Agreement

1912	Reference from the governments to the IJC to study Great Lakes pollution
1918	IJC Report on Reference Great Lakes Pollution submitted to government outlines "perilous" state of the Great Lakes[1]
1918	Proposal for a pollution agreement with enhanced IJC powers
1946	Reference from government to the IJC pertaining to the St. Clair River, Lake St. Clair, Detroit River, and St. Mary's River
1948	Reference extended to include Niagara River[2]
1963	Publication of *Silent Spring* by Rachel Carson warns world of dangers of new man-made organic chemicals, including in communities in the Great Lakes basin
1964–70	Ten semiannual reports and three major interim reports submitted by IJC advisory board
1964	Reference from government dealing with deteriorating conditions in Lakes Ontario and Erie[3]
1967	Media attention and public attention to the view that Lake Erie is "dying"
1970–71	Department of Environment (now Environment Canada) and U.S. Environmental Protection Agency
1970–72	Negotiation for a new bilateral agreement dealing with Great Lakes
1970	IJC Report on Reference[4]
1970	Earth Day; U.S. National Environmental Policy Act/Canada Water Act; IJC Report on 1964 Reference[5]
1971	Canada-Ontario Agreement signed; governors and premiers meet to consider the proposed water-quality agreement
1972	Great Lakes Water Quality Agreement signed by President Richard Nixon and Prime Minister Pierre Trudeau on 15 April[6]

NOTES

1. International Joint Commission, *Final Report on Boundary Waters* (Ottawa and Washington, D.C., 1918). A summary of this report is found in R. B. Bilder, "Controlling Great Lakes Pollution: A Study in United States–Canada Environmental Cooperation," *Michigan Law Review* 70 (1972): 481–91.
2. International Joint Commission, docket 54.
3. International Joint Commission, docket 83.
4. International Joint Commission, docket 55.
5. International Joint Commission, "Pollution of Lake Erie, Lake Ontario, and the International Section of the St. Lawrence," 1970.
6. 23 U.S.T. 301, 24 U.S.T. 2268.

SOURCE: Adopted from Leonard B. Dworsky, "The Great Lakes: 1955–1985," in *Perspectives on Ecosystem Management for the Great Lakes: A Reader*, ed. Lynton Caldwell (Albany: State University of New York Press, 1988), 70–71.

and, in effect, establishes a set of substantive and institutional principles, which worked generally and initially in the Great Lakes. One of the key principles relates to the notion of binationalism (as opposed to bilateralism), where the processes work toward common goals regardless of national interests. Another important principle is that of parity; that is, Canada is in the same position as the United States, although it has only a fraction of the economic power and population of its neighbor. This has provided an opportunity for Canada to persuade the United States to act when it may otherwise not feel compelled to do so, or vice versa.

CHAPTER 3

EVOLUTION OF THE AGREEMENT FROM 1972 TO 1978

IMPROVING WATER CHEMISTRY, ESPECIALLY REDUCING PHOSPHORUS LEVELS, was the main aim of the Great Lakes Water Quality Agreement that Prime Minister Trudeau and President Nixon signed on 15 April 1972. To slow the phosphorus loadings that stimulated algae growth in the process that scientists called "accelerated eutrophication," sewage treatment was improved in both countries, phosphate-detergent bans were adopted in the United States and Canada severely restricted phosphate content, and runoff of agricultural fertilizers was reduced.[1] The result, according to limnologist Alfred Beeton, was an environmental success that had not been achieved until then anywhere else for such a large system through cooperation in so many political jurisdictions across an international border.[2] As algae growth slowed, floating sewage, oil, and debris, and fish kills also virtually disappeared. Within five years, the water had become so clear and the walleye fishing so much better in Lake Erie, along with better conditions in Lake Michigan and Lake Ontario, that the public concluded that Great Lakes cleanup had been achieved.[3] Scientists, however, had become alarmed about new discoveries about the pervasiveness of certain persistent organic chemicals in the Great Lakes ecosystem that were already affecting the health of wildlife and could be a threat to human health.[4]

This period in the life of the agreement also saw the beginning of a sense of community among the people and the institutions and agencies that were working for its implementation as the means to protect Great Lakes resources. The community included the IJC and its staff, officials of agencies with responsibilities for implementation of the agreement, staffs of other agencies and institutions whose missions also related to the agreement, scientists inside and outside government, members and staff of environmental organizations, and certain journalists who regularly covered Great Lakes issues.

The agreement had called for review at the end of five years. By 1978, the growing community welcomed a new version of the agreement that focused on eliminating toxic contaminants from the Great Lakes environment and called for a more comprehensive approach to management that would consider connections between air, water, and land.

The General Context

The first five years of the Great Lakes Agreement coincided with the period in which the governments of both countries responded to public concern about the environment with new laws and programs, mainly to control visible pollution.[5] Most of the new laws stressed pollution control for the separate environmental media, beginning with air and water.

The U.S. National Environmental Policy Act also set up a system for environmental impact analysis that required evaluation of environmental consequences in advance of major actions by federal agencies.[6] Canada then adopted a similar approach, and the foundation was laid in both countries for the development of environmental policy that would evolve from pollution control to include pollution prevention.[7]

The basic approach to regulation of water pollution was different, however, in the two countries. The new U.S. water-pollution law set a goal of stopping discharge of all pollutants into waterways by 1985, with a permit system that set minimal national standards for discharges. The Canadian approach allowed discharges that could be assimilated, depending on conditions at the specific site. The Great Lakes Agreement allowed resolution of disagreements on how these different approaches were used for achievement of common goals and objectives.

The Lead Federal Agencies for the Parties

The lead responsibility for implementation of the new agreement fell upon the USEPA and Environment Canada. Both agencies were new themselves, having been established while negotiations were already underway for the 1972 agreement.

THE U.S. ENVIRONMENTAL PROTECTION AGENCY

The USEPA was established by executive order of President Nixon in 1970. The agency headquarters are in Washington, D.C., with 10 regional offices. The domestic authority for the new agency to take the lead for implementation of the Great Lakes Agreement derives mainly from the Clean Water Act, the law that was first passed as PL 92-500 in 1972. Throughout the life of the agreement, the officials in the USEPA's Washington headquarters have continued to insist that it does not have authority to compel other federal agencies to accept the goals and objectives of the agreement, although their cooperation can be sought.[8]

The rationale for this position is that, as an executive agreement, the Great Lakes compact does not have the force of a treaty and therefore does not supersede domestic law—in this case, the Clean Water Act. The Water Division staff of the USEPA headquarters has also tended to consider obligations under the Great Lakes Agreement as interference with the agency's policy to give priority to national rather than regional issues. Within the agency, day-to-day liaison with the IJC was left to the Office of International Activities in Washington, and the Region 5 office in Chicago took the lead in working with the IJC and Canadian agencies.[9]

From the first years of the agreement, continuing bipartisan Congressional oversight was needed to designate special funding for the Great Lakes because of the view in Washington.[10] Members of Congress from Great Lakes states cited agreement obligations in objecting to President Nixon's impoundment of Congressional appropriations for federal sewage-treatment grants to local communities.[11] They also requested studies by the General Accounting Office (a Congressional auditing agency) about USEPA implementation of the agreement, held hearings, and sponsored new legislative initiatives.[12] By the mid 1970s, the USEPA routinely limited budget requests for Great Lakes purposes, knowing that Congress would restore and even increase total agency funding in order to provide for Great Lakes programs.[13]

The Region 5 administrator, Francis Mayo, became the first U.S. co-chair of the IJC Water Quality Board and continuously sought greater recognition of Great Lakes problems and the agreement.[14] He set up an Office of Great Lakes Coordination to integrate the Great Lakes programs into agency programs under the various legislative mandates for air and water.[15] His successor, George Alexander, said that Congressional support was the reason he was able to convince USEPA headquarters in 1976 to establish the Great Lakes National Program Office (GLNPO) in Region 5 with its own line item in the agency budget.[16]

One of the arguments from headquarters was that the agreement objective of a one-milligram-per-liter effluent limit for phosphorus from large sources violated the U.S. Clean Water Act's ultimate goal of making all the waters of the country "fishable and swimmable" by 1983, with no discharge of pollutants after 1985.[17] Nevertheless, the law served agreement objectives by providing federal grants to local governments for improved sewage treatment, and by the permits limiting effluent discharges for industries and publicly owned sewage-treatment systems. Authority for issuance of the permits is delegated to state governments that meet federal requirements, and federal grants are provided to assist their agreement-related programs.[18]

Authority for setting and enforcing water quality standards was also delegated to the states, which could adopt standards stricter than the required national minimum. In the 1990s, consistency of state standards with objectives of the agreement would be one of the issues that led to development of the Great Lakes Water Quality Initiative.

In addition to the funding designated by Congress specifically for the Great Lakes, funding to meet agreement obligations was provided in two other ways in this early period. First, the Region 5 office of the USEPA used funds from other programs to support its Great Lakes office and the binational activities directly related to implementation of the agreement.[19] Second, appropriations for water programs such as sewage control were counted as Great Lakes expenditures when they were made within the Great Lakes basin.[20]

From 1972 to 1978, approximately $4.5 billion of U.S. state and federal funds were provided to upgrade sewage treatment under section 201 of PL 92-500.[21] Funding for research and interagency projects to demonstrate alternative waste-treatment technologies was also authorized.[22] Section 108(d) gave $5 million to the Army Corps of Engineers to study nonpoint-source control, and led to the involvement of the U.S. Department of Agriculture in trials of conservation tillage as a means to reduce phosphorus in fertilizer runoff in Ohio and Wisconsin.[23] This Great Lakes project was the beginning of the still-growing national movement for conservation tillage.[24]

ENVIRONMENT CANADA

The Canadian federal environment department was established in 1971, just prior to the negotiation of the 1972 Great Lakes Water Quality Agreement. Its first minister, Jack Davis, used the Great Lakes as one of the first issues to further Canada's international agenda. With the new agreement, Environment Canada assumed a mission for the Great Lakes.

Implementation of the agreement played out differently in Canada than in the United States. First, the Canadian federal government had already enacted a ban on phosphates in detergents in 1970 as a provision in the then new Canada Water Act. One factor in this early action was the confidence of decision makers, including Joe Green, then minister of Energy, Mines, and Resources, in the conclusion of Canadian scientists and the IJC that phosphorus was the limiting, or most critical, nutrient for eutrophication.

Second, there was a consensus on the Canadian side that either using a substitute or less phosphate in detergents was acceptable without a total ban. Third, the provinces did not object to the reductions, which would reduce the cost of removing phosphorus for the sewage-treatment systems under their jurisdiction.[25] Finally, Canada may have also used the reductions of phosphates to convince the United States to follow the same course of action.

By the time the 1972 agreement was signed, Canada had already also negotiated the Canada-Ontario Agreement (COA), which specifically designated the responsibilities of the federal government in relation to the provincial government for the water quality agreement. Essentially the accord provided that Ontario would implement the obligations set out in the 1972 agreement if the federal government paid for the needed capital improvements to update the provincial sewage-treatment facilities.

Then, as today, the Ontario region of Environment Canada remained primarily responsible for Great Lakes activities. The first director general of the Ontario region, A. T. Prince, was also the first co-chair of the Water Quality Board. He was followed by James Bruce (who then moved to chair the Science Advisory Board) and Robert Slater. Slater became one of the key negotiators of the 1978 agreement.

There was little issue with funding from Environment Canada through the early and mid 1970s. Although the situation began to change toward the end of the 1970s, most of the decade witnessed a prosperous Environment Canada with its National Water Research Institute, housed at the Canadian Centre for Inland Waters, providing the leading, and some have argued the best, research forum for fresh waters at the time.[26]

Role of the States and Provinces

The role of the states under the agreement reflects their obligation to implement federal policy, but also lack of responsibility beyond their own political boundaries. Research for this project has revealed ambivalence and contradictions in the states' role in implementing the agreement that reflect domestic political changes over time, as well as evolution in the joint institutions and binational relationships that it fosters.[27]

Consistent with the U.S. Constitution, the states did not participate directly in the negotiation of the agreement, and later would complain about obligations imposed without their participation. Some states initially wanted Lake Michigan excluded, but were overruled after Wisconsin governor Pat Lucy joined forces with a representative of the Lake Michigan Federation to obtain approval of a resolution recognizing that the Great Lakes form a single connected system.[28]

Initially, no state had special Great Lakes programs or used state funds except to satisfy matching requirements for federal grants for agreement-related activities.[29] The head of the environmental-regulatory agency generally represented each state on the wqb, and staff from the respective water programs or from other agencies served on committees or work groups.

Satisfaction or frustration of the states with the agreement has generally been tied to the availability of federal funding. At the same time, state environmental agencies have appreciated the collective political power resulting from the regional institutions that have developed around agreement processes. Some state officials have also enjoyed the opportunities for interaction on policy with their peers, and participation in the expanding community on both sides of the border.[30]

The same officials often met each other on other Great Lakes matters, such as meetings of the Great Lakes Basin Commission or of the advisory board for the Army Corps of Engineers winter-navigation project.[31] The growing number of environmental activists who also participated in such events did not distinguish between agreement and non-agreement matters; the focus was on the lakes themselves.[32]

Lyman Wible, a former official of the Wisconsin Department of Natural Resources and a participant in the wqb in the 1970s and 1980s, observed that, in addition to producing visible and easily measurable water quality improvements, the massive new sewage-treatment plants were physical symbols that generated local pride and developed political capital for the state agencies with an approving public. He and officials from other states in this period also talk about how state officials compared notes on development of the new programs required by federal water law, and on provincial policies with their Canadian peers.[33]

State objections to what would now be called "unfunded mandates" grew as federal funding for sewage-treatment grants was decreased following the 1977 Clean Water Act, and more and more problems in the Great Lakes involving persistent synthetic chemicals were being revealed. States other than Michigan also were dissatisfied later about not being involved in the five-year review of the 1972 agreement.

Although in Canada only the federal government can negotiate international agreements on environmental issues, federal-provincial cooperation is required because the provinces have the bulk of legislative and program authority needed for implementation.[34] The necessary cooperation is often facilitated by bilateral federal-provincial agreements, which was why the Canada-Ontario Agreement (coa) was developed for the Great Lakes. Signed eight months before the first Great Lakes Agreement, the coa in effect became the basis for Canada's negotiating position with the United States. Essentially the same persons negotiated both agreements.[35]

The 1971 coa, and those that followed until 1994 were mechanisms (as stated in the 1982 coa) to "provide for the cost sharing of specific programs which the province will undertake to assist Canada in meeting" obligations under the Great Lakes Agreement.[36] Most of the $50 million committed in the original COA was dedicated to the upgrading of sewage-treatment plants on the Canadian side of the Great Lakes.

In addition to providing a way to get the province to satisfy an international obligation negotiated by the federal government, the first COA provided a considerable degree of harmony in federal and provincial goals and actions for the Great Lakes. Although the federal government provided expertise on the nature of the problem and money to take action, it was agencies like the Ontario Water Resources Commission (which dealt with water quality issues prior to the establishment of the Ministry of the Environment in the early 1970s) that had the expertise to deal with sewage-treatment plants and related issues.[37] Quebec had limited involvement in the negotiations, but no COA-type agreement was forged at that time between Quebec and the federal government.

Research-and-Planning Institutions and Programs

The binational research community that developed around the Great Lakes Agreement came to lead world research on large lakes. Research is carried out by government scientists who interact with academic scientists in a wide variety of programs and institutions. Some existing research agencies shifted their focus to agreement-related issues, and new ones were established.

Research in the United States

The USEPA and other agencies also established new institutions for basic research or expanded attention to Great Lakes issues under the 1972 agreement. The USEPA's existing Environmental Research Laboratory in Duluth, Minnesota, carried out some Great Lakes research, and its director served as U.S. co-chair of the SAB.[38] A Large Lakes Research Station was established at Grosse Ile, Michigan, explicitly to manage Great Lakes research and to provide technical assistance to the GLNPO and the IJC for surveillance, research, modeling, and water quality projections.

Established as part of the National Oceanic and Atmospheric Administration's (NOAA) "Regional Seas" program, the Great Lakes Environmental Research Laboratory (GLERL) in Ann Arbor, Michigan, also served agreement purposes. GLERL staff members continue to serve on IJC boards and committees, and the laboratory helped meet USEPA research needs through interagency agreements and contracts.[39]

Other U.S. federally funded research on agreement-related issues was carried out at Argonne National Laboratory at Lemont, Illinois, near Chicago, and by the Sea Grant programs operated by NOAA at public universities in six of the eight Great Lakes states at the time. The Sea Grant programs included data collection, monitoring, and public education through extension services, as well as grants for basic and applied research.[40]

University-based research institutions and programs, some preexisting and some established following adoption of the agreement, also became involved in the expanded binational process of research and information exchange that followed the signing of the 1972 agreement. In addition to resources provided by environmental agencies, they could obtain other state and federal funds for research and education. Their faculties, staffs, and students became part of the emerging Great Lakes community.[41]

Research in Canada

Canadian government research for the Great Lakes was more centralized than in the United States. Canadian research on Great Lakes issues had been carried out at the Experimental Lakes Program in Manitoba long before the agreement. During the mid 1960s, freshwater-resource research was conducted through the Inland Waters section of the Department of Energy, Mines, and Resources. The Canadian Centre for Inland Waters (CCIW) was then established in the late 1960s and moved into its new facilities in Burlington, Ontario, in 1972. Some key scientists for Great Lakes research then transferred to the new location.

Environment Canada continues to administer the National Water Research Institute from Burlington in 2005. Dr. Richard Vollenweider was the first head of the institute, followed by James Bruce. Typically, the head of the institute also chaired the Science Advisory Board, which included Bruce, Al LeFeuvre, and Keith Rodgers.

The CCIW had a relatively modest amount of base funding, which was enhanced for work on the two references to the IJC that accompanied the agreement. By the late 1970s, the CCIW established regional facilities in Winnipeg and Vancouver, which in turn were combined to form the National Hydrology Research Institute in the early 1980s.

Expansion of the Great Lakes Research Community

Earlier, increased concern about the fishery and lamprey problems and the reference on phosphorus had contributed to the establishment of the International Association for Great Lakes Research (IAGLR) in 1967. Its journal and annual meetings became additional forums for attention to scientific issues associated with the agreement, and for interaction between scientists across the border within the broader binational Great Lakes community. Scientists had played a lead role in development of the Great Lakes Agreement, and interaction between Great Lakes researchers and policymakers continued as implementation proceeded. The Great Lakes science community is also interdisciplinary.

Most IAGLR members are physical or biological scientists. Academic political scientists and other experts in institutional arrangements began their own long-term involvement with the agreement in 1971 and 1972, with the first of a series of interuniversity seminars. The chief organizers were Leonard B. Dworsky of Cornell University and George Francis of the University of Waterloo. The seminar resulted in a final report endorsed by 24 academic experts in natural-resource management.[42]

The chief recommendation called for expanding the authority of the IJC, launching an ongoing discussion about whether agreement objectives could be achieved without a stronger regional-governance arrangement. The final report made specific recommendations that the governments in both countries should begin to consider going beyond the terms of the agreement to develop "multiple purpose management of the Great Lakes."[43] In May 1973, a presentation on the recommendations was made to the Subcommittee on Inter-American Affairs of the U.S. House of Representatives Committee on Foreign Affairs.[44] Similar presentations were made to the Standing Committee on Foreign Affairs of the Canadian Senate, in March and December of 1975.[45] The recommendation received no formal endorsements, but could be considered an early articulation of the later call for an ecosystem approach to management.

A second interuniversity seminar on "Improving the Management of the International Great Lakes" was convened under the same leadership in 1976–1977. Several individuals who participated in these events continued their interest in and involvement with the agreement to the present, as academic researchers, as participants in IJC-sponsored activities, and also as advocates with nongovernmental organizations.[46]

IJC Joint Institutions and Binational Processes

In Article VIII, the IJC was given an additional special charge to oversee exchange of information about water quality. Its responsibilities for joint institutions included submission of an annual budget for anticipated agreement-related expenses to the parties. Most of the expenses to the IJC related to the operation of the new regional office, including the activities of the advisory boards, and to carrying out the two special references on nonpoint-source pollution, and pollution of the Upper Lakes.

Great Lakes Regional Office

The Windsor office opened in March 1973 with a binational staff. In contrast to explicit Terms of Reference for the Research Advisory Board and directives within the agreement for how the Water Quality Board would be structured and its members appointed, the 1972 agreement gave the IJC only broad authority to establish the new office at a site to be determined by consultation with the parties.[47] By the end of the first five years, there were nearly 250 members of the boards, their subcommittees, and working groups.[48]

The position of director of the regional office alternated between Canadian and U.S. citizens, with two-year terms (later expanded to four). A staff of three professional positions grew to 33 by 1979, with expertise that included urban planning; limnology; physical, organic, and analytical chemistry; civil and environmental engineering; statistics; and biology.[49]

Public information, and increasingly over time direct involvement of the public in agreement-related activities, became another major function of the regional office for which there was only passing reference in the language of the agreement. Funding arrangements were also vague, with the agreement providing only that each side would pay half the costs of an annual budget that the IJC would submit to the governments. No one disputed that the regional office served "in a highly professional manner" in the first stage of its existence, but questions about its authority and relationships with the boards, agencies of the parties, and the IJC itself led to more detailed terms of reference in the second agreement in 1978.[50]

A 1979 report on a follow-up joint study of the regional office observed that "the responsibilities assumed by the Regional Office, as well as tasks assigned, led it to grow . . . over the years without a great deal of outside scrutiny and accountability . . . and there grew . . . some varying interpretations of its functions, capacities, and directions." This report was called for because of questions raised in connection with the negotiation of the revised GLWQA in 1978. When questions were raised about whether the doctoral degrees of one-third of the staff increased costs for an overqualified staff, the 1979 study found that a high level of technical and scientific expertise was required because of the interaction with expert members of the advisory groups and the high level of competence needed to write the reports.[51]

Independent verification of data provided by the parties or the boards was a more controversial function of the regional office because it related to WQB assessment of whether the parties were making adequate effort to achieve the agreement's objectives. The 1979 study concluded that "there has been no instance where the Regional Office has performed an independent verification function . . . which has proved an embarrassment to [IJC] advisory boards."[52]

As public involvement increased with implementation of the agreement, the Research Advisory Board sponsored a workshop to consider methods for public participation.[53] The 1979 study of the regional office urged the adoption of an explicit policy for the public-information function of the regional office because it had become so important during the first five years of the agreement.[54]

THE ADVISORY BOARDS

Unlike the special boards of experts that disband after providing advice on specific subjects of references from the governments under the Boundary Waters Treaty, the advisory boards under the Great Lakes Agreement are ongoing. In the first phase of implementation under the 1972 agreement, the two boards largely set their own agendas.

The Water Quality Board

The relative functions of the Water Quality Board and the Science Advisory Board were somewhat uncertain. The agreement said simply that the WQB should "assist" the IJC (Article VII). The terms of reference (GLWQA-1972) directed the Research Advisory Board (RAB; later the Science Advisory Board, SAB) "to work at all times in close cooperation with" the WQB, without identifying their specific responsibilities.[55]

Members of both the advisory boards were to be appointed by the IJC "after consultation with the appropriate government or governments concerned." The requirement that the consultation proceed through the foreign-affairs agencies on both sides was mainly a formality, as the custom was established that the U.S. co-chair would be the administrator of Region 5 of the USEPA.[56] In later years, the SAB members came to be appointed by the IJC, and the WQB members by the governments.

The first Canadian co-chair, A. T. Prince, was from the federal Department of Energy, Mines, and Resources, and subsequently was the director of the Inland Waters Directorate of Environment Canada. The total membership of directors and other high-level officials of state and provincial agencies was about 20.

The need to have senior officials serving on the board for "effective development of policy recommendations" was noted in the 1974 report of the Water Quality Board to the IJC. At this stage, attendance was good, with an average of 15 members or "a small number of alternates" at meetings throughout the year.[57]

Increasingly over time, the dual role of serving both as an agency representative and as an individual expert came to be perceived as a built-in conflict of interest for WQB members. The issue was whether staff of an agency could be honest in judging the agency's performance.[58] Some WQB members used their participation on the WQB to advance their ideas or to prod their own agency. One state member admitted that he criticized his home-agency's performance as a member of the WQB, then used the criticism back in his state-capital office to advocate program change.[59] Canadian members made similar statements.

The cost of participation in IJC activities for state and provincial officials was another ongoing issue. The 1974 WQB report noted that the effort and time that members of the board and its subcommittees spent on IJC activities was in addition to their "normal" work loads in the agencies they represented. The report cited agency warnings that "the assignment of staff and material to [agreement] work will be constrained due to competition for available budget funds."[60] This warning foreshadowed events a decade later, when the IJC took greater charge of the commitment of resources to board activities.

This third annual report also foreshadowed the ongoing question of the regional office's role in gathering data on the governments' progress in complying with the agreement. The report said that it was the responsibility of "the several levels of government" to provide needed data, and urged the IJC to allocate funds to cover agency costs of meeting IJC data needs. The commission responded that the governments should cover the costs directly.[61] Beginning with this 1974 report, a summary volume was supplemented by several appendices with detailed reports from the Water Quality Objectives, Surveillance, and Remedial Programs subcommittees of the WQB.

Research Advisory Board

The broader RAB membership called for in the Terms of Reference was to include not only "appropriate" members from federal, state, and provincial agencies but also from "other agencies, organizations, and institutions involved in Great Lakes research." Membership was to be based primarily on an individual's personal qualifications.[62]

In 1975, the RAB had 10 members from each side, plus one ex-officio member. The nine standing committees had up to 14 members each, including private citizens as well as research scientists and agency officials. Many of the members were heads of research agencies or eminent leaders in their fields. For example, the Standing Committee on Eutrophication was headed by Richard Vollenweider, the scientist credited with helping to identify phosphorus as the limiting nutrient for eutrophication and with setting the stage for the phosphorus-reduction efforts fostered by the agreement. The Committee on Lake Dynamics was headed by Clifford H. Mortimer, director of the University of Wisconsin Center for Great Lakes Studies at Milwaukee and a leading expert on Great Lakes hydrology.

The RAB generally set its own agenda and often became the forum where new issues were raised.[63] In its 1977 annual report to the IJC, having laid the groundwork in earlier reports, the RAB called for an ecosystem approach to management, a concept that was later incorporated into the revised agreement of 1978.[64] In 1979, in discussing long-range transport and atmospheric deposition of pollutants, the RAB called attention to acid rain as a potential threat to ecosystem integrity, even though the limestone base of the Great Lakes basin protected the lakes themselves from acidification.[65]

Although travel costs for nongovernmental members of subcommittees and work groups were covered by the IJC, agencies were not compensated for the time or travel costs of their staff who participated in IJC activities. USEPA and other agency concerns about what they considered undue demand on increasingly scarce resources led to review of the regional office in connection with the five-year review of the agreement, followed by the 1979 internal review by the commission.

Evolution of Public Involvement

There had been no direct public involvement in the development of the Great Lakes Agreement, although the decision of the governments to create it was influenced by the growing public concern about pollution in the late 1960s. The negotiators of the first agreement acknowledged citizen concern about the environment by making public information a specific responsibility of the Great Lakes Regional Office that was created as a new IJC institution by the agreement.

The IJC and the Public

Before 1972, the IJC had held public hearings on specific topics in connection with reference investigations, but otherwise conducted its business in private because "internal communications . . . by boards and committees" were only to be made available to the public by permission of the governments.[66] While requiring the IJC to provide public information, the agreement gave the IJC discretionary authority to issue special reports and to publish any documents (Article VI). Over time, increasing public involvement in agreement-related activities that began in the early stage of implementation became one of its most significant results.[67]

The boards were directed to publicize their meetings and permit members of the public to attend them. All board reports to the IJC have automatically been made public throughout the history of the Great Lakes Agreement. The 1975 workshop of the RAB's Standing Committee on Social Sciences, Economic, and Legal Aspects led to establishment of 17 public-advisory panels throughout the Great Lakes watershed for the PLUARG study.[68] The panels included local elected officials and academic experts, as well as environmental activists and representatives of other interests.

The PLUARG public-involvement process had three major results with long-lasting consequences. First, the widespread involvement of individuals with diverse backgrounds and interests throughout the basin broadened knowledge and support of the agreement and the IJC. Second, involvement at the local level helped set the stage for the later Remedial Action Plan process for local areas of concern. Third, recommendations from the panels included in the final PLUARG report influenced the agenda of the IJC. [69]

Mark Reshkin, chairman of the advisory panel for the Calumet region in Indiana, said the persistence of a member who had been active locally on air-quality issues was the reason that the panel recommended the identification of atmospheric deposition, in addition to land runoff, as a nonpoint source of pollution.[70] The attention to atmospheric deposition that began in the Great Lakes Agreement processes led ultimately to the provisions for toxic air contamination in section 112 of the U.S. 1990 Clean Air Act.[71] A contract with the nonprofit organization Great Lakes Tomorrow for pre-hearing educational workshops on the issues addressed by the Upper Lakes Reference Group set another new pattern for seeking public participation.[72]

News-media coverage of the meetings also reminded citizens of both countries at least once a year of the existence of the agreement, because the WQB reports were treated as "state of the lakes" reports to the general public.[73] Paul McClennan from Buffalo and a few other reporters came to be considered members of the community because of their continuing coverage.[74]

Identification by the WQB of geographic "problem areas" (later to be called "areas of concern") where agreement objectives were not being met provided a local angle for press releases based on the regional-office reports.[75] Meanwhile, the regional office expanded distribution of its quarterly newsletter, *Focus*, and audiovisual materials and brochures describing the IJC and the agreement, and provided answers to information requests by letter or telephone.[76]

Biennial Meetings

Starting in 1975, the annual (later biennial) IJC meetings where the boards presented their reports to the IJC became another forum for ongoing citizen participation. Initially, the meetings mainly allowed much informal contact for nongovernmental participants with scientists and agency staffs, as well as with each other. In the first meetings, the audience was allowed only to observe the presentation of the board reports and the discussion between the boards and the IJC commissioners. Later, written questions were submitted for answer during the exchange, and still later, special sessions were scheduled to obtain public comments.

Emergence of a Sense of Community

An emerging sense of community among the growing number of persons in this period who were involved with implementation of the Great Lakes Agreement was an intangible but important phenomenon. More and more people who otherwise would never have encountered each other became acquainted through their common concerns for cleaning up and protecting the Great Lakes.[77]

This sense of sharing mutual interests and efforts resulted from overlapping participation in activities and events organized by governments and the IJC, and by numerous other institutions that engaged in binational activities because of the agreement. It extended across geographic lines, areas of professional expertise, and diverse experience. Government agency staffs, scientists, and environmentalists exchanged information in formal presentations at meetings and workshops, and informally over lunch or dinner or in hallways during meeting breaks. Many individuals came to see each other numerous times during the course of a year as the number of events, activities, and institutions expanded.

The sense of common purpose and concerns among persons involved with the agreement began in this first phase of the agreement, reached its peak in the 1980s, waned somewhat in the 1990s, and appears to have expanded in the new millennium. Many participants believe that evolution of the community that evolved around the agreement has been the most important force behind the political will of the governments for meeting the obligations they accepted in 1972.

Other Institutions with Binational Operations
Great Lakes Basin Commission

In the United States, the Great Lakes Basin Commission provided an additional coordinating mechanism among federal and state agencies, and for public participation in Great Lakes and agreement-related matters. The agency was one of six "river basin commissions" that had been established under the 1965 Federal Water Resources Planning Act to coordinate federal and state policies and planning for development of water resources.[78] Water quality was already the chief Great Lakes issue when the Basin Commission was established in 1967 to develop a regional Framework Plan for water resources in the Great Lakes watershed.

The Basin Commission had eight state and twelve federal members, with the Department of State participating to ensure that the international dimension—effectively, Canadian interests—was taken into account. A representative of the Ontario Ministry of the Environment frequently attended Basin Commission meetings, and staffs of Ontario and federal Canadian agencies participated in workshops and conferences on subjects relevant to the agreement. After the Great Lakes Agreement was signed in 1972, the commission provided planning and analysis, funded in part by grants and interagency agreements with the USEPA, until it was disbanded by the Reagan administration in 1981. The members of the Public Involvement Work Group established by the Basin Commission included environmentalists who also were active on agreement matters.[79]

In effect, the Basin Commission provided another policy forum plus technical analysis for agreement-related issues. One of its projects helped develop modeling techniques applied in developing the target loadings for phosphorus for the lakes.[80] Annual meetings convened for the state heads of the Soil Conservation Service in the U.S. Department of Agriculture served as a forum where skeptics about the value of conservation tillage are said to have become advocates.[81] Binational coordination among the U.S. state coastal-zone management programs and Canadian shoreline management programs did not directly relate to the agreement, but expanded the Great Lakes community. The binational coordination role was reflected by a publication, whose costs were shared by the Basin Commission, U.S. Army Corps of Engineers, and Fisheries and Environment Canada, urging use of vegetation to stabilize shorelines as an alternative to engineered structural erosion-control measures.[82]

When the Basin Commission requested public comment on a draft Framework Plan in a series of public meetings in 1975, many agency officials were astounded by the strong support expressed for "environmental quality" as a regional goal over economic development. The high participation in the meetings had been urged in advance information about the public-consultation process circulated by the Lake Michigan Federation and the Sierra Club. The officials were especially surprised by the turnout of about 300 persons in Marquette on Lake Superior in the Upper Peninsula of Michigan, where the population was very low.[83]

Great Lakes Commission

The Great Lakes Commission was a different U.S. regional body that was originally created in the 1950s through an interstate compact to represent state navigation and shipping interests when the St. Lawrence Seaway was built. It became a member agency of the Great Lakes Basin Commission when it was established later. After the 1972 agreement, the Great Lakes Commission continued to be concerned primarily with navigation matters.[84] Later, the Great Lakes Commission, using funding transferred from the Basin Commission when it was shut down, began to broaden its agenda to environmental issues and to seek to fulfill coordinating functions for the states that the planning agency had formerly provided. The Great Lakes Commission's role continued to expand over the next two decades.

Great Lakes Fishery Commission

The Great Lakes Fishery Commission was established through a joint agreement between Canada and the United States in the 1950s primarily to support a binational effort to eradicate the sea lamprey. Later, its activities expanded to include coordination of fishery management programs and policies. The IJC and the Fishery Commission have separate mandates, but staff and commissioners of the fishery agency participate in the agreement-related community, and came to devote increasing attention to ecosystem management as the focus shifted from the phosphorus-control objective of the original 1972 agreement.[85] The future of the relationship between the efforts of the two binational agencies is one of the issues that needs more attention in the new millennium.

ENVIRONMENTAL ORGANIZATIONS

By the mid 1970s, several environmental organizations had established special Great Lakes programs, and regularly lobbied agencies, legislatures, and officials on behalf of agreement-related actions. The Lake Michigan Federation, for example, worked for phosphate-detergent bans in cooperation with local organizations in Chicago, Indiana, Michigan, and Wisconsin.[86] The League of Women Voters had a Lake Erie Interleague Committee in Ohio and a four-state interleague group for Lake Michigan, and local league members usually covered IJC meetings wherever they occurred.[87]

The Izaak Walton League successfully led the lobbying for the first state phosphate-detergent ban by Indiana in 1973 and set up a special four-state Lake Michigan Committee.[88] The National Audubon Society, which had 68 chapters in the Great Lakes region, in the mid 1970s made the Great Lakes a priority issue for its regional office in Dayton, Ohio.[89] The Sierra Club formed a binational Great Lakes Committee of member volunteers to develop policy recommendations to the group's national board of directors, and then established a Great Lakes program within its Midwest regional office in Madison, Wisconsin.[90] Later, the Sierra Club took the lead in establishing a Great Lakes advocacy presence in Washington, D.C.

The Michigan United Conservation Clubs led the lobbying for a detergent ban in that state. Great Lakes Tomorrow was another binational group that promoted public participation on agreement issues from a different perspective. The Ohio-based group cooperated in carrying out Great Lakes Decisions, an educational program on Lake Erie and Lake Ontario that Elaine Kaplan Beck had first developed for Lake Michigan.[91]

Environmental groups in Canada were neither as large nor as affluent as those in the United States, in part because the population base is so much smaller. Canada's parliamentary system does not lend itself to the lobbying techniques used in the United States. Although access to the courts has been liberalized in recent years, they are still not as accessible as in the United States. The Canadian rule that the loser pays the winner's court costs also discourages litigation, and in particular public-interest litigation. Further, many groups were newly organized. Groups that became very influential, such as Pollution Probe, the Canadian Environmental Law Association, and the Canadian Institute for Environmental Law and Policy, were all first formed in 1969 or 1970.[92]

In Canada, Great Lakes Tomorrow linked up with the Conservation Council of Ontario, itself a coalition of mostly conservation groups. Although such groups did not make a lot of headlines, they did educate and capture the interest of many individuals on Great Lakes issues.[93] Canadian environmentalists also met U.S. activists at events such as the annual meetings of the IJC, forming relationships that would lead to binational environmental advocacy in later phases of the agreement.

The absence of large Canadian environmental groups in the early days of the agreement did not reflect absence of interest by members of the public. For example, many individuals participated in the public advisory panels for PLUARG, and some, like Gil Simmons of Hamilton, remain pillars of citizen activism for the Great Lakes. Finally, some of the Great Lakes' best advocates were scientists who played an enormous role in turning the results of scientific studies into public policy. These scientists interpreted the significance of their findings for environmental advocates who then became active in promoting application of the new science in policy.

In Canada, Jack Vallentyne, Canadian co-chair of the RAB, was noted for the globe he carried on his back at public meetings as a symbol of environmental activism, and for his dedication of time and energy to environmental education in schools.[94] Alfred Beeton, U.S. co-chair of the RAB who had participated in the 1960s research on eutrophication, Wayland Swain, and other scientists on the U.S. side assisted environmental advocacy groups in understanding scientific issues.[95]

Tracking of Progress toward Agreement Objectives

One of the principal functions of the IJC under the agreement is to track progress in implementation and report results to the governments and to the general public. The commission relies mainly on the advisory boards for the information needed to fulfill this obligation.

WATER QUALITY BOARD REPORTS

The annual reports required in Article VI of the 1972 agreement were meant to assist in tracking progress toward achievement of the goals and objectives of the agreement. Since reduction of phosphorus was the main aim at this time, Annex 2 required reports on annual reductions in phosphorus loadings. By 1975, the WQB recommended development of a Great Lakes International Surveillance Plan (GLISP) in order to coordinate water quality monitoring activities of the USEPA and Environment Canada.[96]

Thus progress, or lack of it, in meeting objectives of the Great Lakes Agreement was tracked by the annual reports of the WQB and the reports of the IJC to the governments, which during this period were based mainly on distillation and evaluation of the reports submitted by the two advisory boards. The early WQB reports reflect two aspects of the implementation process that continue to this day.

On the one hand, recommendations reflect common concerns about protection of the Great Lakes, rather than state, provincial, or national concerns. On the other hand, there is criticism in both directions about how programs are structured or how agencies operate. Nevertheless, the activities of the WQB provide evidence that the parties to the agreement have usually continued to work together even while they complain about each other.

The first reports reflect early Canadian complaints about the discrepancy between the proportion of its population for which "adequate" treatment was provided compared to the U.S. residents of the Great Lakes basin.[97] The United States complained about what it considered Canada's lack of regulatory authority to require effluent limits.[98] By July 1976, the 1975 WQB report hailed substantial compliance with the 31 December 1975 deadline for having municipal treatment programs either completed or in place as "one of the first major achievements toward restoration of water quality."[99]

Canada had drastically reduced the phosphate content of household detergents in 1972 by allowing use of nitrilotracetic acid (NTA) as a substitute. The USEPA had been forced to comply with a 1971 ban on NTA by a pronouncement from the Surgeon General's office that NTA was a threat to human health. This action undermined passage of a federal ban on phosphates in laundry detergents sponsored by Senator Gaylord Nelson of Wisconsin, because only NTA was then available as a substitute.

In 1975, as the Canadian experience failed to confirm carcinogenic effects of NTA, and WQB and IJC reports continued to urge all states to adopt phosphate-detergent bans, Region 5 administrator Francis Mayo established a task force to present the arguments in favor of agency support for state bans in the Great Lakes basin.[100] USEPA headquarters' opposition to the Region 5 proposal was overcome after EPA administrator Russell Train attended the 1976 IJC annual meeting, followed by a tour arranged by Region 5 of several of the largest sewage-treatment systems in Buffalo, Detroit, and Milwaukee, as well as industrial sites in Cleveland and northern Indiana.[101]

Over objections of the Soap and Detergent Manufacturers Association and the Proctor and Gamble Company, from then on USEPA staff actively provided technical information in support of state bans as they were being considered by state legislatures.[102] Eventually, such bans were adopted throughout the basin, in part because they reduced sewage-treatment costs for phosphorus removal.[103] The third major source of phosphorus, runoff of agricultural fertilizers, was chiefly addressed in the conservation-tillage demonstration projects carried out by the Army Corps of Engineers.

The WQB also reported on the annexes concerning vessel wastes, dredging, and oil spills. The difficulty of proper disposal of dredge spoils remains a major issue in the United States, but the joint contingency plan for oil spills has been periodically updated by the two coast guards.[104]

The WQB reported that public-opinion surveys in both Canada and the United States found that the public considered water quality in Lake Erie to be improving. The same surveys found that the general public was willing to spend more money to protect Great Lakes water quality, even though there was lack of awareness of existing government efforts.[105]

As the five-year review required by the 1972 agreement was proceeding in 1977, the 1977 WQB report devoted as much attention to the growing evidence of pervasive toxic contamination as to the signs of slowing eutrophication.[106] Through the first years of the agreement, the RAB had increased its attention to toxic contamination.

RESEARCH ADVISORY BOARD REPORTS

From 1975, the annual full RAB report was supplemented by an ever-growing number of reports of workshops, conference proceedings, or special investigations, and by an annual directory of Great Lakes Research and Related Activities supplemented in 1976 by a separate report on research needs.[107] The 1975 report from the Standing Committee on the Scientific Basis for Water Quality Criteria, which described a proposal to link "structure and activity" of persistent bioaccumulative toxic contaminants, was the first step in a long process that eventually led to the USEPA's Great Lakes Water Quality Initiative in 1995.[108] The issue was to identify the compounds whose chemical structure made them likely to persist and bioaccumulate in the tissues of living organisms as the result of exposure in food or the environment.

The board reports in this period reflect the growing scientific concern about how discoveries about the number and extent of toxic contaminants in the Great Lakes by both regulatory and research agencies coincided with other events that heightened public concern. The State of Michigan spent over $100 million dealing with the consequences of contamination of the milk and meat supply by polybrominated biphenyls (PBBS) about the same time that extremely high levels of PCBS were found in the sediments of Waukegan Harbor near a drinking-water intake on the Illinois shoreline of Lake Michigan.[109] Discoveries of ground-water contamination by toxic chemicals in several locations in Great Lakes states added to state-agency concerns about the need to preserve water quality in the lakes for future water supply.[110]

Two events in 1975 added to the growing sense of urgency about the need to control toxic contamination of the lakes as well as eutrophication. The first event was the first-ever national conference on PCBS that was held in Chicago in November. The conference was authorized by top headquarters USEPA management in response to information provided by Region 5 staff about the presence of PCBS in the Great Lakes, and to Congressional pressure that had been stimulated by a letter-writing campaign of the Lake Michigan Federation.[111] The conference agenda covered the recent research on the presence of PCBS in fish tissues, information about effects of feeding fish with PCBS to mink, and research at the University of Wisconsin in which the health of primates was affected by consumption of food with PCBS at levels comparable to those being found in fish. News coverage of the conference noted that the Food and Drug Administration had banned commercial sale of fish from Green Bay for the same reasons.

The second major happening was the discovery of the highest levels of PCBS yet found in fish tissues in small Lake Siskiwit on Isle Royale in the remote northern part of Lake Superior. Atmospheric deposition of PCBS in Lake Michigan had already been reported. This discovery by USEPA research scientist Wayland Swain confirmed that the chemicals were being transported long distances through the atmosphere, because there was no possible source of direct discharge in this location.[112]

PCBS were not the only problem. The RAB also reported how the number of chemicals found in the Great Lakes that were persistent and had the capacity to bioaccumulate was continuing to grow. In the late 1970s, almost a thousand different chemicals had been found, though eventually the list for priority action would be refined to 11 criteria substances.[113]

IJC REPORTS TO THE GOVERNMENTS

The progress reports required in Article VI of the 1972 agreement continued the IJC's traditional principal function of tendering advice to the governments, in this case on achievement of water quality objectives for the Great Lakes. The agreement allows the IJC to make special reports to the governments at any time on new problems, but it has principally relied on the routine annual (later biennial) reports.[114] The IJC water quality reports are in addition to separate annual reports to the governments on all of its activities in relation to levels and flows, and to reports on special references. The agreement reports are made public and go to all eight Great Lakes states and Ontario, as well as to the national governments, but formal responses to the commission come only through the departments of State and External Affairs.

The first report, in 1972, largely concerned the establishment of the binational institutions required by the agreement.[115] The second report, covering 1973 and part of 1974, for the first time raised the ongoing question about whether progress could "be confirmed on the basis of the scientific data and information supplied to the Commission."[116] The Third Annual Report for 1974, published in December 1975, raised another complaint, which became perennial, about the incomplete response of the governments to its earlier reports. The 1975 report cautioned that public perceptions of almost immediate results from Great Lakes cleanup could be overly optimistic because improvement in such a large system might not be measurable for decades. This report also urged the governments to address PCB problems, expressing doubt that the offer to limit sales made by the Monsanto Company, the sole North American manufacturer, would solve them.[117]

In 1976 the IJC noted that, while total phosphorus loadings had decreased, programs were behind schedule. Greater emphasis was put on the need for attention to toxic contaminants. Finally, the commission concluded that "development of coordinated programs for research, surveillance, and remedial measures" was "a major accomplishment on which the Parties should continue to build."[118]

The general annual reports of the IJC, which are separate from the Great Lakes progress reports, reflected the broad range of the commission's other activities outside the Great Lakes Agreement from 1972 to 1978. The agency had received another reference on water quality for the Garrison Diversion project, which proposed to divert water from the Missouri River through a large irrigation project to the Hudson River drainage basin in North Dakota. There were also reports on references on water quality for the Rainy, St. Croix, St. John, and Poplar rivers.[119]

The IJC was also addressing issues relevant to the Great Lakes outside its agreement-based activities. In 1975, the IJC had been given a reference on air quality in Michigan and Ontario in the Detroit–Windsor and Port Huron–Sarnia areas. The IJC's International Air Quality Board had also recommended attention by the governments to alleged transboundary flow of fluoride emissions between Massena, New York, and Cornwall Island, Ontario, and to long-range transport of pollutants from outside the Great Lakes basin, in addition to miscellaneous other items.[120]

Finally, the commission suggested that funding for its own operations should be reviewed in light of a General Accounting Office report that suggested its funding from the United States was inadequate.[121] There was no mention of the exclusion of the commission from the five-year review that the parties had started in compliance with Article ix.[122] No process for the review was specified, but preparations were begun by the governments.

Results of the First Phase of the Great Lakes Agreement

In 1977 the review of the results of the 1972 agreement began in preparation for the possible negotiation of a new agreement.[123] The signs were increasing that eutrophication had slowed enough to meet at least some of the agreement goals, but new information about toxic contamination continued to emerge.[124] The first phase of the Great Lakes Agreement remains perhaps the most dramatic because of the changes that occurred within a few years.

From the growing evidence of the problems in the Great Lakes and the public demand for action, to the negotiation and conclusion of the agreement, visible results were obtained in a relatively short time. Algae growth had decreased, and so had the so-called "dead zone" in Lake Erie. The general public rejoiced that the water appeared clearer throughout the system.

The toxic contamination that worried scientists, officials of government, environmental agencies, and others who understood the problem was not yet comprehended by the great majority of residents of the watershed. Nor did they understand the institutional and international-relations successes.

The agreement not only set common goals and broke new ground in terms of providing binational guidance on controlling pollution, it also extended the role of the ijc by attempting to apply the commission's traditions and operating principles to environmental problems, not just to control of levels and flows. The agreement retained the binational character of the Boundary Waters Treaty in two ways: in the operation of joint institutions, and in allowing each country to achieve the common objectives under its own political system and laws.

The agreement also fostered growth of a binational community by expanding the public-information services of the ijc. The limited public understanding of the ijc's role in decisions for construction of engineering works under the treaty was expanded because the Great Lakes Agreement allowed the ijc to make information available about its progress at any time, both to the governments and to the public at large.

Major gains had been made in scientific understanding, both for how to slow accelerated eutrophication in the lower lakes, and how to prevent its occurrence in the upper lakes. Research had confirmed that the atmosphere, not just direct discharge of industrial or sewage effluents, could be a source of both conventional pollutants and toxic contaminants. Research revealed that toxic substances were pervasive and already affecting the health of fish and wildlife that depended on aquatic organisms. Recognition of long-range transport of organic chemicals in the Great Lakes basin would lead to recognition that persistent organic pollutants are a global problem. Although this first phase can only be interpreted as successful, the most obvious challenge for the future was the alarm of scientists not about what could be seen, but what was invisible.

A requirement for joint monitoring of water quality gave the ijc a new evaluation role and provided accountability between the ijc and the governments, between the governments, and increasingly, over time, directly between the ijc and the citizens of both countries for the objectives of this first water quality agreement. The challenges of controlling toxic contamination in the following years would bring increasing criticism that the binational agency has no powers to enforce its recommendations.[125]

Under the treaty prior to the Great Lakes Agreement, most ijc decisions were reached by consensus, and the governments accepted and acted on most recommendations of the commission. Under the original 1972 water quality agreement, the governments generally accepted ijc proposals, as they had under the treaty. The lead agencies began to resist ijc recommendations after substantial change in goals in the 1978 version, and still later successfully set the stage for diminishing ijc oversight following renegotiation in 1987.

Finally, the foundation for a broadly based binational community was laid in the first few years of the agreement. The existence of the community both facilitated and depended on communication between scientists and environmental advocates. How it also fostered the political will of the governments for action would be demonstrated in the coming decade.

CHAPTER 4

NEGOTIATION OF THE 1978 GREAT LAKES AGREEMENT AND ITS EVOLUTION

THE ORIGINAL 1972 GREAT LAKES WATER QUALITY AGREEMENT HAD CALLED only for restoration and enhancement of "water quality in the Great Lakes system" by improving water chemistry through pollution control. The new version that resulted in 1978 from the first review and renegotiation set a fundamental new goal in the call for "an ecosystem approach to management" based on "virtual elimination" of toxic contaminants.

The first international accord with such broad aims, the new agreement aimed "to restore and maintain the chemical, physical and biological integrity of the waters of the Great Lakes Basin Ecosystem" with elimination of "the discharge of any or all persistent toxic substances." Commitments were made to develop regulatory programs in the "philosophy of zero discharge." An International Joint Commission (IJC) brochure meant to explain the concept to the general public said that the new agreement "recognizes the complex relationships among WATER, LAND, AIR AND LIVING THINGS (plants, animals and man) [emphasis in the original]."[1] Human health was identified as a concern by the definition that said substances are toxic if they can cause behavioral abnormalities "after concentration in the food chain" in any living organisms.

The decade between review and renegotiation of the new agreement in 1978 and another review and renegotiation in 1987 brought major change to the regime that had been formed to implement the first agreement. The changes affected both the operations of the institutions and their relationships. Some came from within the regime and others were due to outside influences. The consequences of most of these changes continue to be issues for Great Lakes restoration and preservation in 2005.

The 1980s saw a shift in the general approach to environmental management in both Canada and the United States, as well as within the Great Lakes regime, from a focus on pollution control to changing processes and products to prevent pollution in the first place. In both countries, the shift was largely related to growing public concern about the use and management of hazardous materials. Great Lakes science continued to lead the way in identifying the consequences of the presence of persistent bioaccumulative chemicals in the environment, such as PCBS, dioxins, and furans.

Inside the regime, the role of the IJC changed as the appointment process was politicized, and members of the commission began to disregard tradition in asserting their own ideas about how the Great Lakes Regional Office and the advisory boards should function. During this period, the government agencies on both sides began to resist the oversight role of the IJC in agreement-related activities as making unreasonable demands on decreasing agency funding and personnel resources.

In the United States, the Washington headquarters of the U.S. Environmental Protection Agency (USEPA) continued to resist the goals of the Great Lakes Agreement as having greater authority than domestic policies and laws. At the same time, certain USEPA officials tried for the first time to impose the U.S. approach to control of pollution discharges on Canada. This effort seems to have caused no lasting damage to the working relationship between the Great Lakes National Program Office of the USEPA and Environment Canada.

Much greater and long-lasting consequences came from the growth of public involvement and the influence of the environmental community. By the time of another review and renegotiation in 1987, the IJC and the lead federal, state, and provincial executive agencies and legislatures were responding to demands for zero discharge of toxic contaminants from an expanding and very vocal constituency. The 1978 agreement was renegotiated in a very different context than the first had been.

The Context of Review and Renegotiation in 1978

Scientists largely led development of the original 1972 agreement because of scientific consensus that reduction of phosphorus loadings could slow eutrophication, and political consensus that public demand for action had been stimulated by conditions in Lake Erie, as well as a general explosion of concern for the environment in the late 1960s and early 1970s.[3] Renegotiation of the agreement in 1978 was triggered by the requirement for "comprehensive review of the operation and effectiveness . . . during the fifth year after its coming into force."[4]

Several convergent factors have been cited as reasons for the political commitment to amend the agreement when the required review became due. There was a sense of success in slowing eutrophication, but growing recognition by policymakers—driven by scientific leaders in the Great Lakes research

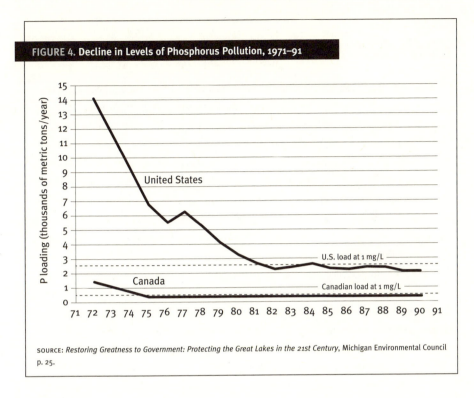

FIGURE 4. Decline in Levels of Phosphorus Pollution, 1971–91

SOURCE: *Restoring Greatness to Government: Protecting the Great Lakes in the 21st Century*, Michigan Environmental Council p. 25.

community—of the problems posed by the presence of toxic chemicals.[5] The expanding involvement of environmental organizations and the absence of a strong lobby against the changes helped create a favorable political climate.[6]

The period from 1972 to 1978 had been exciting for the Great Lakes community. Both governments made major funding available for research, for improving sewage treatment, and for public involvement in addressing the difficult problem of pollution from nonpoint sources in the PLUARG study.[7] As signs of decreased eutrophication became visible, said one Environment Canada official, "everyone was basking in the glow of the 1972 agreement."[8]

As the deadline for the five-year review approached, the attention of the research and regulatory communities was focused on major discoveries about the presence of persistent bioaccumulative contaminants in the environment.[9] The presence of PCBs in fish throughout the Great Lakes was considered a potential threat to human health. Although manufacture and most uses of PCBs had been discontinued, it was realized that such stable chemicals would likely remain in the huge, virtually closed Great Lakes systems for decades if not for centuries.[10]

PCBs were not the only problem. The pesticide mirex was found in Lake Ontario and downstream in the St. Lawrence River.[11] By the mid 1970s,

PCBs: Not Just a Great Lakes Problem

The manufacture and most uses of polychlorinated biphenyls (PCBs) were banned in the U.S. Toxics Substances Control Act (TOSCA) in 1976. The first report of PCBs in fish tissues in northern Lake Michigan was made by Thomas Edsall at the last meeting of the Lake Michigan Enforcement Conference in Chicago in 1971.

Edsall, a fishery biologist from the Great Lakes Fishery Laboratory of the U.S. Fish and Wildlife Service in Ann Arbor, Michigan, said that levels of DDT in fish tissues in Lake Michigan had gone down sooner than expected following DDT bans by Wisconsin and Michigan. (A national ban was adopted in 1972.) He was uncertain whether previous analysis had been distinguishing DDT from its chemical cousins, PCBs, before a new testing technique made the distinction possible.

The announcement alarmed Great Lakes scientists, but not USEPA officials in Washington, D.C., who said it was just a Lake Michigan problem. In an editorial in *Science*, the deputy director of the Office of Research and Development said it was just a Great Lakes problem when the chemicals were found in fish elsewhere in the lakes. For several years, Region 5 administrator Francis Mayo urged a national conference to assess the significance of persistent bioaccumulative chemicals in the Great Lakes ecosystem.

The Lake Michigan Federation urged its members to write to their Congressional representatives about the need to take the presence of PCBs seriously. In 1975, after Mayo made his case at a semiannual policy meeting of headquarters officials and regional administrators, USEPA administrator Russell Train overruled the other officials to direct Region 5 to organize the conference that Mayo wanted. Later, Russell said that he was responding to Congressional pressure.*

The November conference in Chicago was cosponsored by the USEPA with the Department of Interior and other federal agencies. The agenda included description of uses of the man-made PCBs since the 1930s, principally in connection with electricity because of stability in the presence of heat. Dangers of PCBs in the environment because of their toxicity and capacity to bioconcentrate in the food chain were also explained.

A University of Wisconsin scientist described health problems in primates who were fed food with PCBs in the concentrations found in fish. His findings were confirmed by other researchers in a session left open for reports of unpublished research.

Most headlines about the conference concerned the lament of Nathaniel Reed, assistant secretary of the Interior, that many millions of dollars were being spent to restore Great Lakes fisheries while PCBs made them unsafe to eat. Commercial fishermen from Green Bay told on television how their livelihoods had been destroyed by a Food and Drug Administration ban on sale of fish because of PCBs. The 1976 TOSCA ban recognized that PCBs were not after all just a Great Lakes problem.

*Personal communication to Lee Botts.

research fostered by the agreement had found hundreds of toxic contaminants in Great Lakes fish and waters, and more were being found all the time.[12]

Another major factor was the accumulating evidence about the sources and the pathways for toxic contaminants in the Great Lakes ecosystem. As the environmental movement gathered force in the late 1960s and early 1970s, the major source of pollutants was generally assumed to be direct discharge of industrial wastes into waterways or into the air. Sewage as a major source of phosphorus was recognized under the 1972 agreement. The PLUARG study was especially important for the 1978 agreement because it confirmed the significance of nonpoint sources.[13]

A follow-up to the 1964 Great Lakes Reference on the lower Great Lakes and St. Lawrence River that led to the original Great Lakes Agreement, the massive study produced over one hundred published reports and involved hundreds of citizens and local officials in its 17 advisory panels—nine in the United States and eight in Canada.[14] The reasons for its importance included:

- It expanded the scientific understanding of nonpoint and land-based sources of pollution in the Great Lakes;
- It laid the foundation for the development of the ecosystem concept for management and its incorporation into the agreement; and
- It expanded public participation in IJC activities.[15]

Jack Manno explains the importance of PLUARG this way: "The consultation process was unique, characterized by its geographic extent, binational involvement, and use of citizen panels. Citizens advised PLUARG on all aspects of the study. Their involvement not only had a direct impact on the final report but also positively influenced people's attitudes toward the GLWQA. It was successful in gaining both support and credibility, as was hoped."[16]

Similarly, the Upper Lakes reference study also confirmed the atmosphere as a diffuse source of contaminants to the lakes. For example, it was found that 25 percent of sulfates reached Lake Superior from the air; a figure of 1 or 2 percent had been anticipated.[17]

The presence of DDT had been recognized in the 1960s just one year after publication of Rachel Carson's warning in her 1962 book *Silent Spring.*[18] Now in the 1970s, with the expansion of research under the Great Lakes Agreement, evidence of the extent of the problem was coming from many sources, including a Canadian monitoring program that measured the concentrations of contaminants in eggs of the common herring gull.[19] The highest levels of PCBS had been found on remote Isle Royale in Lake Superior, where PCBS could have reached only by long-range transport through the atmosphere.[20]

As government officials contemplated undertaking the first required review of the agreement, they had to consider the implications not just of accelerated eutrophication in the water but also of the accumulation of chemicals that could bioconcentrate in the food chain possibly for several human life spans before decomposing. What had been thought to be a "water quality" problem was understood now by officials, scientists, and environmentalists active in the Great Lakes community to be an air problem, a land-runoff problem, a contaminated-site problem, and potentially a human-health problem for generations. Cleanup of the Great Lakes that had been thought achievable by reducing phosphorus loadings and preventing oil spills and trash littering now turned out to require elimination of possibly hundreds of chemicals that reach the lake from many sources, some of them diffuse and far away.

Changes in Public Awareness and Understanding

Manno found that citizen advisors in the PLUARG study had gained understanding of the complexity of Great Lakes problems that increased their appreciation for the intended purposes of the 1972 Great Lakes Agreement, but the general public did not have the same awareness. As the deadline for the first five-year review approached, there was no general public demand for Great Lakes cleanup because the problems caused by toxic contamination were not as obvious as the algae, sewage, and fish kills had been earlier. To the casual observer, the Great Lakes seemed cleaner because algae growth had declined so much in Lakes Michigan and Ontario with better phosphorus controls. Even on Lake Erie, the Cuyahoga River no longer seemed to catch fire, there was seldom any sign of human sewage, and walleye fishing was getting better.

Toxic contamination could not be seen, tasted, or smelled in the water anywhere, and sport fishermen could not accept warnings that their favorite catch, large coho and chinook salmon that had been introduced from the Pacific Northwest, were unsafe to eat.[21] Public concern was aroused on both sides of the border, however, by news about what was happening at a residential community called Love Canal near the Niagara River in New York. The community got its name from an old canal that had been filled with hazardous wastes before houses and a school were built. The legacy of Love Canal—the land contaminated with chemicals that could be seen leaching into the water from the high river banks, reports of damage to children's health, and the possible need to evacuate an entire community—was said to have had a profound impact on the negotiations. It also spawned the environmental justice movement that has continued to be a major element in the environmental management policy of the USEPA.[22]

The effect of Love Canal on the 1978 review and renegotiation was due to the reaction of scientists and agency officials to the avalanche of new information about contaminants, not to public demands for action. The public did not yet realize, as the researchers and government personnel did, that the long-range atmospheric transport of PCBS that had been confirmed in Lake Superior in 1975 meant that the entire Great Lakes system was vulnerable.[23] The general sense that cleanup of the Great Lakes was underway, and the lack of general public alarm at this stage about contaminants were at least part of the reason that the first periodic review of the Great Lakes Agreement was largely carried out internally within the government agencies as a bureaucratic process.

INSTITUTIONAL ISSUES

The institutional context in which the review occurred was also different than when the agreement was created. The early 1970s were the period of explosive growth of the environmental movement in both countries. The new environmental agencies of the governments when the first agreement was signed now had greatly enlarged agendas that distracted from the Great Lakes commitments. The agencies that now had the lead responsibilities for implementation of the agreement had not existed when the Great Lakes Agreement was conceived. By the time of the first required review in 1976 and 1977, institutional issues had emerged that would persist for three decades through the subsequent history of the agreement.

Environment Canada and the Ontario Ministry of the Environment had been established in 1970 and 1971 respectively, and the Canada Centre for Inland Waters in the same period as the agreement was being developed. The USEPA was established by executive order of President Nixon in 1970, and the original Clean Water Act was passed in October 1972, several months after the agreement had been signed in April.[24]

In both countries, creation of the new agencies was accompanied by new programs and new laws, and the struggle of officials of these agencies to keep a Great Lakes focus was complicated by increasing demands on their budgets for other purposes.[25] For example, in the United States in 1974, USEPA headquarters diverted funding that Congress had intended for Great Lakes programming to establish a new Chesapeake Bay program.

The first agreement review came due as the Great Lakes National Program Office was being established—to be housed at Region 5 in Chicago, but with a mandate now to work also with Region 2 in New York and Region 3 in Philadelphia. The office was created in response to Congressional pressure and in spite of the opposition of high-level USEPA officials in Washington. As the new responsibilities were added, USEPA headquarters continued to try to reduce Great Lakes funding because of the continuing view that the terms of the agreement were subservient to U.S. domestic law.[26]

Love Canal and the Evolution of a Grass-Roots Movement

In 1978, the federal and state governments began evacuating people from the Love Canal neigh-borhood in Niagara Falls, New York. Eventually, 900 families were moved out. During the 1940s and 1950s, Hooker Chemical (now Occidental Chemical) dumped 43 million pounds of hazardous wastes into a canal, covered it with earth, and then "sold" the property to the Niagara Falls school board for $1. A neighborhood developed around the site, and a school was built directly on top of Love Canal.

In the mid 1970s, people living in the Love Canal neighborhood became increasingly alarmed about health problems. Their research uncovered the fact that toxic wastes were buried under the schoolyard that their children played in every day, and that these wastes were leaking from that site into their basements. The community organized into the Love Canal Homeowners' Association under the leadership of a local housewife, Lois Gibbs. Their activism resulted in President Carter declaring Love Canal a federal disaster area.[1]

The Love Canal was only one of an estimated 200 hazardous-waste landfills near the Niagara River. Hooker Chemical had dumped an estimated 350 million pounds of toxic hazardous wastes into three of these: "S" Area, Hyde Park, and 102nd Street. Evidence showed that hazardous wastes, including dioxins, were leaking from these sites into the Niagara River and were flowing downstream into Lake Ontario. In 1985, then Ontario environment minister Jim Bradley said, "There are 2,000 pounds of dioxins in the Hyde Park site. If just a fraction enters Lake Ontario, it will present a serious threat to our drinking water."[2]

The leaking dumpsites on the U.S. side of the Niagara River quickly became an international concern. In the early 1980s, environmental groups from Canada, including Operation Clean Niagara (led by Margherita Howe of Niagara-on-the-Lake), Pollution Probe (led by Moni Campbell and

In the United States, the state agencies were becoming more reluctant to participate in IJC affairs as their federal grants became smaller and had to cover more activities. The pattern in the new environmental laws passed by Congress in the 1970s was to delegate authority to state governments for implementation and to provide grants of federal funding to assist implementation. Under the Clean Water Act, for example, states were given annual program grants to enforce the National Pollution Discharge Elimination System (NPDES) effluent limits, provided the permits met the minimum national discharge limits for specific substances and other conditions set in the federal law. The laws also provided federal grants for specific programs, such as federal grants under the Clean Water Act to local governments for up to 75 percent of the cost of expanding the capacity of publicly owned sewage treatment works to meet the new effluent limits. As the available funding decreased in

Anne Wordsworth of Toronto), and the Canadian Environment Law Association (led by Toby Vigod of Toronto) combined with the Ecumenical Task Force on the U.S. side (led by Sr Margeen Hoffman of Niagara Falls, N.Y.) to fight for a cleanup of these dump sites. These groups played an essential role in pushing the Canadian and Ontario governments to get involved in the Niagara River issue.[3] Their activism resulted in Canada, the United States, Ontario, and New York State signing the Niagara River "Declaration of Intent" in 1987, which committed the governments to a 50 percent reduction in persistent chemicals of concern from point and nonpoint sources in Ontario and New York by 1996.

Love Canal and the Niagara River set off alarm bells in the late 1970s that had permanent effects all across the continent. The U.S. Congress passed the Superfund legislation to require the chemical industry to pay towards the cleanup of hazardous-waste sites. It led to the recognition of the need to move from a pollution-control to a pollution-prevention approach to toxic substances, in order to avoid future Love Canals. Love Canal and the Niagara River were also a birthplace for a grass-roots movement of anti-toxics groups that spread across the continent and also led to the environmental justice movement. Lois Gibbs of Love Canal dedicated her life to supporting this grass-roots movement and founded the Citizens Clearinghouse for Hazardous Waste, which was renamed the Center for Health, Environment, and Justice.[4]

Prepared by John Jackson

1. There are numerous writings on Love Canal. One excellent synopsis is Samuel S. Epstein, Lester O. Brown, and Carl Pope, "Dumping in Niagara Falls," in *Hazardous Waste in America* (San Francisco: Sierra Club Books, 1982), 89–132.
2. Ministry of the Environment, "Environment Minister Bradley Wants Immediate Action to Stop Flow of Deadly Dioxins to the Niagara River," news release, 2 August 1985.
3. Phil Weller, *Fresh Water Seas: Saving the Great Lakes* (Toronto: Between the Lines, 1990), 145–47.
4. Thomas H. Fletcher, *From Love Canal to Environmental Justice: The Politics of Hazardous Waste on the Canada–U.S. Border* (Peterborough, Ontario: Broadview Press, 2003), 46–54.

subsequent reauthorizations, states were pressured to increase their assistance to local governments.

Both of these programs were essential to achievement of specific objectives of the Great Lakes Agreement, but resentment by the states grew over time about the decrease of federal funding available to deal with what the states came to call "unfunded mandates." They also reflected the view of the states that obligations under the Great Lakes Agreement are the responsibility of the federal government because the states are not themselves parties to the compact.[27]

Tension had also developed between the IJC and the government agencies during the first five years about growth in the staff and function of the Great Lakes Regional Office, which had not been spelled out in the original agreement. Budget and personnel constraints were already leading program managers to question the value of the staff time that was spent participating in the advisory-board structure that was managed by the Great Lakes Regional Office.[28] Both state and federal officials complained that the work for the IJC had to be carried out in addition to other staff responsibilities. In spite of the difficulties and the constraints, cancellation of the Great Lakes Agreement was never suggested from either side, and the required review proceeded.

Final Review and Negotiation for a New Agreement

The agreement directed the parties—that is, the governments—to carry out the review and decide whether changes were needed. The review was carried out largely internally, without significant public participation and with no provision for IJC participation. Apparently the national governments viewed the agreement as between them alone.[29] Canadian IJC commissioner Keith Henry's public criticism in the 1978 meeting of the lack of IJC involvement is said to have cost him his position.[30] (The IJC was not to participate in the later 1987 review either.)

Thomas Jorling, USEPA assistant administrator for Water, raised issues in the 1977 five-year review of the first agreement that confirmed Washington's continuing reluctance to accept the agreement goals. Following the election of President Jimmy Carter in 1976, Jorling had become U.S. chair of the WQB—the first, and to date, the only headquarters official to do so. Although he questioned the agreement's objectives when a new agreement was signed in 1978, he seldom attended WQB meetings, and the position was returned to Region 5, whose support of the agreement continued to be backed up by Congress.[31]

The formal process began on 13 April 1977, one day before the fifth anniversary of the original signing and the date actually stipulated for completion of the review. Each side prepared recommendations in advance, followed by consultation and preliminary negotiation by the staffs of agencies involved with implementation of the agreement. Early in 1978, the final review and negotiations were quickly carried out without public oversight by teams of six negotiators on each side.[32] The basic final agreement was in place by May, but the signing was delayed while internal disagreements about funding were resolved on the U.S. side.[33]

Three major issues emerged in the review and advance negotiations: U.S. effluent standards versus Canadian water quality objectives, the Great Lakes Regional Office, and the question of an ecosystem approach to management with the virtual elimination of toxic contaminants. The first two issues were raised mainly by the Washington headquarters of the USEPA and were controversial. The ecosystem approach to management concept was accepted without controversy on both sides.

The Review Process and Negotiation

The final negotiating teams were nominally led by the State Department and the Department of External Affairs, although the USEPA and Environment Canada were actually in charge.[34] The lead negotiators were Robert Slater, director of the Ontario Regional Office of Environment Canada, and George Alexander, who had been asked to stay on as Region 5 administrator following the election of President Carter in 1976 in order to participate in the negotiation.[35]

In preparation for the review, both sides had established their own senior review groups to begin formulating negotiating positions. The U.S. Senior Review Group was headed by Barbara Blum, deputy administrator of the USEPA, with staff from other federal agencies as members. Thomas Jorling, USEPA assistant administrator for Water, appears to have been the actual leader for this group, and raised the major issues that had to be resolved as the review of the agreement proceeded.[36]

Jorling's main interests were to eliminate the Great Lakes Regional Office and to persuade Canada to adopt a regulatory approach compatible with the U.S. approach as embodied in the Clean Water Act. Otherwise, the USEPA Senior Review Group depended heavily on its Sub-Group A for detailed recommendations for changes in the agreement, article by article and annex by annex. Leadership in the final negotiating sessions was left to the U.S. chair, Alexander.

The U.S. Sub-Group A included representatives of the federal and state agencies who participated in implementing the agreement. Seven additional work groups, also headed by USEPA staff directly involved in agreement activities, were formed to address specific topics, including water quality objectives and surveillance, phosphorus, hazardous substances, research, nuclear wastes, and point and nonpoint sources of pollution.[37]

The Canadian negotiating delegation was led by a senior Environment Canada official, with other departments—such as External Affairs, and Fisheries and Oceans—also involved at times. Quebec also maintained a presence at the negotiations.

Effluent Standards versus Water Quality Objectives

The first controversial issue was Jorling's proposal that Canada adopt an industrial pollution-control program like that of the U.S. Clean Water Act, which set uniform effluent limits for direct discharges substance by substance. The U.S. side said that the more flexible Canadian approach of setting water quality objectives that attempted "to tailor the discharge to the assimilative capacity of the receiving water" was like allowing the equivalent of only primary treatment for both sewage and industrial discharges, rather than the minimum "best practicable treatment" required by U.S. law.[38]

The United States also wanted both sides to adopt basin-wide water quality standards. The effect of this proposal would have been to broaden the scope of the agreement to include all tributaries, rather than just water bodies through which the international border runs.[39] Finally, the U.S. proposed language for Programs and Other Measures in Article 5 that would also cause Canada to open up its pollution-control system to public scrutiny, as required in the U.S. Clean Water Act.[40]

Canada rejected all three proposals. Although the U.S. Clean Water Act had been reauthorized in 1977, neither Canadian federal nor Ontario water quality laws were scheduled to be revamped. Canada also considered the tributary rivers to be within domestic, not international, jurisdiction. Munton summarized Canada's arguments against the effluent limit approach as follows:

> The overall water quality objectives approach is, of course, much more compatible with the Canadian position of the two countries' "equal rights" to the use of the Great Lakes than was the effluent standard approach. The latter would require similar source-by-source reductions despite the disparity of the total amounts of pollutants from each side. The Canadians argued each country should be responsible for taking such measures as necessary to ensure both together met the common objectives [of the agreement] in the boundary waters.[41]

The Canadian position on effluent standards was also consistent with the position taken by both sides on phosphate-detergent bans. In the United States, most jurisdictions sought total bans (except for dishwashing compounds for sanitary reasons) of phosphates in detergents. The United States had not objected to Canada's partial bans because the total contributions of phosphorus were so much lower than on the U.S. side.

Great Lakes Regional Office

The United States also proposed elimination of the Great Lakes Regional Office in Windsor. While agreeing that IJC oversight was needed for implementation of the agreement, the USEPA thought the regional office over-reached its role by initiating activities that required staff and resources that could be better used by the government agencies. Without the regional office, the IJC could depend on the Water Quality and Science Advisory boards.[42] The same issue would be raised again in the next review a decade later by Environment Canada, but was strenuously opposed by the Canadian negotiators in 1977.

In the end, it was agreed to define the role of the regional office, which had not been done in 1972. The compromise was that first, the office would provide technical assistance and administrative support and report to the advisory boards. Second, the ijc would oversee public information services by the regional office for both the commission and the boards.

The arrangement was not well received by the ijc members, particularly the Canadian chair Maxwell Cohen and commissioner Keith Henry. Cohen is reported to have believed that the ijc's capacity to provide independent review of the progress of the governments under the agreement required independence for the regional office.[43] In June 1978, the two governments reviewed the staffing and functions of the office, and the ijc made is own review in 1979 after the new agreement was signed.

An Ecosystem Approach to Management and the Goal of Virtual Elimination

The concepts of an ecosystem approach to management and the goal of virtual elimination were included during the final closed negotiations. The Canadian side is credited with providing the "ecosystem" language, and several officials can take credit for supporting the concept during the actual negotiations.[44] It is not clear whether the language was proposed as an alternative to the U.S. preference for specifying the exact levels of reduction required in effluent discharges.

It is also not clear whether the implications of the concept were clearly understood by the negotiators, although one said in 1995 that "some who had a fair idea of the need for a cross-media or more integrated approach downplayed the possibilities to prevent a backlash against its inclusion."[45] Even though the ecosystem-approach concept may not have been fully understood at the time, later it came to be considered one of the most profound contributions of the Great Lakes Agreement.

Paradoxically, the "virtual-elimination" language was noncontroversial at the time, but later became the most contentious feature of the agreement. The U.S. side may have considered it compatible with the goal of the Clean Water Act to stop all discharges of pollutants by 1985.[46] The goal became contentious because of disagreement over its definition. What is called "virtual elimination" in Article II is referred to as "zero discharge" in Annex 12, where there is a commitment by governments to design regulatory programs in the philosophy of "zero discharge."

USEPA FUNDING ISSUES

The signing of the agreement was delayed for several months because of usepa attempts to cut funding for Great Lakes programs by half as the review and negotiation were proceeding. In the actual negotiation, the usepa proposed to reduce federal costs for collecting monitoring data on water quality in the open lakes by submitting instead the data on tributary water quality that the states were required to collect in order to receive annual funding for administration of the NPDES permit system.

In January 1978, Edith Tebo, GLNPO director, reported that Michigan, Wisconsin, Indiana, Ohio, and Minnesota had all refused to accept federal grants for collecting the tributary data. The reason was that they considered the obligations of the Great Lakes Agreement to be a federal responsibility that they might have to assume if the trend towards reduced federal funding for environmental programs continued.

Meanwhile, in the budgeting process of the U.S. federal government, USEPA headquarters reduced its request for Great Lakes programs from $11.1 million to $5.5 million for the following fiscal year. The reduction was protested by the agency's own Office of International Activities and by the U.S. State Department.[47] The cuts were restored by Congress before the agreement was signed after Senator Gaylord Nelson of Wisconsin persuaded all 16 Great Lakes senators to write to President Jimmy Carter.[48]

This incident set the stage for the USEPA to continue to ask for less funding for the Great Lakes in their formal annual budget than they knew that Congress was likely to provide. One problem this practice creates is that the agency's own budget request is related to the number of staff positions that have been authorized within the executive branch before the budget request is presented to Congress.

Congress cannot add staff positions when it authorizes an increase in the funding appropriation. As a consequence, the agency is forced to use sources outside its own staff to carry out work that the additional funding makes possible. The sources may be a private consulting firm, a nongovernmental entity such as the Great Lakes Commission, an academic research institution, or another government agency. Dependence on outside sources raises the question of ability to assure that the work is actually performed in accordance with the terms of a grant or intergovernmental agreement. In 2005, the Great Lakes National Program Office continued to have a small number of staff positions in relation to its total budget as authorized by Congress.[49]

Public Participation

Limited efforts were made on both sides to obtain public participation in the review during the summer of 1977. The lack of public involvement in this first periodic review was remembered when another review became due in the late 1980s.[50] On the U.S. side, no record of significant results of four public meetings, or even their exact locations, has been found.

The USEPA did send the work-group reports to several public-interest groups for comment. Alexander informed Barbara Blum that "no comments of substance were received from the public interest groups because of the short time frame in which comments were requested."[51]

In July 1977, Canadian officials released documents with general descriptions for public hearings in Toronto and Thunder Bay, Ontario. These meetings were coordinated with an Environment Canada–sponsored "Great Lakes Week," a series of activities aimed at making the public aware of issues and threats to the Great Lakes. Release of the official background documents that stated the negotiating positions of the governments was not the Canadian "style," one official said.[52] Neither meeting caused controversy or made headlines.

CONCLUSION OF THE NEGOTIATION

Apart from the issues identified above, negotiations proceeded as planned, with exchanges of drafts of various texts from late 1977 to March of 1978. By 11 May 1978, the basic agreement was in place with only minor differences in text to be finalized. [53]

The cabinet of Prime Minister Pierre Trudeau apparently approved the agreement in mid-July 1978. U.S. approval was delayed by the regional-office issue, and by the efforts to reduce funding for Great Lakes programs.[54] The new agreement was signed for the two governments in Ottawa on 22 November 1978, with no formal ceremony and little notice in the news media.

The major objection to how the negotiations were carried out came from representatives of the states on the U.S. side. The final negotiating team, which operated with great secrecy, had only one state representative as a member: William Marks, of the Michigan Department of Natural Resources. In response to complaints from Illinois and Ohio, Marks said he had not consulted with the other states because of State Department insistence on secrecy. The State Department said it had assumed that Marks had consulted the other states. Although many state officials credit the agreement with beneficial results, this incident is another example of the ongoing ambivalence of the states about their role.[55]

Differences in the New 1978 Agreement

The new 1978 Great Lakes Water Quality Agreement had essentially the same format and framework as the 1972 agreement, but the goals and objectives were different. Two new but closely related goals are generally known within the Great Lakes community as "an ecosystem approach to management" and "virtual elimination." Both goals were retained in the next major review of the agreement in 1987 and have not been changed in 2005, but their meanings have been continuously debated. Figure 5 describes the key features of the 1978 Great Lakes Agreement and differences with the 1972 agreement.

FIGURE 5. Key Differences Between the 1972 and 1978 Agreements

SECTION		DESCRIPTION OF NEW SECTION
Definitions	I(g)	Definition of "Great Lakes Basin Ecosystem" that includes the interacting components of air, land, water, and living organisms including man
	I(v)	Definition of "toxic substances"
Purposes	II	New "purpose" section, namely, to restore and maintain the chemical, physical, and biological integrity of the Great Lakes, and three policy commitments, including the goal to prohibit the discharge of toxic substances in toxic amounts and to virtually eliminate persistent toxic substances
Specific Objectives	IV.1(d)(e)(f) IV.2 and 3	New Specific Objectives
Standards, etc.	V	Various amendments
Programs	VI	New deadlines and various program commitments pertaining to municipal sources, industrial sources, inventory of abatement requirements, land-based sources, persistent toxic substances, airborne substances, and monitoring
Powers of IJC	VII.1(a)(d)	• Additional responsibilities given IJC pertaining to data collection, tendering of advice
		• IJC to report biennially
	VII.3 VII.6	• Recognition of SAB and WQB
Joint Institutions	VIII	Clarification of the roles of the Water Quality and Science Boards and the Regional Office
Consultation	X	Review of Agreement following the third biennial report of the Commission
Annexes		Inclusion of New Annexes

Ecological Integrity versus Water-Chemistry Improvement

The unambiguous goal of the first agreement in 1972 had been "to restore and enhance water quality" by achieving specific objectives through pollution control.[56] The fundamental purpose was to improve water quality with a focus on reduction of phosphorus loadings because of the scientific evidence that its presence in excessive amounts accelerated eutrophication. Research in the process of implementation led to specification of target loadings, or the amount of phosphorus reduction determined to be needed to prevent the excessive algae growth and oxygen depletion that were signs of excessive nutrients.

The 1978 agreement introduced new ambiguities in two ways. First, the purpose was now stated as "to restore and maintain the chemical, physical, and biological integrity . . . of the waters of the Great Lakes Basin Ecosystem."[57] The aim was still to protect water quality, but the definition of the Great Lakes Basin Ecosystem as "the interacting components of air, land, water and living organisms, including humans" seemed to imply a new goal of ecological integrity beyond the waters themselves.[58]

This interpretation is reinforced by the statement in the introduction "that restoration and enhancement of the boundary waters cannot be achieved independently of other parts of the Great Lakes Basin Ecosystem with which these waters interact."[59] The basis for the belief that the new agreement calls for "an ecosystem approach to management" also derives from the statement of purpose in Article II, which pledges the parties "to make a maximum effort . . . for a better understanding of the Great Lakes Basin Ecosystem."[60]

Over time, many members of the Great Lakes community have come to believe that the new language meant that the purpose of the Great Lakes Agreement is now restoration of ecological integrity as the major goal, not just improved water chemistry through pollution control. Differentiation between "an ecosystem approach" and "water-chemistry improvement" is further suggested by the distinction of the Great Lakes system as all of "the streams, rivers, lakes and other bodies of water that are within the drainage basin"—in other words, the entire physical hydrologic system, rather than the ecosystem that includes all living organisms.[61] Both systems extend to where the St. Lawrence River becomes the international boundary between the two countries.

Linking Land Use, Water Quality, and Air Pollution for an Ecosystem Approach

Several converging factors contributed to broadening the purpose of the water quality agreement in the 1978 version. They include the work of the Research Advisory Board (RAB), results of the PLUARG study on nonpoint sources, the rising concern about toxic contamination, and identification of atmospheric deposition and hazardous-waste disposal sites as sources of toxic chemicals to the lakes, as well as new understanding about contaminated sediments and how persistent toxic substances cycle within the ecosystem.

Jack Vallentyne, the first Canadian co-chair of the RAB, was one of the scientists who advocated recognition of the links between water quality and sources of pollution from land and the air. At a meeting in Detroit in the fall of 1976, Vallentyne established a committee to explore an ecosystem approach to management, which the RAB then recommended to the IJC in its annual report in July 1977.[62] The response of the IJC was positive, and then the Great Lakes Fishery Commission endorsed the recommendation in a joint meeting with the IJC in October of the same year.[63]

The Fifth Annual Report of the IJC to the governments said that "the ecosystem approach recommended by the RAB may have significant benefits for the long-term management of the Great Lakes . . . by providing a framework for assessing . . . the significance of changes."[64] In March 1978, the commission asked the RAB to evaluate any difficulties in melding the ecosystem and water quality–objectives approaches, practical means of implementation, and research needs for data collection, management techniques, or other aspects.[65]

In June 1978, the earlier ecosystem report, which had gone into a second printing, was submitted—with the board name changed to Science Advisory Board—as part of the annual IJC report.[66] An observer said that, with the PLUARG reports, the SAB report paved the way for acceptance by the governments of the ecosystem concept into the 1978 Great Lakes Agreement.[67] All but one of six changes in specific wording suggested by the advisory-board report were included in the final document. A name change to "Agreement between the United States and Canada on Boundary Waters of the Great Lakes Basin Ecosystem" was not accepted.

Virtual Elimination

Virtual elimination is the second new concept whose meaning has been debated since its introduction in the 1978 agreement. Its origin is less clear. The new provision states that "the discharge of toxic substances in toxic amounts [shall] be prohibited and the discharge of any or all persistent toxic substances [shall] be virtually eliminated."[68] A toxic substance is defined broadly as "any substance which can cause death, disease, behavioral abnormalities, cancer, genetic mutations, physiological or reproductive malfunctions, or physical deformities in any organism or its offspring, or which can become poisonous after concentration in the food chain or in combination with other substances."[69]

One factor was fear of the negative consequences that scientific studies cited for exposure of wildlife and humans to toxic substances—in particular, for persistent chemicals that bioconcentrate in the food chain. State agencies were alarmed about the implications of long-term availability of the Great Lakes as a source of drinking water. William Marks, the state representative on the final negotiating team, talked about how discovery of 900 sites contaminated by dry-cleaning chemicals had created fear in Michigan about possible dependence on the Great Lakes should groundwater become unusable for drinking water.[70]

The concept of "zero discharge" is thought to have emanated from the U.S. Clean Water Act goal of stopping all discharge of pollutants into waterways by 1985. This law also calls for elimination of discharges "in toxic amounts."

In any case, negotiators have stated that the goals of "virtual elimination" and "zero discharge" made sense at the time, even though they may be operationally difficult.[71] The ongoing debate is centered on whether the "virtual elimination" called for in the statement of policy in the agreement is the same as the "philosophy of zero discharge" called for in Annex 12. To some, "virtual elimination" means reducing discharges and ambient water levels as much as practicable in light of costs and considering whether removal methods, such as dredging of contaminated sediments, may in fact release and create more environmental damage than leaving the materials in place. To others, virtual elimination and zero discharge referred to an attempt to phase out use of the most dangerous toxic substances and otherwise promote pollution prevention and cleaner production processes in industry. The concept became controversial after environmental groups later made "Zero means zero" a rallying cry in accusing the governments of failure to fulfill their obligations under the agreement.[72]

Other Changes

The 1978 agreement also called for revised water quality objectives, including new, more stringent target loadings for phosphorus for each of the lakes, with the exact reductions on both sides to be negotiated.[73] New deadlines were set for adoption of necessary municipal and industrial pollution-abatement programs by the end of 1982 and 1983, and a program to identify sources of toxic pollutants to the atmosphere was called for.[74]

Overview of Differences between the 1972 and 1978 Agreements

The fundamental new features of the 1978 agreement were the introduction of the concept of an ecosystem approach to management and virtual elimination of toxic substances. Additional differences included a shift in focus from phosphorus to toxic contaminants, with a set of new goals together with detailed general and specific objectives. Circumstances that led to the changes included research carried out under the 1972 agreement, concurrent events including Love Canal, and the initiative of farsighted individuals.

One negotiator said that the process had gone "relatively smoothly" in spite of some differences that had to be worked out. Canada resisted the attempt of the usepa to impose U.S. policies and regulatory practices. The U.S. Congress intervened in the usepa attempt to reduce federal funding for

Great Lakes programs. The new goals of taking ecological integrity into account and drastic reduction of toxic contamination met no major objections within the governments and the Great Lakes community, or from the general public. In the end, the 1978 negotiation is remembered for the lack of lasting controversy.[75]

Joint Institutions

Essentially, the joint institutions of the original agreement continued under the 1978 version. The Seventh Annual Report of the IJC described its role as primarily "monitoring, assessing, and subsequently advising the Parties concerning the state of the Great Lakes Basin Ecosystem and the effectiveness of any measures taken by the various Great Lakes institutions to meet the terms of the Agreement." The IJC also asserted that "Any matters that might affect the quality of the Great Lakes Basin Ecosystem, and thereby the quality of the boundary waters of the Great Lakes System, are included" in its mandate.[76]

Increasing criticism by the government agencies and nongovernmental sources led to changes later in the 1980s as the institutions established by the agreement struggled with the challenge of moving from improvement of water chemistry to ecosystem protection. The difficulties were compounded by changes in the operations of the IJC.

Water Quality Board

Remaining as principal advisor to the IJC, the WQB was directed to report every two years on its own activities and evaluation of programs of the governments, with recommendations for improvement.[77] A Program Committee was set up to oversee subcommittees on surveillance, point sources, nonpoint sources, and dredging. The same committee was to assist in designating areas of concern. The numerous meetings and reports required much time for the committee members. In 1980, a new directive outlined its duties and elaborated on the terms of reference in the 1978 agreement. Figure 6 shows the structure of the board's operations.[78]

The persistent dilemma for WQB members was that they were expected to make judgments about the agencies that employed them as independent professional experts in the tradition of the IJC. The potential for conflict of interest was raised by the IJC secretariats, by the commission, by commentators on the IJC as an institution, and by environmentalists. Yet some believe the criticism failed to recognize the real contribution of the WQB.[79]

Ian Jackson summarizes the situation this way:

> Responsibility for implementing the Agreement rests primarily with the two federal governments, and the Commission was therefore appointed as official

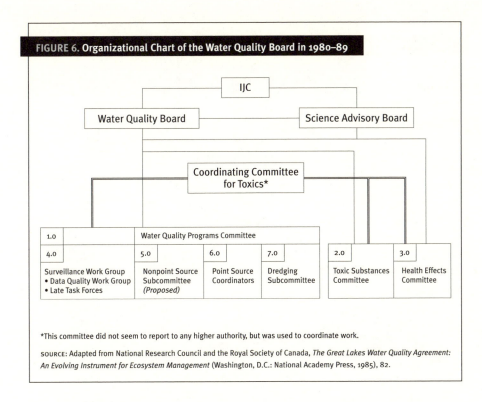

FIGURE 6. Organizational Chart of the Water Quality Board in 1980–89

*This committee did not seem to report to any higher authority, but was used to coordinate work.

SOURCE: Adapted from National Research Council and the Royal Society of Canada, *The Great Lakes Water Quality Agreement: An Evolving Instrument for Ecosystem Management* (Washington, D.C.: National Academy Press, 1985), 82.

critic of the Governments that appoint its members. Perhaps the governments believed that the criticism would be moderated through the device of making "the principal advisor" to the Commission a Great Lakes Water Quality Board that was composed entirely of state, provincial, and federal government representatives. If so, their ingenuity produced an unexpected result. What was created by this provision was an arrangement that was illogical in principle but remarkably productive in terms of making an ecosystem-based Water Quality Agreement actually work.[80]

Former members say that the WQB worked for three reasons: First, as high-level managers of environmental programs, members of the WQB "could make things happen." They could, and did, make recommendations through the IJC that they would have to deal with themselves in the budgets and programs of their agencies. Second, they could use the WQB as a lever for action, discussing policy needed for the lakes with their peers and then arguing for the actions by their home agencies. Third, assisting the fact-finding role of the IJC could help find solutions for problems and implement the agreement.[81]

Still, criticism grew through the 1980s. Evaluation by the National Research Council of the United States and the Royal Society of Canada [hereafter referred to as the NRC/RSC report] concluded that conflict of interest was

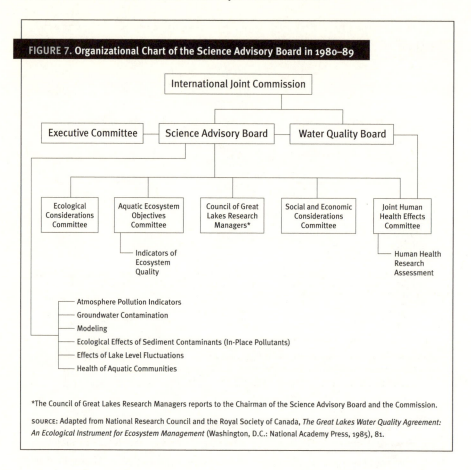

FIGURE 7. Organizational Chart of the Science Advisory Board in 1980–89

*The Council of Great Lakes Research Managers reports to the Chairman of the Science Advisory Board and the Commission.

SOURCE: Adapted from National Research Council and the Royal Society of Canada, *The Great Lakes Water Quality Agreement: An Ecological Instrument for Ecosystem Management* (Washington, D.C.: National Academy Press, 1985), 81.

a factor in the failure of agencies to deal with toxic contamination effectively.[82] The first three biennial reports (replacing the previous annual reports) of the IJC to the governments also commented on this issue.[83]

The strongest criticism was generated by Great Lakes United in a 1987 report, *Unfulfilled Promises: A Citizen's Review of the International Great Lakes Water Quality Agreement*. This document proposed that nongovernmental members be appointed to the WQB, and suggested the creation of a separate Citizens Advisory Board. Both the IJC and the NRC/RSC report questioned the commission's ability to discharge its coordination duties through the WQB and the SAB, in part because of lack of funding that "affected the ability to keep essential levels of personnel in certain activities and have inhibited coordinated research programs."[84] Foreshadowing changes that were to transform agreement processes in the early 1990s, the NRC/RSC report recommended that "the coordinating responsibilities for the control programs that implement the Agreement should be left to the parties, rather than the Water Quality Board. Coordination should be handled through bilateral government-to-government meetings."[85]

Science Advisory Board

The basic mandate of the SAB did not change with its new name under the 1978 agreement to "provide advice on research to the commission and to the Water Quality Board." [86]This board had three committees in 1987: the Ecological Committee, the Societal Committee and the Technological Committee. It also participated in three joint SAB/WQB committees on three topics: Ecosystem Objectives, Human Health Effects, and Toxic Chemicals. Figure 7 shows the organization of the Science Advisory Board.

Two issues have persisted for the SAB from this time. First was the question of how "science" oriented the work of the SAB should be. The agenda was broader than review and assessment of physical and biological science research. The considerable attention to the "societal" and "technological" side of science led to many policy accomplishments of the board, especially during the latter part of the 1980s.

Board membership was another ongoing issue. From the beginning, the board had included not only biologists and water chemists but also social scientists, and later, citizens and representatives of industry. The NRC/RSC report supported this appointment philosophy, which was consistent with the interpretation of its wide mandate.[87] This issue has also persisted to the present.

Council of Great Lakes Research Managers

The broadened agenda of the board left a gap for assessing and meeting research needs. This gap, and the continuing need to engage research scientists directly, led to the establishment of the Council of Great Lakes Research Managers (CGLRM) as a new advisory body to inventory and evaluate research programs for the Great Lakes. This board is not called for in the agreement and was created by the IJC. Initially it reported to the commission through the SAB, and later as a third independent advisory board.

Established in 1984, the council includes managers of research programs pertaining to the Great Lakes. To date, it has been more successful in inventorying than in identifying research needs and promoting coordination. An earlier attempt by the Great Lakes Basin Commission in the late 1970s to promote coordination had been perceived by scientists and the research agencies as an attempt to set research agendas.[88] Some scientists still suggest that the tasks of identifying research needs and preventing duplication of efforts assigned to this body belong to the SAB.[89]

Great Lakes Regional Office

From the beginning in 1972, there was an undercurrent of tension about who was in charge of the Great Lakes Regional Office. The 1978 agreement included a subtle but significant change. Originally, the regional office reported to the IJC itself through the secretariat offices in Ottawa and Washington. Now Article VIII said that the regional office would report to the advisory boards in providing technical and administrative assistance, but to the IJC in providing public-information services. For a period in the early 1980s, the person in charge of public information worked out of the Washington office rather than the regional office in Windsor.[90]

One objection to the change was that the governments, rather than the IJC, would now have the power to select the director and staff, since it was the governments that named the co-chairs of the boards. The reviews of the regional office by the parties and by the IJC that had been agreed to in negotiation of the agreement were reported on in 1979. The parties' report clarified the roles of the director and board secretaries, and recommended that board chairmen be consulted on IJC requests for verification of data in board reports. Several positions were eliminated, including a deputy director, and the director's term was extended to up to four years. No changes resulted from the IJC internal review, but questions about the operation of the regional office continued. The 1985 NRC/RSC report reiterated the debate and recommended that the regional office report directly and solely to the IJC.[91]

Actions of the Governments

In the 1980s, the Great Lakes regime was affected by actions of the governments in addition to the negotiation of the 1978 agreement. Some of the changes affected the regime directly, such as appointments to the IJC and new initiatives by the states and provinces. Others resulted indirectly from changes in domestic environmental management policy and funding reductions.

INTERNATIONAL JOINT COMMISSION

The 1980s began with the largest gap in membership on the IJC in the life of the Boundary Waters Treaty as the new conservative governments delayed making appointments. This period began a pattern of replacement of IJC commissioners with every change of administration on the U.S. side, with a similar, although less consistent, trend in Canada. First, the entire membership has been replaced with every change of federal administration on the U.S. side and a similar but less consistent trend has followed in Canada. Second, the appointments have been exclusively given to political allies, and in some cases as political-patronage awards.

President Ronald Reagan took office in January 1981. On March 4, he abruptly dismissed all three of the commissioners that had served in the Carter administration. One of them, Charles Ross, had served under five presidents, both Democratic and Republican. A new U.S. panel of members did not take office until more than six months later. Two of the three had been state campaign chairmen for Reagan in the 1980 election, and the third was a former Republican congressman from New York.[92]

Prime Minister Brian Mulroney appointed Richard Olson in January, and Charles Bedard in August. Only J. R. Roy was in office through the uncertain transition period. None of the appointees had past experience with Great Lakes issues, knowledge of how the IJC operated, or understanding of the traditions that protected its status as an independent advisory body committed to binationalism.

The new commissioners were appointed by governments that were struggling with the effects of inflation, and who sought to reduce government expenditures in general and spending on environmental programs in particular. The Reagan administration disbanded the Great Lakes Basin Commission, and federal funding was reduced for university and agency research and for regulatory programs.

As jurisdictions coped with meeting agreement obligations with reduced budgets, agency managers on both sides of the border questioned the commitment of personnel time and money to attend meetings and write reports for a multiplicity of subcommittees, task forces, and work groups—particularly for the WQB.[93] One WQB member and agency head thought the early 1980s were an "empire-building stage," when the IJC tried to provide the sole framework for jurisdictions to address water quality issues.[94] Questions about efficient use of resources continued through the decade to become a major issue for the next review of the agreement in 1987.

The Provinces and States

New Canada-Ontario agreements were negotiated in 1982, and again in 1986.[95] Both essentially continued the same money-transfer structure, with the federal government committing to provide about 15 percent of the costs, the province about 40 percent, and the municipalities the balance of 45 percent for actions required by the Great Lakes Agreement.[96]

In this period, the Progressive Conservative Party that had been in power in Ontario for 40 years was replaced in 1985 with a Liberal/New Democratic Party minority coalition government. As the new government took over, public outcry occurred over discovery of a large mysterious "blob" of toxic contaminants in the St. Clair River near Sarnia that corroded a diver's helmet.[97]

Ontario established a new water quality regulatory program called the Municipal-Industry Strategy for Abatement (MISA) in 1986. The purpose of the new program was to set technology-based effluent limits that would "virtually eliminate" discharge of toxic substances into Ontario waterways. Most observers link this program to the Great Lakes Agreement.[98]

Quebec had not been included in most Great Lakes activities, even though the jurisdiction of the Boundary Waters Treaty and the Great Lakes Agreement stop at Cornwall/Massena on the St. Lawrence River, just short of the Quebec border. During this period, a prominent Montreal environmentalist wore black armbands at Great Lakes events to symbolize Quebec's absence. Although downstream and affected by results of the Great Lakes Agreement, Quebec remained a silent partner in the Great Lakes regime, according to one Canadian activist, because it did not want to be committed to the agreement's goals within its jurisdiction.[99] In 1988, the federal government and Quebec signed an agreement concerning measures to address water quality in the St. Lawrence.[100]

In the United States, most high-level state resource managers continued to participate in the WQB. Yet the states also criticized "a proliferation of committees and subgroups" for the WQB. There were also complaints about too much time in the boards spent on budget and administrative matters, rather than policies and programs.[101]

At times, state environmental agencies would work with environmental advocacy groups to use the Great Lakes Agreement to prevent weakening of state laws for the water quality standards adopted for compliance with the Clean Water Act. Indiana environmentalists cited the agreement in fighting repeal of the state's phosphate-detergent ban in nearly every biennial session of the legislature.[102] In Wisconsin, a paper company attempt to weaken PCB discharge limits was defeated with nongovernmental lobbying.[103]

Most state officials of the time credit the agreement with creating a sense of community and a climate that promoted more action on water quality in the region than otherwise would have occurred. The Great Lakes Charter, signed by the states in 1985, dealt with diversion, not water quality.[104] Yet the charter on diversions set the stage for a Great Lakes Toxic Substances Control Agreement in 1986, in which the governors committed to achievement of the Great Lakes Agreement goals for contaminants.[105]

The call of the states' Toxic Substances Control Agreement for "coordinated regional action" echoed the spirit of the binational accord, but went further in committing the governors to lobby the federal government for uniform national standards to discourage competition for economic development, as the Great Lakes region struggled with the decline of its economic base in manufacturing.[106] It should be recalled that a number of important studies were being released on the impacts of toxic chemicals. For example, in May 1986, Kate Davies of Toronto's Department of Public Health released at the World Conference on Large Lakes on Mackinac Island, Michigan, results of a study that she had carried out comparing the relative contributions of persistent toxic substances in the bodies of people living in Southern Ontario from air, water, and food. To help in estimating toxins from food sources, she had samples analyzed of five types of fresh food sold in Toronto supermarkets. She concluded that food was a much more significant source of persistent toxic contaminants in people than were water and air.[107]

The agreement called for "coordinated regional action" in accordance with six principles. In addition to recognizing the "economic and environmental importance of water resources that transcend political boundaries," the agreement called for management of the Great Lakes "as an integrated ecosystem" to satisfy requirements of both the Clean Water Act and the binational agreement "to virtually eliminate" the discharge of all persistent toxic substances. The agreement's purposes were to be achieved by cooperation among "local and state agencies, regional groups, the federal government, the International Joint Commission, and the public."

The states' agreement went even further than the Great Lakes Agreement in committing the governors to lobbying the federal government "through appropriate national associations and their Congressional delegations." The reason was that "the toxic substances threatening the Great Lakes are not confined to the region . . . and yet the federal government has historically been unable to establish . . . uniform national standards [whose] absence may encourage competition for economic development to the detriment of the Great Lakes Region and endanger public health and the environment."

The agreement included an action plan for the states themselves. Among the principal actions were "Various measures to increase the role of the States," including "an active role for the States should renegotiation of the Agreement be agreed to by the federal governments of the United States and Canada." Other actions pledged state support for activities in support of the Great Lakes Agreement, such as research, monitoring, and surveillance programs as well as coordination in collection of compatible water quality and health data.

Presumably, in light of the view of the states that obligations for such activities under the binational agreement are the responsibility of the federal government, the toxics agreement did not mean that the states would undertake such activities themselves. Yet some of the other actions were subsequently initiated, including establishment of the Great Lakes Protection Fund as the "Great Lakes Water Quality Fund" to permit "continuing progress toward a healthier Great Lakes ecosystem." Neither the states nor the federal governments have been able to secure consensus for the uniform health advisory called for.

The Council of Great Lakes Governors that had been organized in the early 1980s was given responsibility for coordination and oversight duties for the toxics agreement. On 3 November 1986, the premiers of Ontario and Quebec and the governors signed a Memorandum of Understanding on the Control of Toxic Substances in the Great Lakes Environment that was similar to the states' agreement. In 2005 the agreement has not lived up to its potential, but is considered to have provided the basis for later development of the Great Lakes Water Quality Initiative by a federal/state task force.[108]

The Great Lakes states, with Ontario, also helped begin development of remedial action plans. The geographic areas that the WQB had identified as "problem areas" where objectives of the agreement were not being achieved were now called "areas of concern." In 1983, a "Master Plan" for cleanup and restoration of the Grand Calumet River and the Indiana Harbor and Ship Canal in Lake County, Indiana, had been produced by the Indiana Board of Health, Region 5 of the USEPA, and the Grand Calumet Taskforce of the Lake Michigan Federation.[109] The WQB proposal that such plans be developed for all the areas of concern was conceived as a way to involve local governments and other stakeholders in the ecosystem approach called for in the 1978 agreement.[110]

When the question of another review of the agreement was raised in the mid 1980s, the states decided that the agreement should not be altered in any major way, but that it required "minor technical adjustments."[111] The growing Great Lakes community concentrated on implementation until the next review in 1987.

The Public and the Great Lakes Agreement

The Great Lakes Agreement was developed in part in response to public concern about Lake Erie and water pollution as the environmental movement gathered momentum in the late 1960s. Citizen attendance as observers at the annual IJC meetings grew slowly in the early years of the agreement.

In 1979, the IJC established a standing committee to assist in providing the public-information service called for in the 1978 agreement.[112] By November, the two-member committee (American Jean Hennessey and Canadian Bernard Beaupré) had worked with the public-information officer in the Windsor office to develop a formal public-information policy.[113]

The basic concept was that citizens have rights to participate in IJC activities and should be encouraged to do so. The new policy stressed that information ought to be provided while studies and activities are being carried out, not just after decisions are already made. The aim was to increase the commission's credibility by taking public opinion into account. More funding to support public participation was urged.[114]

The IJC's public-information activities expanded through the 1980s, beginning with production of a slide show about the 1978 agreement called

Promises to Keep. Several environmental organizations helped distribute the slide show throughout the basin, but the "unfulfilled promises" that the binational coalition Great Lakes United later complained about referred to its title.

Growth in Organization and Advocacy

Citizen action for the environment usually begins out of concern for an issue or a problem close to home. Advocacy activities of environmental organizations for the Great Lakes increased throughout the 1980s for the system as a whole, and seemed to reflect the call for an ecosystem approach.[115] Groups became more demanding within the Great Lakes basin and in Ottawa and Washington, in accordance with the tradition in each country.

Differences in Advocacy Practices

The differences in advocacy practices across the border did not prevent partnerships between environmental organizations. U.S. environmental groups lobbied lawmakers, insisted that opportunities to take part directly in regulatory actions such as setting discharge standards be included in environmental laws, and filed lawsuits against both governments and polluters. The Canadian tradition is for advance consultation with representatives of organizations before new policies are announced. Consultations became more frequent as the Canadian citizens linked up with U.S. groups to advocate on Great Lakes issues.

Membership dues seldom entirely support environmental groups in either country, and citizen groups obtained support for their Great Lakes activities from different sources in the two countries. U.S. groups depend more on philanthropic foundations. In Canada, the government often directly funds citizen participation in policy debates.

Evolution of a Great Lakes Environmental Network

By the 1980s, activists from both sides were increasingly working with each other and with the ijc and government agencies in a growing environmental network. As they came together on various issues, environmental activists began to develop common strategies specifically for the Great Lakes. These included staffs of national, regional, and local environmental organizations, and member volunteers.[116]

Some of the environmental leaders had started working together in the Public Involvement Work Group of the Great Lakes Basin Commission in the 1970s. The Sierra Club included Canadian members in its volunteer Binational Great Lakes Committee. The staff of its Midwest Office in Madison, Wisconsin, gave greater priority to Great Lakes issues and sought support from its California headquarters and lobbying office in Washington, D.C. The Midwest

Regional Office of the National Audubon Society moved from Dayton, Ohio, to Michigan City, Indiana, because its director wanted to work more on Great Lakes issues. In 1982, the National Wildlife Federation established a new Great Lakes Resources Center in Ann Arbor, Michigan, to take legal action and work on policy development. The Lake Michigan Federation became involved in issues for the whole Great Lakes system.

Threat of possible diversion of water from the Great Lakes to the Southwest was a unifying issue for virtually the entire Great Lakes community, including the state and provincial governments. In signing the Great Lakes Charter in 1985, the governors of the Great Lakes states pledged to consult with each other before agreeing to any new diversion from the Great Lakes watershed, and invited the premiers of Ontario and Quebec as observers for the new regional policy.[117]

Acid rain was another issue outside the water quality agreement that brought Great Lakes activists together across the boundary on what was initially considered a Canadian issue. Ontario established a lobbying organization to work with U.S. environmentalists for acid-rain controls in U.S. law.[118]

Toxic contamination was the issue most directly related to the agreement that inspired new advocacy in this period. The Great Lakes groups found new allies in the local organizations that were developing around hazardous-waste-disposal controversies in both countries.[119] Much of the scientific evidence cited in opposition to siting of landfills or incinerators was based on Great Lakes research.

Pollution Probe of Toronto worked with the Ecumenical Task Force in New York to organize residents of the Love Canal region. That work led to intervention of Canadian groups in the litigation for cleanup of the sister sites to Love Canal across the border.[120] Other groups such as the Société pour Vaincre la Pollution of Montreal and the Toronto-based Canadian Environmental Law Association continued their work on Great Lakes issues.

The anti-environmental views of the national administrations in both countries also brought advocacy groups together. The Lake Michigan Federation and other groups had protested funding cuts for Great Lakes programs throughout the 1970s. In the 1980s, U.S. environmental groups joined the Northeast-Midwest Institute and the Center for the Great Lakes in citing obligations of the agreement to justify maintenance and expansion of funding for Great Lakes cleanup. Strategic planning for advocacy increased as the influence of environmental leaders grew.

The conservative approach to environmental matters inadvertently gave profile to a number of issues. For example, Dr. Douglas Hallett, an Environment Canada scientist, gave scientific advice to citizens' groups working for the cleanup of the leaking landfills along the U.S. side of the Niagara River. This

work led to his receiving the United Nations 1984 Silver Medal for Environmental Stewardship. In 1985 he put together a small publication entitled *Storm
Warning* that outlined the health dangers posed by airborne toxic chemicals.
The 9,500 glossy copies of this report were banned from distribution in part
because Health Canada considered human health to be a matter solely within
its jurisdiction, and not in Environment Canada's.[121] A year after the furor that
arose when news of the publication being banned leaked out, Environment
Canada released the document. Hallett resigned from Environment Canada in
1986 as the conflict between him and Environment Canada escalated.[122]

ESTABLISHMENT OF GREAT LAKES UNITED AS A BINATIONAL COALITION

The foundation for creating Great Lakes United as a binational coalition was
laid in New York. The U.S. Great Lakes environmental community expanded
when a group called "Save the River," from the Thousand Islands region,
formed an alliance with the Michigan United Conservation Clubs (MUCC) to
oppose the Army Corps of Engineers' proposal for its winter-navigation project that aimed to assure year-round shipping.[123] With funds provided by the
Joyce Foundation, about 50 persons gathered at the Grand Hotel on Mackinac
Island in May 1982 to consider MUCC's proposition for formation of a "Great
Lakes Federation." They included representatives of the United Auto Workers
in addition to staff and members of local and national, large and small environmental organizations.

The new binational coalition that resulted was called Great Lakes United
(GLU) and soon became a new force in Great Lakes advocacy after surviving
acrimonious controversy about its structure and operations. The GLU agenda
was largely based on policy proposals submitted by member organizations at
annual meetings whose locations alternated across the border, in the tradition
established by the Boundary Waters Treaty. Its first major influence resulted
from its support for the state and provincial agreements on toxic substances,
and in opposition to diversion of water from the Great Lakes to other regions.

Different organizations continued to take the lead on specific policy issues,
but the influence of the Great Lakes environmental community increased
with its coming together in this period. The ability to influence policy and to
lobby for legislation was assisted by exchange of information with scientists
and government-agency staffs in the processes associated with the Great
Lakes Agreement—especially the IJC meetings, where the Water Quality Board
and Science Advisory board reports were presented to the commission.

IJC MEETINGS AS A FORUM FOR THE GREAT LAKES COMMUNITY

The 1980s was the decade when the IJC biennial meetings became the major
forum for communication and exchange of information within the Great

Lakes community. The 1980 public-information policy included guidelines for the IJC annual meetings (that later became biennial events), calling them "the most important public information event of the year." [124] From 1975, attendance at the annual meetings had gradually increased from 135 to about 400.

The first biennial meeting in Indianapolis, Indiana, in 1983 was also the first meeting to be called "a circus" by some observers. The comment referred to the lack of attention to the presentation of the reports of the advisory boards to the commission, and distraction by side events and entertainment of attendees.

This meeting was also the first, and to date the only, IJC meeting for the agreement to be held outside the Great Lakes watershed. The IJC paid for chartered buses to increase attendance by citizens. The location was selected by Keith Bulen, who wanted to increase awareness of the commission and its mission in his hometown, the state capital. The local Republican Party women's committee provided hospitality to out-of-town visitors, including dinners in private homes for selected attendees.

The arrangements for the 1985 meeting in Kingston, Ontario, and the 1987 meeting in Toledo, Ohio, were more traditional, but still attracted significant attendance. The WQB reports continued to receive widespread media coverage as "state of the lakes reports." Resentment grew about the practice of requiring questions from the audience to be submitted in writing.

Throughout the 1980s, criticism from environmentalists also increased about the apparent failure of the governments to achieve either the ecosystem approach to management or the virtual elimination of toxic contaminants called for in the 1978 agreement. Discussions were begun at the Toledo meeting about how to increase public involvement in the next biennial meeting to be held in Hamilton, Ontario, in 1989.

INFLUENCING LEGISLATION AND POLICY

The Sierra Club has more freedom to lobby as an organization for legislation under U.S. tax law.[125] Beginning in 1986, as the strength of the Great Lakes environmental community grew, this organization took the lead for an annual Great Lakes Week, usually the last week in March, in Washington, D.C. The week was scheduled to coincide with the annual meeting of the Great Lakes Commission and the briefings that were provided to Congress by the Northeast-Midwest Institute. Participants included staff from other environmental organizations, and about two dozen U.S. citizen volunteers representing environmental organizations from throughout the Great Lakes basin. Through GLU, a few Canadians attended to demonstrate the binational importance of the issues.

The week's agenda began with briefing on current issues, followed by training in lobbying techniques. Then, members of Congress from the Great

Lakes region were visited in their offices, preferably by residents of their home states. Meetings were also scheduled with officials of the USEPA, the State Department, and other agencies.[126] Social events included a reception at the Canadian embassy, and receptions sponsored by the Great Lakes Commission for members of Congress in either the Senate or the House of Representatives. On occasion, individual sponsors of legislation met with the group, such as Senator Robert Kasten of Wisconsin as the chief sponsor of a proposed new Great Lakes section for the Clean Water Act.

Contact was then maintained with participants throughout the year in a Great Lakes Washington Report that tracked legislative and budget developments and encouraged continuing contacts with members of Congress on specific legislative proposals. At the urging of their members from the Great Lakes region, the Washington offices of other national organizations began to give more attention to Great Lakes issues.[127]

Contaminated sediments became a national issue after the Lake Michigan Federation teamed up with the Coast Alliance, a national coalition of environmental groups concerned with marine shorelines and the Mississippi River. The national organization used Great Lakes information to inform other environmental organizations about the problems of contaminated sediments. Then the national group led the lobbying of the USEPA to create national policy and a program for addressing the issue.[128]

Legislative victories included adoption of an amendment of the 1987 Clean Water Act, whose purpose was to respond to the ongoing reluctance of USEPA headquarters to accept the agreement's goals. Section 118 codifies the Great Lakes Agreement into U.S. law by stating that "It is the purpose of this section to achieve the goals embodied in the Great Lakes Water Quality Agreement . . . through improved organization and definition of mission on the part of the Agency, funding of state grants for pollution control in the Great Lakes Area, and improved accountability for implementation of such agreement."[129]

The growing political strength of the environmental coalition was acknowledged in the 1980s by inclusion of environmentalists in an informal annual meeting of Great Lakes leaders convened by the Center for the Great Lakes. Staffs of regional environmental groups such as the Lake Michigan Federation, the Sierra Club Midwest Office, and the National Wildlife Federation office in Ann Arbor frequently were consulted by the USEPA Great Lakes National Program staff and other federal and state agencies. [130]

Philanthropic Foundation Contributions

The Great Lakes community that evolved around the agreement in the 1980s owes much to the philanthropic foundations of the region. Such support had first been provided to environmental organizations such as the Lake Michigan Federation, which was created in 1970 as a project of the Openlands Project with grants from two local foundations in Chicago—Chicago Community Trust and the Wieboldt Foundation.

FOUNDATION SUPPORT FOR ENVIRONMENTAL ORGANIZATIONS

Like other not-for-profit organizations in the United States, the Lake Michigan Federation has also been sustained by membership dues and contributions, and by government contracts for specific projects, but its long-term survival is due mainly to ongoing support from foundations.[131] In Canada, the government often directly funds policy debates, but not-for-profit organizations also receive foundation support.

In the 1980s, philanthropic foundations in the Great Lakes region both strengthened the capacity of existing organizations and led to the establishment of new ones. The Chicago-based Joyce Foundation began operating in 1976 with assets that make it one of the largest foundations in the United States. The foundation devotes most of its resources to the Midwest. In 1981, the foundation decided to commit major resources to a 10-year program to promote Great Lakes cleanup and protection, and economic diversification.[132]

One of the first activities was a 1981 conference to encourage similar programs by other Midwest foundations. The conference was held at the Kellogg Center of the University of Chicago. Since then, the George Gund Foundation of Cleveland, Ohio; the Charles Stewart Mott Foundation of Flint, Michigan; and the Joyce Foundation have provided major funding to numerous Great Lakes environmental organizations, institutions, and special projects in the United States and Canada.

The Laidlaw Foundation in Canada has been another ongoing participant on a smaller scale. Both the Canada Donner Foundation and the U.S. Donner Foundation also supported Great Lakes projects. The Johnson Foundation's Wingspread Conference Center in Racine, Wisconsin, continues to be the site of numerous significant discussions of Great Lakes issues.[133]

The ongoing interest of these regional foundations also appeared to increase the willingness of other foundations to fund activities in the Great Lakes region. The availability of funding also encouraged projects for the Great Lakes by national environmental groups. The Washington, D.C.–based Environmental Defense Fund, for example, obtained foundation funding for a project to promote pollution prevention in the Great Lakes region.

FOUNDATION ASSISTANCE FOR NEW NONGOVERNMENTAL ORGANIZATIONS

One theme at the 1981 Joyce Foundation conference was the need to increase capacity for coordination, in part to replace coordination among the states that had been provided by the Great Lakes Basin Commission. The idea that emerged from the conference for a binational center for policy research that would address both environmental and economic development issues led to the establishment of the Center for the Great Lakes, with offices in Chicago and Toronto. Former Michigan governor William Milliken served as president, but the center ceased operation in 1993.

The Joyce Foundation assisted establishment of the Council of Great Lakes Governors, which also seeks to engage Ontario and Quebec on issues of binational significance. In the mid 1980s, a proposal to create a unique, permanent regional endowment fund with state funds to benefit the Great Lakes emerged from the Center for the Great Lakes and the agreement on toxic contaminants signed by the governors. Efforts to create a similar fund in Canada have not been successful to date.

The Great Lakes Protection Fund was established with an endowment of $100 million U.S. The contribution from each state was determined by a formula that considered the population of the state that depends on the Great Lakes for drinking water and total withdrawals for other purposes. Seven of the eight states completed their contributions, with Indiana as the only holdout.[134]

The income on one-third of each state's contribution is returned to be used as the state decides. New York, Michigan, and Ohio have all used this funding to create their own Great Lakes State Protection Funds that make grants for projects within the states. The income on the other two-thirds is pooled to support programs and projects of regional significance and to pay administrative costs. Members of the board of directors are appointed by the governors.[135]

The Northeast-Midwest Institute was established with foundation help as a not-for-profit research agency to assist the Congressional delegations from these regions. A special Great Lakes Task Force with members from the Great Lakes states continues to lead bipartisan actions for the region in Congress.[136]

In 1982 the Joyce and U.S. Donner foundations supported a third interuniversity seminar, managed by Northwestern University in Evanston, Illinois, and the University of Toronto. Faculty from 24 universities attempted to define the elusive "ecosystem approach" called for in the 1978 agreement.[137] In 1983 seminar discussions inspired Philip Jessup of the Donner Foundation staff to propose an assessment of progress under the Great Lakes Agreement by the Royal Society of Canada and the National Research Council of the U.S. National Academy of Science.[138]

Funded by both Donner foundations, the first joint study of the two preeminent scientific bodies of both countries covered both scientific and institutional issues. The study's final report in 1985 stated that residents of the Great Lakes basin are exposed to "more toxic chemical burden" than the residents "of other similarly large regions of North America."[139] This controversial statement received the most news-media coverage and attention in the Great Lakes community.

The NRC/RSC report helped inspire a second major binational study by the Conservation Foundation of Washington, D.C., and the Institute for Research on Public Policy (IRPP) of Ottawa "to assess environmental conditions and trends and the adequacy of government programs." This study was also funded by foundations, as well as by Canadian government agencies and industry contributions. The report also raised the issue of "intergenerational equity" that was addressed later in the book *Our Stolen Future*, which outraged the chemical industry in the early 1990s.

The first result was a book titled *Great Lakes, Great Legacy?* that provided comprehensive information on what was known at that time about the implications for human health of the presence of toxic contaminants in the Great Lakes, and by implication, everywhere in the world. The book did not agree with the NRC/RSC report that residents of the Great Lakes basin generally have higher levels of toxic substances in their bodies than persons anywhere else.[140]

The integration of information from cross-disciplinary sources inspired ongoing research that led to new global attention to this issue in the 1990s. As the Conservation Foundation/IRPP study was being carried out, new negotiations resulted in the 1987 Protocol for the Great Lakes Agreement.

Progress under the 1978 Agreement

Following adoption of the 1978 agreement, progress in reduction of phosphorus loadings continued, as well as progress in understanding the effects of toxic contamination in the Great Lakes ecosystem. Through the 1980s, research disclosed how toxic contaminants could cause reproductive and developmental problems for aquatic organisms, birds, and mammals, including humans. The levels of PCBs declined somewhat, but positive consequences were not as visible as they had been with the phosphorus declines.

PCBS continued to be considered a major problem because of their pervasiveness in the environment, their multiple sources, and their chemical stability. The SAB continued to try to determine which of the nearly one thousand toxic chemicals that had been found to be present in the Great Lakes posed the greatest long-term danger. Eventually, agreement was reached on a list of 11 critical contaminants and classes of chemicals that continue to be the principal targets for virtual elimination.

The early concentration of attention on the kinds and numbers of contaminants was followed by more attention to effects. Tumors in both bottom-feeding and wide-ranging fish were linked to exposure to polyaromatic hydrocarbons, and high concentrations of PCBS were found in sediments accumulated in nearshore waters. Birth defects and reproductive disorders in birds and mammals were found to be associated with exposure to dioxins and other chemicals. In the early 1980s, a connection was found between blood levels of PCBS in humans and consumption of certain fish from Lake Michigan by sport fishermen and their families.

The Great Lakes community and nongovernmental involvement continued to grow through this period, along with tension between the governments and the IJC. The IJC biennial meetings provided major forums for communication and exchange of information among environmentalists, scientists, government officials, and IJC commissioners and staff. The political influence of a binational network of environmental organizations also grew.

As another review of the agreement was being considered in the mid 1980s, GLU took the lead through its growing binational network to involve citizens in considering what needed to be done about the growing dissatisfaction of the environmental community with government action to control toxic contaminants. When a new review began in 1986, all sides agreed that the fundamental features that had been adopted in the 1978 agreement should be preserved. Almost no one in the Great Lakes community recognized what would be the consequences of the changes proposed by the USEPA and Environment Canada and adopted in the 1987 review.

CHAPTER 5

EVOLUTION OF THE GREAT LAKES REGIME FROM 1987 TO 1997

T HE GREAT LAKES WATER QUALITY AGREEMENT WAS REVIEWED AND RE-negotiated again in 1987. The few changes made in the agreement itself by the 1987 Protocol were followed by profound, unanticipated changes in the Great Lakes regime during the next decade. The institutions, the issues for water quality in the lakes, and the character of the Great Lakes community that had grown up around the agreement were all affected.

Toxic contaminants remained a major issue, but during this period attention shifted to new threats, including invasive species, swimming bans on beaches, and the possibility of global warming. Phosphorus levels rose again in Lake Erie and, while levels of already-known contaminants declined, little progress was made in controlling atmospheric deposition or removing contaminated sediments, which were necessary for virtual elimination.

The principal expansion of the Great Lakes community in this period was around development of Remedial Action Plans (RAPS) and Lakewide Management Plans (LAMPS). The RAPS were meant to involve local governments and other stakeholders in designated areas of concern where objectives of the agreement were not being achieved in nearshore waters. The LAMPS were intended to provide management planning for the open waters of each lake. By the end of this period, the lengthy planning processes and incomplete results contributed to growing dissatisfaction with progress under the Great Lakes Agreement itself.

New binational institutions were created by the governments as they decreased their participation in the familiar processes managed by the International Joint Commission. By the end of this decade, even the fundamental character of the agreement and the ways in which its goals could be achieved were beginning to be questioned. This period of change began with review and renegotiation of the 1978 version of the agreement during a time of growing political conservatism and changes in government programs for the environment in both countries. The new version was called the 1987 Protocol because the new provisions were considered minor.

The General Political Context

Conservative political and social views prevailed in the governments of both countries as the second major review of the agreement was carried out in 1986 and 1987 and in the following decade. In 1988 former Vice President Bush succeeded Ronald Reagan as president and promptly replaced the Reagan appointees to the IJC, even though they were of the same political party. His campaign chairman in Indiana, Gordon Durnil, became the new U.S. co-chair. Prime Minister Brian Mulroney and President George Bush shared conservative political views and were committed to the "special relationship" between Canada and the United States.

In 1992, President Bill Clinton took office as a Democrat whose centrist political views were a pragmatic response to the generally conservative times. From 1994, he had to contend with extremely conservative Republicans in control of Congress who made weakening of environmental regulations a major goal. Clinton also appointed a new panel of IJC commissioners, continuing the trend that President Reagan had begun of awarding the appointments only to political allies.

The strength of the Great Lakes community in the early 1990s led to new legislation and regulatory initiatives for the Great Lakes in the United States. Otherwise, a general trend toward preference for voluntary action over regulatory enforcement continued through the whole period.

In Canada, the Progressive Conservative government of Prime Minister Mulroney, elected in 1984, continued to forge a more formal economic relationship with the United States through the U.S.–Canada Free Trade Agreement in 1988, and then the North American Free Trade Agreement between the United States, Canada, and Mexico in 1992.[1] Both of these agreements were the subject of intense and divisive political debate. Many of the issues related to fears of the impact of the agreements on the ability of Canada to retain and protect cultural, social, and economic identity. The Mulroney government was also attempting to forge a new relationship within Canada by pursuing constitutional amendments to redefine and further evolve the role of the provinces within the federation, particularly Quebec. However, both the Meech Lake Accord (1987) and the Charlottetown Accord (1992) were defeated, ending the last attempts at constitutional reform to date. Ironically, the environment rose through the late 1980s to be one of the key public-policy issues in the nation.

In 1993 the Liberal government won a majority, with Jean Chrétien becoming the new prime minister.

At the provincial level, the Liberal/New Democratic Party partnership that formed the coalition government in 1985 lasted two years, with the Liberals winning a majority in 1987. However, three years later, the NDP won a majority in Ontario, ushering in an ambitious environmental agenda, which was severely hampered by a serious economic recession that lasted most of its terms of government.

Changes in Environmental Programs and Policies

New ideas about how to protect the environment generally, as well as the Great Lakes, were another factor in the third phase of the evolution of the Great Lakes regime between 1987 and 1997, when the next review of the agreement was carried out. Experience in the Great Lakes was not only affected by some of the new concepts but also a contributor to the development of new ideas.

POLICY EVOLUTION IN THE UNITED STATES

Concepts in the United States about environmental management moved from pollution control to greater reliance on voluntary action and pollution prevention, and then evolved further to embrace preservation of biodiversity and restoration of habitat in the 1990s. A USEPA policy of reliance on risk analysis to determine the level of cleanup required at disposal sites of hazardous materials, or where industrial activities had damaged natural resources, challenged the virtual-elimination goal of the Great Lakes Agreement.

The political power of the Great Lakes community was reinforced when members of the Great Lakes Congressional delegation noted the insistence of more than 800 citizens at the 1989 biennial IJC meeting that steps be taken to meet the agreement's objective of zero discharge of toxic contaminants.[2] Members of the National Wildlife Federation, backed by members of smaller groups throughout the region, led the lobbying for the 1990 Great Lakes Critical Programs Act.[3] The law reinforced the directive to the USEPA in section 118 of the 1987 Clean Water Act that the agency's programs recognize the objectives of the agreement by setting deadlines for several programs required under the 1987 Protocol.

The federal environmental agency now had a legislative mandate for Remedial Action Plans, for Lakewide Management Plans, for five major demonstration projects on technology for removing contaminated sediments in five Great Lakes harbors, and for providing guidance to the states for adopting water quality standards consistent with the virtual-elimination requirement of the agreement.

The 1990 U.S. Clean Air Act included new requirements for attention to atmospheric deposition and identification of toxic contaminants that would reach the lakes from this nonpoint source. The strengthening of section 112 of the 1990 Clean Air Act under the Sierra Club's leadership was based substantially on legislation originally introduced to address problems with atmospheric deposition in the Great Lakes.[4]

The new laws also required regular reports to Congress on progress in response to the Great Lakes environmental community's demand for greater accountability for government efforts for the Great Lakes Agreement. Agreement obligations were also used in 1990 to explain the ecosystem-approach-to-management principle of a new Great Lakes Fish and Wildlife Restoration Act.[5]

Geographic Initiatives

In 1989, soon after William Reilly became head of the USEPA, he announced that the agency would use the Great Lakes experience as a model for a new approach to policy based on preservation of ecological integrity.[6] This action gave the Great Lakes Agreement more acceptance in agency headquarters.[7] Reilly then followed up with a 1990 directive that the regional offices should institute "geographic initiatives," beginning in the areas with the most environmental degradation in each of the 10 regions nationally. The Region 5 office in Chicago began the first such program in the Calumet region of Northwest Indiana, where there was already an area of concern under the Great Lakes Agreement.[8]

The new approach began with major enforcement actions seeking compliance with all federal environmental laws, which applied a multimedia approach for air, water, and land pollution. Court decisions in these cases resulted in consent decrees in which companies on the shoreline of Lake Michigan agreed to clean up pollution and change processes for pollution prevention. Major companies, such as the Gary Works of U.S. Steel, began to agree to go even beyond regulatory requirements as they learned that pollution prevention increased production efficiency. The first area designated for priority cleanup effort was Northwest Indiana, followed by Southeast Michigan and Northeast Ohio, all in the Great Lakes basin.

Voluntary Action

The USEPA undertook new initiatives to encourage voluntary pollution prevention by major industries in the Great Lakes region. Several major companies agreed to eliminate PCBs in the manufacture of autos, and three large steel producers agreed to identify and eliminate sources of mercury.[9] The Council of Great Lakes Governors worked toward the same ends with the printing industry.[10] Industry representatives supported the new policy trend on the grounds that it allowed more flexibility to control pollution efficiently.

Some environmentalists considered reliance on voluntary reduction and prevention of pollution to be a retreat from essential use of regulatory powers.[11] The trend continued to gain importance at the USEPA after Bill Clinton was elected president in 1992, especially when Republican leaders sought to reduce funding for environmental programs after they gained control of Congress in 1994.

The new Republican leadership attempted to weaken all the federal environmental programs established by laws adopted since the 1970s, including the Clean Water Act. By 1996 and another presidential election, a backlash had developed in response to strong public support for environmental programs. Still, the second Clinton administration continued to return more authority to the states for implementation of environmental laws and did not seek any major new federal environmental-regulatory initiatives.

New Emphasis on Restoration

The USEPA's Great Lakes National Program Office (GLNPO) instituted an Ecological Protection and Restoration Program that provides grants for research and demonstration projects for restoration of habitat and preservation of biodiversity, all serving GLWQA goals. From 1992 to 1995, a total of $8,519,219 in grants was made to 36 local, tribal, state, and federal agencies, and nongovernmental organizations. An additional $9 million from other sources was also spent on 87 projects. Both of these programs reflect the new emphasis on restoration of natural areas and protection of biodiversity, in addition to pollution control, adopted by the GLNPO in this period.[12]

New Toxics Management Policy

The USEPA's principal activities for control of toxic contamination were to work with the states for the Great Lakes Water Quality Initiative, a large mass-balance study for Lake Michigan, and, with Environment Canada, initiation of a new Binational Toxics Strategy. The Water Division of the USEPA, Region 5 initiated development of the Great Lakes Water Quality Initiative, later called the Great Lakes Initiative (GLI), in 1989 by setting up a task force of representatives of the Region 2 and 3 offices in New York and Philadelphia, respectively, and of state environmental agencies. An advisory committee was established, with co-chairs representing the environmental community and industry interests.

The federal agency sought a new regulatory approach for chemicals that bioaccumulate in organisms and are called "persistent" because they do not break down in the environment as conventional organic pollutants do. The approach recognized the ecological aims of the agreement by requiring that harm to wildlife and threats to human health be considered as well as danger to aquatic life. The Council of Great Lakes Governors also supported the aim of consistent state water quality standards for toxic substances among the states, so that states with weaker standards would not have an advantage in attracting new economic development.

Sued by the National Wildlife Federation for missing the statutory dead-line for completing the complex regulatory process, the USEPA finally promul-gated the GLI guidance in 1994. The states were given a 31 March 1997 deadline for making their water quality standards consistent with the federal requirements. In spite of the new acceptance of pollution prevention, indus-try interests set up the Great Lakes Water Quality Coalition to organize oppo-sition to the GLI because of fear that the new regulatory approach might be applied nationally if adopted in the Great Lakes states.

ENVIRONMENTAL MANAGEMENT IN CANADA

In 1988 the Canadian federal government had combined five statutes into a new Canadian Environmental Protection Act (CEPA). Part 2 of the act required assessment of the toxicity of substances as a precondition for the government to impose controls.[13] One of the most controversial federal initiatives was the imposition of effluent limits for the pulp-and-paper industry, including limits for organochlorine discharges.[14] Not surprisingly, Great Lakes activists lamented that the regulations were not sufficiently stringent to meet the goal of virtual elimination under the GLWQA.[15]

To respond to the wave of environmental interest in Canada, the federal government announced the Green Plan, a 1990 plan to invest over a billion dollars on environmental issues. Despite its fanfare, the plan dissipated with only a fraction of new money being actually allocated to the environment. At the 1991 biennial meeting, the new environment minister, Jean Charest, made two very important announcements. First, he committed the government to developing a national emissions inventory, similar to the U.S. Toxics Release Inventory.[16] Second, Mr. Charest announced a process to further the goal of phasing-out persistent toxic substances. The process, eventually called the "Accelerated Reduction/Elimination of Toxics" (ARET), commenced the next year and carried on for a number of years, although the nongovernmental groups withdrew in the second year.[17] Nevertheless, the process established a policy dialogue on the goal of virtual elimination and toxics.

In 1994 the five-year review of the Canadian Environmental Protection Act commenced, with virtual elimination being a key issue. When the statute was revamped in 1999, the goal was incorporated into the law establishing a direct correlation between the Great Lakes Agreement and Canadian domestic legislation.

Ontario

The 1985 Canada/Ontario Agreement (coa), which was crucial for the Great Lakes Agreement, was to have expired in March 1991, but was extended for two years when the federal and provincial governments were not able to conclude a new version. A new agreement was signed in 1994, but the delay demonstrates the complexity of federal/provincial relations for Great Lakes purposes.[18] In this instance, the federal government refused to pay the additional costs of upgrading sewage-treatment systems in fulfillment of GLWQA obligations on the grounds that such costs should be completely recovered through fees on water and sewage-system users.[19]

The second controversial issue echoed the chronic complaint of the U.S. states, namely that the province is forced to pay the costs of commitments made by the federal government.[20] It was reported that Ontario either wanted more control in the making of the Great Lakes commitments or greater federal involvement in paying for specific environmental programs.[21] Another issue was that the province wanted RAPs to have priority, while the federal government wanted priority for LaMPs, especially because of indications that the United States wanted to move ahead with the LaMPs.[22]

The 1994 coa differed from its predecessors in having an ecosystem perspective and measurable targets for achieving basic objectives.[23] Another difference is that it assigned responsibility for achieving Great Lakes objectives to both levels of government.[24] Unlike the early coas, the 1994 version did not specify the federal share of costs.[25] Subsequent severe cutbacks in both federal and provincial budgets created uncertainties about whether the commitments were realistic.

Implementation of the Ontario water quality program, the Municipal-Industrial Strategy for Abatement (MISA), moved slowly, but technology-based effluent regulations for the large direct dischargers commenced with petroleum refineries in the early 1990s, with eight other sectors following by 1994.[26] Again, the pulp-and-paper effluent regulations, adopted in 1992, were the most controversial since they aimed for the zero discharge of organochlorines.[27] In announcing the tough new limits, the Ontario environment minister relied heavily on information developed for the agreement through the IJC.[28]

Quebec

Quebec is not within the Great Lakes watershed and has preferred not to be bound by the Great Lakes Agreement. It has had a role in the development of the regime because the St. Lawrence River is the outlet of the Great Lakes to the Atlantic Ocean, that is, downstream of the Great Lakes. From the late 1980s, the federal and Quebec governments entered into agreements derived from the COA and the Great Lakes Agreement.

A 1988 St. Lawrence Action Plan committed to a 90 percent reduction by 1993 in toxic effluents discharged from 50 priority industrial plants, as well as restoration of contaminated sites and wetlands, creation of a marine park, and programs to assist recovery of threatened species, including the beluga whale. The plan received $110 million from the federal government and $65 million from the Quebec provincial government. It was replaced in 1993 by a Quebec program "to restore degraded sites in the St. Lawrence ecosystem" through 23 Zones of Priority Intervention (ZIPs), which are similar in function to RAPS for areas of concern.[29]

Deregulation and Downsizing

By the mid 1990s, the political context for environmental issues was quickly changing. Both federal and provincial governments were set to downsize government bureaucracies because of the major decline in fiscal resources. At the federal level, a "program review" led to a dramatic downsizing of Environment Canada (an over 30 percent reduction in staff from 1994 to 1997), with the consequence of challenging the agency to do more, or even the same, with less. A "harmonization agreement" between the provinces and the federal government had been a source of controversy since the first draft was released in 1993.[30]

Harmonization meant that only one level of government would deal with a specific issue. Environmentalists feared that harmonization would lead to devolution of responsibilities over the environment from the federal to provincial governments, particularly with respect to the setting of environmental standards and even enforcement of federal laws.[31] The harmonization agreement was eventually concluded, but had fewer long-term consequences than anticipated. Nevertheless, the influence of Great Lakes policy innovations was evident during the parliamentary review of the Canadian Environmental Protection Act when the federal responsibility for meeting binational obligations was acknowledged.[32]

At the provincial level, the Ontario Ministry of the Environment and Energy was bracing for funding reductions of more than 35 percent between 1996 and 1997. The Ontario government undertook an ambitious regulatory reform by rewriting statutes and consolidating the 80 environmental regulations into 47 regulations.[33] The zero-discharge goal in the pulp-and-paper regulations was one target for change.

As in the United States, both federal and provincial governments began emphasizing voluntary action by industry. In fact, despite the skepticism of the environmental community, regulation seemed to give way to voluntarism, such as memorandums of understanding and emission reduction challenges with industry. In mid 1996, the Ontario government proposed a regulatory code of practice where voluntary measures would be considered first before new regulations were made.[34] One of the reasons for the withdrawal of non-governmental groups from ARET was the emphasis on voluntary measures.[35]

As the 1990s proceeded, the focus of attention within the environmental sector was changed from the ambitious forging of new concepts and policies to struggling to retain existing laws, policies, programs, and institutions. The fact that fewer government resources were now committed to environmental protection than in the previous decade had major implications for addressing new priorities, continuation of scientific research, and maintenance of effort to achieve the goals of the Great Lakes Agreement.

Other Influences in the Great Lakes Regime

In spite of the apparent acknowledgement of its importance by the governments, the Great Lakes Agreement was ignored in the 1991 U.S.–Canada transboundary air-quality accord on bilateral reductions of the emissions that cause acid rain.[36] Neither the governments nor the IJC had responded to suggestions from the academic and environmental communities that an ecosystem approach would seem to require coordination in implementation between the water quality and air accords, which could be provided through the IJC.[37] The only role assigned to the IJC was to organize public hearings on progress under the acid-rain agreement.[38]

By 1993, the issue of trade again dominated the U.S.–Canada bilateral relationship. Questions about the environmental consequences of the North American Free Trade Agreement (NAFTA) between Canada, Mexico, and the United States led to a side agreement establishing a new trilateral North American Commission for Environmental Cooperation (NACEC), now called the Commission for Environmental Cooperation (CEC). Under the North American Agreement on Environmental Cooperation Between the Government of Canada, the Government of the United Mexican States, and the Government of the United States (1993), the CEC is governed by a council comprising the heads of the environmental agencies in all three countries. The day-to-day activities of the CEC, however, are managed by a secretariat with three directors, one appointed by each country. One of the directors serves as the executive director. The council appoints a Joint Public Advisory Committee. The functions of the council include developing recommendations on pollution prevention, scientific research, public awareness of the environment, protection of endangered species, and many other matters.[39]

Although the CEC is addressing issues of importance to the Great Lakes, including transboundary transport of air emissions, and a 1995 resolution

called for the elimination or reduction of four major toxic substances in all
three countries, no role was assigned to the IJC in the trilateral agreement.[40]
There was little formal contact between the two commissions to coordinate
work plans in the first years of the CEC, even though one of its major programs calls for Sound Management of Chemicals in North America and is
based largely on Great Lakes science.[41] There has also been little participation by Great Lakes organizations in the United States in the CEC's public-
outreach efforts.

Growing Evidence of Harm from Toxics

While environmental programs were being challenged in this period, evidence continued to accumulate about the effects of persistent bioaccumulative toxic contaminants on the environment and on human health. In the
1970s, initial concern about the cancer-causing effects of exposure to toxic
contaminants for humans seemed to be supported by the discovery of widespread fish tumors.[42] Ongoing research throughout the world continues to dis-
close links between exposure to dioxin and other substances, and birth defects
and reproductive failure, with increased understanding of immune-system
suppression and other hormone-like effects of toxic contaminants on wildlife,
and potentially on humans. A background paper on toxic contaminants prepared for the 1994 State of the Lake Ecosystem Conference reported that in
the Great Lakes, reproductive or other problems attributable to toxic contaminants have been documented for 11 species.[43]

In 1996 the results of research on development of infants born to mothers
who had high levels of PCBs in their bodies due to consumption of fish from
Lake Ontario were reported to be consistent with the ongoing Jacobson studies that show developmental effects due to maternal consumption of Lake
Michigan fish with high concentrations of PCBs.[44] Major scientific consensus
on the gravity of the problem that the endocrine-disruption effects of certain
toxic substances poses for humankind is shown by the 1991 Wingspread consensus statement of 20 renowned scientists.

In 1996, following a workshop in Erice, Italy, an international group of scientists issued a new consensus statement about the effects of exposure to certain industrial chemicals on development of the brain and nervous system.[45]
A few weeks earlier, an article published in *Science* magazine seemed to
confirm the validity of the language concerning additive effects that had been
added in the 1987 Protocol. This article reported on research that showed that
the effects of combinations of hormone-disrupting chemicals were far more
dangerous than the effects of exposure to single chemicals.[46]

While scientific uncertainties remain, what was thought to be a potentially serious environmental problem for the Great Lakes in the 1970s had become a serious human-health issue that may explain multifold increased cancer risks, learning disabilities, and even behavioral problems for industrial society. The IJC's biennial reports in the first half of the 1990s reflected this growing catalog of evidence of the problems associated with persistent toxic substances.

No longer quoting entirely from advisory-board reports, and citing public concern, the reports had a new tone of urgency about the need to address toxic-substance problems. The Fifth Biennial Report concluded that "there is a threat to the health of our children emanating from our exposure to persistent toxic substances."[47] The Sixth Biennial Report concluded that humans are "in danger" from these substances,[48] while the Seventh Biennial Report concluded that "there is sufficient evidence now to infer a real risk of serious impacts in humans."[49] Citing that the evidence of the dangers of persistent toxic substances is being reinforced, the Commission in its Eighth Biennial Report concluded that such evidence justified concerted and effective action.[50]

With reductions in direct discharges, contaminant concentrations in 1996 generally met the 1978 objectives in the open waters of the lakes, but remained higher in the tissues of fish and birds.[51] The fact that bald-eagle reproduction continues to be less successful on the shores of the Great Lakes than inland confirms that the ultimate agreement objective of waters free of substances harmful to human, animal, or aquatic life has not been achieved.[52]

The evolution of the Great Lakes regime is related to the pace of research and growth of public understanding and concern about the toxic contaminants in the environment. Toxic contamination was the chief reason for increased public participation in the biennial meetings, as well as the new involvement of industry in IJC processes. In the same period, emerging new issues that competed for attention included new invasions of exotic species, especially the zebra mussel, and the need for preservation of habitat and biodiversity. This period of profound change began with negotiation of the 1987 Protocol.

Negotiation of the 1987 Protocol

The advance consultation, review, and renegotiation that produced the 1987 Protocol were far more open and inclusive than the closed process for the 1978 review, which essentially had included only government officials. This time, five nongovernmental observers from environmental organizations participated in the final negotiation. The states were represented by officials from Michigan, Wisconsin, and New York. The Canadian negotiating team included two representatives from Ontario and one from Quebec.

The governments also considered three external sources of commentary and recommendations: the 1985–1986 study by the Royal Society of Canada and the National Research Council (RSC/NRC) for the National Academy of Sciences in the United States, the report by Great Lakes United (GLU) based on public hearings throughout the basin, and the Third Biennial Report of the IJC. The first two were referred to most often in the actual negotiations.

All three of the advance external reviews agreed in urging that the 1978 agreement be continued, but that amendments were needed to strengthen it. The detailed recommendations of the RSC/NRC report covered agreement objectives, joint programs, the advisory boards, the regional office, the role of the IJC and of the lead agencies for the parties, and the responsibilities of the parties for both implementation and communication with the public.

The GLU report, *Unfulfilled Promises*, was based on the 19 citizens' hearings attended by 1,200 persons throughout the basin in 1986. This document stressed the need for faster and stronger efforts to control toxic contamination, and for more involvement of the public and accountability for actions by the governments. The recommendation for the concept of zero discharge, already in the agreement since 1978, laid the groundwork for a later campaign for more explicit attention to zero discharge in water quality management programs and schedules for achievement. Both the RSC/NRC and the GLU reports urged creation of a citizen's advisory board for the agreement, and inclusion of non-governmental representatives on the Water Quality Board (WQB).

The IJC's Third Biennial Report to the governments drew upon the other two documents in urging that the coming renegotiation "clarify, strengthen, and support the various provisions of the 1978 agreement."[53] While acknowledging that the less-than-satisfactory progress under the agreement was due in part to unrealistic timetables and objectives, the IJC nevertheless urged the governments to expand their efforts for point-source discharges, air quality, contaminated sediments, wetlands, and monitoring. The theme that ran through all three reports was that the parties should try harder and be more accountable for their efforts on behalf of the agreement's goals. This report was the IJC's only opportunity to contribute to the negotiation.[54] The commission was not asked to comment on draft versions or the final language of the 1978 agreement.[55]

As before, Canada's Department of External Affairs and the U.S. State Department formally oversaw the process, but deferred to Environment Canada and the USEPA throughout. The USEPA and Environment Canada began by each proposing their own amendments to each other. Following exchange of drafts over the summer, they had reached substantial agreement before the formal negotiations began in October. The final version reflected changes that each side had wanted, as well as concessions made to each other.

Canadian and U.S. Proposed Changes

Canada initially proposed far more detailed amendments for both the body of the agreement and Annex 1, most of which were not agreed to in the final version. Canada also proposed the addition of human health concerns, which was accepted by the United States.

Canada thought the Specific Objectives of Annex 1 should be strengthened by adding six substances, but instead agreed to the U.S. proposal to include a process for updating the objectives. The United States proposed the addition of a requirement for Lakewide Management Plans (LAMPS) as well as Remedial Action Plans (RAPS), and Canada agreed. Both sides added topics as annexes, including contaminated sediments, nonpoint-source pollution, and airborne toxic substances.

For the joint institutions, the United States proposed to strengthen the role of the Water Quality Board by allowing the board, rather than the IJC, to make final decisions on designating areas of concern and "approval" of RAPS and LAMPS. Some U.S. agencies joined Canada in viewing this proposal as a weakening of the IJC. In the end, the federal governments were given approval power, with the IJC allowed to review and comment.

Echoing earlier USEPA objections to federal funding of more advanced sewage-treatment systems to meet agreement requirements, Canada proposed to amend Article II to remove the federal obligation to help finance publicly owned treatment plants. This proposal was not supported on the U.S. side, and was dropped because of opposition from Canadian environmental groups.

The Role of Nongovernmental Groups

In addition to the advance hearings and the *Unfulfilled Promises* report, over the summer of 1987 GLU and other environmental groups tracked the preliminary development of the agreement and organized pressure for the inclusion of nongovernmental representation in the final negotiation. Environmental organizations on both sides of the border stressed the need to achieve the objectives of the existing 1978 agreement, and to make any changes primarily through the annexes and appendices rather than the body of the agreement.

The lack of industry attention reflected this sector's limited participation in the Great Lakes community in the first two decades of the agreement's history. After the Soap and Detergent Manufacturers Association and companies such as Proctor and Gamble of Ohio opposed phosphate-detergent bans in the 1970s, industry had little presence in agreement-related activities until the early 1990s. Then, the interest of the chemical industry was stirred by debate over the IJC proposal for a chlorine ban and by the opposition of corporations that need discharge permits under the U.S. Clean Water Act to the Great Lakes Water Quality Initiative on toxic contaminants.[56]

The environmental groups mainly sought to increase the accountability of the governments for progress toward achievement of objectives of the agreement. They also wanted more public participation in identifying additional areas of concern, which would mean additional RAPS and new annexes on contaminated sediments, groundwater, nonpoint sources of pollution, and atmospheric deposition of contaminants. They urged the inclusion of the St. Lawrence River and again proposed appointment of nongovernmental representatives to the WQB.

Great Lakes United, the Sierra Club, and the National Wildlife Federation were invited to provide U.S. observers for the final negotiation. They were, respectively, Tim Eder, Jane Elder, and Mark Van Putten. John Jackson and Kate Davies of Great Lakes United were also invited. Although officially only observers, all five participated directly in discussion during a formal bilateral negotiation session on 16 October 1987.

FINAL NEGOTIATION

Quick agreement was reached on several changes proposed by the observers, including ecosystem objectives for the St. Lawrence River and connecting channels, and a requirement for public involvement in RAPS and LAMPS. Addition of the words "singly and in combination" or "synergistic or additive" was also accepted wherever toxic contaminants were mentioned. The nongovernmental observers did not object to the language the government negotiators proposed for Article x.

Issues that had to be resolved included mixing zones for effluent discharges, the relationship between dredging and sediments, and an annex on airborne pollution. Controversial language on what had been called "limited use zones" was changed to "point source impact zones." The title "Airborne Toxic Substances" was finally agreed to in order to avoid what appeared to be U.S. concerns that the agreement might be used to strengthen the Canadian push for stricter control of acid-rain sources. Ambiguous language also resolved differences between the parties on dredging. After final review and formal approval by the federal governments, the new version was adopted and signed on 18 November 1987 at the IJC biennial meeting in Toledo, Ohio

KEY PROVISIONS

Most of the changes in the 1987 Protocol added to or reinforced provisions of the 1978 version, except for those relating to the role of the parties and the relationship between the parties and the IJC. Figure 8 outlines the changes.

The most important changes were the new reporting process for the lead federal agencies called for in Article x, and the provisions in Annex 1 for how the parties pursue the specific objectives for toxic substances. New annexes also called for the development of RAPS and LAMPS. RAPS are processes that are intended to identify problems, review remediation options, and then implement those options for 43 "areas of concern" or toxic hot spots in the basin. The intent was to include all levels of government and the public in this planning process, since it is the local communities that have the largest stake in the outcome of the initiative. The same applies to LAMPS, except the action plans are based on a lakewide scale.

The thrust of the new language was that the lead agencies of the parties could, or even should, pursue joint activities on behalf of the agreement and communicate with each other directly, rather than through the IJC. This change in relationship was sought by the USEPA and Environment Canada because of their commonly held view that participation in the joint institutions managed by the IJC, especially the multiple-committee structure of the WQB and the SAB, consumed too much staff time and travel funds that might be better used otherwise. The nongovernmental observers believed the new approach would make the governments more accountable for results.

Changes in the Regime following the 1987 Protocol

To many observers, the changes with the 1987 Protocol were minor compared to the substantial expansion of aims that occurred between 1972 and 1978 when the emphasis shifted from phosphorus control to elimination of toxic contaminants from the ecosystem. Yet, more change occurred in the relationship between the governments and the IJC and in the part that the government agencies play in the binational institutions and activities than in any other period since the agreement was originated in 1972.

One of the important changes relates to the historic role of the Water Quality Board in assessing the adequacy of the parties' programs to meet GLWQA goals. The board's role changed to that of a policy advisor, and it no longer was required to undertake an assessment role. Since that time, programmatic assessment seems to be a weak link in the evaluative role of the IJC. Although the IJC can still comment on the parties' programs, in the new relationship the binational advisory boards will not provide data and information for this purpose. Experience in the Binational Executive Committee (BEC) to date suggests that the agencies are unlikely to engage in self-evaluation, since observers report a shift from a "mutual search for solutions" frame of mind that formerly existed in the WQB to that of "negotiation on the common position to be presented to the IJC in the BEC."[57]

Some observers blame the 1987 Protocol itself for the changes. At least one commentator believes that the changes in Article x were made by the parties to weaken the IJC.[58] Former government officials who were involved in the

FIGURE 8. Key Amendments to the GLWQA by the 1987 Protocol

SECTION #	DESCRIPTION OF NEW SECTION
Specific Objectives	
III(f)	Commitment of parties, in cooperation with states and provinces, to work toward the elimination of Areas of Concern, Critical Pollutants, and Point Source Impact Zones under Annex 2.
Standards, Regulatory Meaures, and Research Programs and Other Measures	
V	Parties to undertake best efforts to ensure "research priorities are undertaken in accordance with Annex 17."
VI	Parties commit to such programs "in cooperation with State and Provincial Governments."
VI.1(e)(ix)	Amendment to recognize new nonpoint Annex 13.
VI.1(l)	Amendment to change subheading to "airborne toxic substances" and recognize new air Annex 15.
VI.1(n)	Amendment to recognize Remedial Action Plans in Annex 2.
VI.1(o)	Amendment to recognize Lakewide Management Plans in Annex 2.
VI.1(p)	New subsection on contaminated sediments with recognition of new Annex 14.
VI.1(q)	New section on contaminated groundwater and recognition of new Annex 16.
Consultation and Review	
X.3	Provision added requiring parties, in cooperation with states and provinces, to meet twice a year to coordinate their work plans with respect to implementation of the Agreement and to evaluate progress made.
X.4	Agreement to be reviewed after every third biennial report.
Specific Objectives to Supplement Annex 1	
Annex 1	Supplement Annex 1 to include:
	(a) objectives development process
	(b) a review process for a biennial review of objectives
	(c) establishment of an ecosystem objective for Lake Superior.

1987 review on both sides have confirmed that the intention was to decrease expenditure of resources for IJC activities.

Not all the changes within the regime were due to the new language in the Protocol; some resulted from decisions of IJC commissioners who took office later or were influenced by external factors. Implementation of decisions of an

Remedial Action Plans and Lakewide Management Plans

    Annex 2   Revised Annex 2 that:

        (a) designates Areas of Concern

        (b) advocates development of Remedial Action Plans

        (c) designates Critical Pollutants

        (d) advocates development of Lakewide Management Plans

        (e) designates Point Source Impact Zones.

Discharges from Vessels

    Annex 4   Various revisions.

Review of Pollution from Shipping Sources

    Annex 6   Various revisions.

Joint Contingency Plans

    Annex 9   Various revisions.

Hazardous Polluting Substances

    Annex 10   Adds pollutants.

Surveillance and Monitoring

    Annex 11   Revisions to include:

        (a) surveillance programs

        (b) defined expansion of programs

        (c) development of health indicators for the Lakes.

Persistent Toxic Substances

    Annex 12   Revision to include principle to reduce production.

Pollution from Nonpoint Sources

    Annex 13   New annex.

Contaminated Sediments

    Annex 14   New annex.

Airborne Toxic Substances

    Annex 15   New annex.

Pollution from Contaminated Groundwater

    Annex 16   New annex.

Research and Development

    Annex 17   New annex.

individual commissioner deviated from the traditional operation of the commission by consensus, a trend that would continue. The reasons included new concerns about the environmental consequences of a global economy, the decline in fiscal resources allocated to environmental programs by the national governments, and national politics. In this period, increasing conservatism in the governments in both countries responded to apparent growing conservatism of a majority of voters, who seemed more worried about their own economic futures and social well-being than the environment.

Invasion of exotic species became a major concern following the introduction and rapid spread of first the zebra mussel in the Great Lakes ecosystem and beyond, and then of several other new species. Meanwhile, new attention was being given to habitat protection and biodiversity, even while new information about potential threats to human health from toxic contamination was almost constantly being made public.

Changes in Operations by the Parties

The fundamental new principle in Article x of the Protocol was that the lead agencies of the parties, Environment Canada and the USEPA, should consult directly with each other twice a year. While the new requirement did not prohibit the previous practice of contact between agency personnel and IJC staff through the advisory boards and their committee structure, the governments' interpretation of the new provision led to establishment of new institutions of their own and less interaction in IJC activities.

First, the parties established a new coordinating institution, the BEC, to respond to the Protocol directive for two meetings a year to coordinate their work plans for implementation of the agreement and to evaluate progress. The meetings are open to the states and provinces and to other federal agencies. Co-chaired by the USEPA and Environment Canada, the BEC did not begin functioning until 1991. Until the July 1996 decisions to open BEC meetings to observers, only government personnel attended the meetings.

Second, the agencies began to have their own biennial meetings, independent of the IJC, called the State of the Lake Ecosystem Conference (SOLEC). The stated intention in forming SOLEC was to complement the IJC biennial meetings by providing information that would help the IJC develop its required progress reports to the federal governments. The SOLEC agendas are determined solely by the BEC with no input from the IJC.

Third, the lead agencies began to make their progress reports directly to the IJC rather than through the WQB. This practice was not specified in the Protocol. The stated intention here was to avoid possible bias or conflict of interest for officials who represent their agencies as members of the WQB. In practice, one result has been more separation between activities that Environment Canada and the USEPA carry out for the Great Lakes and the binational activities that are coordinated through the IJC. Another result is that lower-level staff now participate in the WQB instead of just agency managers with policymaking authority, as before 1987.

As directed by the IJC, through SOLEC the BEC has been trying to develop indicators for ecosystem health since 1997 to assist monitoring of progress and to detect possible new problems. Improvements in water chemistry, such as reductions in the levels of phosphorus or increases in dissolved oxygen, were the chief measures under the 1972 agreement. The IJC has not specified information it would need in order to evaluate progress through the indicators.

Much effort was made under the 1978 agreement to expand the binational Great Lakes International Surveillance Plan (GLISP) to track toxic contaminants in fish and animal tissues as well as the waters of the system. In the 1990s some of the effort formerly given to GLISP was concentrated on a huge mass-balance study for Lake Michigan.

Changes in Operations of the IJC

It is not possible to determine which changes in operations of the IJC were intended to respond to the 1987 Protocol, because some of the changes were due to personal views of IJC commissioners. IJC members in the early 1990s said that the operation of the library was discontinued to save overhead costs. The Protocol did not directly require change in the function of the WQB or disbandment of the committee structure of both the SAB and the WQB. It has also been pointed out that the commission's assumption of an advocate role on chlorine in these years was not related to the Protocol.

Elimination of the committee structure for the two advisory boards had major consequences. The decrease in exchange of information between agencies of the parties and IJC staff appears to give the IJC less basis for evaluating the effectiveness of government programs.

Another change not mandated by the Protocol was the IJC's greater reliance on independent nongovernmental sources, rather than on recommendations and supporting evidence from the advisory boards. Language in Article VII where the powers, responsibilities, and functions of the IJC are prescribed can, however, be interpreted as allowing discretion in using outside sources.

Directives to the IJC in the 1987 Protocol

With new evaluative functions assigned by the Protocol, the commission was directed to:

- Review progress in preparation of the Remedial Action Plans (RAPS) in the areas of concern and recommend designation of additional areas of concern by each party;

- Review progress in control of critical pollutants and recommend additional designation of additional critical pollutants; and
- Review the biennial reports submitted by the parties and assess them in the commission's own reports to the governments and by other means.

A working paper by IJC staff on the implication of these changes noted that they would require a clearer definition of IJC roles and additional or reallocated resources. The paper also pointed out that changes in the operations of the boards, the regional office, and the commission itself would be required because the effectiveness of the increased accountability required of the governments would depend on the adequacy of IJC audits of the information received from Environment Canada and the USEPA.[59]

The commission responded with an *IJC Policy Statement on Its Approach to the Revised Great Lakes Water Quality Agreement*, dated 14 September 1988. The statement noted that the commission's overall workload would increase. Requests for additional funding had already been made through the budgetary process in both countries by the time the IJC's Fourth Biennial Report was published.

The 1988 policy statement also reviewed the IJC's traditional role as advisor to the governments. Traditionally, the commission had depended on information provided by the boards to determine the state of the lakes and the progress toward achieving the improvements sought by the agreement, as well as the effectiveness of the government programs. The policy review also considered the functions the IJC had served under the previous versions of the agreement, including providing a policy forum, managing all the binational activities and some coordination of research, and the development of Great Lakes agendas by the parties. Though not intended as a directive for change, the policy statement was followed by major alterations in the commission's internal procedures and in the structure that had been established in 1972.

The strong opinions held by Gordon Durnil, the first U.S. co-chair following adoption of the protocol, about his responsibilities as a manager and an administrator for the commission was one force in the transformation.[60] Another factor was evolution in the relationship between the commission and the parties. The change was in part a reaction to complaints from environmentalists about the perceived conflict of interest for agency representatives on the WQB, and about inadequate government action against toxic contaminants.

Many of the public comments at the 1989 biennial meeting in Hamilton, Ontario, criticized the WQB, as an agency of the IJC, for failure to address the problem of toxic contamination. The commission thought that the public simply did not understand that the governments, not the wqb as an ijc insti-tution, were responsible for implementation of the agreement. This confu-sion was also consistently apparent to the commissioners in their day-to-day activities and was the reason for seeking clearer delineation of roles in the language of the 1987 Protocol.

Reconstituted Task Force on Commission Role and Priorities

The formal process of reform commenced in 1989 with a Task Force on Role and Priorities established to examine the role of the commission and the role and structure of the advisory boards.[61] The original task force was reconsti-tuted, and again reviewed the operation of the ijc, including the three direc-tives of the 1987 Protocol. In 1991 a *Report of the Reconstituted Task Force on Commission Role and Priorities* was accepted on the following topics:[62]

- Establishment of a biennial planning and priority-setting process to set the agenda for agreement-related responsibilities, including for the advisory boards;
- Redefinition of the functions and composition of the advisory boards, with the wqb to serve as a policy advisor, the sab to provide advice on the issues identified in the priority-setting process, and the Council of Great Lakes Research Managers to track research;
- Definition of the purpose of the biennial meetings;
- Redefinition of the role of the regional office to include the provision of secretariat services to the boards, and administrative services to the task forces, roundtables, and other activities initiated by the commission;
- Clarification of the ijc's role in reviewing raps; and
- Clarification of the ijc's public-involvement purposes.[63]

While not directly defining how the ijc interpreted its role under the 1987 Protocol, the report called for a new division of roles between the work of gov-ernment-agency staff for their home agencies, and the work of the same staff for the ijc in a "personal and professional capacity." As the report stated, "It is now clear to the commission and a growing number of agency officials from both countries that government officials should no longer play both the role of implementing and assessment of progress and effectiveness of that implemen-tation."[64]

By and large, this document appeared to be used as an organizational blueprint for the ijc following replacement of the Bush-appointed panel with the 1993 appointments by President Clinton. Figure 9 shows the organization of the ijc as it came to be understood in the 1990s.

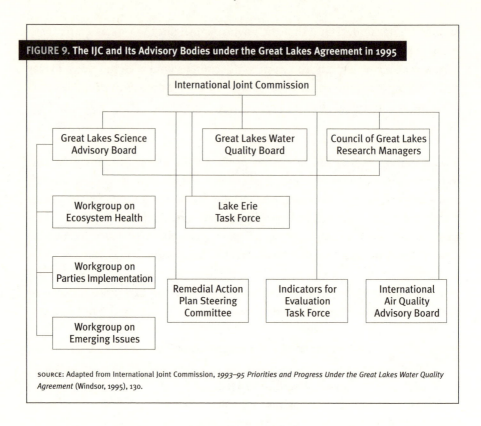

FIGURE 9. The IJC and Its Advisory Bodies under the Great Lakes Agreement in 1995

SOURCE: Adapted from International Joint Commission, *1993–95 Priorities and Progress Under the Great Lakes Water Quality Agreement* (Windsor, 1995), 130.

New Priority-Setting Process

The new agenda and priority-setting process that the IJC adopted was not called for in the 1987 Protocol, but was initiated by Commissioner Durnil. The minutes of a 1992 SAB meeting quote him as saying that the priorities process is necessary to fulfill the responsibilities of the commission and to manage limited funding more efficiently.[65]

Previously, the boards had set their own agendas, although often in consultation with commission staff and members. Beginning in 1991, commissioners, some IJC staff, and co-chairs of the advisory boards set priorities for both the commission and the boards according to specified criteria in a Planning and Priorities Group report.

One result was that the boards lost autonomy. Now they spent most of their time addressing issues determined primarily by the IJC and its staff as the issues to be reported on two years hence in biennial reports to the governments. Both boards addressed essentially the same issues, with less capacity to identify emerging issues that would need attention.

The change was especially significant for the SAB, which earlier had initiated attention to such issues as atmospheric deposition, acid rain, and an ecosystem approach to management.[66] One former SAB member said the new approach deprived the IJC of the special expertise that a scientist might bring, and made participation less interesting for scientists with special knowledge.[67] A former WQB member said in 2003 that withdrawal from IJC processes during the 1990s was reaction in part to the efforts of IJC staff "to take charge."[68]

A board could still address issues not on the priority list if the activity did not depend on IJC funding. In practice, board members now had an indirect, and some suggested too modest, role in the priority-setting process. They were less likely to seek resources from other sources, including their home agencies, for priorities set by others.

One product of this process was the Priorities Report presented to the IJC at the 1995 biennial meeting in Duluth. Instead of separate reports, as in the past, the priority reports of the advisory boards were combined into a single document with a "priority summary" that addressed issues that had been marked for attention in 1993.[69] Some SAB members felt that the SAB had lost status within the IJC family with this format.[70] The question remained of how issues of interest to a board, but not the IJC, would be addressed.[71]

Another dilemma resulted from the creation of three different sets of priorities: for advisory boards, for task forces created by the IJC, and for internal commission purposes. In the 1995–1997 biennial cycle, for instance, it would seem that prior to assumption of this role by the IJC, the boards would have identified such priorities as nuclear inventories and transition planning. The changes in status and function of the boards date from 1991.

Water Quality Board

The 1991 Task Force Report provided three rationales for changing the mandate of the WQB to policy advising, rather than evaluating programs. First, it noted (without explanation) that government personnel would no longer be generally available to participate in substructures of the board.[72] There was no discussion of whether alternatives to disbandment of the subcommittee structure were considered. Second, the reform was said to be needed to remove the perceived conflict of interest in asking the same persons to be "doers and reviewers." The third explanation was the need to distinguish between the role of the parties as implementers of the agreement, and the role of the IJC as evaluator of progress.

Delegation back to the parties of the traditional WQB role in setting water quality and ecosystem objectives and in planning surveillance and monitoring programs essentially created a vacuum for the WQB. The 1989 WQB report was the last evaluation of progress by the board.[73] The first WQB effort in its new policy-advisory role was a 1991 workshop in Toronto that produced a "vision statement" about "future desirable characteristics of the Great Lakes," and suggestions to the Priorities Planning Group of the IJC.[74]

The differences in WQB reports in the mid 1990s seem to reflect uncertainty about the board's new role. The 1991 report, written by journalist and author Michael Keating, discussed three general policy recommendations in only 47 pages.[75] The 1993 report considered review of the agreement, legislative and regulatory issues for virtual elimination of toxic contaminants, and risk assessment, among other topics.[76] The 1995 report analyzed several topics in depth, in particular pollution prevention and recent developments in the pulp-and-paper industry.[77]

Former members and other observers within the Great Lakes community have noted that participation in the WQB changed after it no longer had a specific mission.[78] Other than the co-chairs or their representatives, high-level agency officials seldom attended. Some heads of state agencies say they now find the WQB, the IJC, and even the agreement irrelevant, and some have made the same observation for SOLEC. Most such comments are by persons with no experience with the agreement prior to the 1987 Protocol.[79]

Science Advisory Board

The SAB's mandate was neither altered by the 1987 Protocol nor the focus of reform efforts by the IJC, but its function also changed in this period. The board is still charged with reviewing scientific information, assessing the adequacy of research, and identifying research needs and programs for which binational cooperation is desirable.[80] In the 1990s, the SAB revised its structure to have three work groups, on Ecosystem Health, Emerging Issues, and Parties Implementation. Membership of the work groups includes both SAB members and others with relevant expertise.

Several issues for the mandate of the SAB had persisted from adoption of the 1978 agreement to the 1990s. First, the SAB interpreted "science" broadly to include both basic and applied sciences, but also social sciences, ethics, law, and economics, especially following the 1978 agreement. Membership in the 1980s under the leadership of co-chairs Jack Vallentyne and Alfred Beeton reflected this trend. In the mid 1980s, the four subcommittees were on Human Health, Ecology, Society, and Technology.

Four IJC commissioners attended a workshop on *The Role of the Science Advisory Board* in 1991. One member questioned whether the SAB could continue its former role as "a primary advisor" since it now had to compete for "the attention, the priorities, and the budget" of the commission.[81] Although the role of the board was not officially changed either in the agreement or by the IJC, some SAB members felt their role was confused when the commission began to set up special task forces to address topics it had determined for the 1990s.

The 1991 report again raised the issue of SAB membership, leading to one disgruntled comment that "recent appointments of nonscientist policy analysts and advocates of special interests are evidence of IJC preoccupation with attaining political balance in lieu of attention to science."[82] The "specific interests" represented on the SAB continued to include industry and environmental advocacy.

Council of Great Lakes Research Managers

When it was established in 1984, the Council of Great Lakes Research Managers (CGLRM) assumed responsibility for part of the tracking of research that had been assigned to the SAB in the original agreement. This third advisory board was not called for in the Great Lakes Agreement, but was given full board status in 1992. In effect, the existence of the council allows the SAB to continue its broad policy-oriented work without having to focus on such work as inventorying research projects.

The stated reason at the time for its creation was to enhance the ability of the IJC to provide leadership, guidance, support, and evaluation of Great Lakes research programs. Nelson Thomas, the first co-chair, said that the difference is that "the SAB interprets research while the CGLRM aims to make certain there is enough and appropriate research."[83] In 1986, the SAB co-chairs Vallentyne and Beeton assisted in creating terms of reference for the council. The council reports directly to the IJC at least annually instead of through the SAB, and its secretariat service is provided by staff of the regional office.

Members are to include persons responsible for research programs, plus two SAB members. They are to serve "in their personal and professional capacity and not as representatives of their employers or organizations," a challenge that one member said laid them open to the same charges of conflict of interest that had plagued the WQB.[84]

While he was overseeing modification of the board roles at the beginning of the 1990s, former U.S. chair Durnil said the aim of the council was to facilitate more effective use of research budgets and to direct research to the priorities determined by the IJC.[85] The council reports directly to, and obtains funding and work-plan approval from, the commission. Its principal activity has been to develop and maintain an inventory of research about or relevant to the Great Lakes.

Other Advisory Mechanisms

Since 1990, the commission has initiated several other advisory mechanisms not specified in the agreement. Earlier, special workshops or events had been sponsored by the wqb, sab, or one of their subcommittees. The commission began to initiate such events as it assumed a more direct managerial role for the regional office and the agreement processes. One commissioner noted that, although the boards remain primary advisors, the commission can seek advice from a variety of sources.[86]

Task forces are time-limited, narrowly focused on a single issue, and representative of a broad spectrum of opinion. Membership is drawn from the boards and research council, or from outside "the ijc family." The subjects of task forces include virtual elimination and the state of the Great Lakes basin ecosystem. In 1995 task forces were operating for Lake Erie and for the development of Indicators for Evaluation. The Virtual Elimination Task Force was the most controversial.

The Virtual Elimination Task Force was set up "to investigate the requirement of the amended Great Lakes Water Quality Agreement to virtually eliminate the input of persistent toxic substances into the Great Lakes basin ecosystem."[87] Confusion was created by the fact that, while it began as a joint body of the wqb and sab, it was soon obviously a separate advisory body reporting directly to the ijc.

A major difference from earlier special committees or work groups of the boards was that the Virtual Elimination Task Force was designed to provide consultation with multiple interests or stakeholders, with members representing federal, state, and provincial governments; industry; and environmental groups. Another difference was the increased participation of industry in reaction to the commission advocacy of a chlorine ban.

In contrast to the consensus that had usually emerged from events such as the Hiram, Ohio, workshop on an ecosystem approach to management a decade earlier, the final recommendations of the Virtual Elimination Task Force were the result of lengthy negotiation among the participating scientists, environmentalists, and agency and industry representatives.[88] The commission accepted the task force recommendations on strategy in its Seventh Biennial Report.

"Roundtables" are another innovation for consultation by the ijc that was not originally called for in the agreement. At the 1989 biennial meeting, the commission announced an intention to undertake a number of roundtables concerning agreement obligations for persistent toxic chemicals. The first "Zero Discharge Roundtable" was held in 1990 at Dartmouth College, in Hanover, New Hampshire. The next roundtable occurred a few months later in Washington, D.C., on legislative issues for the goal of zero discharge.

A third roundtable in this period was held in Thunder Bay, Ontario, just prior to the 1991 biennial meeting in Traverse City and the subsequent Fifth Biennial Report. The topic was zero discharge in the pulp-and-paper industry. In 1993, another set of roundtables were held under the joint sponsorship of the Physicians for Social Responsibility. Its purpose was to inform the health-care profession about the potential human health effects of toxic contaminants.

Great Lakes Regional Office

The role of the Great Lakes Regional Office was defined in the 1978 agreement.[89] In addition to the government-agency questions about the resources required for the enlarged staff to coordinate with the advisory boards, there had been tensions between the secretariat staffs in Washington and Ottawa about who was in charge within the IJC.[90] The changes in functions of the regional office after the 1987 Protocol resulted from administrative decisions of the commission following the Reconstituted Task Force, not from protocol language.

Two major changes were made. First, instead of managing board functions, regional-office staff were assigned as chairs, working members, or managers of the task forces that the commission began to establish on topics such as virtual elimination.[91] Second, the regional-office staff and the secretariat staffs are considered a single staff to the commission. With this change, the commission itself became directly involved in day-to-day management of the regional office in new ways.

Donation of the IJC library to the University of Windsor in 1992 was coupled with a proposal to move the regional office to Detroit. The library held approximately 38,000 books and 300 periodicals. The library of the former Great Lakes Basin Commission had been contributed to the IJC in order to make it available for public use.[92] The action provoked debate inside and outside the IJC, including a protest rally in downtown Windsor, and was clouded by an ongoing labor dispute between the library staff and the commission.[93]

The environmental community saw the library closing as a symbol of reduced capacity of the regional office. For some scientists and academic experts, the closing of the library reduced accessibility to important Great Lakes documents and information assembled by the research community.[94] For the commission, the savings in rent and personnel costs freed resources for programs.[95]

Part of the material is now held in a separate "Great Lakes Collection" at the university, and other material was merged into the university library's general collection. A staff member at the university's Great Lakes Institute said that parts of the collection have not been kept updated, and that students and others are referred to the IJC collection only for historical information.[96] The controversy has now been largely forgotten.

RESPONSIBILITIES OF THE PARTIES

The responsibilities of the parties, through the USEPA and Environment Canada, also changed after the IJC made the WQB a policy advisor instead of an evaluator of programs. As articulated in May 1991, the change meant that the USEPA and Environment Canada had agreed to provide data needed for reporting on the following activities:

- Coordination of work plans for specific purposes;
- Progress toward meeting GLWQA requirements;
- Progress in completing RAPS;
- The state of the lakes, including conditions and trends;
- Enforcement actions for compliance with regulations;
- Use of quality-assurance and quality-control methodology in monitoring;
- Monitoring of pollutant loadings; and
- Coordination of research.[97]

The issues raised by these and other continuing changes in the implementation process under the Great Lakes Agreement are discussed in the following chapter. Establishment of the Indicators for Evaluation Task Force in 1993 recognized the new challenge faced by the IJC to assess the information provided by the governments on the state of the lakes. The report on indicators that the task force issued in 1996 did not answer the question of how government programs could be evaluated without recommendations from the WQB.[98]

The Public and the GLWQA

Following adoption of the 1987 Protocol, environmental groups increased their advocacy activities for the Great Lakes inside and outside the Great Lakes region. Many publications assisted information exchange and other activities, including the Sierra Club's *Washington Report* (published until 1994), Great Lake United's newsletter, and the membership publications of the Lake Michigan Federation and numerous other organizations.

Special reports from nongovernmental groups promoted binational activity across the border, such as Pollution Probe's mid-1980s map of "Toxic Hotspots" and the *Prescription for Healthy Great Lakes*,[99] produced jointly by the National Wildlife Federation and the Canada Institute of Environmental Law and Policy. *The Great Lakes: An Environmental Atlas and Resource Book*,[100] originally produced by the USEPA and Environment Canada in 1986, became such a standard source for Great Lakes information that two updated editions have been published since. More recently, it was the inspiration for *An Atlas of Biodiversity*, published in 2003 by Chicago Wilderness, a consortium of nearly 200 public and private agencies working to restore natural areas in the greater Chicago metropolitan area.

Several series of fact sheets were widely distributed within and beyond the community directly involved with agreement processes, including information about each of the lakes by the Great Lakes Basin Commission and the University of Michigan Sea Grant program. In the early 1990s, the Center for the Great Lakes issued fact sheets for each of the 43 areas of concern where RAPS are being developed. Through the years, agreement issues have also been addressed in the research supported by the Sea Grant programs at public universities in all eight Great Lakes states.

Apart from the information networks and stakeholder contacts, the period from 1987 to 1993 in the Great Lakes regime was marked by expansion of the role of nongovernmental participants in the biennial meetings of the IJC, and by dramatic change in how the IJC responded. The new era of participation in these meetings began in 1989 in Hamilton, Ontario, as a continuation of efforts to force more action on toxic contamination by the governments.

The Biennial Meetings as an Institution

The Great Lakes Agreement requires the IJC to report to the governments on progress in achieving the goals, annually until 1978 and biennially thereafter. From 1975, the IJC held public meetings to receive the reports of the advisory boards prior to drafting its own required reports to the governments.

The IJC meetings served as the most important gatherings for the ever-expanding community that was evolving around the Great Lakes regime. Attendance increased nearly every year, and formal agendas expanded as well as special events associated with the meetings.[101] The most dramatic meetings followed adoption of the 1987 Protocol, when the involvement of environmental leaders in the renegotiation was followed by their decision to organize for greater participation in the 1989 meeting in Hamilton, Ontario.

The early meetings in the 1970s were mainly spectator events for environmentalists and other members of the public, although attendance allowed interaction with agency and IJC staffs, scientists, and others who were involved in activities of the boards, their subcommittees, and work groups.[102] Other diversions were provided at the 1983 meeting in Indianapolis, but generally attendees not directly involved in presentation of the board reports remained observers of the exchanges between presenters and commissioners. Answers to questions from the audience were provided only for questions submitted in writing.

Beginning in 1989, the meetings became more interactive and participatory for a much larger and broader audience. Special presentations, interruptions by demonstrations, and comments by attendees came to overshadow submission of the board reports.

A new change occurred in 1995 when the biennial meeting in October was preceded by debate over whether to have formal presentation of board reports at all. In effect, the pendulum had swung completely from the early meetings that were held solely for the purpose of receiving board reports, to events that provided a stage for stakeholders—including industry, environmentalists, First Nations or tribal councils, and labor—to lobby the IJC.

Another change was the combining of the reports of all three advisory boards into one document for publication, with an introduction that summarized the priorities determined by the commission. This one-volume report contrasted with an earlier practice of including reports from each committee or task force as appendices to the main reports.

The commissioners thought the condensed format would assist public understanding of the relation between the advice from the boards and the IJC's own priorities. According to members, the issue for the SAB was whether the board could maintain a distinctive identity and independence from other IJC bodies, and whether distinguished scientists would continue to be willing to participate.[103] Increased importance of the meetings as a forum for interaction within the Great Lakes community began in 1989.

The 1989 Meeting in Hamilton

Public concern about hazardous materials and uncontrolled release of toxic contaminants into the environment grew in both countries throughout the 1980s. Through contacts within the community that had formed around the Great Lakes Agreement, environmentalists were assisted by scientists in dramatizing the effects of contaminants on wildlife in Congressional hearings.[104] Established environmental groups also formed alliances with the new local "grass-roots" groups that had formed to protest siting of waste facilities following the Love Canal tragedy.[105]

The decision of a working coalition of environmental groups to increase the public's presence at the 1989 meeting resulted from frustration about the limited public role in earlier meetings, and was a follow-up to the basin-wide hearings organized by GLU in preparation for the 1987 review of the agreement. Planning began more than a year in advance, for the first time with the participation of Greenpeace, which had recently instituted a Great Lakes program of its own. This international advocacy organization provided funding to augment the resources of the Sierra Club, the Lake Michigan Federation, the Canadian Institute for Environmental Law and Policy, the National Wildlife Federation, and Great Lakes United.

Another possible factor may have been the negotiations with the IJC staff over whether the environmentalists would hold a separate meeting. A senior IJC member stated that in the late 1980s, IJC staff discussed how to increase IJC attention to the inadequate efforts by the governments to control toxic contaminants.[106] David LaRoche, then head of the U.S. secretariat, had attended the Mackinac Island meeting where GLU was launched, and was well connected with the environmental network. The format of the 1989 meeting was determined after consultation between the commission and an environmental-planning group.

The environmentalists had originally intended to hold a parallel meeting at an adjacent site at the same time as the official IJC meeting. The commission made a counterproposal to allow direct public participation in its own event. It was agreed that time would be allowed for three types of presentations: (1) presentations by local groups; (2) a coordinated presentation by the environmental-planning group; and (3) statements by any attendees. The IJC also agreed to cooperate in making arrangements for activities outside the formal meeting sessions, including briefing sessions for attendees, press conferences, and tours to local sites of interest.

Five organizational meetings were held across the basin. For several months in advance, the planners, assisted by groups in the Hamilton area, worked to organize events and attract new participants to the meeting. GLU and its member organizations widely distributed its report critiquing existing toxic-substance control programs.[107] Greenpeace toured the Great Lakes in its ship, the *Moby Dick*, urging attendance at the meeting.

The cooperating environmental organizations encouraged their members to attend through newsletters and mailings about lodgings and the availability of Greenpeace-subsidized charter buses from several locations. A bus arranged by the Lake Michigan Federation started in Milwaukee and picked up passengers in Chicago and Indiana before proceeding across Michigan to Hamilton. Most of the riders, including students from the University of Wisconsin in Madison, had never before attended an IJC meeting and learned about the agreement in a rolling "workshop." The roundtrip fare was $25.[108] Other buses came from across the region, and help was also provided in arranging carpools. Results exceeded expectations.

Nearly a thousand persons attended the meeting, about twice as many as had attended any previous IJC meeting. The great majority were private citizens. In contrast to the usual polite and quiet IJC affairs, this meeting was noisy, in part because of the crowd and in part because of the nature of the presentations by the nongovernmental participants. Well-orchestrated presentations were made by Great Lakes United, Greenpeace, the Canadian Institute for Environmental Law and Policy, the Canadian Environmental Law Association, and others. Signs and songs added theater to substantive statements on issues, many presented with intense emotion. At times, the noise level of the audience response made it seem like a sporting event.

Following the group presentations, dozens of individuals spoke, often with great feeling, during 19 hours of citizen testimony over two days. Many statements demanded that the governments and the ijc act to eliminate toxic contamination from the Great Lakes. Both ijc commissioners and official board members who were present remember the long hours of listening as an ordeal.[109]

They were also surprised at the cohesion of the message delivered by persons of all ages (including children) and many different backgrounds from throughout the basin. Some statements were so accusatory of the wqb that the U.S. chair still felt years later that his personal integrity had been attacked.[110]

The keynote speech at a luncheon sponsored by the ijc was another major surprise. The usepa's William Reilly had originally been scheduled to speak, in the tradition of featuring a political or a senior government official on such occasions. When Reilly canceled a few days before, Joyce McLean, director of the Greenpeace Great Lakes office in Toronto, agreed to take his place.[111] Her speech was supplemented by a theatrical demonstration with wildlife costumes and music intended to arouse emotion.

The Hamilton meeting is remembered as a defining event throughout the Great Lakes community.[112] The environmentalists considered the whole affair a major triumph in opening up the formal meetings of the ijc to public participation. Some staff of both the ijc and the government agencies resented what they considered attempts to stir up emotions against them. There is agreement that this and subsequent meetings with a similar format led still later to deliberate efforts to prevent a "circus" atmosphere.

The 1991 Meeting in Traverse City

The 1991 meeting in Traverse City, Michigan, followed essentially the same format as the 1989 meeting in Hamilton, but with a more complex agenda. A total of 1,600 persons registered at the meeting in spite of the rather inaccessible location, and the enthusiasm of the nongovernmental participants was again high. Release of various reports by environmental groups was timed to provoke new media attention on the Great Lakes and the event.[113] For the first time, a significant number of industry representatives were present.

This was the first ijc meeting for the Great Lakes Agreement where presentation of the traditional wqb report on the State of the Lakes was not a major agenda item. The board report, written by a journalist, outlined general issues related to toxic contaminants with some broad recommendations.

A conference on pollution prevention sponsored by Environment Canada and the usepa overlapped with the ijc meeting. In cooperation with the Center for the Great Lakes, the Council of Great Lakes Industries also sponsored a session on pollution prevention. With other concurrent events including a major workshop on health effects of toxic substances, attendees commented that it was difficult to know which event belonged to which meeting.[114]

More high-level officials from both sides attended this meeting than any other to date. Both Canadian Minister of the Environment Jean Charest and USEPA Administrator William Reilly spoke. As noted above, Charest announced that his government would sponsor a consultation to examine how to phase out use of persistent toxic chemicals.[115] Ontario Minister of the Environment Ruth Grier committed her ministry to pollution prevention and identification of toxic substances to be banned for general use. Government officials resented an accusatory banner hung by Greenpeace outside the hotel, but this time nongovernmental groups were given a location away from the official meeting place for their own activities.

The 1993 Meeting in Windsor

The intensity of the 1993 biennial meeting in Windsor, Ontario, was close to the fervor of the Hamilton meeting. About 2,000 persons attended at least part of the meeting, including 300 representatives of corporations and industry trade associations and 500 members of environmental organizations. The main event was an intense debate between a Greenpeace spokesman and a staff member of the Chlorine Institute, which had been established to combat attempts to ban the use of chlorine in industry. The theater at this meeting was provided by performances by the Trinity Theater of Toronto, plus the wearing of paper-mâché animal heads by members of the audience.

The WQB report reflected its new mandate from the IJC to provide policy advice, rather than reporting on the status of programs. In response to the absence of the traditional review of government efforts in earlier WQB reports, two dozen citizen groups endorsed an evaluation of government performance that gave both sides a "D" grade.[116]

Many attendees considered the format of this meeting to be "typical." Others, especially government officials, characterized it as "another circus." The differences seem to have influenced the organization of the 1995 meeting in Duluth, Minnesota.

The 1995 Meeting in Duluth

The Duluth meeting was the first official meeting for all six newly appointed IJC commissioners. About 1,700 persons registered in spite of the distant location.

The IJC was said to have deliberately structured the agenda to change the tone.[117] Another factor may have been less advanced organization by the large environmental groups. The lack of excitement may be the reason that one IJC commissioner dozed off in full view of the audience.

Still, several environmental organizations made a joint presentation on current significant issues for the lakes, and local organizations arranged special activities for visitors.[118] Many government officials attended in order to sign the Lake Superior Binational Agreement, which had been in development for several years. The goal of the agreement was to demonstrate how to achieve zero discharge and preserve the pristine character of the largest of the Great Lakes.

The Changing Biennial Meeting Format

Following the 1995 meeting, the commission undertook an examination of the format and content of the biennial meetings. Evaluations of each meeting, a mail-out survey, and a number of selected interviews convinced the commission that the events should be redesigned. From the collected responses, the IJC decided to seek positive news-media coverage and a more informal, less staged, and more interactive format.[119]

The commission also concluded that the format of the earlier meetings had not provided the full range of information and views needed for preparation of the required biennial report to the governments.[120] The IJC contracted with a public-relations firm for assistance.

In September 1996, the commission announced that public involvement in the meetings would expand from education and information feedback to include consultation and limited joint planning.[121] Mechanisms to achieve the changes included:

- Development of sector papers by IJC invitation to key leaders;
- Commission visits to sites where information could be obtained about RAPS and LAMPS;
- Two roundtables, each with the commissioners and 12 sector group representatives, to consider a vision for the next 25 years of the GLWQA;
- Focus-group interviews with representatives of sectors that had not previously been involved, such as foundations, First Nations and tribal councils, and communities at risk from toxic contamination;
- Annual public meetings for the advisory boards;
- A total of 13 workshops and conferences by the boards and council;
- IJC public meetings prior to formulation of recommendations to the governments; and
- A Great Lakes Summit to discuss findings of sector papers and other consultation sessions at a visible basin-wide event.

The overall thrust of the proposed new consultation process was to replace the biennial meetings with a series of other events. The "Great Lakes Summit" was seen as a one-day event, not a scaled-down biennial meeting. The practice of having board and government presentations in public was to be eliminated.

Some industry representatives supported elimination of the biennial meeting on the grounds that the format of the 1989–1995 meetings did not allow adequate presentation of the "facts" needed for the ijc annual report.[122] Environmental groups almost immediately criticized the proposal to substitute the new approach for the biennial meetings.[123] They said the new consultation mechanisms should be adopted in addition to, not instead of, the biennial meetings that had made all members of the Great Lakes community more accountable in face-to-face contact, and strengthened the sense of community.[124]

The ijc responded that insufficient funding was available to support both biennial meetings and the proposed new consultation processes. In October 1996, the ijc decided to continue the biennial meetings.

Changes in the Biennial Reports

The style and substance of the ijc reports submitted to the governments changed following the 1989 meeting. Earlier reports had relied principally on the board reports and the ijc's analysis, and required that the reader have knowledge of the ongoing implementation process for the Great Lakes Agreement for full understanding.

The Fifth Biennial Report that followed the 1989 meeting was more comprehensible outside the Great Lakes community, but also did not rely wholly on the advisory-board reports. Part 1 outlined public concern as articulated at the meeting. Part 2 responded to those concerns by urging that the governments set timetables for achieving the zero discharge of toxic contaminants that had been demanded so forcefully at Hamilton.

The Sixth Biennial Report that followed the 1991 meeting in Traverse City became the most controversial, mainly because of the recommendation that the governments develop timetables to "sunset"—that is, to discontinue use of—chlorine and chlorine-containing compounds in industrial feedstocks. The Seventh Biennial Report that followed the 1993 meeting suggested that the governments report on progress in eliminating toxic contaminants with a biennial State of the Lakes Ecosystem Report starting in 1995. For the first time, this report included recommendations to the business community, labor, and the news media that they join in seeking virtual elimination of persistent bioaccumulative toxic substances from the Great Lakes ecosystem.

The Eighth Biennial Report in 1996 followed a format similar to the previous three reports. The report noted a trend toward deregulation in favor of voluntary action in both countries, and the possible effects for Great Lakes laws, policies, and programs. By this time, Environment Canada and the usepa had begun to give more attention to land use and habitat restoration, while the ijc continued to stress elimination of toxic contamination.

New Policy Developments for Toxic Contamination

A major trend in evolution of the agreement process following the 1987 Protocol was the attention in the ijc biennial reports to policy innovations for management of toxic contamination. Some of the ijc recommendations concerned the need for a reverse-onus process, use of the weight-of-evidence approach, the use of "sunsetting," and most controversial of all, the call to eliminate use of chlorine as a feedstock.

Reverse Onus and Weight of Evidence

The 1989 report recommended use of reverse onus as a means of achieving virtual elimination. As described by the ijc, reverse onus means that "when approval is sought for the manufacture, use or discharge of any substances which will or may enter the environment, the applicant must prove, as a general rule, that the substance is not harmful to the environment or human health." The recommendation was made again in the 1996 report.[125]

The "weight-of-evidence" approach had been discussed generally by the sab and in the ijc reports, but the 1992 Sixth Biennial Report explicitly called for its use. This approach attempts to deal with the problem of making legislative and policy decisions in the face of scientific uncertainty. The Seventh Biennial Report in 1994 repeated the recommendation and suggested that the use of the principle should be pragmatic.

The 1996 report noted that the weight-of-evidence approach should trigger reverse-onus procedures by producers, rather than leaving the burden of proof to environmental management agencies with limited resources. Both approaches, the report said, would further the prevention, or precautionary approach, that is necessary if a society dependent on chemicals is to escape the burden of management after the fact of the damage caused by substances that turn out to be too dangerous to use. "Governments must lead this process," concluded the report, by "a carefully planned and deliberate process of transition away from the persistent toxic substances we now produce and use to more environmentally and humanly sustainable patterns of production and consumption."[126]

The "Sunsetting" Approach

Following on earlier discussion, the 1994 report also urged "sunsetting" of chemicals to achieve zero discharge for the worst substances. Use of such chemicals would be restricted, banned, or phased out. The concept had already been applied for ddt and pcbs as evidence of their threat to wildlife and human health was developed. The ijc recommended systematic application of criteria to identify when sunsetting should be applied to additional substances.[127] The ijc urged extending the concept to classes or families of substances, even to industrial feedstocks. Application of these concepts to chlorine created controversy within and outside the Great Lakes community.

Banning Chlorine as a Feedstock

Reverse onus, weight of evidence, and sunsetting challenged existing policy frameworks. The 1992 recommendation to sunset the use of chlorine and chlorine-containing compounds as an industrial feedstock challenged a large sector of contemporary commerce that includes drug, paper, pesticides, and plastic manufacturing. It also concerned the substance used most widely to prevent bacterial disease in drinking water and for other sanitary purposes. Detailed discussion of the IJC's action on chlorine can be found in a 1995 law-review article and a book by Gordon Durnil, the U.S. co-chair when the recommendation was made who became the chief spokesman for the IJC in the resulting international controversy.[128]

The proposal had several consequences. First, the action galvanized industry to lobby against the proposal inside and outside the IJC. From 1992, industry, particularly through the Chlorine Institute and the World Chlorine Chemical Council trade associations, began to devote considerable financial resources (reportedly over $10 million per year) to discredit the recommendation. About 300 industry personnel supported the industry position in the nearly day-long debate between representatives of Greenpeace and the Chlorine Institute at the 1993 biennial meeting in Windsor.

Second, active debate continued about the scientific justification for the recommendation. While the problems caused by some chlorine compounds are recognized, industry and others reject phasing out the use of chlorine as an industrial feedstock. The scientific community is divided on whether use of the whole family of chlorine compounds should be phased out.[129] Operators of drinking-water supply systems argue that more lives would be lost than saved if chlorine could no longer be used for disinfection. In recognizing the controversy, the IJC explicitly applied the weight-of-evidence approach, where science remains uncertain in its resolve to deal with chlorinated substances as a class rather than on a substance-by-substance basis.

Third, questions were raised about how the recommendation was developed. The IJC had considered the information and views provided in its task forces and public testimony in the biennial meetings.[130] Whether enough scientific justification had been provided was questioned.

Some observers believe that the advocacy role assumed for chlorine undermined the IJC reputation for objective judgment, based on expert advice derived from joint fact-finding. Others both defend the recommendation and believe that the use of evidence from a variety of sources allowed the commission to be more bold and aggressive than had been its tradition.[131]

Still, the IJC pointed to a string of recommendations from the SAB for phasing out use of persistent toxic substances—in particular, halogenated organics.[132] The interim report of the Virtual Elimination Task Force made a similar proposal.[133] In-depth review of the decision-making process in 1991 concluded:

- Taken together, these comments suggest that in at least some cases, the commissioners pursued an issue on the basis of public testimony;
- Sought the support of their scientific advisory boards before committing themselves; and then
- Having received such support, genuinely perceived subsequent comment on this issue from the public as simply confirming their scientifically based beliefs.[134]

The recommendation gave the IJC a new high profile during the early 1990s.[135] Many environmentalists praise the commission for its action. Others have expressed concern that its boldness undermined the credibility of the commission and contributed to its loss of stature in later years.

In any case, the chlorine debate proved larger than the IJC and the Great Lakes, as it continued in Europe and elsewhere in connection with development and plans for implementation of the Stockholm Convention on Persistent Organic Pollutants. The IJC itself continued to consider next steps on toxic contamination. In 1995 GLU established a Clean Production Task Force that continued to put forward ideas about how to achieve virtual elimination.[136]

Evolution in the Operations of the Parties

After adoption of the 1987 Protocol, the role of the parties to the agreement changed in formal and informal ways. As the lead agencies, the USEPA and Environment Canada sought to respond to the charges of a conflict of interest for agency officials who served on the WQB while also deciding how to participate in the IJC process in light of fiscal and budgetary constraints and IJC criticism. For all three reasons, the governments interpreted the 1987 Protocol to mean that they should formally assume functions that had formerly been under the domain of the WQB.

Before the Protocol, Environment Canada and the USEPA provided information to the WQB on progress—such as, for example, the number of municipal treatment systems that had or had not achieved the level of removal of phosphorus required by the agreement. Results of the monitoring of water quality and other conditions in the lakes were gathered by the WQB's surveillance committee. The IJC then used information provided by the WQB in preparing its biennial reports to the governments. Under the 1987 Protocol, the lead agencies undertook these functions.

Another primary difference between the former and newer roles of the two agencies was that they now reported directly to the IJC, rather than through the WQB. The two sides would report separately for some functions, such as their national programs, but together on others, such as their joint assessment of the state of the lakes.[137] This new reporting process raised questions about the capacity of the IJC to evaluate or to respond to the reports from the parties. The decision for both separate and joint responses to the IJC was made by the Binational Executive Committee in May 1994 as a new binational structure continued to evolve.[138]

THE BINATIONAL EXECUTIVE COMMITTEE

The Binational Executive Committee (BEC) is the chief new binational institution that was created by the parties outside the IJC framework under the 1987 Protocol. In the first four years following adoption of the 1987 Protocol, USEPA and Environment Canada personnel and representatives of other federal agencies on both sides met twice a year for a total of eight times.[139] Then, at the end of 1991, a "Parties Framework" was established that included a Binational Executive Committee that would meet twice a year to resolve policy issues and determine priority actions for meeting agreement requirements.[140]

The co-chairs would be the Ontario regional director general for Environment Canada, and the administrator of Region 5 of the USEPA. Canadian membership was to include directors of the federal Great Lakes Environmental Office (GLEO) and the Water Resource Branch of the Ontario Ministry of the Environment, as well as representatives of several other agencies. U.S. membership was to include the director of the Great Lakes National Program Office (GLNPO), two state representatives, and officials from several additional federal departments. The GLEO and GLNPO would provide secretariat services such as arrangements for the locations of the meetings that alternate between Canada and the United States.

A Binational Operations Committee (BOC) was also formed to oversee coordination of the binational planning and program priorities identified by the BEC. The BOC could establish small task forces and forward information, progress reports, and plans to the BEC for review and approval. It usually met quarterly. In effect, the BEC is for policy-level officials, while the BOC was for mid-level managers with operational responsibilities for their agencies. Figure 10 shows this management framework.

Problems in the initial bilateral structure led to the elimination of the BOC in March 1995.[141] A discussion paper outlined how the BEC would maintain its role, with provision for associate membership of additional federal agencies

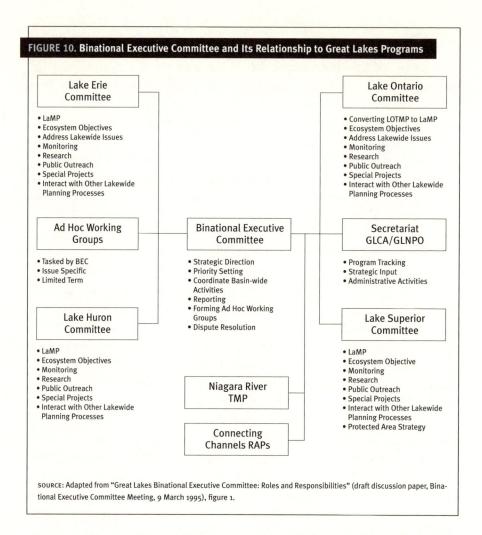

FIGURE 10. Binational Executive Committee and Its Relationship to Great Lakes Programs

Lake Erie Committee
- LaMP
- Ecosystem Objectives
- Address Lakewide Issues
- Monitoring
- Research
- Public Outreach
- Special Projects
- Interact with Other Lakewide Planning Processes

Lake Ontario Committee
- Converting LOTMP to LaMP
- Ecosystem Objectives
- Address Lakewide Issues
- Monitoring
- Research
- Public Outreach
- Special Projects
- Interact with Other Lakewide Planning Processes

Ad Hoc Working Groups
- Tasked by BEC
- Issue Specific
- Limited Term

Binational Executive Committee
- Strategic Direction
- Priority Setting
- Coordinate Basin-wide Activities
- Reporting
- Forming Ad Hoc Working Groups
- Dispute Resolution

Secretariat GLCA/GLNPO
- Program Tracking
- Strategic Input
- Administrative Activities

Lake Huron Committee
- LaMP
- Ecosystem Objectives
- Monitoring
- Research
- Public Outreach
- Special Projects
- Interact with Other Lakewide Planning Processes

Lake Superior Committee
- LaMP
- Ecosystem Objective
- Monitoring
- Research
- Public Outreach
- Special Projects
- Interact with Other Lakewide Planning Processes
- Protected Area Strategy

Niagara River TMP

Connecting Channels RAPs

SOURCE: Adapted from "Great Lakes Binational Executive Committee: Roles and Responsibilities" (draft discussion paper, Binational Executive Committee Meeting, 9 March 1995), figure 1.

on both sides of the border.[142] The BEC operates by consensus and continues to meet at least twice a year. The secretariat provided by the two special Great Lakes agencies provides strategic input to the BEC and assists in the coordination and tracking of the binational program activities and provisions of the Great Lakes Agreement.

A Lake Committee was also set up for each lake. Membership includes staff of Canadian and U.S. environmental and natural-resource agencies with jurisdiction for the respective lakes. The Lake Michigan Committee members are from U.S. agencies with a Canadian observer. Figure 10 outlines the basic structure of the BEC.

For a time, the relationship between the parties appeared to be complicated by controversy about the outspoken views of the director of the USEPA's GLNPO office about what he considered to be the inadequacies of the Canadian approach to pollution control.[143] This official had worked in USEPA headquarters prior to being given the GLNPO position. Twice, the Canadian government lodged diplomatic protests regarding his public statements urging Canada to adopt the U.S. regulatory approach.[144] In 1992 he reiterated complaints about the costs of participation in the IJC board and committees. In 1995 he took another position in the USEPA not related to the Great Lakes program.

Lake Committees oversee development of LAMPs for the open waters of the lakes. The BEC can also create ad-hoc bilateral work groups for basin-wide issues. BEC work groups have been formed for the State of the Lake Ecosystem Conferences (SOLEC), review and proposed revisions of the specific objectives of Annex 1 of the GLWQA, implementation of the Integrated Atmospheric Deposition Network (IADN), the Binational Toxics Strategy, and binational responses to IJC biennial reports.

In late 1994 and early 1995, work began on a binational strategy for toxic substances that the IJC had called for in every biennial report since the 1978 agreement.[145] A draft strategy was presented to the IJC at the Duluth meeting. Although environmental groups were not entirely satisfied, they applauded features such as deadlines for specific reductions of certain substances and periodic reporting requirements.[146] The final strategy was completed in 1997 and is discussed in chapter 6.

The first 1994 SOLEC was held in Dearborn, Michigan, by Environment Canada and the USEPA to provide information on the physical, chemical, USEPA biological integrity of the Great Lakes system to assist in setting program priorities. SOLEC was said to be designed to complement the IJC biennial meetings, and the 1994 event was meant to set the pattern for follow-up conferences in alternate years.

The organizers said the event was not to be "political," but rather to make scientific information available to managers and decision makers.[147] Industry and GLU representatives were invited to participate with scientists and agency representatives in planning the agenda. Six background papers on aquatic-community health, human health, habitat, contaminants, nutrients, and the economy were commissioned. Approximately 350 persons attended, with a far smaller proportion of nongovernmental participants than the IJC meetings.

A summary of the six background papers was presented at Duluth as the first State of the Lakes Ecosystem Report, called for by the IJC.[148] The report makes it clear that it does not address the state of programs created to deal with stresses to the ecosystem. The program information was to be provided in a different series of reports, prepared separately by the lead agencies for the governments.

The second SOLEC meeting was held in November 1996 in Windsor. This time, the focus was on nearshore waters and how land use affects water quality. Attendance nearly doubled from 1994, with about 600 persons registered. The majority were agency officials at all levels, plus a number of environmentalists and industry representatives, as well as staff of research agencies. The five sitting ijc commissioners and regional-office staff attended solec events, as well as meeting separately. Again, the background papers described conditions and problems more fully than the adequacy of programs designed to address them.[149] The ijc created an Evaluation Task Force in May 1995 to establish a framework to review data submitted by the parties, such as the solec reports.[150] The task force submitted a final report in April 1996.[151]

Review of Programs

Prior to the 1991 change in mandate, the wqb assessed the adequacy of the parties' programs to meet agreement goals. In the new relationship since 1987, the binational advisory boards did not provide data and information for this purpose. After the bec was formed, the agencies did not engage in self-evaluation or respond fully to ijc requests for information about programs. As the relationship between the ijc and the parties changed in the 1990s, observers reported that the apparent shift from "a mutual search for solutions" frame of mind, which had formerly existed in the wqb, to "negotiation of the common position to be presented to the ijc" was confirmed in the bec.[152]

Binational Programs under the GLWQA

Three unique institutions called for in the 1987 Protocol require federal plus state or provincial participation—or both, depending on the geographic location. All three continued through the third phase of the agreement and still had uncertain outcomes.

Remedial Action Plans

Remedial Action Plans (raps) are locally developed plans for remediation in areas where the objectives of the agreement have not been achieved, called Areas of Concern (aoc). Based on efforts to develop a local cleanup plan for the Grand Calumet River in Northwest Indiana, the concept was recommended by the wqb to the ijc in 1985 and made part of the agreement in Annex 2 with the 1987 Protocol.[153] The intent is for governments, industry, and local residents, known as stakeholders, to participate in development of a remediation plan.

Initially, 42 (and later 43) areas of concern were identified where raps should be developed, most in urban industrial areas. Slow progress under Annex 2 was a major disappointment almost from the beginning.

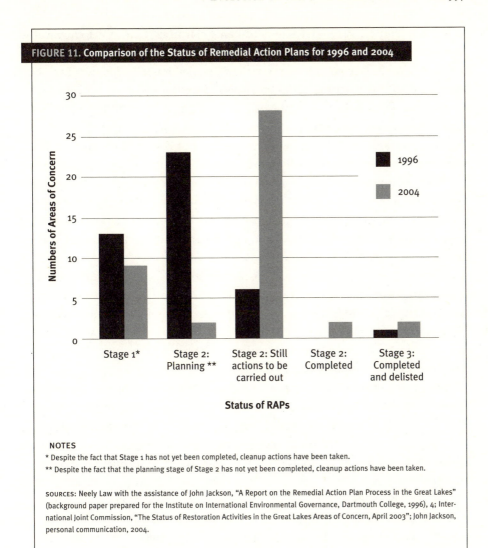

FIGURE 11. Comparison of the Status of Remedial Action Plans for 1996 and 2004

NOTES

* Despite the fact that Stage 1 has not yet been completed, cleanup actions have been taken.

** Despite the fact that the planning stage of Stage 2 has not yet been completed, cleanup actions have been taken.

SOURCES: Neely Law with the assistance of John Jackson, "A Report on the Remedial Action Plan Process in the Great Lakes" (background paper prepared for the Institute on International Environmental Governance, Dartmouth College, 1996), 4; International Joint Commission, "The Status of Restoration Activities in the Great Lakes Areas of Concern, April 2003"; John Jackson, personal communication, 2004.

Three "binational" RAPS were undertaken for the St. Mary's, St. Clair, and Detroit rivers, 17 in Canada and the remainder in the United States. For both the Niagara and St. Lawrence rivers, two separate RAPS were undertaken because New York and Ontario did not agree on a binational process. In 2004 Collingwood Harbor and Severn Sound in Ontario had been removed, or "delisted" as areas of concern, with IJC approval of completed RAPS. The RAP for Waukegan Harbor in Illinois had been completed but not yet approved.

Annex 2 calls for the federal governments to cooperate with the states and provinces to ensure that the RAPS incorporate a comprehensive ecosystem approach, with public consultation on all actions. The purpose of the final plans is to correct 14 "impairments of beneficial uses" that affect chemical, physical, or biological integrity. The ijc has two rap responsibilities: to recommend new areas of concern, and to review and comment on the adequacy of each phase of the rap process for each area of concern.

The rap process has three stages. The first phase is identification of the impairments and their causes. The second phase includes identification of appropriate remedial measures and designation of responsibility for correction. The third phase requires monitoring of the results.

Initial enthusiasm was high for the raps, which were called "a blueprint for action" and a means to achieve "ecological democracy."[154] Yet frustration grew as the planning process continued. In 1995, only 71 percent of raps had completed stage 1, 18 percent stage 2, and only 2 percent stage 3. Figure 11 illustrates progress with raps between 1996 and 2004.

A growing literature on the rap process identifies issues and analyzes reasons for the slow pace of progress. Lack of information is a major reason for slowness in completing stage 1. On the other hand, identification of linkages between water quality, direct and nonpoint sources of pollution, and atmospheric deposition demonstrates how raps can be mechanisms for implementing the ecosystem approach at a practical level.[155]

Intergovernmental cooperation proved difficult to achieve, especially between New York, Michigan, and Ontario for the connecting-channels raps. Yet the efforts made on both sides by the public-advisory committees to develop their own coordinating mechanisms in the St. Lawrence and Niagara areas of concern were examples of citizen commitment to the process in many locations.

Lack of committed resources at all levels of government was a continuing problem. In Canada, the rap program was initially sustained by the 1990 Great Lakes Action Plan, with $43 million invested in 200 projects. When Environment Canada's budget was reduced by more than 25 percent starting in 1995, Ontario was told that the commitment to restore 70 percent of impaired uses would be extended. Contracts with coordinators for public involvement were canceled.

In 1995 and 1996, the continuing ambivalence of the states about agreement-related programs could be seen in the withdrawal of state support for development of the raps. Earlier, the states had mainly passed through federal funds received from the usepa with a proportion of state matching funding. After the usepa announced that it would no longer provide funds to the states for raps, Michigan took the lead in announcing in late 1994 that it would discontinue state support over the following three years. Then Wisconsin withdrew from three of its five raps, and Minnesota from its single rap.

Confusion continued over the IJC role in evaluation of the reports on progress, which was carried out slowly. Problems that the IJC identified with the overall effort included insufficient accountability, lack of enforcement of needed actions, need for improved communication among RAPS, and insufficient means to sustain RAP institutions including public participation.

The question remains as to how to measure the progress of the RAPS. One view is that they should be measured not only by the proportion of uses restored but also by the level of community participation in RAP development. Most RAPS have some sort of stakeholder group, coordinating group, public-advisory council, or other body to help facilitate public participation, coordinate RAP development, and build institutional capacity. However, the level of community participation in each RAP is different, with clear variations in terms of technical support and relationships among the stakeholders.[156]

In some locations, RAP constituencies appeared more interested in having their areas removed from the AOC list than in achieving the goals of the agreement or correcting the beneficial-use impairments. No new actions specifically intended for the RAP were identified in the stage 2 report of the Calumet RAP in Indiana, which listed only activities already under way or being undertaken for another purpose.

LAKEWIDE MANAGEMENT PLANS

Annex 2 of the 1987 Protocol noted that lakewide management efforts were already under way for the open waters of Lakes Michigan and Ontario, and stated the parties' intention "to endorse and build . . . existing efforts for Lakewide Management Plans, or LAMPS." The grand plan was that results of RAPS for local areas of concern and LAMPS at the whole lake level eventually could be integrated into a total basin-wide effort on behalf of the entire Great Lakes ecosystem. This is the concept that was ignored in the so-called restoration legislation introduced in the U.S. Congress in 2003 and re-introduced in 2005.

The United States has sole responsibility for a Lake Michigan LAMP, but binational coordination is required for the other lakes. In a sense, inclusion of such an ambitious, long-range commitment by the parties affirmed their continuing commitment at the time to the fundamental goals of the agreement.

By 1996, processes for development of the LAMP had been established for all five lakes, but no environmental results could be identified. On the other hand, both local officials and citizen participants believed there was value in the interaction between a wide range of interests in the "forums" that had been set up for each lake.[157] The 1996 Lake Michigan Forum work plan described this then new institution as "a diverse stakeholder group organized to work in partnership and supported by the USEPA and the four states to protect and enhance environmental quality . . ."[158]

This language reflected the broader agenda for the USEPA's Great Lakes programs that had developed in the 1990s to include ecological integrity beyond toxic-contaminant control and water quality improvement. The first draft of the work plan in 1993 had stressed toxic-contaminant control. The 1996 version added objectives and "action steps" to deal with relationships between land use and water quality.

This report also reflected the new involvements with industry, citing a "pollution prevention/toxics reduction" plan with the primary metals industry. The Lake Michigan Mass Balance Study (a study that attempts model input, pathways, and outputs of toxics within a defined ecosystem) was cited as an attempt to provide information on movement of contaminants into and through the basin that could be used to construct programs to reduce "loadings of critical pollutants."[159]

Lake Superior Program

In 1991 both federal governments, Ontario, Michigan, Minnesota, and Wisconsin signed a special agreement to carry out a demonstration for how to achieve zero discharge in Lake Superior. Both voluntary and regulatory actions were to be used "to achieve zero discharge and zero emission" for nine chemicals.

In general, the same difficulties were encountered in this program as in those established under the Great Lakes Agreement: difficulties in accountability and lack of resources in spite of original intentions. The process by which a citizens advisory group developed recommendations to the governments was similar to the forum process for LaMPs.

Other Great Lakes Programs

During this period, some Great Lakes institutions outside the agreement process disappeared, but new ones developed. The Center for the Great Lakes shut down in 1993 because of funding difficulties. Industrial interests organized a Great Lakes Water Quality Coalition to oppose the GLI. A Council of Great Lakes Industries was organized to represent business interests in policy debates. A Great Lakes Research Consortium within the State University of New York system was added to academic research centers.

The Great Lakes Commission expanded its agenda by establishing a binational Great Lakes Information Network (GLIN) to provide an ongoing source of Great Lakes news and information through the Internet. Both Environment Canada and the USEPA made electronic Great Lakes databases available, and exhibits and training were provided at SOLEC meetings for use of both systems.[160]

In 1994 the Great Lakes Commission also issued an Ecosystem Charter articulating principles for achieving and maintaining ecological integrity. A number of environmental organizations declined to sign the charter because they said it lacked mechanisms for implementation, but by 1996, 175 endorsements had been received from diverse sources.[161]

The Period of Change

The years following adoption of the 1987 Protocol brought more change to nearly all aspects of the Great Lakes regime than had occurred in the two previous decades. Many changes are still evolving. They can be considered in terms of changes—first, to the operations of the IJC; second, to the relationship between the parties and the IJC; and third, to the greater community that has developed around the Great Lakes Agreement.

Alterations have occurred in both the internal operations of the IJC and the way the commission relates to other parts of the community. The major internal changes include the restructuring and change in mandate of the original advisory boards, the SAB and the WQB, plus the establishment of new advisory mechanisms that include the CGLRM and task forces. Others are the new direct management of the regional office by the secretariats of the parties, and the change in role of the office staff. The use of a commission-directed priority-setting process demonstrates the new role of the IJC itself in overall management of the binational institutions.

In addition to a new internal-management framework, other initiatives of the IJC include reaching out to, and inclusion of, new constituencies, including corporations, for the agreement process. The IJC broke new ground in seeking to broaden the basis for its recommendations beyond the advisory boards, and in its advocacy for using the weight of evidence, precautionary principles, and response to public input. One result was the series of recommendations on the use of chlorine, which brought the IJC unprecedented national and international attention and made it the focus for direct intensive lobbying by the chemical industry. With all the internal changes, questions arose about the relations with other international institutions whose jurisdictions overlap with those of the IJC, including the Great Lakes Fishery Commission and the Commission for Environmental Cooperation for North America.

Identification and evaluation of changes in the relationship between the IJC and the governments and in the role of the lead agencies for the parties is made more difficult by the lack of a framework or a plan for institutional development following the adoption of the protocol. Much seems to have depended on the views of agency administrators such as the director of the USEPA's Great Lakes National Program Office. The agencies have also had to operate during a period of growing rise of political conservatism and decreasing fiscal resources.

In any case, the staffs of the USEPA and Environment Canada were much less involved in the activities and processes coordinated by the IJC than in previous years. The functions of the BEC and SOLEC were still evolving, and are further described in the next chapter. The change in participation in the WQB raised three questions: First, can the IJC adequately assess the separate or joint reports by the parties? Second, does the IJC have any fact-finding or reviewing functions in the new separate bilateral processes that are comparable to its evaluation role prior to 1987? Third, without the IJC as a forum, how can the binational community participate in assessment of the adequacy of programs? Unfortunately, as the history of the agreement is further described in the next chapter, these questions remain as relevant today.

The delegation in this period of authority and responsibility for environmental management to both the states and the provinces raised new questions about their role in meeting national obligations under the Great Lakes Agreement. Yet, in a period in which governments seemed to be withdrawing from agreement processes, RAPS, LAMPS and the special efforts for Lake Superior expanded participation by local governments, business and industry, and citizens.

Finally, this phase of the Great Lakes Agreement was marked by an increased role for nongovernmental participants, especially environmental activists and representatives of industry. The regional and national environmental organizations that had become involved in the 1980s were joined at the biennial meetings, starting in 1989, by numerous local grass-roots organizations concerned about toxic contaminants. Their presence changed the character of the meetings from exchanges of information between the advisory boards and the IJC to major demonstrations of public opinion. The increased activism enhanced political support for Great Lakes programs and led to new, strong U.S. legislation in support of the agreement in the United States, and to major policy developments in both countries.

From 1991, industry participation grew in both biennial meetings and other agreement-related activities. Industry representatives also began lobbying IJC members and staff as never before.[162]

In the 1990s, environmental groups in both countries were struggling to maintain their organizational capacity, with much uncertainty about the continuing role of the philanthropic foundations that had earlier been the major source of funding for Great Lakes protection activities. Yet participation in development of the RAPS and LAMPS were evidence of continuing vitality in the community concerned with the Great Lakes Agreement.

In the United States, bipartisan support for Great Lakes protection remained in the Congress, although it seemed diminished by changes in membership and leadership. In Canada, controversy over national unity and cutbacks in government funding for the environment diluted focus on Great Lakes issues.

CHAPTER 6

THE CONTINUING EVOLUTION OF THE GREAT LAKES REGIME FROM 1997 TO 2005

In 2003 much of the U.S. Great Lakes community became so preoccupied with legislation introduced into the U.S. Congress that the relevance of the Great Lakes Water Quality Agreement seemed in doubt for the first time since it was signed in 1972. The so-called "restoration legislation" ignored the binational thirty-year-old regime by proposing to authorize substantial new federal funding, to be managed by the governors of the eight Great Lakes states.[1]

The enthusiasm for the new approach provoked attention to the possibility of renegotiation and renewal of the agreement following the periodic review by the governments that was due to take place in 2004.[2] No changes had been made in the agreement since the 1987 Protocol, which laid the foundation for the strengths and weaknesses manifested in the regime between 1997 and 2004.

The question was whether the new review would lead to renewal and possible renegotiation, or whether the agreement would fade away as past history. There was universal agreement that substantially more effort would be needed to restore the integrity of the Great Lakes ecosystem, but new disagreement about how this goal could be achieved.

The State of the Lakes

Water quality of the Great Lakes generally continued to improve throughout the 1990s into the new millennium. Yet scientists warned that new threats could undermine future ecological integrity, even if the original goals of the agreement were achieved.

By the 1990s the levels of some of the most dangerous contaminants such as PCBS and dioxins had dropped to new lows with control of direct discharges.

The bioconcentration in fish tissues made health advisories against consumption of certain species still necessary.[3] Virtual elimination will not be possible until atmospheric deposition by long-range transport is stopped. The new international Stockholm Convention offers hope that this will eventually be possible. Discharge of toxic pollutants within the basin remains a concern because hundreds of thousands of tons continue to be released into the Great Lakes basin every year. [4] A major source continued to be reservoirs of toxic chemicals in contaminated sediments, which had been removed from about a third of the sites waiting for cleanup, always with great cost and controversy over disposal of the sediments.

Phosphorus levels remained low, except for puzzling fluctuations and expansion of a dead zone in Lake Erie in the 1990s. Concerned scientists believed these changes could be due to the presence of zebra and quaqqa mussels, non-native species that had been introduced in ballast water from ocean-going ships only a few years earlier. Increasingly, scientists referred to "biological pollution," which included continuing introduction of invasive species in the 1990s—mainly in ballast water, and possibly linked to globalization of trade.[5]

Local governments became more concerned about beach closings because of levels of fecal *E. coli* bacteria that exceeded the existing health standard. The greater frequency of swimming bans was due, at least in part, to better monitoring of water quality with funding under the U.S. Beaches Environmental Assessment and Coastal Health Act, also known as the Beach Act. Increased research to identify sources confirmed that bird and animal, as well as human wastes could be at fault. The difficulty of linking violations of the *E. coli* standard to disease in humans was one of the topics of a conference sponsored by the City of Chicago and the USEPA in 2001. The publicity about beach closings made the presence of *E. coli* a major economic as well as a public-health issue.[6]

Loss of habitat, including shoreline wetlands, that causes loss of biodiversity is another form of increasing biological pollution. New attention was given to land use and urban development as critical issues for Great Lakes water quality and ecosystem integrity.[7] Climate change was also perceived as another pervasive threat with unknown but likely major ecological consequences.[8]

The goal of restoration of ecological integrity, not just improvement of water chemistry, was being accepted more and more widely in both public and private activities. First articulated in the 1978 agreement as a requirement for an ecosystem approach to management necessary to eliminate toxic contaminants, the concept now seemed to include the pollution prevention, habitat restoration, and watershed management planning that were being practiced more generally in public and private activities.

Frustration with two of the major programs instituted by the 1987 Protocol was part of the reason for enthusiasm about the new approach to restoration proposed in the U.S. Congress. After development of Remedial Action Plans (RAPS) had been underway for 15 years, only Collingwood Harbor and Severn Sound in Ontario had been removed from the list of 43 areas of concern. Lakewide Management Plans (LAMPS) were drafted for three of the five lakes: Michigan, Erie, and Ontario.

Overall, through the 1990s, the state of the Great Lakes as a whole had seldom made headlines as an environmental issue within the region, or nationally in either country (although some attention was given to the issue of significant fish die-off in Lake Erie). Beach closings, the spread of zebra mussels, declines in yellow-perch populations, and occasional reports on PCBs or mercury were mainly treated as local news, not general alarms. In Canada, the general public had seemed indifferent to a decade of major decreases in funding for environmental protection, even though that situation changed as the public begun to understand the implications of downsizing.

The 2001 Report of the Commissioner of the Environment and Sustainable Development highlighted these points by noting that the state of most of the lakes was "mixed," with Lake Erie considered to be "mixed deteriorating," with funding to deal with many issues in the Great Lakes as declining and insufficient to meet the government objectives.

While disturbing to boaters and navigation interests, low lake levels did not disturb the public at large. The water looked cleaner, and most people, unlike the scientific community, seemed to have the impression that all was more or less well with the lakes.[9]

The General Political Context

A deep political conservatism had settled into both Canada and the United States by the mid 1990s. Environmental issues were of less concern than economic and other social issues. No major new environmental laws were adopted, nor were there any significant new Congressional initiatives for the Great Lakes until the Great Lakes Legacy Act in 2002. State and local governments continued to receive less federal funding to help them cope with environmental regulations and the consequences of continued growth and development.

The United States' hesitation to accept the proposed goals of the Kyoto Treaty on climate change in 1997 was turned around by intervention of then Vice President Albert Gore, and President Clinton had signed on for the United States. The Clinton administration then followed the lead of the chemical industry in opposing the treaty on Persistent Organic Pollutants proposed by the United Nations Environmental Program in 1997, until agreeing with the majority of nations in the final negotiations in South Africa in 2000.

President George W. Bush canceled U.S. acceptance of the Kyoto climate-change treaty soon after taking office in 2001. A short time later, he signed the Stockholm Convention on Persistent Organic Pollutants rather than risk the kind of criticism he had received from environmentalists for the Kyoto action. No move had been made by 2005 to seek ratification of either treaty by the U.S. Senate, as required by the U.S. Constitution.

As the 2004 presidential election approached, the Bush administration was accused of having "initiated more than 200 major rollbacks of America's environmental laws, weakening the protection of our country's air, water, public lands and wildlife."[10] The same source quoted a pollster for the Republican Party as cautioning that "The environment is probably the single issue on which both Republicans in general and President Bush in particular are most vulnerable." This statement was made before President Bush began to receive lower approval ratings in public-opinion surveys because of the economy and the war in Iraq. It was this potential vulnerability that members of the Great Lakes Congressional delegation sought to exploit with bipartisan support in the so-called Great Lakes restoration legislation in 2003 and again in 2005.

During the mid 1990s, tensions remained high within the Canadian confederation between the federal and provincial governments. In 1998, a "harmonization accord" was concluded between the provincial and federal governments (with the exception of Quebec) to clarify federal-provincial roles with respect to the environment.[11] The agreement, which was negotiated through and administered by the Canadian Council of the Ministers of the Environment (CCME), called for a process where only one order of government would act over a certain area of the environment, including the development of "Canada-Wide Standards." [12] The agreement was widely opposed by the nongovernmental community.[13] Essentially, there was concern that it was another step towards diminishing the federal role in environmental decision-making, especially with respect to toxic contaminants, and providing more power to provinces that were still undergoing very dramatic budget cuts to environmental budgets.[14] What is interesting is that work under the agreement was, in effect, removed from the various processes within the Great Lakes (such as the Canada-Ontario Agreement or the Binational Toxics Strategy).

Federal-provincial conflicts continued, but stabilized after Jean Charest was elected premier of Quebec in 2001. He had been environment minister for Canada and attended the 1991 IJC biennial meeting in Traverse City, Michigan, where toxic-contaminant issues dominated the agenda.

During this time, the focus of the federal government was more on water quantity than quality. A proposal by a small company in Sault St. Marie,

Ontario, to export water from Lake Superior by tanker caused a robust national debate on water. Eventually, a federal-provincial accord was debated at length, although it failed to materialize. The federal government amended its statute implementing the Boundary Waters Treaty to the effect that export of water outside of designated water basins was not permitted.[15] This action also created a bilateral debate on diversion, which was one of the triggers for development of the Great Lakes Annex 2001, discussed below.

Prime Minister Chrétien announced that he would be stepping down as prime minister. One of the legacies he left was the ratification of the Kyoto Protocol, over and above the protest of many provinces. Paul Martin, the new prime minister, allocated significant resources in 2005 to implement the protocol. Canada was a strong supporter of the Stockholm Convention.

In Ontario the Progressive Conservative government continued downsizing and budget cuts, in effect diluting the Great Lakes focus and losing much of its capacity to take an active role in Great Lakes matters. The public awoke to these problems with the tragedy at Walkerton, Ontario, a small town near Owen Sound. In the summer of 2001, seven persons died and over 2,000 became ill, some critically, because of *E. coli* contamination of drinking water. In October 2003, the provincial government lost an election to the Liberals and new Premier Dalton McGuinty. The new premier committed to the implementation of the recommendations flowing from an inquiry into the tragedy.

The 1998–99 Review

Another periodic review by the governments had been anticipated in 1992 following the 1987 renegotiation of the Great Lakes Agreement.[16] The nongovernmental environmental groups, the Council of Great Lakes Industries, and the Science Advisory Board all recommended against review. The governments agreed with an IJC recommendation that efforts should instead be devoted to implementation of the existing agreement.[17] The commission commented that "the present Agreement is sound, effective and flexible. Review and renegotiation are not necessary. Rather, the Parties need to renew and fulfill their commitments and focus on implementation, enforcement and other actions, including review of institutional arrangements, to achieve the Agreement's purpose."[18]

When the next periodic review came due in 1998, the Binational Executive Committee (BEC) set up an ad-hoc work group to prepare a scoping paper on review issues.[19] Discussion of the paper in July revealed growing debate over whether the agreement should remain focused on water quality,[20] or whether (and how) it should be expanded. When both coast guards and Transport Canada proposed specific amendments for the several annexes for which they had responsibility,[21] a Great Lakes Water Quality Agreement Binational Steering Committee was formed to consider possible changes.[22]

By early 1999, the committee had developed a plan for internal review of the agreement, and work groups were assigned to consider possible changes for each annex.[23] The preliminary findings were presented at the July 1999 BEC meeting, as follows:

- The annexes were out of date and needed to be revised;
- Issues pertaining to science, programs, and interpretation of language in the agreement needed to be clarified or updated;
- The agreement was confusing to the public, involved stakeholders, and those responsible for implementation;
- Improvement was needed to make the agreement a better tool for program managers; and
- Needed changes include factoring "ecosystem management" into objectives.[24]

In reviewing the annexes, the BEC made a number of recommendations on preferred options. In concluding, the BEC co-chairs agreed that the agreement is "out of date." Although they did not intend to undertake such an extensive review, they recognized "the findings of the BSC and its experts that substantial changes should be considered to bring the document up to date and make it more relevant to the future."[25]

The review momentum was dramatically slowed, despite support for a formal review and possible renegotiation by some interests. The Great Lakes Commission had urged "an open, objective and thorough review" and possible amendment.[26] The Environment Canada and USEPA BEC co-chairs announced at the July 2000 meeting in Chicago that there was no interest by the parties in possible renegotiation.[27] Despite this communication from the governments, in May 2001 a report from a Science Advisory Board (SAB) workshop concluded that Annex 1, on specific objectives for toxic contaminants, needed to be revised.[28] Still, this review was effectively put to bed.[29]

The BEC also considered a paper on improving reporting and sharing of information between the IJC and the parties. BEC members asked whether "there would be a reasonable return for the effort" to meet reporting demands of the IJC. It was noted that review of reporting processes aimed to improve the relationship with the IJC, which was invited to begin sending a representative to BEC meetings.

A follow-up report at the June 2002 BEC meeting criticized the reporting requirements of the agreement and noted that the parties were not meeting, or were only partially meeting 15 such requirements (or 31, if reporting was offered "in the spirit of the agreement" rather than the specific obligations)."[30]

At the December 2002 meeting, it was agreed that the parties would not report under Article IV (progress on specific objectives) and Annexes 1 (specific objectives), 7 (dredging), and 10 (hazardous polluting substances) until these parts were brought up to date.[31]

Thus, despite the clear communication about the lack of interest by the governments in revising the agreement or the annexes, the issue remained alive within the BEC and the IJC through 2002. A new wave of enthusiasm for revisiting the issue emerged in 2003.

Development of the Stockholm Convention Treaty

Meanwhile, new international negotiations had begun under the auspices of the United Nations Environmental Program on a new treaty calling for global action to control persistent organic pollutants in the environment.[32] Several IJC biennial reports had noted that toxic contamination could not be solved solely within the Great Lakes watershed because of long-range transport and atmospheric deposition from sources outside the drainage basin. Presumably, the Great Lakes situation contributed to recognition that the presence and world-wide distribution of persistent organic pollutants (POPS) required international action.[33]

The negotiations began at Montreal, Quebec, in July 1998. John Buccini, an official from Environment Canada, chaired the seven negotiating sessions until the treaty was concluded in Stockholm, Sweden, in May 2001.[34] Officially called the Stockholm Convention on Persistent Organic Pollutants, the accord is also referred to as the POPS Treaty.

Canada was the first country to ratify the agreement, and contributed $20 million to assist implementation. The ratification needed by 50 countries was concluded in 2004. Seven regional plans for implementation had been completed, and the first Conference of Parties, a forum for parties to the treaty, was expected to occur in May 2005.

Efforts to eliminate toxic contaminants in the Great Lakes had several connections to the Stockholm Convention. Great Lakes science had provided fundamental understanding of how persistent chemicals with the capacity to bioaccumulate can damage human and wildlife health. A major motivation was the recognition that the Arctic region is the ultimate sink for such substances as dioxins and PCBs in the northern hemisphere, where they affect the health of the indigenous Inuit populations and the wildlife on which they depend for food.[35] Research has confirmed that the sources are other parts of the world, possibly including the industrial centers in the Great Lakes.

Throughout the negotiations, the Great Lakes region contributed human resources in addition to scientific understanding of how such chemicals are distributed through long-range transport in the atmosphere, and bioaccumulate in blood and fatty tissues of people and animals. Nongovernmental groups that advocated for the convention included the World Wildlife Fund, Greenpeace, the Canadian Environmental Law Association, and the Delta Institute of Chicago. Back in the United States, members of the National Wildlife Federation, Great Lakes United, the Lake Michigan Federation, and other environmental groups successfully lobbied members of the Congressional Great Lakes delegation, who then influenced the Clinton administration to support the treaty in the final negotiating session in South Africa.

Individuals with experience as Great Lakes advocates who played key roles included Craig Boljkovac and Julia Langer of the World Wildlife Fund, and Morag Carter and Jack Weinberg of Greenpeace. Weinberg led the organization of an International POPs Elimination Network (IPEN) that linked nongovernmental advocacy groups from other countries, including in Europe and Asia, with the North American activists. IPEN continued to be involved in seeking ratification and planning for implementation. In addition to the nongovernmental leaders, participating government officials from Canada and the United States, industry representatives, and scientists also had Great Lakes connections.

The international negotiating meetings in Bonn, Germany; Nairobi, Kenya; Geneva, Switzerland; and Johannesburg, South Africa were forums for consideration of concepts that had been debated in the Great Lakes Agreement process for two decades.[36] They included the goal of elimination, not just control, of contaminants; the precautionary principle; public participation in environmental decision-making and oversight; and the need for pollution-prevention planning in the use of persistent toxic substances. In a presentation at the 2003 annual meeting of the International Association for Great Lakes Research, Weinberg's assertion that control of toxic contaminants would be determined globally rather than in the Great Lakes raised the question of how implementation of the Great Lakes Water Quality Agreement should be related to implementation of the new international treaty.[37]

Domestic Actions in Canada and the United States

The mid 1990s was a quiet time for the Great Lakes in the U.S. Congress, but a stormy time in the Canadian Parliament. The situation reversed following the election of President George W. Bush in 2000 and the Walkerton tragedy in 2001.

As in the United States, Canada's environmental laws are subject to periodic legislative review. The 1994 required review of the Canada Environmental Protection Act (CEPA) resulted in the introduction of a new version of the law and intense parliamentary debate.[38]

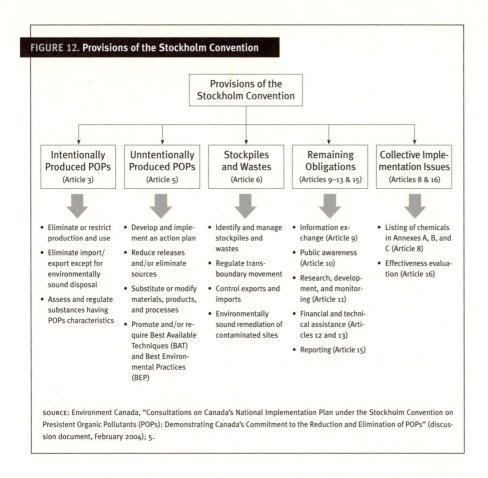

FIGURE 12. Provisions of the Stockholm Convention

Provisions of the Stockholm Convention

Intentionally Produced POPs (Article 3)	Unintentionally Produced POPs (Article 5)	Stockpiles and Wastes (Article 6)	Remaining Obligations (Articles 9–13 & 15)	Collective Implementation Issues (Articles 8 & 16)
• Eliminate or restrict production and use • Eliminate import/export except for environmentally sound disposal • Assess and regulate substances having POPs characteristics	• Develop and implement an action plan • Reduce releases and/or eliminate sources • Substitute or modify materials, products, and processes • Promote and/or require Best Available Techniques (BAT) and Best Environmental Practices (BEP)	• Identify and manage stockpiles and wastes • Regulate transboundary movement • Control exports and imports • Environmentally sound remediation of contaminated sites	• Information exchange (Article 9) • Public awareness (Article 10) • Research, development, and monitoring (Article 11) • Financial and technical assistance (Articles 12 and 13) • Reporting (Article 15)	• Listing of chemicals in Annexes A, B, and C (Article 8) • Effectiveness evaluation (Article 16)

SOURCE: Environment Canada, "Consultations on Canada's National Implementation Plan under the Stockholm Convention on Presistent Organic Pollutants (POPs): Demonstrating Canada's Commitment to the Reduction and Elimination of POPs" (discussion document, February 2004); 5.

THE CANADA ENVIRONMENTAL PROTECTION ACT (CEPA)

The Canada Environmental Protection Act is the primary federal mechanism for dealing with toxic substances. The new version in 2000 precipitated battles between government, industry, and environmental groups, as well as within Parliament, over policy concepts resulting from experience with toxic contamination.[39] The major controversies were over inclusion of virtual elimination as a goal and how it could be achieved, the precautionary principle, and pollution prevention—the same concepts that were also being debated internationally in the POPS negotiations and that were issues under the Great Lakes Agreement. During the 1998 debate on Bill c-32 before the House of Commons Standing Committee on Environment and Sustainable Development, more amendments were proposed than for any other bill in the twentieth century.

Some of the most controversial provisions approved by the committee were due to an unusual alliance between members of the governing Liberal Party and opposition parties. This is highly unusual, since the Canadian

Parliamentary system traditionally requires committee members to vote according to government direction. Despite some extremely progressive changes to the bill proposed by the Standing Committee, the chemical-industry lobby worked very hard to "undo" the committee's hard-fought gains.

When the bill was introduced into Parliament for a third and final reading, the environment minister persuaded Parliament to change a number of provisions in the final reading in 1999, to take effect in April 2000 and dilute many of the proposals put forward by the committee. Nevertheless, the new law included a goal of virtual elimination and its definition, the precautionary principle and its meaning, a directive for increasing the role of the public in environmental decision-making, and directions on how to further pollution prevention. Visionary—some would say naïve—goals of the Great Lakes Agreement were now part of the legal fabric of Canada. With adoption of the Stockholm Convention in 2001, Great Lakes goals are now part of an international legal regime. Interestingly, the Canada Environmental Protection Act was scheduled to be reviewed by Parliament again in 2005, roughly the same time as the Great Lakes Agreement.

THE WALKERTON TRAGEDY AND ITS AFTERMATH

The tragedy in Walkerton, a small town with about 5,000 residents, was a turning point in the environmental history of Ontario. Local officials could not identify the cause when many people became ill a few days after heavy rainfall in May 2000. Eventually, it was determined that the local water supply was contaminated with *E. coli* H:157 because the water was not chlorinated and the contamination had not been reported to health authorities. In the end, seven persons died and over 2,000 became ill, several critically.

By early June, public demand forced formal official inquiry with two parts. The first part concerned both the physical causes and whether government policies had contributed to the event. The second part examined whether government practices, including funding cuts, were a factor. The 2002 reports on results of the inquiry made a total of 121 recommendations for prevention of another such incident.[40]

The results of the inquiry were significant for the Great Lakes because they linked the adequacy of funding to the effectiveness of programs. First, the inquiry found that the province's budget cuts for the Ministry of the Environment from $461 million in 1991–92 to $174 million in 1999–2000 contributed to reduced capacity of the agency. These cuts had resulted in a 43 percent reduction in professional staff positions. [41]

Second, the human tragedy, followed by the inquiry and its resulting recommendations, forced the government to realign its priorities. New regulations and a Safe Drinking Water Act were adopted for the province.[42]

The Liberal government that was elected in October 2003 inherited the downsized ministry and a host of recommendations still to be implemented. Policy reviews and legislative initiatives for environmental protection that were in full swing in 2004 provided a new setting for consideration of Great Lakes issues.

WATERSHED PLANNING IN ONTARIO

A key set of the recommendations from the Walkerton inquiry related to the need for source protection of drinking water. In November 2002, the provincial government appointed a multi-stakeholder committee to further a source-protection approach for the province. This committee reported in April 2003.[43] Based on this report, the new provincial government issued a white paper on source-protection planning, that is, a proposal that would eventually translate into legislation.[44]

The implications of this strategy, if implemented, could be profound. The report calls for the implementation of a watershed-planning approach for the province by requiring the development of watershed plans for each of 36 designated watersheds in the province. Led by a conservation authority, a Source Protection Planning Committee, with a local, multi-stakeholder membership, would coordinate the development of the watershed plan for the watershed. This plan would be based upon a source-protection assessment that would provide information on existing and prospective water supplies, water use and demand, and sources of contamination. This committee would forward the plan to a Source Protection Planning Board, which would be composed of the board of directors of the local conservation authority. Upon review, the plan would have to be approved by the Ministry of the Environment. Once approved, land-use decisions would have to be consistent with the watershed plans. Passage of the legislation setting up the new process is expected by the end of 2005, with full implementation within five years.

2001 REPORT OF THE COMMISSIONER OF ENVIRONMENT AND SUSTAINABLE DEVELOPMENT

The Office of the Commissioner of Environment and Sustainable Development is a unique institution of the Canadian federal government, somewhat comparable to the General Accounting Office in the United States. The office carries out comprehensive reviews of federal programs in accordance with the legislative mandate, policies, and practices of the Office of the Auditor General of Canada. Results are reported to the House of Commons. The 2001 report focused on the Great Lakes and the St. Lawrence River Basin.[45]

One of the key questions asked by the environmental commissioner was: What role does the federal government play in protecting and preserving this key ecosystem, and how is it performing that role?[46] The answer concluded that, although there have been some positive results, the job is far from complete. The report noted:

> . . . our overarching concern is the ambiguity of federal commitments. We often see federal departments doing things without having clearly articulated what they wanted to achieve. Cleaning contaminated sediments, getting areas of concern delisted, promoting realistic water pricing, and protecting public health by ensuring that people know when it may not be safe to drink the water or eat the fish—all are areas where the federal commitment is unclear. Indeed, federal departments often define their role as supporting the priorities of others rather than their own.
>
> The government does not have some of the basic information it needs to develop priorities and action plans. For example, it has no overall picture of the many contaminants in the basin or the contribution of groundwater to the basin. Consequently it is involved in many remedial actions with no way to determine which are the most important and what they will contribute.[47]

The report was critical of budget cuts and reallocations within the federal government. It noted that, while the Minister of the Environment committed in 1994 to spend $150 million for the Great Lakes 2000 program (covering 1995–2000), including $125 million in new funds, only $14.9 million was distributed to departments participating in the program.[48] The environmental commissioner noted that there is lack of clarity of the government's commitments and priorities, and that there is a mixed record with respect to government's achievements in meeting the commitments under the agreement. The mixed record cannot be attributed only to a lack of resources. The report states that the "limited use of federal powers, weaknesses in basic management and accountability, and the politics of federal-provincial relations have all played a part."[49]

The report was particularly critical of the government's relationship with the IJC. It found that the government has not provided the IJC with enough information to assess Canada's progress properly under the Great Lakes Agreement. It also noted that the government "has delayed answering the commission's requests for information and responding to its recommendations."[50] Similarly, it noted that the contribution of the government to the commission's technical and advisory boards has diminished, so that "the loss of scientific and technical capabilities as a result of budget cuts is putting this support at risk."[51]

This report provides one of the few, perhaps the most powerful, third-party reviews of the Canadian federal government's approach to the agreement and to the federal government's relationship to the ijc in decades. One of the most difficult questions was:

> What is the value of making domestic and international commitments when in some cases there is no capacity to deliver? When the federal government signed the glwqa, for example, it assumed an obligation to ensure that action would be taken. The government decided to rely on others, and when others failed to deliver, it did not assume the lead. In our view, the federal government remains accountable for its obligation to ensure that the job gets done. The time has come for it to either take responsibility for its commitments or change them.[52]

Environment Canada Program Renewal

The Great Lakes program of the Ontario region of Environment Canada operates on a five-year cycle for funding and program activities. The Action Plan for the Great Lakes covers federal obligations, joint federal-Ontario activities, and cooperative actions with U.S. federal and state agencies.[53] The plan also covers the role of the eight federal departments who participate in meeting commitments under the Great Lakes Agreement.

According to one official, the previous 2000–2005 Action Plan received only $40 million of the $160 million requested.[54] Of the $40 million granted, $30 million was dedicated to providing technical and financial support to development of Remedial Action Plans for the 17 Canadian areas of concern.[55]

In 2004, as part of planning for renewal of the Great Lakes program, Environment Canada recommended adoption of a watershed-planning approach to advance the binational objectives of the Great Lakes Agreement.[56] The rationale is based on recognition that land use in upstream drainage basins affects the health of the Great Lakes. It is also consistent with Ontario planning initiatives to protect drinking-water sources. The purpose of the watershed plans is to reduce nutrient and pollutant loadings, conserve habitat and biodiversity, prevent introduction of alien species, and restore beneficial uses in areas of concern. This approach is also consistent with a similar trend for local watershed management planning in the United States.

In late February 2005 a new Canadian federal budget was announced for the Great Lakes, again for $40 million over five years. About $6 million per year was for such programs as Remedial Action Plans and $2 million for other miscellaneous purposes such as participation in coordination activities under the Great Lakes Agreement. This allotment was the same as for 2000–2005, without any adjustment for inflation. Some observers speculated that the government had decided to channel its resources to implementing the Kyoto Treaty on climate change rather than the Great Lakes. In any case, a lower priority had been given for restoration of the Great Lakes than had been expected.

Accountability for USEPA Great Lakes Work

In the United States, accountability and reporting requirements have continued to be issues in the Great Lakes regime, not just for the IJC but also for the U.S. Congress and for the public. In 1990 the U.S. Congress tried to increase the accountability of the USEPA for its Great Lakes efforts by requiring two major periodic reports on the state of the Great Lakes. Originally, these reports were to be in addition to the biennial joint reports by the USEPA with Environment Canada to the IJC.

The Great Waters Report is required under section 112(m) of the 1990 Clean Air Act, and concerns atmospheric deposition of toxic contaminants.[57] Although first intended to cover Great Lakes issues, the requirement was expanded to include Lake Champlain, Chesapeake Bay, and certain other sites in the National Estuarine Research Reserve. Three such reports had been issued by 2004, mainly describing results of ongoing research rather than any programs to deal with atmospheric deposition or results of such efforts. In the first Great Waters Report, the agency said explicitly that it had all the authority needed to deal with atmospheric deposition.[58]

An annual Great Lakes Ecosystem Report was required under the 1991 Great Lakes Critical Programs Act, which amended section 118 of the Clean Water Act. The purpose of the law was to give the USEPA a legislative mandate to take the lead for preparation of the Remedial Action Plans and the Lakewide Management Plans that were called for in the 1987 Protocol for the Great Lakes Agreement. In 1995, the requirement for this report was eliminated by a law that sought to reduce unnecessary paperwork for federal agencies.

Knowing that Congress likes to have information on how federal funds are spent, the Great Lakes National Program Office of the USEPA decided to use the required biennial reports for the IJC also as reports to Congress.[59] The most comprehensive version to date, *Great Lakes Ecosystem Report 2000*, was issued in January 2001. It is described as "the sixth Biennial Progress Report to the IJC, Congress and the citizens of the Great Lakes Basin."[60] In 2002, the requirement for such a report to Congress was reinstated in the Great Lakes Legacy Act.

This document integrates reporting on the physical state of the lakes and other resources within the watershed with descriptions of programs and discussion of policy issues. It contains the most complete overview of activities within the United States aimed at achieving "significant environmental improvements through the implementation of a multimedia, ecosystem-based approach in the Great Lakes."[61] It does not relate the information specifically to U.S. obligations under the agreement. It does, however, discuss in detail the policy framework for the agency's Great Lakes program.

The management structure for the Great Lakes requires "cross-program and cross-agency integration" at various scales, from the local level to lakewide issues with "basinwide policy coordination," and beyond the drainage basin to a global scale. The foundation is said to be local planning and implementation through RAPS and special geographic initiatives in Chicago, Northwest Indiana, Southeast Michigan, Northeast Ohio, and the Niagara River frontier. The need for partnerships of all kinds at every level is emphasized— between local, state, and federal government agencies, with industry, and with nongovernmental institutions and organizations.

Many special projects and initiatives are described, including wetlands restoration at the local level, statewide programs to collect and dispose of pesticides, and the commitment of the three largest automakers to reduce and prevent pollution during vehicle manufacturing and assembly. Federal partnerships include joint strategies by the U.S. Department of Agriculture and the USEPA to control animal waste and fertilizer runoff, and Army Corps of Engineers assistance to local governments with dredging and disposal of contaminated sediments.

Overall, this report reflects efforts during this period to broaden government efforts beyond pollution control to include restoration and land-use management. It also links physical issues, such as response to low lake levels and the initiative of the Council of Great Lakes Governors to improve diversion-management policy, to water quality issues such as improved chemistry, to biological issues such as increased introduction of invasive species, and to ongoing efforts at fishery restoration.

Results of monitoring and changes in conditions are reported, such as the stabilization of nutrient levels (except in Lake Erie) and the basin-wide decrease in levels of toxic contaminants. Still, the report does not provide a sense of general ecological improvement in the lakes, or explain in ways that the general public will understand how results of the multitude of programs will combine to restore and maintain ecological integrity of the Great Lakes. The effort to provide this perspective was undertaken in the late 1990s by the SOLEC meetings.

Proceedings of the biennial SOLEC events were the other major new report series initiated following adoption of the 1987 Protocol. Prepared jointly by the USEPA and Environment Canada, the 1996 SOLEC report on land use made the case for greater emphasis on wetlands preservation and habitat restoration in order to preserve biodiversity.[62] Subsequent SOLEC reports have dealt primarily with the complications of developing a set of environmental indicators that would satisfy both the need for scientific accuracy and the need for understanding by the public and policymakers.[63] By 2005 the SOLEC struggle to provide meaningful indicators that could be understood by the public was overshadowed by the excitement generated by the restoration legislation in Congress and by a Bush administration effort to control restoration initiatives from Washington.

THE GREAT LAKES LEGACY ACT AND THE U.S. POLICY COMMITTEE

Two events roused the Great Lakes community in the United States in 2002. One was passage of the Great Lakes Legacy Act, the first significant legislation for the Great Lakes in a decade. The bill had 21 co-sponsors in the House of Representatives, and five more in the Senate. The other was announcement of a new U.S. Policy Committee and a federal strategic plan.

The stage was set for passage of the Legacy Act by a GAO report chastising the USEPA for failing to provide the leadership, oversight, and resources needed for completion of the Remedial Action Plans called for in the 1987 Protocol and the 1991 Great Lakes Critical Programs Act.[64] The central issue was disagreement between the USEPA and the states over responsibility for completion of the RAPS.

The report said that each state had approached the RAP process differently after the USEPA reduced its funding, but that generally the resources for completion of the RAPS had declined over the previous 10 years. Meanwhile, the report noted that the federal agency had shifted its focus to other activities— some required under the Great Lakes Agreement, such as reduction of toxic substances, and others initiated outside the agreement process, such as development of the SOLEC indicators and habitat restoration.

The USEPA said it had reduced its support for RAPS on the assumption that the states would continue to fund RAP completions. The states then reduced their support because they considered the RAPS to be a federal responsibility as a requirement of the Great Lakes Agreement. Meanwhile, no RAPS had been completed for any of the 26 areas of concern in the United States.[65]

Introduced in May, the same month the GAO report was published, the Legacy Act passed in November with intensive lobbying by the nongovernmental organizations and the Great Lakes Commission. It authorized $50 million per year for five years from 2004 through 2008, principally for cleanup of contaminated sediments, the most costly needed action in many areas of concern. Only $15 million was provided in the fiscal 2004 budget by the Bush administration, which was then reduced to $10 million in a Congressional conference committee, but the USEPA administrator announced that $45 million would be requested for 2005.[66]

The second major action in 2002 was the USEPA's announcement in November of a new *Great Lakes Strategy 2002: A Plan for the New Millennium*, developed by the U.S. Policy Committee. Earlier, the GLNPO had operated under its own internal five-year strategic plans. Then, in 1988, it had established a U.S. Policy Committee that was disbanded in 1995 after other agencies complained that they had not been consulted in the development of a strategic plan for the period 1992–1997. A new, similar U.S. Policy Committee formed in 1999 that was involved in development of the new strategy announced in 2002.

The stated aim of this plan was to guide the efforts of nine federal agencies, the eight Great Lakes states, the binational Great Lakes Fishery Commission, and tribal governments to achieve "measurable outcomes for environmental improvement for the Great Lakes Basin Ecosystems." The Policy Committee was described as providing a forum for key representatives of all the member agencies.

A draft version of the strategy was presented in four workshops, open to the public, in 2001. The workshops took place in June and July in Duluth, Minnesota; Detroit, Michigan; Niagara Falls, New York; and Chicago, Illinois. At the end of July, a consortium of 17 nongovernmental environmental organizations submitted collective comments on the draft.

The strategy document began by citing the Great Lakes Agreement as "a world-wide model for inter-jurisdictional cooperative environmental protection and natural resource management."[67] The introduction states that the purpose relates "to fulfilling the goals of the GLWQA." The overarching vision was cited as seeking to assure that:

- The Great Lakes Basin is a healthy natural environment for wildlife and people.
- All Great Lakes beaches are open for swimming.
- All Great Lakes fish are safe to eat.
- The Great Lakes are protected as a safe source for drinking water.

The four priority goals listed to achieve the vision related more directly to the goals of the agreement.

- Chemical Integrity, with virtual elimination of toxic contaminants "over time."
- Physical Integrity, supporting habitats for healthy and diverse species, and protecting the lakes from unsustainable diversion.
- Biological Integrity, protecting human and biological health, restoration of predominantly native species, prevention of introduction and spread of invasive species.
- Working Together, in an environmental community for effective programs, coordination of authorities, reporting of progress, information exchange, and collective decision-making.[68]

The body of the strategy described the environmental threats that must be dealt with for each goal, set key objectives, and listed key actions to be taken, chiefly by the USEPA alone or in cooperation with others. In general, the actions relate to existing programs rather than new initiatives. The emphasis on efforts already underway, rather than new initiatives, was underscored by two sentences: "The Strategy should not be construed as a commitment by the U.S. government for additional funding and resources for its implementation. Nor does it represent a commitment for the U.S. government to adopt new regulations."[69]

When asked how the ambitious goals could be achieved with such limitations, a USEPA official said that the restrictive language had been required by the U.S. Office of Management and Budget as a condition for approval by the Office of the President.[70] A 2003 GAO report also noted that this strategy did not include any estimates of funding needed to achieve its objectives or clarify the relative responsibilities of the states and the federal government.

The nongovernmental comments urged numerous changes and additions to the draft policy, most seeking greater specificity or clarification for an objective, a shorter timeline for achieving a target change, or a more aggressive goal. The goal of restoration of 100,000 acres of coastal wetlands in 10 years, for example, was said to be "woefully low."[71] There should be a better rationale for that definitive number, including determination of the total number and quality of existing wetlands. Similarly, 2007 was said to be too long to wait for Great Lakes Water Quality Initiative standards to be applied in National Pollution Discharge Elimination System permits required by the Clean Water Act, and priorities should be set for cleanup of contaminated-sediments sites in every state.

Finally, the environmental groups complained that the strategy "did not include actions by states, federal agencies other than USEPA, tribal governments nor . . . highlight areas of cooperation between these levels of government."[72] The USEPA was encouraged to gather more definite commitments from the various partners.

The 2003 GAO Report

In May 2003, the GAO released another report criticizing the USEPA and setting the stage for introduction of additional legislation.[73] This report's central theme was lack of coordination within the federal government and between the federal government and the states and local governments, and the need for "an overarching strategy" for restoration of the Great Lakes.

Almost two billion federal dollars had been spent since 1992, but, unlike restoration efforts in the Florida Everglades and Chesapeake Bay, the GAO report said that the Great Lakes cleanup was piecemeal and without an overall strategy. Furthermore, the GAO concluded, it is impossible to assess progress in restoring the Great Lakes because of the lack of measurable results.

The report referred to U.S. commitments under the Great Lakes Agreement, but did not analyze whether or how the agreement itself provides the "overarching strategy" that is needed. Instead, the GAO cited the history of the reluctance of the USEPA to accept responsibility for fulfillment of U.S. obligations under the Great Lakes Agreement, as chronicled in the ongoing series of Great Lakes reports. The report referred to how initially, the responsibility for meeting agreement obligations was assigned to the Region 5 office in Chicago, which met resistance in the Washington headquarters over the need for phosphate-detergent bans and removal of phosphorus in sewage-treatment systems.

The report said that refusal to accept the goals of the agreement continued after establishment of the Great Lakes National Program Office in the mid 1970s. In 1982 the GAO recommended that the GLNPO be allowed to coordinate actions within the agency, with other federal agencies, and with the states.[74] For the next several years, the Region 5 office still had to provide staff for the GLNPO because of inadequate budget requests by USEPA headquarters. Each year, Congress restored the funding until amendment of the Clean Water Act in 1987.

Section 118 was added, the GAO report said, to require the USEPA, through the GLNPO, to lead and coordinate efforts of USEPA headquarters with the other regional offices, as well as with other federal agencies and state and local authorities, to meet the goals of the agreement. The agency was also directed to include a separate line item for the GLNPO in its annual budget request to Congress. The 1990 Critical Programs Act "further defined GLNPO's role . . . and assigned additional responsibilities" for RAPs and the Lake Michigan LaMP as well as Great Lakes water quality standards and contaminated sediments."[75]

This report also described the GLNPO's unique status within the USEPA, and how its function differs from the other national programs for specific environmental mediums, such as the air or water divisions. The GLNPO has a small staff of only about 40 positions in its office in Chicago, where the politically appointed administrator of Region 5 is the Great Lakes National Program manager. Congress appropriates funding for the GLNPO to make grants to state agencies, research institutions, and nongovernmental organizations that enable it to address a wide range of environmental issues within the Great Lakes watershed. The partnerships with the states are essential for carrying out U.S. responsibilities under the Great Lakes Agreement. Its working relationships with the federal and provincial governments of Canada and the IJC are another unique feature of this USEPA program.

Still, the GAO found that the GLNPO had not exercised its statutory authority and unique responsibility for coordinating Great Lakes restoration programs, citing a 1999 report by the USEPA's Office of Inspector General. That report said that the GLNPO had not complied with the Clean Water Act's direction for developing agreements with other program offices within the USEPA, or with other federal agencies and the states.[76]

The 2003 GAO report acknowledged that size, complexity of issues, and numerous political jurisdictions make development of an overarching strategy for the Great Lakes more difficult than for the Florida Everglades and Chesapeake Bay watersheds. For example, the Great Lakes basin covers 201,000 square miles, compared to 64,000 for Chesapeake Bay and 18,000 for the Everglades.

Two countries, eight states, two provinces, and half a dozen of the largest cities in North America have governance responsibilities within the Great Lakes watershed. Many programs already exist for cleanup and restoration within the basin, but most have different purposes, approaches, and scopes. The GAO found that other federal and state officials, Great Lakes institutions such as the Great Lakes Commission, and nongovernmental environmental groups all share disappointment in what they consider the lack of leadership by the USEPA for the Great Lakes.

Lack of adequate funding is the other major complaint, with 24 of 33 federal programs and 3 of 17 state programs reporting insufficient funding for specific Great Lakes activities. Michigan reported that in 2001, for example, it received requests for $10.4 million and was able to provide only $700,000 from its own Great Lakes Protection Fund.

The report's recommendations set the stage for follow-up by Congress and the explosion of effort on behalf of new "restoration" legislation in 2003, 2004, and 2005. The recommendations urged the administrator of the USEPA to:

- Ensure that the GLNPO fulfill its coordinating responsibility within the Great Lakes basin;
- Charge the GLNPO with developing an overarching strategy; and
- Submit a time-phased funding requirement proposal to Congress necessary to implement the strategy.[77]

The GAO report is, in an approximate way, consistent with the Canadian environmental commissioner's report issued in 2001 and discussed above.

U.S. POLITICS AND RESTORATION OF THE GREAT LAKES, 2003–2004

Presidential and regional politics, not the Great Lakes Agreement, were behind the question by Senator George Voinovich of Ohio in a July 2003 Congressional hearing in Washington, D.C. "Is there an orchestra leader that knows what all of you are doing and coordinating? Is there?" he asked the panel of speakers on proposed legislation that was causing almost as much excitement in the Great Lakes region as when the Cuyahoga River seemed to catch fire near Lake Erie back in the 1960s.[78]

The speakers on the panel had all been describing what their agencies or organizations were doing for restoration of the Great Lakes ecosystem. They were also telling why they wanted Congress to approve billions of dollars of new funding called for in separate bills introduced in the U.S House of Representatives and the U.S. Senate. Through the summer, the agreement seemed irrelevant in the excitement across the Great Lakes community about the possibility of the $6 billion called for in the Senate bill, or even the $4 billion requested in the House version.

The 2003 eruption of Congressional concern for the Great Lakes had two sources. First was Congressional approval in 2000 of $14.8 billion of federal funding for restoration of the natural hydrology of the Florida Everglades by the U.S. Army Corps of Engineers. Immediately, the Great Lakes Commission, environmental leaders, and members of the Great Lakes Task Force in Congress had all seen the Florida commitment as a potential precedent that could be exploited for the Great Lakes.[79]

The link with presidential politics came with the victories of new Democratic governors in Michigan, Illinois, Pennsylvania, and Wisconsin in the mid-term elections in November 2002. Where Indiana had had the only Democratic governor in the previous decade, now the Democrats had five of the eight Great Lakes governorships. The new Democratic strength was seen as evidence of the importance of the key Midwest region in the 2004 presidential election. Perhaps, both Republican and Democratic members of the Great Lakes delegation thought, the situation could be exploited to obtain major new federal funding for the Great Lakes. The news media linked the hearing to the 2003 GAO report.[80]

Then Senator Voinovich asked Thomas Skinner, the USEPA's manager of the GLNPO and administrator of the Region 5 office in Chicago, why the agency was not the orchestra leader for federal Great Lakes programs. "We do not have the authority," Skinner said, and the Senator replied, "We (Congress) thought that was what we gave you in Section 118 of the Clean Water Act." The exchange demonstrated the insistence of the USEPA headquarters throughout the life of the agreement that its binational goals were secondary to the agency's goals under domestic law. The answer reflected the USEPA position that the agreement does not have the treaty authority, and that the lead agency can request cooperation but cannot direct other federal agencies to comply with its requirements.

The GAO report to Congress stressed lack of coordination among 33 federal programs and 17 state programs specific to the Great Lakes as the cause of failure to prevent invasion of exotic species, slowness in removing contaminated sediments, and increases in beach closings that headed the list of current Great Lakes problems. Results cannot be determined because of inadequate monitoring and lack of indicators of environmental change. Most programs report "outputs," or actions taken, rather than results achieved by actions.

The main problem, the report concluded, is need for "a coherent approach to attain overall ecosystem restoration." The GAO did not consider whether the Great Lakes Agreement itself provides a unified vision and strategic framework, or how U.S. efforts could be linked to Canadian efforts, and this was not discussed in the Senate hearing. Neither the GAO report, Congress, nor the Great Lakes community in its response to both considered the need for an effective binational approach that was the reason for the Great Lakes Agreement and the evolution of a powerful Great Lakes community around the processes of its implementation.

THE U.S. RESTORATION LEGISLATION

The legislation introduced in the U.S. Congress laid out a new approach to Great Lakes protection, and the interest it inspired was almost immediately labeled "a restoration movement" and also ignored the existence of the Great Lakes Agreement. Both bills proposed similar new arrangements that would put the states in charge of distributing, and presumably using themselves, billions of U.S. dollars outside the binational partnership with Canada. Neither bill considered the states' historic insistence that the obligations of the Great Lakes Agreement are a federal responsibility, not theirs, and whether even more funding would be needed for federal programs under the proposed new arrangement.

The House of Representatives bill was originated by another winner in the 2002 election, first-term Congressman Rahm Emanuel, a Democrat from Chicago who had worked on the White House staff of the Clinton administration. Emanuel saw responding to what he believed was the Bush administration intention to use apparent commitment to the Great Lakes to firm up President Bush's Midwest political base as an opportunity to fulfill his own campaign promises on the environment.

Soon after taking office, he told Illinois environmentalists that he intended to introduce a bill that would do for the Great Lakes what Congress had already done for the Florida Everglades—commit a lot of federal money. Making clear that he had little knowledge of Great Lakes issues himself, he stressed his personal interest in the politics of getting a Great Lakes bill approved in Congress.[81]

By July 2003, Emanuel had introduced HR 2720 with Illinois Republican Mark Kirk and 14 other co-sponsors. Almost simultaneously, SR 1398 was introduced in the Senate with Senator Carl Levin, a Democrat from Michigan and long-time champion of the Great Lakes, and Senator Michael DeWine, a Republican from Ohio, as chief sponsors. Both bills soon gained many additional sponsors, in large part because of lobbying by members of the "Blue Group," as the informal consortium of leaders of the major Great Lakes environmental organizations call themselves.

The House "Great Lakes Restoration Financing Act of 2003" called for a new "comprehensive Great Lakes management plan," to be developed in two years by a new Great Lakes Advisory Board with the state governors as the voting members, to distribute grants. The Senate bill proposed a "Federal Coordinating Council" led by the GLNPO, in addition to a "Great Lakes Environmental Restoration Advisory Board" with the eight governors, eight chief executives of local governments, and five federal officials as members.

Both bills called for Canadian representatives as nonvoting observers, along with representatives of other Great Lakes interests such as environmental organizations and industry. They cited entities created by the Great Lakes Agreement process such as areas of concern, RAPS, and LaMPS, but seemed to disregard the difficulty without binational coordination that fish and water would have in honoring the boundary between restoration in U.S. territory and the Canadian half of the system.

Overall, neither bill seemed to recognize why the Boundary Waters Treaty and later the Great Lakes Water Quality Agreement had been created. The binational partnership and the constitutional responsibilities of both federal governments for international affairs did not seem to matter in what some called "Everglades fever."

Surprised and worried Canadian officials who sought a meeting with Senator Voinovich in Washington after the July hearing were told that the partnership would be recognized, but the senator did not say how. One high-ranking Canadian official went to Chicago to ask USEPA colleagues in the Binational Executive Committee, "What should we do?"

The answer was that the future would depend on Congressional action on the proposed legislation, but that existing joint activities would continue meanwhile. They returned home to consider, however, how Canada would respond should the proposed legislation put the states rather than the federal government in charge of Great Lakes cleanup in the United States.[82]

In spite of the excitement and lobbying stirred up by the legislative proposals, by April 2004 there was wide agreement that the bills would not be passed in the current Congressional session due to end before the November presidential election. There was simply too much distraction by controversial domestic issues such as health care, the war in Iraq and threats of terrorism, and the economy's struggle to overcome a deep recession. Following the election the prospect of new funding continued to excite both federal and state research and management agencies in state and local governments and the nongovernmental advocacy groups. The Bush administration continued to respond.

A New Regional Collaboration

During the 2004 presidential campaign President George W. Bush made frequent visits to the Great Lakes states where public opinion polls showed almost evenly divided voter support for the Democratic candidate John Kerry and the Republican Bush (Ohio, Wisconsin, and Michigan). In May the president issued Executive Order 13340 calling for creation of yet another strategic plan to save the Great Lakes by a task force to be led by USEPA administrator Michael Leavitt. This one aimed "to bring an unprecedented level of collaboration and coordination . . . among federal agencies, states, local communities, tribes, and other interests in the Great Lakes region.

Canada was also mentioned but was not invited to participate in planning for a ceremonial event to follow the November election. In contrast to the history of primary initiative for the Great Lakes from within the region, this initiative was controlled from the national capital.

Through the summer of 2004 Leavitt and White House staff met with GLNPO and city officials to plan an event to be held on 3 December in Chicago with "cabinet-level" officials representing nine federal agencies. That morning five governors and representatives of the other three, plus several cabinet officials (although no secretaries), four members of Congress, Mayor Richard M. Daley of Chicago, and other state and local officials followed a bagpipe and drum corps for a ceremonial signing. The "Great Lakes Declaration" called for "Protecting and Restoring the Great Lakes through a Regional Collaboration of National Significance."

In the afternoon, nongovernmental observers and lesser officials met in small work groups to receive direction for preparation of reports on eight "priority issue areas" that had been identified earlier for the Council of Great Lakes Governors as chapters of a new document. The format for each chapter was prescribed in a page-and-a-half outline with the finished product to be no longer than four or five pages.

The volunteer Regional Collaboration teams were to communicate principally through the Internet and conference telephone calls but meet "face-to-face" in July 2005 with release of the completed document by the end of the year. Skeptics about the potential benefits of the plan pointed out that again no commitment was made for funding to implement this plan either.

The Healing Our Waters Project

The Great Lakes environmental advocacy organizations that call themselves the Blue Group developed a strategy of their own to use in the Regional Collaboration in lobbying for passage of the restoration legislation, and in the 109th Congress if at all possible. The effort would be supported by a $5 million grant from the Wege Foundation following a meeting that had been convened in May 2004.

The convener was Mark van Putten, the first director of the National Wildlife Federation Great Lakes Resources Center in Ann Arbor, later president of the national organization and then part-time staff advisor to Peter Wege, vice president and son of the founder of the Steelcase office furniture manufacturing company of Grand Rapids, Michigan. The purpose was to organize a new coalition, under the leadership of the National Parks and Conservation Association out of Washington, D.C., and the National Wildlife Federation through its regional office in Ann Arbor, Michigan.

In contrast to earlier efforts that promoted Great Lakes advocacy within the watershed, the new aim was to build a national constituency for the Great Lakes as "a national treasure" that would support the efforts for more funding in Congress. By early 2005 a funding goal of up to $20 billion was being discussed.

The State of the Great Lakes Community

The sense of community that had seemed to decline in the mid 1990s began to be renewed in this period in new ways that did not relate to the agreement processes and the IJC, as it had earlier. At the same time, divisions within the community began to threaten its coherence. The divisions were between the governments and the IJC, between the environmental community and the Great Lakes Commission, and within the IJC itself.

These divisions increase the urgency of addressing all aspects of the binational process established by the agreement in the review of the water quality agreement scheduled to begin in 2005.

Annex 2001 to the Great Lakes Charter

The threat of diversion had been a unifying issue in the mid 1980s that led to the 1985 Great Lakes Charter among the states. Amendment of the charter became a unifying force in the new century.

The proposed amendment was put forth by the Council of Great Lakes Governors in 2001, with the aim of achieving a new binding agreement by the end of 2004.[83] The purpose of the amendment was to strengthen the ability of the states to defend future decisions against new diversions from legal challenge. Ontario and Quebec were invited to participate in the expectation that they would also join in opposing future diversions.

The process began with a round of public hearings in every state. As it proceeded, each state undertook to document water withdrawals and usage, and to develop policies that would be consistent with the regional policy established by the charter. With the Great Lakes Commission, representatives of nongovernmental environmental organizations from both sides of the border were deeply involved in working out details of how the new policy would be applied. Although the annex has not been finalized at the time of this writing, all sides agree on the constructive value of the process by which it has been addressed.

The most immediate pressures for new diversion came from growing suburbs just outside the watershed but still within metropolitan areas of major cities, such as Waukesha, Wisconsin, near Milwaukee. The proposed new policy would require treatment and return of water withdrawn above a minimum amount as well as proof of "ecological improvement." Approval would be required from only six of the eight governors, instead of the unanimous assent required under the existing system.

Controversy in both countries delayed completion of a binding agreement by the original deadline. More than 10,000 comments were received during the public review, most urging stricter prohibition against diversion. The debate stimulated new attention to the connections between groundwater and the lakes and the need for water conservation to meet anticipated future needs. The attention to restoration of ecological integrity seemed consistent with the call for an ecosystem approach to management in the 1978 Great Lakes Agreement.

RALLYING AROUND THE PROPOSED RESTORATION LEGISLATION

On the U.S. side, the proposed legislation provoked a sense of immediacy and opportunity that energized the Great Lakes community from its introduction in 2003. All eight governors signed a letter supporting the legislation.[84] Mayors and other local officials joined in lobbying for the legislation through the new Great Lakes Cities Initiative, organized by Mayor Richard M. Daley of Chicago.[85] The new institution was established in 2003 as a not-for-profit project of the Northeast-Midwest Institute, with funding from the Joyce Foundation. David Ullrich, former deputy regional administrator for Region 5, USEPA, was hired as the executive director.

In the early years of the Great Lakes Agreement, there had been almost no direct participation by local governments in seeking implementation of the objectives of the agreement. Making use of federal grants to improve sewage-treatment systems was related to the Clean Water Act in the United States.

Chicago became the first jurisdiction to adopt a phosphate-detergent ban in order to reduce costs of phosphorus removal; the ban had virtually no effect for Lake Michigan because of the reversal of the flow of the Chicago River but led the way for eventual adoption of phosphate bans throughout the basin.

Getting local governments involved had been one of the goals when RAPS were initiated, but Chicago was not an area of concern. Chicago's role in achieving the goals of the agreement was complicated by the fact that most of its waste effluents were discharged into the Mississippi watershed through reversal of the flow of the Chicago River and the connecting canal system.

Despite Chicago's location on Lake Michigan, only a part of the city is actually within the Lake Michigan watershed because the Mississippi drainage basin begins at places only a mile or so from the lake. In the 1990s, Mayor Daley's concern for Great Lakes cleanup was stimulated by unexpected frequency in violations of the *E. coli* standard and need to ban swimming at the city's beaches. His frustration grew as the city tried but failed to find a solution for the problem.

When Mayor Daley learned that the Association of Mayors of the Great Lakes and the St. Lawrence included only smaller cities, Chicago joined. Then when he discovered that this organization had not been politically active in Great Lakes affairs, in 2003 he established the new organization, Great Lakes Cities Initiative. The growing membership includes numerous other local governments, as well as cities. The membership of local governments had grown to fifty-five in both countries by 2005.

The aim of the organization, as described by Mayor Daley and Ullrich, was "to get local governments to the table for Great Lakes decisions." Within a few months, the new organization had launched a "best practices initiative" for cities and was working with the Blue Group in lobbying for the restoration legislation.

The Blue Group includes the leadership of environmental groups such as the National Wildlife Federation, the Midwest Office of the Sierra Club, Great Lakes United, and the Lake Michigan Federation that had long been active on Great Lakes issues. It also includes two Canadian groups, the Canadian Environmental Law Association and the Canadian Institute for Environmental Law and Policy.[86] Leaders of environmental organizations that had not previously been involved joined the new activity of the Blue Group for the proposed legislation. Newcomers included the student-led Public Interest Research Groups (PIRGS) at several of the public universities in the region and the long-time leader in preservation of natural areas, The Nature Conservancy (TNC).

In the 1990s, TNC had established its own regional Great Lakes program after publishing a report on the importance of preserving and restoring biodiversity.[87] TNC began offering technical and scientific assistance to other groups in restoration projects after identifying significant natural areas throughout the Great Lakes watershed. Now, for the first time, it became involved in political efforts to protect Great Lakes resources.

When GLU's Green Book, summarizing "A Citizen's Action Agenda for Restoring the Great Lakes–St. Lawrence River Ecosystem,"[88] was released, then executive director Margaret Wooster had declared that "something stronger is needed" than the partial successes of the previous 30 years under the agreement. Now she took the lead in working with other Blue Group members to organize detailed comments on the legislation on behalf of the environmental community.

In 2003 the Biodiversity Project announced a new effort to increase public understanding of threats to the Great Lakes that would lead to a larger role of the public in implementing solutions. In developing a new campaign called "Great Lakes Forever," the Biodiversity Project found that many organizations and institutions have existing public-education materials and programs that reach a limited audience. The new campaign will use public-education and marketing techniques that have proved successful for other purposes in an effort to reach members of the public who do not belong to environmental organizations and who have limited understanding of ecological science and the complexities of Great Lakes problems.

Advance research revealed that most persons who do not perceive problems for the lakes still have a strong sense of pride and of personal responsibility for protecting them. A pilot project in Wisconsin was carried out in cooperation with the state park system to inform the public at large about water quality and water-supply issues, and government actions to address them. The intention is then to use results in Wisconsin to carry out similar educational campaigns throughout the Great Lakes region. In preparation for launching the Great Lakes Forever Campaign basin-wide, in February 2005 the Biodiversity conducted workshops in Chicago, Illinois, and East Lansing, Michigan, for communications and education staff of environmental organizations, institutions such as the John Shedd Aquarium, and agencies such as the university-based Sea Grant extension service and the U.S. National Park Service.

THE GREAT LAKES COMMISSION

The Great Lakes Commission was another lead advocate for the legislation. This quasi-governmental agency had been established by a congressionally authorized interstate compact in the mid 1950s to represent the interests of Great Lakes states in navigation and shipping, which were expected to grow with completion of the St. Lawrence Seaway. The GLC continued to concentrate its attention on navigation until 1981, when the Great Lakes Basin Commission was dismantled by the Reagan administration.

The authorizing legislation for the Basin Commission provided that the state members could decide on disposition of remaining resources of the agency should it be disbanded. The Great Lakes Commission received the remaining funding and other resources of the Basin Commission, despite opposition by several states. The lack of support for the commission's narrow mission by Wisconsin, Michigan, Minnesota, and New York was a factor in the subsequent formation of the Council of Great Lakes Governors.[89]

Navigation interests remained a primary concern, even as the shipping industry declined during the 1980s and 1990s. Beginning in the late 1980s, after Michael Donahue was named executive director, the Great Lakes Commission expanded its agenda to include environmental issues. Under Donahue's leadership throughout the 1990s, the agency successfully obtained more and more funding from the USEPA, philanthropic foundations, the Army Corps of Engineers, and other sources for a wide variety of projects.

In 2003 one USEPA official asked why there was so much distrust between the Great Lakes environmental organizations and the commission. The official was informed that the distrust related to the close ties of the commission to the shipping industry, which refused to control introduction of invasive species in ballast water, and its support for the Army Corps of Engineers' expansion of the St. Lawrence Seaway, which would likely lead to even more biological pollution. Aggressiveness in competing for scarce funding for Great Lakes projects was also noted. The official expressed regret about the distrust, but said that the Great Lakes National Program Office relied on the Great Lakes Commission because "no one else has comparable capacity."[90]

Not surprisingly, the Great Lakes Commission was ready with its own Great Lakes restoration plan when the new legislation was introduced.[91] With the motto "Restore the Greatness!" the commission had formulated a "Great Lakes Program to Ensure Environmental and Economic Prosperity" with seven "restoration" priorities. In 2004 the Great Lakes Commission sponsored several workshops in cooperation with the Great Lakes Council of Governors to solicit public comment on restoration priorities. In spite of the mistrust, the environmental organizations were cooperating with the Great Lakes Commission to lobby for the legislation in 2004, but became wary of a GLC proposal to give leadership to the Army Corps of Engineers for developing a new restoration plan. Donahue's resignation as president and CEO of the agency was announced in February 2005.

By summer, there was agreement that the legislation would not be approved by Congress in the session that would complete authorization for the fiscal 2005 federal budget before recessing for the fall campaign season.

An article in the *Northeast-Midwest Economic Review* had cautioned that "Instead of simply chasing the money, the Great Lakes region should carefully evaluate what it wants for the watershed in 20, 50, or 100 years."[92] Following the re-election of President Bush for a second term, the states, the local governments, and the Blue Group seemed determined to seek again major new appropriations in the U.S. Congress for Great Lakes restoration. The question was whether the fragmented community distracted by the Regional Collaboration, disagreements over the Annex 2001 proposal, and confusion over leadership could overcome the lack of commitment by the Bush administration to this goal.

GREAT LAKES COMMUNITY "ON HOLD" IN CANADA

While the U.S. community focused on the U.S. restoration legislation in Congress, there was no similar initiative to catalyze the environmental movement or spark new momentum in Canada. Still, the Great Lakes were not totally off the public-policy or activism table. Pollution Probe organized a major conference examining a variety of issues in 2002.[93] Although environmental groups were very active, the Great Lakes were not the organizing theme for any groups in Canada except Great Lakes United.

Several factors explain the lack of focus on the Great Lakes by the Canadian environmental community during the latter part of the 1990s and the early part of the new century. The downsizing and deregulatory trends in the previous years diverted attention from the Great Lakes to a fight to retain core services at environmental agencies. A number of groups changed their programmatic priorities. Greenpeace, which had played such a key role in the late 1980s and early 1990s, gradually pulled away from both a Great Lakes focus and the toxic-contaminants issue. The Walkerton tragedy had raised public concerns for the environment in general, and perhaps news-media reports suggesting the death of Lake Erie would remind the Canadian public of the vulnerability of the Great Lakes and revitalize interest in their protection. Another possible explanation is that the IJC was neither encouraging public involvement nor providing a forum for organizing and networking, as was the case a decade before. Despite this lack of focus on the Great Lakes, considerable ongoing work was being undertaken for RAPS and LAMPS, local environmental-restoration efforts, and other directly or indirectly related issues.

THE INTERNATIONAL JOINT COMMISSION

During this period, the challenges for the International Joint Commission grew from inside the agency and in its relationship with the governments. The U.S. membership had changed again following the 2000 election and coincided with the appointment of new members from Canada. Herb Gray, a long standing member of Parliament from the Windsor area and former cabinet minister, was appointed to the Canadian chair by the Liberal government. With the new panel, the trend that began in the early 1990s for abandonment of the traditional operation by consensus, and for individual commissioners to assert their personal views was exacerbated by the strong opinions and personal style of the new U.S. chair, Dennis Schornack. In 2003 and 2004, it was said that virtually no IJC decisions were reached by consensus, and that virtually all votes were five to one against the U.S. chair. It was also said that Schornack was not deterred by opposition from imposing his personal decision in many instances.[94]

By 2004 observers inside and outside the commission said that relations between the Ottawa and Washington offices of the IJC had never been so hostile, and ascribed the situation to Schornack's insistence on unilateral, individual decisions. One major problem was his refusal to authorize full payment to meet the U.S. share of the cost of operation of the Great Lakes Regional Office in Windsor for two consecutive years. This meant that the office had only the Canadian share to cover salaries and other operational costs. By his order, staff vacancies due to retirement could not be filled, and there was uncertainty about ability to cover day-to-day operating costs.

Another contentious issue was Schornak's insistence that the IJC should be given a major role in the upcoming review of the agreement, though he had abandoned an earlier proposal that the review should be conducted by the IJC on behalf of the parties. In establishing a Scoping Committee for the review, the BEC had proposed that the IJC oversee public consultation in connection with the review, but Schornack continued to demand a larger role.

The Separate Government Operations

The 1987 Protocol marked the beginning of decreased government involvement in IJC processes and corresponding development of new and sometimes parallel institutions.

Not until the mid 1990s did Great Lakes environmental leaders recognize how the relationship between the governments and the IJC had changed as a consequence of the language inserted by USEPA and Environment Canada officials in Article x of the 1987 Protocol. As is now admitted by officials who were involved in the review process that led to the change, the purpose of the new provision was to diminish IJC oversight and allow the lead agencies to fulfill their implementation obligations by working directly together, rather than through the binational institutions provided in the original agreement.[95]

The environmentalists had seen inclusion of requirements for Remedial Action Plans and Lakewide Management Plans as the way to increase public participation and involvement of local governments in working for the agreement's goals. The lively IJC biennial meetings and the IJC chlorine ban in the early 1990s were seen as victories at the time by the environmental organizations, even after the events stimulated an enormous industry presence in Great Lakes affairs and backlash against the concept of virtual elimination.

Awareness grew in the late 1990s of the consequences of the smaller presence of government agencies in IJC activities, and the ongoing consequences of politicization of the appointment process for IJC commissioners. By 2005 the gap between the governments and the IJC had widened so much that it was clear that institutional arrangements should be included in the next review of the agreement.

Binational Executive Committee

The Binational Executive Committee (BEC) was formed in the early 1990s to provide coordination for the work of the government agencies under the agreement. The membership includes key federal agencies from both countries, with USEPA and Environment Canada officials as co-chairs. Affiliate members include state and provincial agencies, and First Nations and tribal governments. Nongovernmental observers have been allowed since 1995.

During the late 1990s, the BEC seemed to be preoccupied with the actual BEC roles and responsibilities. In a 1998 meeting, there was discussion of updating a 1995 document that had articulated the primary functions. The new version said that the BEC would meet twice a year in order to:

- Set priorities and strategic direction for binational programs;
- Coordinate binational programs and activities;
- Respond to new and emerging issues in existing or new work groups;
- Evaluate progress under the agreement; and
- Provide advice or comment on preparation of binational reports and presentations.[96]

The document also identified BEC priorities to be:

- The Binational Toxics Strategy;
- The Integrated Atmospheric Deposition Network;
- Lakewide Management Plans for Lakes Superior, Ontario, and Erie;
- Lake Superior Binational Program;
- Niagara River Toxics Management Plan;
- Remedial Action Plans for the Connecting Channels; and
- The State of the Lakes Ecosystem Conference.

The basic organization of the BEC includes secretariat service shared by the USEPA and Environment Canada, Lake Committees (whose key responsibility includes the development of LAMPs), and work groups. The three established work groups deal with SOLEC, implementation of the Integrated Atmospheric Deposition Network, and implementation of the Binational Toxics Strategy.

By mid 1999, an issue paper was discussed, entitled *Reinvigorating the Binational Executive Committee*, that said that the effectiveness of the BEC needed to be improved. It noted that BEC activities should add value to binational actions for the Great Lakes.[97] The key recommendation, which was adopted, said that fewer topics should be covered in the meetings with more in-depth discussion. It was agreed that a work plan should identify a major topic for each meeting, such as a LAMP. Even with the new plan, the BEC meetings appear to function mainly for information sharing—between the agencies within each side, and between the two sides—about the status of ongoing activities, with little in-depth discussion of existing or needed policies or programs.

BINATIONAL TOXICS STRATEGY

Repeatedly in the 1980s and the 1990s, the IJC biennial reports to the governments recommended better coordination between the parties. A 1990 report specifically recommended that the parties develop and implement "a binational toxics management strategy to provide a coordinated framework for accomplishing, as soon and as fully as possible, the Agreement philosophy of zero discharge."[98]

By the mid 1990s, the rationale for this recommendation seemed to be reflected in several disconnected and uncoordinated programs. The United States had a Virtual Elimination Pilot Project for Lake Superior and the USEPA Water Quality Guidance for the Great Lakes System, which had resulted from the Great Lakes Water Quality Initiative. Canada had the 1994 Canada-Ontario Agreement and the 1995 Toxic Substances Management Agreement.

In February 1995, Prime Minister Chrétien and President Clinton committed to the development of a new Great Lakes toxics-control strategy by the two countries. In April 1997, the Great Lakes Binational Toxics Strategy was developed to achieve the virtual-elimination goal of the Great Lakes Agreement, concluding: "the Strategy seeks to reduce and virtually eliminate the input of persistent toxic substances to the Great Lakes. Virtual elimination will be sought within the most expedient time frame through the most appropriate, common sense, practical and cost-effective blend of voluntary, regulatory or incentive-based actions. All feasible options will be considered, including pollution prevention, phase-outs and bans."[99]

To further this goal, the parties proposed a four-step process:

- *An information-gathering step* to identify both point and nonpoint sources and examine which sectors may be contributing to the presence of the substances in the basin;
- *An analysis of the current laws, initiatives, and programs* to identify gaps and opportunities to further effective and appropriate reductions of the substances;
- *Identification of cost-effective options* to achieve further reductions, including emission trading schemes, pollution prevention, or other alternative approaches; and
- *Recommendation and implementation* of actions that work toward the goal of virtual elimination using cost-effective measures.

The strategy focuses on what are called "Level 1" substances for primary efforts.[100] There is no specific program for "Level 2" substances until they are placed on the Level 1 list. Instead, stakeholders are encouraged to adopt pollution-prevention measures to reduce levels of all contaminants in the environment and to conform to the laws and policies of each country.

The core component of the strategy is a set of "challenges" or reduction goals for Level 1 substances.[101] For instance, Canada committed to a 90 percent reduction in releases of dioxins and furans from human-based sources within the Great Lakes, while the United States committed to a 75 percent reduction of all U.S. air sources by 2006. A more specific list of the challenge goals is given in figure 13.

Under the auspices of the BEC, stakeholders from industry, academia, state and provincial and local governments, tribes and First Nations, and environmental organizations are participating in the strategy. Work groups are established for each Level 1 substance, such as a Mercury Work Group and a PCBS Work Group. An Integration Work Group is charged with dealing with overall issues. Occasional workshops are held on specific issues, such as long-range transport in the atmosphere. Each year, the governments release a report on progress under the strategy.[102]

The purpose of the strategy has been debated since its inception. The issue is whether the strategy was an attempt to further the virtual-elimination goal of the agreement, or a method of diverting attention and resources away from the agreement in favor of more limited goals. In effect, the latter view assumes that the governments as well as industry wished to counter the strong support of the environmental community for "zero discharge" and the phaseout of chlorine as an industrial feedstock that the IJC had recommended.[103]

The annual progress reports demonstrate that both the United States and

Canadian governments have made considerable progress in dealing with the bioaccumulative and persistent toxic contaminants in the Great Lakes (figure 12). The most extensive review of the strategy was carried out by the Water Quality Board in 2001 and is of special interest for several reasons.[104] First, the fact that the wqb undertook the study is reminiscent of its historical review function. In effect, agency personnel put on their ijc hats to evaluate a program undertaken by their governments. Second, the "Process Review Work Group" included members from academia, industry, and a nongovernmental organization, as well as members of the wqb.[105]

The wqb report to the ijc was based on a consultant's report and the board's evaluation.[106] The report had only 10 recommendations, compared to 45 in the consultant's report, but the wqb urged the governments "to evaluate the insight presented."[107] The wqb recognized the benefits of the strategy, including enhancement of the database, networking among stakeholders, coordination and collaboration by sharing of information and experience among the jurisdictions, and the attention focused on persistent toxic substances.[108]

The wqb report also identified important issues and several weaknesses. It questioned the contribution of the strategy for some substances, such as lead and pesticides, where the base year for the challenge was 1988 and the goal had been met prior to the signing of the strategy in 1997. It noted that lack of appropriate quantitative baselines for other challenge goals, such as for dioxins and furans, made gauging of progress difficult, and that some others lacked specific targets.[109] Other issues related to the voluntary nature of the strategy and lack of clear reporting on progress. Finally, the report noted that work on the strategy appears to be bilateral rather than binational, with Canada and the United States conducting separate rather than joint programs and reporting.[110]

The wqb cited the consultant's report in questioning whether the strategy is contributing to achievement of virtual elimination. Some members felt that the strategy "has contributed to achieving virtual elimination by spurring existing programs and spawning new initiatives, as well as stimulating work to fill information gaps." Others said that the initiative is one of many that were well underway when the strategy was signed. While the strategy may have influenced other initiatives, "a cause-effect relationship cannot necessarily be established."[111]

The Eleventh Biennial Report of the ijc noted the wqb report and reiterated many of the key findings. The commission report noted that "the role of the Strategy in fulfilling the Parties' commitments under the agreement is uncertain, particularly in its relationship with Remedial Action Plans and Lakewide Management Plans."[112]

FIGURE 13. Challenge Goals—Binational Toxics Strategy

■ **Challenge Goal 1**

CANADA Report by 1997 that there is no longer use, generation or release from Ontario sources that enter the Great Lakes of five bioaccumulative pesticides (chlordane, aldrin/dieldrin, DDT, mirex, and toxaphene), and of the industrial byproduct/contaminant octachlorostyrene. If ongoing, long-range sources of these substances from outside of Canada are confirmed, work within international frameworks to reduce or phase out releases of these substances.

U.S. Confirm by 1998 that there is no longer use or release from sources that enter the Great Lakes Basin of five bioaccumulative pesticides (chlordane, aldrin/dieldrin, DDT, mirex, and toxaphene), and of the industrial byproduct/contaminant octachlorostyrene. If ongoing, long-range sources of these substances from outside of the U.S. are confirmed, work within international frameworks to reduce or phase out releases of these substances.

■ **Challenge Goal 2**

CANADA Seek by 2000 a 90 percent reduction in use, generation, or release of alkyl-lead consistent with the 1994 COA.

U.S. Confirm by 1998 that there is no longer use of alkyl-lead in automotive gasoline. Support and encourage stakeholder efforts to reduce alkyl-lead releases from other sources.

■ **Challenge Goal 3**

CANADA Seek by 2000 a 90 percent reduction of high-level PCBs (› 1 percent PCB) that were once, or are currently, in service and accelerate destruction of stored high-level PCB wastes which have the potential to enter the Great Lakes Basin, consistent with the 1994 COA.

U.S. Seek by 2006 a 90 percent reduction nationally of high-level PCBs (› 500 ppm) used in electrical equipment. Ensure that all PCBs retired from use are properly managed and disposed of to prevent accidental releases within or to the Great Lakes Basin.

■ **Challenge Goal 4**

CANADA Seek by 2000 a 90 percent reduction in the release of mercury, or where warranted the use of mercury, from polluting sources resulting from human activity in the Great Lakes Basin. This target is considered as an interim reduction target and, in consultation with stakeholders in the Great Lakes Basin, will be revised if warranted, following completion of the 1997 COA review of mercury use, generation, and release from Ontario sources

U.S. Seek by 2006 a 50 percent reduction nationally in the deliberate use of mercury and a 50 percent reduction in the release of mercury from sources resulting from human activity. The release challenge will apply to the aggregate of releases to the air nationwide and of releases to the water within the Great Lakes Basin. This target is considered as an interim reduction target and, in consultation with stakeholders, will be revised if warranted, following completion of the Mercury Study Report to Congress.

■ **Challenge Goal 5**

CANADA Seek by 2000 a 90 percent reduction in releases of dioxins, furans, HCB, and B(a)P, from sources resulting from human activity in the Great Lakes Basin, consistent with the 1994 COA. Actions will focus on the 2,3,7,8 substituted congeners of dioxins and furans in a manner consistent with the Toxic Substances Management Plan.

U.S. Seek by 2006 a 75 percent reduction in total releases of dioxins and furans (2,3,7,8-TCDD toxicity equivalents) from sources resulting from human activity. This challenge will apply to the aggregate of releases to the air nationwide and of releases to the water within the Great Lakes Basin. Seek by 2006 reductions in releases that are within, or have the potential to enter, the Great Lakes Basin of hexachlorobenzene (HCB) and benzo(a)pyrene [B(a)P] from sources resulting from human activity.

■ **Challenge Goal 6**

CANADA Promote pollution prevention and the sound management of Level II substances, to reduce levels in the environment of those substances nominated jointly by both countries, and to conform to the laws and policies of each country, including pollution prevention, with respect to those substances nominated by only one country. Increase knowledge on sources and environmental levels of these substances.

U.S. Promote pollution prevention and the sound management of Level II substances, to reduce levels in the environment of those substances nominated jointly by both countries, and to conform to the laws and policies of each country, including pollution prevention, with respect to those substances nominated by only one country. Increase knowledge on sources and environmental levels of these substances.

■ **Challenge Goal 7**

CANADA Assess atmospheric inputs of Strategy substances to the Great Lakes. The aim of this effort is to evaluate and report jointly on the contribution and significance of long-range transport of Strategy substances from world-wide sources. If ongoing long-range sources are confirmed, work within international frameworks to reduce releases of such substances.

U.S. Assess atmospheric inputs of Strategy substances to the Great Lakes. The aim of this effort is to evaluate and report jointly on the contribution and significance of long-range transport of Strategy substances from world-wide sources. If ongoing long-range sources are confirmed, work within international frameworks to reduce releases of such substances.

■ **Challenge Goal 8**

CANADA Complete or be advanced in remediation of priority sites with contaminated bottom sediments in the Great Lakes Basin by 2006.

U.S. Complete or be advanced in remediation of priority sites with contaminated bottom sediments in the Great Lakes Basin by 2006.

SOURCE: U.S. Environmental Protection Agency, "The Great Lakes Binational Toxics Strategy: Canada–United States Strategy for the Virtual Elimination of Persistent Toxic Substances in the Great Lakes" Attachment 1, Technical Support Document, "Actions under the Binational Strategy" available at: *www.epa.gov/cgi-bin/epaprintonly.cgi.*

The State of the Lakes Ecosystem Conferences

The State of the Lakes Ecosystem Conferences (solec) were designed in the early 1990s to fulfill the requirements of the Great Lakes Agreement for a report on the state of the Great Lakes every two years. The thrust of the solec process is a biennial conference, followed by State of the Great Lakes reports that are based on ecosystem health indictors. solec meetings have been held every two years since 1994, with reports issued approximately one year later. The more recent focus of solec is the development of ecosystem health indicators.

The enthusiasm for solec by many stakeholders has continued to be mixed. On one hand, since the Water Quality Board no longer undertakes either an assessment of the conditions of the Great Lakes or an assessment of governmental programs, solec is the only binational forum for these issues. On the other hand, neither the conferences nor the subsequent reports have filled the void left by the changing mandate of the Water Quality Board. For example, the conferences tend to focus on one theme, rather than a comprehensive scan of the conditions of the lakes. There is no thorough assessment, if at all, of government programs directed to achieving the goals under the agreement.

In 2003 a peer review of the solec process concluded that solec has made an "extraordinarily important contribution." However, to improve the process, it should result in "environmental management recommendations." In other words, solec needs to evaluate the type of information it needs to develop "to provide groups with material needed to affect change."[113] The indicators project remained the chief topic of the 2004 solec meeting.

The Canada-Ontario Agreement

As a new Canada-Ontario Agreement was being contemplated, the Canadian Institute for Environmental Law and Policy (cielap) issued a report in 1999 detailing the major ways in which the two governments had failed to live up to the commitments that they had made when they signed the 1994 coa.[114] Wary of such criticism, the two governments did not begin serious discussions until around the time that the agreement expired in March 2000. The agreement was not ratified and signed for another two years—until June 2002, although it is dated March 2002.[115]

The negotiation of the 2002 coa was extremely difficult because of the tensions between the Liberal federal government and the provincial Progressive Conservative government. One of the key issues within the coa process was a conflict between the parties, with Ontario arguing that there should not be a formal advisory committee to the coa during its implementation.[116] Finally, the coa was released without any reference to such a committee, although the two governments announced in a joint news release that they would later develop some type of committee. It was another two years before that committee had its inaugural meeting. Significantly, it was called the "Great Lakes Innovation Committee."

Unlike the previous COA, the 2002 COA had almost no specific timelines or numeric targets in it. One can suspect that this was done to avoid the kind of criticism made by CIELAP noting the lack of progress under the previous COA. The governments also made no financial commitments within the COA. In 2001, the federal government had announced $30 million over five years for Great Lakes cleanup. A couple of months before the formal signing of the COA, the federal government announced $50 million over five years for the Great Lakes; the same amount was committed again in 2005.

Changes in Role and Function of the IJC

The changes made internally to the IJC processes, and particularly the changes to the mandate to the WQB and the planning and priorities process, continued, and perhaps even accelerated, with the appointment of new commissioners in 2002. One of the longest serving parliamentarians, Herb Gray, was appointed as Canadian chair of the IJC, while Dennis Schornack assumed the duties of U.S. chair.[117]

The IJC Biennial Reports

The format had changed with the Fifth Biennial Report of the IJC to make the reports more accessible to the public in terms of approach and language. The Fifth, Sixth, Seventh, and Eighth Biennial Reports can also be characterized to varying degrees as sources of policy innovation and promotion. Policy concepts like chemical restriction and the weight-of-evidence approach are good examples. The Ninth, Tenth, and Eleventh Biennial Reports follow essentially the same format established with the publication of the Fifth Biennial Report, but they are far more risk-averse in terms of policy.

The Ninth Biennial Report focused on the need for action on contaminated sites, particularly in areas of concern; the need for a binational approach to deal with toxic air pollution; and required action for specific toxics such as dioxins and furans, mercury and PCBS.[118] Three recommendations were made with respect to toxics and nuclear facilities within the Great Lakes.

The Tenth Biennial Report, issued in 2000, followed similar themes with respect to contaminated sediments and air pollution.[119] The report also made recommendations for improving fish advisories and making them more understandable. The commission also adopted many of the recommendations of the Water Quality Board for improving the Binational Toxics Strategy. In addition, other recommendations dealt with invasive species, land use, and other issues.

The Eleventh Biennial Report, issued in 2002 focused on three issues.[120] It made recommendations on how to improve the indicators of progress for cleanup discussed at the State of the Lakes Ecosystem Conferences, further recommendations to limit invasive species, and, as in the previous report, specified actions required for contaminated sediments. The commission called for a restoration plan for the Great Lakes with a focus on sediment cleanup. It was assumed that funding and priority action within each country would not happen unless such a plan was in place. Submission of the Twelfth Biennial Report in the fall of 2004 was the official prelude to the next review of the agreement. Invasive species was the chief topic but a follow-up report was promised on the role that the IJC wanted to play in the review.

The IJC and the Public

In the 1980s, the significance of the biennial meetings of the IJC increased as they came to be considered as a mechanism for public accountability of the governments' actions and a conduit for expression of public aspirations for Great Lakes cleanup. The large attendance, demonstrations, release of board reports, and the holding of parallel activities at meetings in Hamilton, Ontario, Traverse City, Michigan, Windsor, Ontario, and Duluth, Minnesota, were evidence of the enthusiasm brought to the meetings by the public and the organizing for the meetings by environmental groups.

In response to resentment of some officials about the criticism they felt was unfairly directed at the WQB, the IJC contemplated an alternative to holding several regional meetings on different issues during the two-year cycle. Although the IJC restored the tradition of biennial events, in part due to objection by the public participants, the die was cast for change.

Niagara Falls, New York, 1997

The format of the Niagara Falls biennial meeting was ostensibly the same as for the most recent earlier meetings, but actually differed in a number of ways. First, the environmental organizations felt that its importance was diminished because the IJC did not promote the meeting as it had in the past. The meeting was reduced to two days, with one day essentially devoted to board reports and the second day to a public forum.

GLU held workshops on the Friday and a press conference on Saturday. By the time the public got to speak on Sunday, many persons had already left. Attendance was under 500, a substantial drop from the 1,900 in Duluth and over 2,000 at Windsor.

Milwaukee, Wisconsin, 1999

The Milwaukee biennial meeting again was not intended to have a high profile, and again the attendance was less than 500 in total. Unlike Niagara Falls, this meeting included concurrent workshops on several issues. Board reports followed, and then a few hours of public statements. As at Niagara Falls, most participants had already departed.

At a press conference, GLU urged the governments not to renegotiate the agreement. The governments, which had been conducting an internal review, took the advice.

Montreal, Quebec, 2001

The Montreal meeting was scheduled for 13–14 September, but was postponed until October following the September 11 terrorist attack in New York City. The Montreal meeting followed essentially the same format as in Milwaukee, with workshops, reports from the advisory boards, and then public testimony. Few public interest groups were represented

As a GLU board member noted, had GLU not held a board meeting in conjunction with the IJC event, it would have been difficult to find any nongovernmental participants (including local residents).[121] The low registration prior to September 11 makes it difficult to blame the terrorist attack as the reason for the low turnout of approximately 400.

Ann Arbor, Michigan, 2003

The Ann Arbor meeting again followed the same format, with more emphasis on workshops than on nongovernmental presentations. By the time set for public comment on Saturday afternoon, fewer than 100 persons were in the room.

One new feature was that, on the day prior to the formal meeting, IJC commissioners met in private with small groups representing various stakeholder interests. The commission viewed these meetings as opportunities for the groups to speak directly to them. What was lost in the process, however, was opportunity for the various groups to hear each other's points of view and to learn from each other, an example of the decrease in information exchange and community building that formerly was a major feature of the biennial meetings.

The trend for the biennial IJC meetings over the past decade demonstrates subtle but profound changes for the role of the IJC. The meetings no longer have the visibility they formerly had for either the public or the news media. They are no longer considered the source of authoritative information on the state of the lakes. Neither are they the circuses they were accused of being in the early 1990s. There is the question, however, whether the Great Lakes community has lost unique and productive opportunities with these changes. The next biennial meeting is scheduled for June 2005 in Kingston, Ontario, to focus on the review of the Great Lakes Agreement.

Lakewide Management Plans

LAMPs are being developed for each of the Great Lakes pursuant to Annex 2 of the agreement, with the exception of Lake Huron. A Lake Huron Initiative Plan is being developed, but the governments have been careful to specify that this is not an official LAMP. The stated reason is that they do not have the resources to now develop a formal LAMP for Lake Huron.[122]

Because the governments have not been reporting in the four-stage reporting format laid out in Annex 2, a review of the status of LAMPs according to the GLWQA is not possible. Instead of reporting according to the four stages, the governments release an update every two years. The governments believe that this approach will be less resource intensive and allow them to focus on actions rather than reporting.[123]

Since the governments have not been reporting on the progress on LAMPs as specified in Annex 2, the IJC cannot report progress on each LAMP. In fact, by 2005 the IJC had only reviewed and commented on the Lake Superior LAMP (in 1996 [stage 1] and 2000 [stage 2]), and Lake Ontario in 1999 (stage 1). The IJC has never formally reviewed and commented on the other LAMP.

There is a lakewide multi-stakeholder forum for each of the LAMPs, except Lake Ontario. These have been useful mechanisms. Periodic meetings are held for Lakes Ontario and Huron. However, the lack of federal, provincial, and state support and engagement in the processes is causing frustration among many of the participants.

A number of issues pervade LAMPs.[124] The IJC has noted the "the inadequate integration of human health issues related to critical pollutants" in LAMPs.[125] Although the governments established the Great Lakes Human Health Network, the concern still continues. Another concern is whether LAMPs actually add value to existing or ongoing programs. For the most part, the lack of new resources and funding cuts by federal, provincial, and state governments has meant that LAMPs are rarely the source of new initiatives or programs.[126] There are exceptions, though, such as the mass-balance work for the Lake Michigan LAMP. The mass-balance work in effect establishes a model to better understand the inputs, pathways, sinks, and outputs of the pollutants within the system.

The IJC has repeatedly expressed concern about the limited and often reduced resources that the governments are making available for Annex 2 activities. For this reason, they have expressed concern over the tendency to move LAMPs beyond the issue of critical pollutants, as outlined in Annex 2, to include a broad range of other issues. The concern is that this will divert already limited resources away from actions on critical pollutants.

Overall, the LAMPs are seen as a useful and needed tool to understand and act upon Great Lakes cleanup. From a scientific point of view, understanding the whole processes within the lake, rather than just areas of concern, is fundamentally important. It is also extremely useful for citizens from around the lake to get together and network.

Remedial Action Plans

During this period, government funding was reduced for RAPS. In 1997, the Ontario government dropped all funding for public-advisory committees and for education around RAP programs, and eliminated several RAP coordinator positions.[127] At approximately the same time, the U.S. federal government cut funding for RAP programs. This devastated state involvement in many areas of concern because the states depend on federal funds for much of the money for their state staff. For example, in Michigan, federal funding supported 16 state employees in 1995, but by 2000 this had been reduced to less than two staff dedicated to RAPS.[128]

Figure 11 in chapter 5 provides a summary of the status of Remedial Action Plans (RAPS) committed to in 1987 in Annex 2 of the agreement (with a comparison to their status in 1996). After over a decade and a half of effort, progress on RAPS is considered by many to be too slow, and perhaps even stagnant. To date, cleanup and restoration actions have been completed for only four of the 43 areas of concern. Two of these have been delisted; the other two are defined as in a stage of recovery.[129]

Both parties have established goals to move RAPS forward. The U.S. Great Lakes Strategy commits to:

- Delist at least three RAPS by 2005;
- Delist a total of ten by 2010;
- Confirm all RAPS are in implementation stage (stage 2) by 2005.[130]

The Canada-Ontario Agreement commits to:

- Delist two RAPS by 2007;
- Complete all actions in six RAPS (be in natural-recovery stage) by 2007;
- Make progress in all other RAPS by 2007.[131]

Issues arose both with delisting existing RAPS and adding new ones. One of the innovations is that rather than "delisting" some of the RAPS, a term was developed called "area of recovery." The governments' proposal was to use this term in order to avoid calling a locality where progress is underway an "area of concern," but met severe public opposition. The criticism was that they are still areas of concern where extensive monitoring is required to assess progress, and the public needs to know whether cleanup or restoration actions still need to be taken.[132] As a compromise, the governments agreed that an area in which all cleanup actions had been taken would be said to be in a "stage of natural recovery" while still being called an "area of concern."

Despite a 1998 IJC recommendation, the governments did not designate new areas of concern that the IJC proposed, namely, Lake St. Clair and the St. Joseph River. In a review of RAPS, one commentator noted:

> As with the Lake Huron LaMP, the governments have been avoiding introducing anything that is in the formal GLWQA Annex 2 processes. This is why they refuse to call these AOCs and why they are not developing a LaMP for Lake Huron. The main reason they give for this is that it introduces a new level of bureaucracy and reporting requirements. The impact it has for the public is that it makes the IJC less and less of a body that they can turn to for another view of the status of these areas.[133]

In fact, the IJC is now less influential and less depended on for review of RAPS than previously. Of the 28 RAPS for which a stage 2 plan has been developed, only 11 have been submitted to the IJC for formal review. The IJC has conducted formal reviews on its own on four areas of concern: Detroit River, Hamilton Harbour, St. Mary's River, and the Niagara River.

The slow progress of RAPS can be attributed to a number of challenges that most face. These include the cost of waste-water treatment upgrades and sewer separation, with Canadian estimates requiring $1.9 billion for eight areas of concern and with a price tag of over $7 billion in the United States;[134] the cost of cleaning up contaminated sediments as well as determining the best cleanup approach (for example, removal or capping);[135] the emergence of new or recurring problems, such as algae problems;[136] the declining participation by the public in the processes with the complaints that governments are not giving enough support to the RAPS and citizens; and the lack of clarity as to how decisions are made and the role of public-advisory committees.

One of the crucial issues facing both LaMPS and RAPS is the trend to move these processes more to watershed-planning approaches. While they then may take on more issues and attempt to integrate more threats, there is fear that the move to this approach will dilute efforts on critical pollutants (which is the basis of Annex 2) and further weaken government engagement with virtual elimination of toxic contaminants.

Lake Superior Zero-Discharge Demonstration Program

In 1991, as noted in chapter 5, the parties established a "zero-discharge demonstration program" following a recommendation by the IJC in its Fifth Biennial Report. The Lake Superior Binational Forum, which was formed five months prior to the signing of the Zero Discharge agreement, acts as a binational advisory committee to the governments. As a result of the work of the forum, the federal, provincial, and state governments adopted load-reduction schedules for nine toxics in 1999.[137]

By 2000, the initial interim reduction targets were met, or close to being met: 60 percent reduction in releases of mercury, 33 percent destruction of PCBs, and retrieve and destroy all cancelled pesticides in the basin.[138] The load-reduction targets have created a number of challenges. First, there is either an absence of, or incomplete data to determine progress and the achievement of all interim targets. Data from a variety of sources (such as barrel burning) are not complete, while historically unrecognized sources have little data (such as crematoria, landfills). At times, the U.S. and Canadian data are not compatible.

Perhaps the biggest challenge in meeting the next round of interim targets in 2005, 2010, and 2015 (with zero discharge to be achieved in 2020) is ensuring that governments retain their commitment to the program.[139] For example, the Lake Superior Task Force (that is, federal, state, provincial, and tribal agencies responsible for implementing the program) repeatedly has raised a warning to both the Binational Executive Committee and the Binational Toxics Strategy Integration Group about the inability of meeting the interim targets based on the LaMP 2000 commitments, particularly with respect to mercury emissions from mining and power-generation sectors.[140] The government people working on this program have repeatedly called for more funding support and integration of the zero-discharge program with regulatory programs. In frustration, the representative from the National Wildlife Federation resigned from the Binational Forum, citing the lack of commitment by the governments and noting that in all rulemaking and permitting processes, the governments from both sides of the border "are unfamiliar with their government's Binational Program commitments."[141]

2004 Review of the Great Lakes Agreement

The 1997 review was mainly carried out internally, with little fanfare by the governments. An open review and revision of the goals of the agreement was urged, principally by the Great Lakes Commission.[142] The nongovernmental environmental groups lobbied against revision because of fear of weakening the influence of the agreement on the conservative governments. The following years brought major change in opinions about the agreement within the Great Lakes community.

In early 2003, a report that interviewed a number of leaders concluded that there was now a broad consensus that a comprehensive, transparent review should be undertaken.[143] In January 2004, the issue was considered at a meeting at the Wingspread Conference Center in Racine, Wisconsin, co-sponsored by the Lake Michigan Federation, the Canadian Environmental Law Association, and the Johnson Foundation. Participants included government officials, scientists and representatives of nongovernmental organizations, and institutions active within the Great Lakes community, including industry. A summary of discussion noted that there "appeared to be general acceptance of the proposition that formal review should take place in order for change in scope and processes to be considered."[144]

It was agreed that the Great Lakes Agreement provides an essential shared vision for the future of the Great Lakes, and the basis for binational action, but that the implementation process does not have the same vitality as in earlier times. Acceptance of the need for a review did not provide a consensus that the agreement should be renegotiated. Some environmental leaders believe that decision for renegotiation should depend on the results of a review. Others are convinced that the agreement needs to be updated, and still others think that a thorough overhaul is in order.

Reasons for a review include:

- Emergence of new issues and threats, including climate change, invasive species, and loss of biodiversity;[145]
- Opportunity to use the review to reverse the lack of interest by government agencies and the public in the agreement;
- Need to relate the restoration legislation introduced in the U.S. Congress to the agreement;
- Use of the review to consider the status of implementation; and
- A sense that the IJC and its institutions are foundering and in need of review and renewal.

Although the review was scheduled to follow the 2004 IJC Biennial Report to the governments, neither Environment Canada nor the USEPA seemed prepared to begin a detailed review or renegotiation immediately.

Nevertheless, in response to growing momentum, the USEPA and Environment Canada announced a three-stage approach to the scheduled review after discussion at a BEC meeting in Niagara Falls early in 2004:

- Stage One: Design and scope of the review process led by government with consultation;
- Stage Two: Review and Analysis led by government involving the Great Lakes community;
- Stage Three: Implementation of the review; that is, renegotiation, revision, or do nothing.[146]

For stage 1, a Scoping Committee was formed with senior managers of the lead agencies and other BEC members, including a representative of the IJC. The committee was charged with recommending the scope for the review and an open, transparent, and inclusive process. The committee was also charged with reporting to the BEC in July 2004.[147] No detail was provided for stages 2 and 3.

In early January 2005 a draft of a proposed process for the review was released for public comment. An agreement Review Committee would have co-chairs from USEPA and Environment Canada with representatives of federal, provincial, and state agencies as members. Several working groups would also be formed to review the articles and annexes of the existing agreement. The members of the working groups could represent federal, state, provincial and municipal agencies, Tribes, First Nations, industry, academic experts, and other members or organizations of the Great Lakes community. Special working groups would also be formed to examine other issues not now in the agreement, such as climate change and invasive species. The draft document also included mechanisms for public consultation.

The working groups would be directed to consider three overarching questions:

- Does the agreement achieve the desired effect of restoring and maintaining the chemical, physical, and biological integrity of the waters of the Great Lakes?
- Is the agreement sufficient to protect and restore the lakes, or does it fail to address critical issues? If so, what are they?
- In which situation/case does the agreement successfully fulfill its current goals and where does it fall short? Are there common features that characterize successes or best practices and are there areas needing improvement?

The proposed review process was much more transparent and inclusive than earlier ones. This time there appeared to be a genuine effort for inclusion of stakeholders outside the government and the general public.

The June 2005 biennial meeting in Kingston, Ontario, would be the first opportunity for formal nongovernmental participation in the review process.

The formal government review is scheduled to begin in the fall of 2005 with the establishment of work groups. No date was set for completion.[148]

The IJC and Its Role in the Review

The Great Lakes Agreement specifies that the periodic reviews should be carried out by the parties—in practice, mainly by the USEPA and Environment Canada, with some oversight by the U.S. Department of State and the Canada Foreign Affairs Department. The IJC had no part in the 1978 or 1987 reviews, but sought a major role in the review scheduled for 2004.

The Science Advisory Board had both advocated for review and played a role in the review in 1999 through its U.S. chair, Michael Donahue, who also headed the staff of the Great Lakes Commission.[149] The SAB report to the IJC at the 2003 biennial meeting recommended that the governments "conduct a comprehensive review of the operation and effectiveness of the Great Lakes Water Quality Agreement, and seek public input, with a view to substantially revising it to reflect a current vision of water quality goals, priorities and institutional arrangements."[150]

At the end of the 2003 biennial meeting, the commission issued a resolution requesting "a special mandate from the governments that defines an appropriate and substantial role for the commission in the review of the Great Lakes Water Quality Agreement."[151] In a presentation to the Standing Committee on Environment and Sustainable Development in Parliament, the Canadian co-chair, Herb Gray, outlined five responsibilities that should be given to the IJC for the review:

- An operational review by the Water Quality Board;
- Review of the scientific underpinnings by the Science Advisory Board;
- The IJC to act as a conduit to the public for the review;
- The IJC to provide advice to the governments; and
- The IJC to provide guidance as to its own role.[152]

The next issue of the IJC newsletter, *Focus*, following the 2003 biennial meeting noted that the IJC would outline its advice to the governments in a special report in 2004.[153]

During the fall of 2003, the Windsor office also undertook work examining what changes to the agreement would be appropriate, and the process to further discuss these changes. A roundtable was proposed on the issue, but it was not clear how this work would fit into the commission's work or the government review process.[154] The date of the biennial meeting was moved from September to June to ensure its relevancy to the review.

Science Advisory Board Workshop

In early February 2004, the SAB held a workshop entitled "Science and the Great Lakes Water Quality Agreement" to develop advice to the IJC and complement advice from the other advisory bodies.[155] The workshop consisted of an annex-by-annex review, and seemed to assume that both the body of the agreement and the annexes need revision. Some of the presenters, however, did not see the existing agreement as an impediment to ongoing action.

Milton Clark, a USEPA official, said that issues for Annex 12, which concerns toxic contaminants, "are less about science and more about overcoming obstacles and political will."[156] Others lamented the lack of resources, lack of monitoring, and need for political leadership that impedes implementation.

The Status of the Agreement in 2005

This period saw continuing disconnect between the activities of the IJC and the governments for implementation of the Great Lakes Agreement, and growing uncertainty about its relevance for the future. The question of relevance extends to the IJC, which no longer has the information or the capacity necessary for evaluation of government efforts, and itself has lost status and respect within the Great Lakes community.

The distance between the governments and the IJC seemed to grow as the governments communicated primarily through the new binational institutions established outside the institutional structure of the agreement following adoption of the 1987 Protocol. The arrangements include the Binational Executive Committee, the State of the Lake Ecosystem Conferences, and the Binational Toxics Strategy.

Progress during this period included continuing decline of levels of toxic substances in the lakes with reductions of releases into the environment under the Binational Toxics Strategy. The SOLEC indicators project had so far failed to provide the means to measure progress called for in a critical 2003 GAO report. Even with the Binational Executive Committee, the governments seemed to be moving in the direction of bilateral, rather than truly binational, efforts on behalf of the lakes.

There was also a trend toward broadening the issues for cleanup and restoration beyond the virtual elimination of toxic contaminants. This trend was underscored by the introduction of new so-called restoration legislation in the U.S. Congress that sought major increase in federal funding for the lakes to be administered through the states. The excitement generated by the legislation galvanized the broader Great Lakes community and contributed to the possibility for comprehensive evaluation of the more than thirty-year-old agreement in the periodic review scheduled to begin in 2004.

CHAPTER 7

PAST SUCCESSES AND NEW CHALLENGES

THE GENERAL CONSENSUS WITHIN THE GREAT LAKES COMMUNITY AND BE-yond is that the chief objectives of the 1972 agreement have been real-ized, and that substantial progress has been made toward the goals of the 1978 version. Success has been more limited for some provisions added in the 1987 Protocol, particularly the Remedial Action Plans (RAPS) for specific geographic areas and cleanup of contaminated sediments.

Less tangible disappointments include decline in the sense of community during the 1990s, a loss of confidence of the governments in the IJC, and decreased participation by the nongovernmental environmental community in agreement-related affairs. A growing division between government and the IJC agreement-related activities appears to have contributed to these changes, but is not the only cause.[1]

Residents of the region in both Canada and the United States value the beauty of the Great Lakes and consider them important to their own quality of life. U.S. residents of the region are twice as likely as Ontario residents to view the condition as good or better than it was in the past, but a significant proportion in both countries are concerned about protecting the lakes for future generations. Pollution remains a major concern in both countries.[2]

The parties to the agreement and the Great Lakes community still face major challenges for protecting the future of the lakes. Several factors create opportunities for renewing the agreement and bringing the Great Lakes com-munity together with greater strength than ever for responding to both old and new problems of the Great Lakes themselves.

Successes under the Agreement

Success has occurred in six categories:

- Reduction of phosphorus and other pollutants;
- Reduction of toxic contaminants;
- Promotion of an ecosystem approach to management;
- Contributions to science;
- Evolution of a Great Lakes community; and
- Contributions to partnership between Canada and the United States.

Reduction of Phosphorus and Other Pollutants

Visible change in the physical condition of the water, with more clarity and relative lack of debris that is taken to mean better water quality, is the most obvious change for residents of the Great Lakes watershed since 1972. The chief objectives of the original 1972 agreement were the reduction of the loadings of phosphorus—which had been identified as the limiting nutrient for triggering algae growth and accelerated eutrophication—together with elimination of "floating debris, oil, scum . . . that was unsightly" and "materials [that create] a nuisance" because of color or odor.[3]

Success in lowering phosphorus loadings depended on multiple kinds of actions by all levels of governments—local, state and provincial, and federal. The agreement provided the unifying goal, and its institutions provided the mechanisms for information exchange, policy debate, action, and accountability. The Science Advisory Board informed both government agencies and the environmental community about how excessive phosphorus led to Lake Erie's "dead zone," and to decaying piles of algae on beaches in Lake Ontario and Lake Michigan. In the Water Quality Board, state and federal officials considered the need, and then advocated stricter effluent standards, for water-treatment systems in their home agencies. The WQB reports to the IJC measured progress and identified necessary additional action.

In 2003, the total target loadings set for each lake and the target levels set for concentrations in the open waters had been maintained for 18 years, except in Lake Erie, where they were exceeded in 1982, 1984, and 1990.[4] Scientists believe that the disconcerting rises in phosphorus levels in Lake Erie that began in the 1990s are due to the presence of zebra mussels rather than changes in phosphorus loadings. The presence of zebra mussels, together with other invasive species, is considered an emerging threat to the ecological stability of this lake.[5]

The general reduction in phosphorus loadings was achieved by improved sewage treatment, which was initiated because of the agreement, or went beyond what was required under existing national laws. In Canada, new federal funding was provided under the Canada-Ontario Agreement. In the United States, major sewage-treatment systems in the Great Lakes basin were upgraded to tertiary treatment to achieve the one-milligram-per-liter effluent level required by the agreement, when secondary treatment would have satisfied the Clean Water Act.

In both countries, the phosphate content of detergents was drastically reduced in the Great Lakes basin. The outcome of every legislative battle for a phosphate ban depended on public support, and on environmental advocacy by local and statewide organizations. Measures to reduce runoff of agricultural fertilizers launched a national movement toward conservation tillage in the United States.[6] Within a few years, algae growth had declined throughout the system and fewer beaches were closed. This Great Lakes experience in improving water quality by reducing phosphorus loadings continues to assist the development of management policies for other water systems. Great Lakes sources were consulted when phosphate-detergent bans began to be considered for Chesapeake Bay in the 1980s, for example.[7]

Increases in beach closings due to high *E. coli* counts excited public outcry in the 1990s, but many of the beaches had been considered unsafe for swimming at any time prior to the 1970s. It remains uncertain whether the more recent increase is due to better monitoring for *E. coli* bacteria or to other causes.[8] Even so, most beaches are considered safe for swimming most of the time.[9] The Great Lakes remain the primary source for drinking water for 35 million people, and water quality is considered to be better than it would have been without the Great Lakes Agreement.[10]

Promotion of Toxics Control

The expanding global response to the threat of toxic contamination for nature and humankind is based on knowledge gained from experience in the Great Lakes. Research stimulated by the agreement brought new understanding about the presence and the consequences of toxic contaminants in the Great Lakes.[11] Previously, direct waste discharges were assumed to be the principal source, and pollution control the main management mechanism. Great Lakes research showed that many toxic chemicals were also being deposited from the atmosphere and leaching from landfills inside the watershed to bioaccumulate in fish tissues throughout the whole Great Lakes system. The agreement was reviewed and revised in 1978 to call for virtual elimination of contaminants and an ecosystem approach to management.[12]

Concerns about the relationship between fish tumors and abnormal reproduction of wildlife to exposure to a wide range of toxic contaminants led to research that identified human health effects linked to fish consumption.[13] Ongoing research confirmed effects on development of babies born to mothers with high levels of PCBs in their bodies, and on the endocrine system of adults.[14]

Earlier it was thought that settling into sediments removed pollutants from the water column. Then fish tumors in bottom-feeding fish led to recognition that sediments can be reservoirs of toxic contaminants. Great Lakes scientists found that PCBs released from sediments can enter the atmosphere from the surface of the water to be carried by long-range transport for deposition again, in what they labeled a "grasshopper effect."[15]

During the 1980s, declines in levels of contaminants in both open waters and fish tissues followed decrease in direct discharges of waste waters, but now the reservoirs in contaminated sediments proved to be a continuing source in addition to atmospheric deposition. The fundamental objectives from the 1978 agreement were retained, with a new review in 1987. New annexes were added to assist virtual elimination of toxic contaminants by Remedial Action Plans in the local areas of concern, and by Lakewide Management Plans in the open waters of each lake.

The U.S. Congress amended the Clean Water Act in 1987 to direct the USEPA to recognize the objectives of the Great Lakes Agreement in domestic programs. Further amendments in the 1991 Great Lakes Critical Programs Act led to extensive but not very successful efforts to develop cost-effective methods for removing and treating contaminated sediments. The 1990 Clean Air Act included a new section on toxic air contaminants introduced on behalf of the Great Lakes.

Language was also added in the 1987 Protocol that affected the relationship between the lead agencies for the parties and the IJC as they struggled with the complexities of the virtual-elimination (or zero-discharge) goal. Earlier bans for DDT and PCBs were followed by bans on some pesticides and efforts to decrease use of others. Use of the weight of evidence and the precautionary principle were considered. The chemical industry organized national and international trade groups to counter the IJC's call for a ban on use of chlorine in commerce.[16]

In the United States in 1994, the Great Lakes Water Quality Initiative introduced a policy of regulating bioaccumulative chemicals in a different way than conventional pollutants that break down in the environment. Canada adopted a Chlorine Action Plan in 1994 and a Toxic Substances Management Plan in 1995 following recommendations of the IJC.

In Canada, the province of Ontario used the Great Lakes Agreement as a rationale for tough new limits for the pulp-and-paper sector, as well as developing a list of candidate substances for phaseout. From the early 1990s, federal ministers and policymakers have attempted to respond to calls for "virtual elimination of persistent toxic substances," with the goal eventually to be legislatively incorporated in the Canadian Environmental Protection Act, 1999.

International negotiations for a treaty calling for elimination of persistent organic pollutants from the global environment began in 1996 in Montreal. Presumably, Canada's call for the "virtual elimination" of such substances was based on experience under the Great Lakes Agreement. Nongovernmental participation, up to the final adoption of the Stockholm Convention on Persistent Organic Pollutants in 2001, was led by Jack Weinberg, who had gained his expertise as head of the Greenpeace Great Lakes Program, while Canadian environmentalists participated in the ongoing negotiations fostered by the United Nations Environmental Program. With Tim Brown of the Delta Institute in Chicago, Weinberg continued to participate in development of regional implementation plans, including for North America.[17]

Great Lakes science was also applied by the Commission for Environmental Cooperation for North America (CEC), a tripartite agency organized in 1991 under the environmental side agreement to the North American Free Trade Agreement (NAFTA). In 1993, the CEC launched its Sound Management of Chemicals in North America program under the leadership of Andrew Hamilton, former science advisor to the IJC Ottawa office.[18]

DDT transported by air from Mexico and Central America was still being deposited into the Great Lakes. In 2002, Mexico banned the use of DDT after receiving assistance from the World Health Organization through the CEC to find alternative methods of controlling malaria-bearing mosquitoes. In 2004, Mexico was sharing information about its success with several countries in Central America.

By 2001, George Kuper of the Council of Great Lakes Industries argued that the very low levels of some contaminants in open waters meant that "virtual elimination" had been achieved. Others insisted that toxic contaminants would remain a threat as long as they were accumulating in fish tissues. By this time, concepts of restoration of ecological integrity and protection of biodiversity were increasingly competing with toxic contamination for attention on the Great Lakes agenda.[19]

An Ecosystem Approach to Management

In addition to "virtual elimination," the second major goal of the 1978 agreement was an ecosystem approach to management. The concept was based on identification of multiple sources of contaminants to the lakes and widespread, subtle, and long-lasting effects in the environment. Sometimes called a "cross-media" or an "integrated" approach, the concept also recognized that regulation under some of the early environmental laws had moved pollution around in the environment rather than eliminating it. Again, Great Lakes experience has had wide influence.

In 1989, USEPA administrator William Reilly cited Great Lakes experience in calling for ecological integrity, not just compliance with regulatory standards, as the new policy objective for the agency, as he explained to the National Press Club in 1990.[20] The Sierra Club assigned Jane Elder, who had been a leading advocate for the Great Lakes in Congress in the 1980s, to a new position where she could use the Great Lakes as a model in restructuring the organization's advocacy program around ecosystems rather than single issues.[21]

Attention to habitat restoration, preservation of biodiversity, and fishery issues were meant to be part of the development of RAPS and LAMPS called for in annexes to the 1987 Protocol.[22] One observer said that this meant that implementation involved "bottom-up planning with top-down planning with the Great Lakes in the middle."

Although the results of these formal planning processes have been at best only partially successful, during the 1990s the concept of seeking ecological integrity gained throughout the Great Lakes community and beyond.

In 1993, the Great Lakes Commission had developed an Ecosystem Charter. Later, the agency established the Great Lakes Wetlands Consortium to promote information exchange among research programs and government agencies as part of a growing trend to recognize the ecological importance of such resources.[23]

The theme of the 1996 State of the Lakes Ecosystem Conference (SOLEC) was the relationship between the lakes and land use in the watershed. Whether the agreement should be made into an "ecosystem agreement" instead of a "water quality agreement" was the major issue in the 1998–99 internal review of the Great Lakes Agreement by the governments.

In the nongovernmental community, the Tip of the Mitt Watershed Council in Michigan created the Great Lakes Aquatic Habitat Network and Fund to give small grants for restoration of wetlands in local communities. The grants are distributed through organizations identified as the "hubs" of the network in each state and Ontario.[24] Toxic contamination remained a major issue, while restoration of natural areas on shorelines became a new priority for the Lake Michigan Federation.[25]

Great Lakes United took the lead in linking with the tribes and First Nations on their initiatives for protection and restoration of natural areas and waterways in the Great Lakes watershed.[26] In 1994, The Nature Conservancy established a basin-wide Great Lakes program after identifying critically significant areas for preservation of biodiversity.[27]

Many projects and programs are undertaken through partnerships between state agencies, local governments, nongovernmental organizations, and sometimes corporations. One major example is the Chicago Wilderness coalition of almost 200 public and private partners that seeks to preserve biodiversity from southeastern Wisconsin, through Illinois and Indiana, to Southwestern Michigan around the southern tip of Lake Michigan.[28]

Another growing major trend that reflects ecological concerns in the 1990s is the many new initiatives to preserve existing natural areas and restore natural functions by means of watershed management planning. Both the Lake Erie and Lake Michigan LaMPs call for watershed management planning in tributaries as necessary to improve water quality in the open lakes.[29] Ontario has made local watershed planning a priority. In 2003, the USEPA, regional planning agencies, the Great Lakes Commission, and Western Michigan University co-sponsored a three-day workshop for local government officials and others on this kind of planning.[30]

The Great Lakes Fishery Commission broadened its mission from the original narrow mandate to control the sea lamprey, to "healthy ecosystems" in its updated 2001 Joint Strategic Plan. In the plan, state and provincial fishery-management agencies who had formerly acted unilaterally agreed to ongoing consultation for consistent management policies system-wide, "because natural resources do not respect human boundaries."[31]

The goals of ecological restoration and integrity are also reflected in the work on the Annex 2001 initiative by the Council of Great Lakes Governors to amend the 1985 Great Lakes Charter. Proposed criteria for approval of diversions immediately adjacent to the Great Lakes watershed, or even for new large withdrawals within the watershed, include the requirements "for ecological improvement" and return of all water after treatment to the source.[32]

Even the formal mission statement of the Council of Great Lakes Industries now says the aim is sustainable development, with "biological diversity restored and wetlands restored, with well planned land use and sustainable forests."[33] While increased efficiency in production and reduction of costs for waste disposal have helped drive the acceptance of pollution prevention as a way of doing business by major industries throughout the Great Lakes basin, the need for ecological integrity has also been recognized.

Earlier, three major steel companies had pledged to eliminate mercury in their operations, and the auto industry agreed to eliminate PCBs in its operations. In 2004, the Wildlife Habitat Council had established two field offices in the Great Lakes region, a Great Lakes office in Detroit, and another field office in Hammond, Indiana. The purpose of both offices is to work with corporations to restore natural functions to former industrial lands.[34] An ecosystem approach to management, integrating control and prevention of pollution from land, air, and water, was not yet being universally applied in the Great Lakes basin, but the water quality agreement continued to promote this end.

Contributions to Science

Most of the environmental-management efforts and innovations under the Great Lakes Agreement have been assisted by the network of individuals and research institutions the IJC in 1993 called "a large community of knowledgeable committed environmental scientists."[35] Their influence is magnified by the features of the agreement that encourage scientists to share their information not just with each other, but with program managers, policymakers, legislators, and environmental activists in the larger community.

In the 1960s, scientists initiated the binational joint fact-finding work on eutrophication that led to the original agreement. The 1970 International Field Year for the Great Lakes added more basic understanding of the ecology of Lake Ontario.[36] In Lake St. Clair and the St. Clair River, scientists identified the factors that make mercury in fish tissue dangerous to human health. More pioneering research provided new information about pollution sources in the work of the Pollution from Land Use Reference Group.

Discovery of concentrated contaminants in fish tissues was followed by continuing identification of the multiplicity of ways in which persistent organic pollutants enter the lakes and affect not just aquatic organisms, but wildlife that depend on the lakes for food, as well as human health through fish consumption. Through the life of the agreement, scientists have continued to collect, analyze, and disseminate information needed to develop appropriate measures for reducing loadings, and then to measure results.[37]

Building on measuring and modeling techniques used first to do a mass-balance study in Green Bay, in the 1990s academic researchers worked with the USEPA to carry out a mass-balance study for Lake Michigan.[38] The primary purpose of mass-balance studies is to provide information that can make management policies more precise and efficient. The Lake Michigan results are still being analyzed, but they are also being applied in an effort to develop indicators for ecological health through the State of the Lakes Ecosystem Conferences that were begun in the 1990s. One factor in the decline in vigor in the Great Lakes community as a whole in the 1990s may be that the SOLEC meetings have tended to be what one observer called "occasions for academic discussions rather than sharing of information with environmental advocates."[39]

Still more recently, Great Lakes scientists sought to continue their tradition of contributing to policy development with an innovative project managed through the International Association for Great Lakes Research (IAGLR).

Beginning in 2001, an IAGLR Science-Policy Project sought to strengthen the science-policy link in three ways. First was to build a directory of IAGLR experts on the World Wide Web who agreed to be available to answer questions from policymakers. The second was to make all back issues of the IAGLR *Journal of Great Lakes Research* available electronically, and the third was to develop advice for policymakers on three specific, major ongoing and emerging threats to the Great Lakes.

Three policy papers were subsequently released on contaminated sediments, on ecosystem management, and on invasive species. Each paper summarized the state of scientific understanding on the topic and laid out specific policy proposals. All are now references for policymakers such as U.S. Senator Carl Levin of Michigan, a long-time leader in Congress on Great Lakes issues who used the invasive species report to policymakers to develop a new legislative proposal.[40]

Earlier scientists shared information with the rest of the Great Lakes community through the implementation processes of the agreement. The IAGLR project shows that Great Lakes scientists have a sense of responsibility for assisting development of public policy based on science. It also demonstrates how their shared knowledge continues to lead to support for policies and programs to achieve the agreement goal of chemical, biological, and physical integrity. Finally, the reliance on Great Lakes science in development of the Stockholm Convention on Persistent Organic Pollutants demonstrates the continuing contribution to the rest of the world as well.

Evolution of Community within the Regime

Several Great Lakes organizations and institutions that were binational or addressed Canadian as well as U.S. concerns existed before the Great Lakes Water Quality Agreement was signed in 1972, beginning with the IJC under the Boundary Waters Treaty of 1909. The Great Lakes Fishery Commission and the Great Lakes Commission were established in the mid 1950s as the St. Lawrence Seaway was being built. The University of Michigan began sponsored conferences on Great Lakes science in the same period, and the International Association for Great Lakes Research was formally organized in 1967. The Great Lakes Basin Commission was set up in 1967 to coordinate state and federal policies for water resources, to cooperate with Canadian agencies on specific projects of mutual concern, and to contribute planning and analysis for setting target loadings for phosphorus and other issues.[41]

These earlier experiences provided the foundation for the evolution of a much broader community around implementation of the Great Lakes Agreement. The source of the sense of community was exchange of information and camaraderie among government-agency officials, IJC staff, scientists, staff and members of environmental organizations, and political leaders such as members of Congress and their staff. Many individuals came to know each other personally through events and activities related to the agreement, especially the IJC biennial meetings.

Beginning slowly in the 1970s, nongovernmental participation gained momentum in the 1980s after the IJC made it a major goal. The sense of community seemed greatest around the end of the first two decades of experience, from the late 1980s into the early 1990s. This was the period of large attendance by members of nongovernmental organizations in the IJC biennial meetings. It was also the period of most active collaboration within the community to advocate for policies, programs, and legislation needed to assist achievement of agreement goals and objectives.

Formation of Great Lakes United (GLU) in 1982 provided an accessible mechanism to voice the grass-roots and community concerns and aspirations concerning the ecosystem. The work of GLU, nongovernmental groups, including local, regional, and international organizations and important labor groups from across the basin, erased the international, state, and provincial borders. Elimination of toxic contaminants was a common concern everywhere.

The kind of basin-wide community that developed among environmental organizations also can be found among scientists and scientific institutions, the funding institutions, and industry. Within each community of interest, the Great Lakes are the organizing theme and focus of efforts that often transcend national borders and cultural differences. By the late 1980s, Canadians participated in lobby days in Washington, and Americans could be found engaging Canadian policymakers in Toronto and Ottawa on Great Lakes issues.

Both public and private bodies made use of each other's courts and tribunals to further environmental-protection interests.[42] In the development of these communities, the Great Lakes Agreement provided the "code of conduct," but each community had different, often overlapping, interests and opinions as to how those goals and objectives ought to be met.

Strengthening the Canada–U.S. Partnership

The U.S. Department of State calls the bilateral relationship between the United States and Canada overall "perhaps the closest and most extensive in the world." Larger than the United States in area, Canada has only about 31 million people, compared to the 292 million in the United States. The two countries are each other's largest trading partners, exchanging the equivalent of a billion dollars a day in goods, services, and investments. About 200 million people cross the border each year, most without a passport until the era of fear of international terrorism began in 2001.[43]

Canada's equal role with the United States under the Boundary Waters Treaty, and later the Great Lakes Agreement, reflects the intention of creating an equal partnership by dividing four of the five Great Lakes with the international boundary. As the possibility for competition grew for all the waterways that cross the boundary, the first challenge was to establish a stable, ongoing process by which two sovereign nations with different political systems and cultures and unequal economic power could share the use of such a bountiful resource. The triumph of using the IJC to avoid disputes about use of the waters under the treaty set the stage for the challenge of restoring ecological integrity under the Great Lakes Agreement.

Even when they disagreed on other issues such as acid rain, or adopted different approaches to pollution control, the parties to the water quality agreement worked together through the joint institutions of the IJC until after the 1987 Protocol. Even after the lead government agencies began to work directly together, rather than through the IJC, the agreement continued to be the focus of a stable relationship. Nevertheless, there came to be a sense of "us against them" between Environment Canada and the USEPA and the IJC in the 1990s.[44]

The 30-year-old working partnership was the reason that Canadian officials were shocked by how legislation introduced in the U.S. Congress in the summer of 2003 did not acknowledge Canada's role in management of the Great Lakes. A series of earlier General Accounting Office reports had focused on the role of the USEPA in the implementation of the agreement. The February 2003 report focused on the need for greater coordination in U.S. domestic programs, and was used to set the stage for the new so-called restoration legislation that ignores the necessity for a binational, shared effort for cleaning up and restoring the Great Lakes.

Both the House of Representatives and Senate versions proposed to put the governors of the Great Lakes states in charge of distributing billions of dollars to accomplish the cleanup and restoration that were the ultimate goals of the agreement. The prospect of major new funding seemed to revitalize much of the Great Lakes community, generating major lobbying efforts by environmental groups, local and state officials including all the governors, and the Great Lakes Commission.

When Environment Canada officials inquired in Washington and Chicago about what the new governance approach would mean to the agreement, they received only general, nonspecific assurances that Canada's interests in the Great Lakes would be recognized.[45] The seeming indifference to the agreement raised new questions about its future.

By 2004, the USEPA and Environment Canada began internal preparations for the periodic review by the parties that would be required following submission of the Twelfth Biennial Report by the IJC to the governments. Whether the agreement will continue to contribute to the Canada–U.S. partnership may depend on the results of the review.

Factors in Success of the Great Lakes Regime

Seven features of the Great Lakes Agreement account for its effectiveness and the vitality of the Great Lakes regime in its first 25 years. The question is whether these factors are sufficient to meet the challenges of new external political, economic, and social factors as well as the internal changes within the regime since the early 1990s. They are:

- Binationalism;
- Promotion of community;
- Equality and parity in structure and obligations;
- Common objectives;
- Joint fact-finding and research;
- Accountability and openness in information exchange; and
- Flexibility and adaptability to changing circumstances.

BINATIONALISM

The binationalism that historically characterized the operations of the IJC under the Boundary Waters Treaty has been essential to the success of the Great Lakes Agreement. The most singular feature of the IJC has been its function as a joint independent agency on which the two governments depended for advice to solve problems and avoid disputes in the use of transboundary water resources. The Great Lakes Agreement applied the spirit, the principles, and the processes of the treaty to set joint goals for the Great Lakes.

The theory of binationalism in this context is that it creates a forum in which the IJC commissioners and government officials on both sides can serve in effect as international civil servants. This approach provides opportunity for agency policymakers to discuss matters without home-agency constraints, and fashion solutions that can then be presented to the home agencies with an understanding of how other jurisdictions will approach the problem. Binationalism is conducive to consensus, since separate interests are set aside for the broader mutual purposes.

Binationalism is not the same as bilateralism. With binationalism, the common interest supersedes separate interests. Bilateralism involves negotiation between two parties with national interest as the controlling factor. Experience under the Great Lakes regime has demonstrated the strength of the binational approach for dealing with such a large ecosystem across an international border, but it has also confirmed challenges.

The ways that later changes in relationships and operations within the Great Lakes regime have affected its binational character are the reason that this critical feature should be considered in review and potential renegotiation of the agreement. The consequences for binationalism should also be weighed in unilateral actions by the governments for the purpose of restoration of ecological integrity in what is a single, interconnected system. Even the fate of Lake Michigan, the only one of the lakes entirely within the United States, is linked to the fate of all the other four.

The binational approach that was important to the early success in slowing eutrophication began to be diminished in the early 1980s in the operations of the IJC and in the commitment of government resources. The leadership of the IJC was undermined by the practice of turning the appointment of new commissioners into political patronage awards with every change of administration (United States) and government (Canada).

The result has been lack of continuity at the policy level, with less decision making by consensus on the basis of personal expertise and more responsiveness to national interests. This trend was exacerbated in the 1990s as the operation of the IJC came to be driven by the views and aims of individual commissioners, until it ceased to operate by consensus in the new millennium.

With growing resource constraints on both sides, in the mid 1980s the USEPA and Environment Canada sought to commit fewer agency resources to IJC activities in the review that resulted in the 1987 Protocol. At the same time, the strong consortium of environmental organizations led by Great Lakes United sought to increase the accountability of the governments for the lack of progress toward virtual elimination of toxic contaminants.

Both efforts converged with a new requirement in the 1987 Protocol directing the USEPA and Environment Canada, with other federal agencies and the states and provinces, to confer twice a year on progress and work plans. Officials who urged this requirement on both sides have confirmed that their purpose was to reduce involvement in IJC processes. The environmental observers of the review thought the change would mean the greater accountability that they sought, and did not perceive other consequences.

Slow to start, the Binational Executive Committee led by the USEPA and Environment Canada is the mechanism for the twice-a-year meetings of the governments. The major early activity, with no public involvement, was to plan the 1994 and 1996 SOLEC meetings with "decision makers" as the intended participants. In practice, senior level policymakers and scientists have participated less in both the BEC and SOLEC events than formerly in the Science Advisory and Water Quality boards and the IJC biennial meetings.

Few environmental-organization staff or other persons have taken advantage of the July 1996 decision to allow outside observers of BEC meetings. Later BEC agendas have consisted principally of ongoing discussion of the SOLEC effort to develop environmental indicators for the Great Lakes, and reports of agency activities. In general, the meetings are poorly attended by agency heads or senior-level federal policymakers, with few state representatives at all. Meanwhile, withdrawal of policymakers from the WQB has left this critical component of the earlier binational process without a mission, and the SAB is no longer the source of major policy innovations.

The lead agencies for the governments still seem to accept the need for a binational approach to Great Lakes management as the purpose of the agreement, notwithstanding the so-called restoration legislation introduced to the U.S. Congress. Yet interaction between the lead agencies for the parties, outside the joint institutions of the IJC and without nongovernmental oversight, appears to be leading to regression into country-to-country negotiations and traditional exchanges of views through diplomatic channels.

In other words, change in the relationship between the USEPA and Environment Canada and the IJC appears to have been undermining binationalism in the institutional framework. It appears to be a factor in the diminished vitality of the broad community that developed out of a unified process serving the goals of the agreement and the Great Lakes, rather than just national interests. As it was proposed, the U.S. restoration legislation fosters bilateralism rather than the binationalism whose value to the Great Lakes has been demonstrated by the first 25 years of experience under the water-quality agreement.

Canada, in particular, should be concerned about the potential loss of binationalism. Its leverage to influence U.S. policy is far greater within a binational context than through party-to-party negotiations. The United States should also be concerned about losing the opportunity to maintain its "special relationship" with its northern neighbor, especially in a period of increasing resentment and hostility from elsewhere in the world.

Finally, all members of the Great Lakes community should be concerned about the replacement by a conventional country-to-country relationship of a successful binational process that recognizes the importance of ecosystem integrity and contributes to the growing need for international effort to protect the global environment. The next review of the agreement must include open consideration of the consequences of withdrawal of the parties from the binational process, and how to restore the vigor of the binational community that it created.

Promotion of Community

Direction to the ijc to provide information to the public was the feature that contributed most to evolution of the broad sense of community that is one of the successes of the Great Lakes Agreement. The withdrawal from ijc processes that has undermined binationalism may have been inspired in part by reaction against what the governments considered too much nongovernmental pressure for actions they were not prepared to undertake, especially "zero discharge" of toxic contaminants.

By the 1990s, a backlash from the parties against noisy and theatrical demonstrations organized by Greenpeace in the ijc biennial meetings caused the ijc to change the format of the meetings to calm them down.[46] The desire to defuse public influence was exacerbated by international attention to the ijc recommendation to the governments for a chlorine ban.

The chemical-industry response included a greater presence of industry in ijc activities, such as the sab and the biennial meetings. Resented by some environmentalists as evidence for a corporate-takeover attempt of the ijc, over time industry broadened its participation in the Great Lakes community beyond opposition to acceptance of certain contaminant-control concepts. Several Council of Great Lakes Governors projects have depended on cooperation by the auto and other industries. There is a growing trend for industries to go beyond regulatory requirements in preventing pollution, or voluntarily reducing or eliminating use of toxic substances.

Still, the vigor of the community around the agreement processes had declined by the late 1990s. The wqb was attended by lower-level staff rather than agency heads and had no definitive mission. The sab was less provocative, and the activist scientists of earlier times were no longer involved. Almost no environmentalists attended any bec meetings, and only a handful went to the solec meetings. The endless arguing over appropriate indicators for change in the status of the Great Lakes in the solec meetings was more tiresome than inspiring.

The environmental leadership no longer used the ijc biennial meetings as opportunities to rally members of their organizations around Great Lakes issues. Great Lakes Week in Washington became two separate Great Lakes days, one sponsored by the Great Lakes Commission, the other by the Northeast-Midwest Institute, without the organized lobbying led by the Sierra Club. Only a token number of nongovernmental environmental leaders attended either event.

At the start of the new millennium, the lakes seemed cleaner and less vulnerable to most of the public at large—an inexhaustible resource. Most people who live in the Great Lakes region were unaware of, or did not understand, the complex factors that caused continuing scientific concern about the future of the lakes. This meant that the kind of general public concern that had supported creation of the original Great Lakes Agreement no longer existed, and that its absence undermined the political will of the national governments to achieve the agreement's goals.

In the early years of the new millennium, few of the new political and environmental leaders had the same strong sense of shared purpose in a binational community around the water quality agreement that had accomplished so much in the 1980s. Now, more attention was being given to local issues such as beach closings and wetlands restoration than to basin-wide policy issues such as zero discharge. Many local environmental advocates were weary of what seemed to be a perpetual process to create Remedial Action Plans with no end in sight, although in some cases local citizen groups were using the process to push for local action.

News seemed to keep coming about the possibility of climate change and ecological collapse due to invasive species, but without the sense of urgency caused by the reports back in the 1960s that Lake Erie was dead and the Cuyahoga River on fire. The IAGLR public-policy project tried to recapture the old spirit of influencing policy by science with reports to explain major complex, continuing, and emerging new threats to policymakers, and convincing scientists to make themselves available as experts through the Internet. The reports are useful for reference, but do not appear to be stimulating action.

The role of the Binational Toxics Strategy in stimulating corporate action is difficult to document, but close observers agree that industry response to environmental concerns has been changing from automatic rejection to growing recognition that old methods of dealing with wastes and pollutants are not sustainable. Certainly it would have been difficult in the 1970s or 1980s to imagine DaimlerChrysler, Ford, and General Motors accepting the challenge to reduce PCBs in electrical equipment by 90 percent by 2006 as they have. Or that electric utilities and steel producers would be joining in.

Meanwhile, diversion again became a unifying issue among the states as the governors considered how to reinforce their authority to say no with Annex 2001 to the Great Lakes Charter. Ontario and Quebec were kept fully informed as the process proceeded. The leadership of Chicago's Mayor Richard Daley in organizing local governments for Great Lakes protection is another sign that subnational levels of government are no longer willing to leave action on Great Lakes problems up to the national governments.

The headline of a 21 April 2004 column in the *Toronto Star* was "Think Smaller to Solve Canada–U.S. Problems." The column cataloged a growing number of examples for how the provinces and states are working directly together across the border in "pragmatic relationships" that manage cooperative efforts better than can be done "by long distance from national capitals."

As the time approached for the next review of the Great Lakes Agreement, need for coordination (but the lack of it among the many disparate programs and efforts for restoration of the Great Lakes) was a new theme. It was the central message of the 2003 GAO report, and was echoed in a draft discussion paper prepared for the Council of Great Lakes Governors in 2004:

> The quality of life in the Great Lakes region depends on the quality of the Great Lakes themselves. The Great Lakes support competing activities and uses, including drinking water, tourism, commerce, recreation, economic development, and biological diversity . . . the Great Lakes could be better served through coordinating efforts among federal, state, local and binational policies and programs that serve these many uses.[47]

Clearly, the implementation processes of the Great Lakes Agreement were no longer providing the sense of community that had contributed so much to past successes. But the view expressed here suggests that it may be even more important in confronting the complex new threats. The coming review must encompass the importance of involving states, provinces, and local governments, as well as binationalism by the federal governments. In light of the steadily weakening capacity of the IJC to provide the common framework, it may even be necessary to consider an alternative arrangement for binational cooperation on behalf of the lakes.

EQUALITY AND PARITY

Like the Boundary Waters Treaty on which it is based, the Great Lakes Agreement assumes equality and parity between the parties in the structure of its institutions and their obligations. Each side has the same number of members on the IJC, the advisory boards, and any special task force, committee, or work group. Costs, such as for the Great Lakes Regional Office, are also shared equally for binational actions, though trust in this provision is currently threatened by the unilateral refusal of compliance by the chair of the U.S. section of the IJC.

The intention of the provision for equality is meant to assure equal respect when there is such disparity between the economic resources, political power, and population size of the United States and Canada. It may be more important psychologically to Canadians, but this principle is important to both sides because mutual respect helps maintain stability and commitment in the relationship.

Nearly all the governmental, private, and nongovernmental institutions and organizations in the Great Lakes community have sought to operate in accordance with this principle in the past. Both the IAGLR and GLU, for example, alternate their meetings between each country and divide governance responsibilities equally on their boards of directors. Meetings were even alternated in the mid-1980s study on progress under the agreement by the Royal Society of Canada and the National Research Council, and in the series of interuniversity seminars convened during the life of the agreement. The practice is even honored in processes not connected to the agreement, such as a joint meeting of planning associations of Ontario and Michigan in the early 1980s at Sault Ste. Marie, where daily sessions alternated on each side of the border.

The principle is also being applied in the joint activities of the parties separate from the ijc since the 1987 Protocol. There is equal participation in planning and preparing for the solec meetings, and the bec meets once a year in each country. The principle should continue to be applied in all activities pertaining to the Great Lakes to preserve the mutual respect and sense of community that are so valuable.

The differences in the roles of the provinces and the states in the governmental structures will complicate maintenance of equality and parity if a current trend of decentralization of responsibility from the federal governments continues. It is not considered in the proposed U.S. "restoration legislation" that would give state governors control of a new regional approach to planning and management of federal funding for the Great Lakes. The principle is also difficult to apply with the First Nations in Canada and tribal councils in the United States, who are increasingly seeking recognition of their status as separate sovereign entities. But equality and parity as well as binationalism remain important to maintaining the special relationship essential for restoration and protection of the Great Lakes.

Common Objectives

Common objectives adopted by both parties are another key feature of the agreement. Mutual respect allows each side to achieve the objectives under its own laws, management programs, and differing structures of government.

Each side can complain about the adequacy of the other's efforts without forcing acceptance of the same approach. Disagreement need not lead to a parting of the ways, and has not on the few occasions when individual officials have tried to impose their own ideas. In practice, this principle has allowed negotiation toward mutual agreement, and in some cases adoption by one party of the other's approach.

Canada, for example, adopted a national standard that reduced but did not eliminate phosphates from laundry detergents. In the United States, states and local governments banned all detergent phosphates, except in dishwashing compounds, for sanitary reasons.

The parties agreed that the difference was justified because of the much higher total loadings from the U.S. side. Both approaches served the common objective of reducing phosphorus loadings to the Great Lakes and achieving a one-milligram-per-liter effluent limit for large municipal sewage-treatment systems.

Canada moved toward the U.S. approach of setting specific limits for direct discharges of toxic chemicals in industrial effluents in Ontario with the pulp-and-paper industry. The change allowed Canada to continue to set effluent limits that are negotiated for each source in Canada, but set as minimum uniform national standards in the United States.

In other cases, both sides have taken essentially the same action in banning most uses and manufacture of DDT and PCBs. The bans are not required by the agreement, but serve its aims. Additional bans and phaseouts of uses of toxic contaminants have more acceptance in Canada than in the United States, where current policy tends to stress risk reduction rather than elimination of all use. Binationalism does not demand identical policies so long as actions are based on common goals and objectives and mutual respect.

Joint Fact-Finding

The water quality agreement applied the principle of the Boundary Waters Treaty in the requirements for joint fact-finding and research, though in a different way. Under the treaty, the fact-finding process is used on a case-by-case basis to respond to a reference or a request from the governments for advice on a specific problem. Study boards of experts provide their advice for the subject of a particular reference, and are then disbanded.

Technically, the executive agreement for the Great Lakes is a standing, or ongoing, reference, and the WQB and SAB are the boards of experts. The agreement obliges both sides to contribute to research and monitoring needs identified through the IJC, in addition to carrying out their own research programs. It also allows joint monitoring and research projects when both sides agree that they are needed or more efficient. The sense of community among the scientists, no matter where they work, is a valuable asset for the agreement process.

Joint fact-finding for the advisory boards formerly was generally coordinated through the Great Lakes Regional Office. The SAB is most likely to undertake a special fact-finding process similar to the way the ad-hoc expert boards operate for a reference. For example, such a fact-finding process was carried out on the human health effects of exposure to toxic contaminants, and on the cause-and-effect linkages between exposure to contaminants and the reproductive consequences for wildlife.[48] In another example, the WQB asked the SAB to help determine a list of critical pollutants.[49]

The agreement goes beyond the treaty in recognizing that ongoing research, not just short-term investigations of a specific problem, is needed to achieve the ultimate goals of water quality restoration and ecological integrity in such a large and complex system. It also calls for joint monitoring to measure progress toward meeting the agreement's objectives and to help identify new problems.

Research that serves agreement purposes is carried out by programs established to serve agreement needs, as well as by agencies not dedicated only to Great Lakes research. Most physical and biological research is funded by the federal, state, and provincial governments. Policy research (as well as advocacy and public education) is also funded by philanthropic foundations.

The Great Lakes National Program Office is a major source of funding for agreement-related research in the United States. The Great Lakes Protection Fund supports research for other Great Lakes purposes as well as the water quality agreement, such as the Annex 2001 project for the Great Lakes Charter. The mission of the Protection Fund is to support projects that identify, demonstrate, and promote regional action to enhance the health of the Great Lakes ecosystem.

All eight states now have Sea Grant programs at one or more public universities that support research and provide educational extension services. State universities in Minnesota, Wisconsin, Michigan, and New York all have major Great Lakes research programs that are linked to the government-funded Sea Grant centers. There is extensive cooperation in sharing the use of research vessels. In 2003, a new proposal was made to house several major Great Lakes research programs and agencies in a new building to be constructed in Ann Arbor, Michigan, with the lead being taken by the Great Lakes Environmental Research Laboratory of the National Oceanic and Atmospheric Administration.

The agreement directed that the regional office help coordinate research, but this function has been mainly limited to the inventory of agreement-related research periodically compiled by the Council of Great Lakes Research Managers. Efforts to maintain the binational GLISP monitoring program in the 1990s were eventually abandoned, but the International Atmospheric Deposition Network was expanded. One sign of the distance that was developing between the IJC and the governments in the 1990s was the lack of knowledge by the regional office staff of the huge multiyear Lake Michigan mass-balance study by the USEPA after it had been underway for five years.[50]

Joint fact-finding and research serves agreement purposes in several ways. First, just as joint fact-finding has enhanced the credibility and objectivity of the IJC throughout its history, it has generally provided an objective basis for IJC recommendations to the governments for the agreement. Even for the controversial recommendations on chlorine, the IJC had a large database about the effects of chlorinated compounds in the Great Lakes ecosystem.

Second, research has assisted accountability by identifying progress, or lack or progress, toward agreement objectives. Research confirmed slowing of eutrophication and reduction of toxic-contaminant levels, as well as reduction of their effects on living organisms, and continues to provide critical information about sources and ecological change, such as the role of invasive species.

Third, research identifies problems not previously recognized. Repeatedly, systemic problems found first in the Great Lakes, such as toxic contaminants, have subsequently been found elsewhere. This is why Great Lakes science is the basis for global action through the Stockholm Convention for Persistent Organic Pollutants that was negotiated under the auspices of the United Nations Environmental Program.

Fourth, research assists the flexibility that characterizes the Great Lakes regime and is essential to the goal of an ecosystem approach to management, identifying threats and changing conditions as they occur. Fifth, research is the basis for participation by scientists and integration of the research community into the larger Great Lakes community. Long-time Canadian environmentalist John Jackson reminded the SAB in September 2003 how much the willingness of scientists to work with citizen activists had earlier helped the activists to stimulate policymakers to act.[51]

Fact-finding has evolved with the regime and contributed to the development and acceptance of new concepts. The articulation of the need for an ecosystem approach to management responded to discoveries about toxic contaminants. The precautionary approach, now being applied globally, and the weight-of-evidence approach stimulated debate about how to make decisions in the face of incomplete knowledge.

Such policy innovations are contributions of the regime within and beyond the Great Lakes region, but the decline in the capacity of the IJC to collect and analyze data makes additional contributions uncertain. The change in the role of the WQB—from evaluator of government programs and progress toward meeting agreement objectives, to policy advisor to the IJC—created a gap in gathering and analyzing information. The question is who now assesses the adequacy of government efforts, or oversees data collection and monitors ecosystem integrity, since neither the IJC nor the governments are doing so.

The lack of oversight by the IJC for these tasks means that comprehensive information about the results of programs is not systematically gathered and shared within the regime. The information given to the IJC by the parties is no longer subject to the joint review of agency policymakers as a function of the WQB. Without the knowledge of programs that comes from interaction and exchange of information between the IJC staff and agency staffs, the IJC has little ability to assess the information that is provided.

The SOLEC events were meant to replace the WQB's former "state of the lakes" review, but they also do not provide assessment of programs. The results of the ongoing solec struggle to develop indicators for the state of the Great Lakes ecosystem have been unsatisfactory. The effort does not result in recommendations by the wqb to the ijc about deficiencies in programs, suggestions for changes, or possible new actions. Neither, to date, has the solec process provided meaningful information in a form that can be used by the news media to communicate the "state of the lakes" to the general public in a way that leads to appreciation for progress or reasons for deterioration.

This failure of communication may help explain why the 2003 gao report reflected such lack of appreciation for the real accomplishments of the existing Great Lakes regime, and at least in part the proposals to Congress for a new governance structure for Great Lakes cleanup and restoration. Neither the House nor the Senate bill included any measures for tracking, assessing, or reporting results of the proposed new arrangement in the United States, let alone to Canada, the other stakeholder in the health of the Great Lakes.

Flexibility and Adaptability

One of the most unusual characteristics of the Great Lakes Agreement is its built-in flexibility. Most international agreements are adopted to solve a specific problem or resolve a specific dispute. This feature is carried over from the Boundary Waters Treaty, and gives the parties the capacity to apply new knowledge and to adapt the objectives of the Great Lakes Agreement to changing circumstances. This flexibility also provides the opportunity for potential renewal and revitalization of the Great Lakes community and institutional arrangements to meet tomorrow's challenges rather than yesterday's.

The flexibility is the result of the periodic reviews of the agreement that are required to assess progress and to allow consideration of changes. The capacity for adaptability depends on the ongoing research and monitoring, and on open information exchange within the broad community, including political leaders. These features are critical for an ecosystem approach to management because they acknowledge that change is the most constant feature of both the natural and man-made environment.

Change includes identifying new problems and recognizing any that have been solved. New problems do not have to be addressed in the same way as in the past, and new approaches can be taken. This is why, after the earliest efforts to slow eutrophication were underway in the 1972 agreement and the seriousness of toxic contamination had been identified by research, the first required review after five years resulted in a very different version in 1978.

Again in 1987, review resulted in some changes in process without major change in objectives. The changes in Article x resulted from the desires of the parties to rely less on the ijc regional office for coordination, and from environmentalists' concerns about the need for greater accountability on the part of the governments for control of toxic contamination.

The next review should consider the results of those changes, including the consequences of the lead agencies working directly together through the BEC outside the IJC framework. It should also consider whether the SOLEC process is meeting the requirement for the parties to identify toxic substances that should be subject to "virtual elimination," and how the virtual-elimination goal will be sought.

The strong agreement that the annexes requiring development of RAPS and LAMPS should be revised is reflected in the minutes of the BEC meetings. The intention for RAPS was to involve local as well as state, provincial, and federal authorities with other stakeholders in meeting agreement objectives in geographic areas of concern. For some, the RAP process has resulted more in endless planning than remediation, except in a few locations.[52] Review of these requirements should take into account the local government interests in the Great Lakes Cities Initiative that was launched in 2003.

Progress has also been slow in the LAMP process, which was intended to achieve agreement objectives in the open waters of each lake. Attention should be given to the fact that a major outcome of the Lake Michigan and Lake Erie LAMPS is new watershed management planning in tributaries. This result recognizes that protection of water quality in the open lakes depends on land use in the drainage basin. This is only one example of outcomes and activities that raise the question of whether water quality alone should continue to be the focus of the agreement.

Another review topic should be the need for greater coordination among the multitude of Great Lakes programs that was stressed in the 2003 GAO report, and the resulting legislation that proposed to give states new leadership responsibilities for restoration of the Great Lakes. The ignoring of the agreement and the IJC in the legislation underscores the urgency for attention to institutional arrangements in the next review.

Changes in the institutional arrangements and their functions have been made by both the governments that are the parties and their lead agencies, and by the IJC. The governments politicized the appointment of IJC commissioners and undermined the commission's continuity of leadership and independence. The lead agencies substantially withdrew from the binational process envisioned in the agreement, and undermined the public involvement that is so important for stimulating the political will of the governments.

The IJC itself has reduced public participation by diminishing its efforts to disseminate public information, and with changes in the format of the biennial meetings. The IJC has also allowed changes in the functions of the advisory boards and diminished its own staff capabilities. The result has been loss of stature and respect for the IJC, which contributed to the reduced vigor of the agreement processes and the reduced involvement of the Great Lakes community in the 1990s. The opportunity for involvement of the entire Great Lakes community in evaluating the need for change depends on how the parties conduct the next review.

ACCOUNTABILITY AND OPENNESS

Several features of the Great Lakes Agreement are intended to foster accountability and openness, which in turn promote involvement and sense of community among many diverse interests. One such feature is the requirement for periodic review. Another is the requirement for regular progress reports by the advisory boards to the IJC and the IJC to the governments, to be followed by the governments' responses to the commission. All parts of this process are open to public scrutiny.

A third feature is the directive to the Great Lakes Regional Office to provide a public-information service for the programs of the agreement. Earlier, the IJC expanded the concept and the practice of providing public information to include active promotion of citizen participation in its biennial meetings. Beginning in the 1970s and extending into the 1990s, the IJC included representatives of environmental organizations, professional organizations, and industry on the SAB and as participants in special activities and events. Such participation has diminished since the mid 1990s.

In general, the governments have also maintained a policy of openness, including allowing observers to attend BEC and SOLEC meetings. They have not, however, actively sought or promoted public participation in these events.

The agreement itself requires accountability in several ways. Article VII requires at least biennial progress reports. Article IX is entirely concerned with "submission and exchange of information" between the IJC and the parties, and between the parties themselves. Full disclosure to the public has been the practice, but the public, including the environmental leadership, has paid less attention to IJC reports since the mid 1990s.

Efforts of the U.S. Congress to enhance accountability have been marginally successful. The General Accounting Office has made several special studies of progress over the life of the agreement. Congressional hearings have offered nongovernmental groups opportunity to testify about actions needed to further agreement objectives. At times, USEPA officials have been required to explain their programs, and testimony has been provided by IJC members, including Canadians.

Testimony on legislation intended to support agreement goals has also assisted accountability. Legislation such as the Clean Water Act and the Clean

Air Act has then required special reports from the USEPA to Congress, and in theory the public.

Unfortunately these reports to Congress have proved expensive to produce, are usually overdue, and because they concentrate more on what is being done by the bureaucracies rather than results, do not contribute to broad public understanding of the issues or programs.

In summary, the agreement's accountability mechanisms furthered the development of the binational community so critical to its success in the past, but have not been working so well in recent years. The scope and substance of the reports of the USEPA and Environment Canada to the IJC have been less ambitious since the 1987 Protocol. The SOLEC indicator reports have been both too complex and too simple to mean much to either the general public or the environmental community.

Lack of understanding by environmental leaders, the general public, and even by members of Congress of the changes in the roles of the parties (and the consequences) will inevitably lead to a decline in political support and available resources for the agreement. Making additional funding available for the Great Lakes without a binational process, as Congress is considering, will undermine the decades of experience and binational process inherent in the Great Lakes regime.

Challenges and Opportunities for the Regime

The past history of success for the Great Lakes regime is clearly at risk in the early years of the new millennium. Unless there are significant and rapid changes, the Great Lakes Agreement is at the brink of irrelevancy, and the Great Lakes themselves subject to an onslaught of existing and new threats without a binational regime in place to deal with them. Some of the uncertainties and challenges to the regime that suggest such risk to the Great Lakes Agreement include:

- Diminished political commitment and resources to the Great Lakes;
- Reduced political power of the Great Lakes community;
- Lack of implementation of current agreement;
- New threats to the Great Lakes;
- Decreased funding for science;
- Changes in the operations of the IJC and in the relationships between the IJC and the governments;
- Lack of communication with other international institutions.

Opportunities for the Great Lakes regime to confront the problems and reinvigorate its capacity include the possibility of building on the cohesion and determination exhibited in the process of obtaining agreement for Annex 2001 for the Great Lakes Charter, and the excitement generated by the introduction of the "restoration" legislation into the U.S. Congress. The coincidence of a required periodic review coming due and the renewal of the Canadian five-year plan for the Great Lakes makes it easier to contemplate possible changes in goals and objectives, and is useful even if existing goals are retained. Finally, the launching of the Biodiversity Project's "Great Lakes Forever" opens the opportunity to expand the understanding of the general public and generate new public concern that could translate into strengthening of the political will of the governments.

DIMINISHED POLITICAL COMMITMENT AND RESOURCES

Almost since adoption of the 1987 Protocol, there has been a gradual change in the relationship between the Great Lakes regime and the federal governments. By and large, neither Washington nor Ottawa retained into the 1990s the political commitment and priority for the Great Lakes that had prevailed earlier, despite the economic, social, and recreational importance of the resource. The withdrawal of agency effort from the IJC processes is a practical consequence, one which may also have contributed by undermining the sense of community that had bolstered the political will of the governments in the first two decades of the agreement.

The governments' diminished commitment to and overt complacency about the agreement then seems to have led to decreased capacity to address Great Lakes issues. In its Eighth Biennial Report, the IJC urged that government efforts to reduce regulatory burdens and spending "should not be allowed to . . . compromise the ability of Canada and the United States to meet their Agreement commitments."[53] In both countries, reductions in federal funding for environmental programs are related to struggles over weakening of federal environmental laws, and relinquishment of responsibility for environmental protection to state and provincial governments.

In earlier periods, conservative political trends that resulted in decreased fiscal resources and attention to Great Lakes priorities were in part countered by strong public involvement. The vigorous support of the Blue Group environmental consortium for the proposed U.S. restoration legislation is intended to increase funding for the Great Lakes, but comparable effort has not been devoted to the water quality agreement for some time.

In Canada, issues of national unity and fiscal concerns continue to distract from other issues. At the federal level, the 30 percent and greater recent reductions in the mid 1990s signaled an era of diminished commitment and attention to a host of environmental issues, with the Great Lakes at the top of the list. Many expressed hope that the election of Paul Martin as the new Canadian prime minister in 2004 would reverse the trend of the 1990s, and that he might seek new commitment to environmental protection, including for the Great Lakes.

In a way, the situation has been more dismal at the provincial level, with far more dramatic cuts: over a 30 percent reduction in staffing from the mid 1990s, without new reinvestment in recent years. Moreover, the Great Lakes, as an issue, left the radar screen in the mid 1990s, and the real significance of the new political attention remains to be seen. The newly elected Ontario premier, Dalton McGuinty, was slow to raise the profile or the resources of the Ministry of the Environment, with the exception of drinking-water issues following the Walkerton tragedy. In 2005, both levels of government continue to extol their fiscally conservative approaches.

In the United States, effects for the Great Lakes of the reductions for environmental programs in general may not be so obvious. Still, diminished attention to agreement processes by environmental organizations in the mid 1990s meant less effort on behalf of the Great Lakes until the Legacy Act of 2002. The trend toward a "new federalism" that began in the 1980s is reflected in how the USEPA began deferring more to the states for implementation and enforcement of environmental laws from the early 1990s to the present. Funding reductions threatened research programs in the 1990s, and could do so again.[54] As already observed repeatedly, these issues were not addressed in the restoration legislation introduced to Congress in 2003. The U.S. Great Lakes Legacy Act in 2002 was not followed by significant increase in funding, not even anything near what the law had called for. The lack of political commitment to the Great Lakes Agreement within the states and the nongovernmental community raises serious warning signals for the future of the existing Great Lakes regime.

LACK OF IMPLEMENTATION

As new scientific evidence confirms the potential threat to human health by chemicals that affect hormonal systems, and other implications of toxic exposure even at very low levels, toxic contamination continues as the major current water quality issue. Industry continues to oppose the regulatory approaches for toxic substances proposed by the governments.[55] However, as that battle continues, new substances are being found in the Great Lakes that were not recognized as problems in the past. Hence, although major progress has been made, issues remain with ongoing loadings and toxic legacies, such as contaminated sites and sediments.

There are even new questions about conventional pollution. Questions are being raised about an appropriate balance of phosphorus inputs to maintain the productivity of the fishery.[56] Although reversing eutrophication is the greatest success to date under the Great Lakes Agreement, the 1996 SOLEC working paper on nearshore waters said that "Human sewage effluent in the lakes will be a management issue for the foreseeable future" because of population growth and the need to control combined sewer overflows in cities.[57]

Many aspects of the Great Lakes Agreement remain to be implemented. The RAPS, the LAMPS, air deposition, and contaminated sediments cannot be considered "dealt with" yet under the agreement. The challenge is that many policymakers, some of the public, and the news media assume that cleanup and restoration is complete, or that perhaps it is not feasible to make any further progress. In any case, the momentum for action slowed in the 1990s and must be increased.

NEW THREATS TO THE GREAT LAKES

While progress is still needed against toxic contamination, many additional issues now occupy the attention of government officials and the environmental community. Loss of habitat is recognized as being due to land use as well as pollution, but neither country has yet successfully controlled pollution from nonpoint sources.[58] Fisheries continue to decline as exotic species compete with native species and affect water quality in ways that some scientists expect to cause more profound change in the aquatic ecosystem than has occurred from any other cause.[59] Climate change is now considered a significant issue for the Great Lakes that requires serious attention.

REDUCED POLITICAL POWER OF THE GREAT LAKES COMMUNITY

The political power of the Great Lakes community was reduced in the 1990s as environmental groups in both countries struggled with organizational issues, and the general public had less understanding of current complex environmental issues. Jane Elder, director of the Sierra Club Great Lakes Program and a leader in legislative and lobbying activities in the 1980s, thinks that mistrust of government is another factor in lower participation in efforts to affect policies in the 1990s. She says that research shows a link between a decline in political activism among young adult members of the Sierra Club and a lack of belief in government's capacity to solve social problems.[60]

Other reasons that attention to the Great Lakes does not have the political urgency of previous decades may be a complacency that the improvements made are sufficient, without recognition of the significant needs that still must be met, or of the new and emerging threats to the lakes. In comparison to the 1980s and early 1990s, the news media have focused less on Great Lakes issues in recent years. Journalists that had a long history with Great Lakes issues are either retired, or no longer pursue this topic because they have been given other assignments. Paul McClennan in Buffalo has retired, Doug Draper who was with the *St. Catharine's Standard* worked for GLU, and neither Brian McAndrew with the *Toronto Star* nor Casey Bukro at the *Chicago Tribune* still cover Great Lakes issues.

All of these factors have contributed to the lack of attention, profile, and influence of Great Lakes issues in Washington, Ottawa, and the state and provincial legislatures. A hopeful sign may be the formation of a new communication network among members of state legislatures for sharing of information about legislation needed for the Great Lakes. The network was inspired in part by the work on the proposed Annex 2001 for the Great Lakes Charter, and in part by the introduction of the restoration legislation to Congress.

STRAINED CAPACITY OF THE NONGOVERNMENTAL COMMUNITY

One of the key changes in the past decade is the increase of demands on the nongovernmental community coupled with its declining or static capacity. Many environmental groups struggled to maintain funding and leadership during the 1990s in the face of decreased public and governmental concern for the environment. In the 1990s and early into this century, no single issue united the Great Lakes community or triggered public concern.

None of the environmental organizations has the staff capacity to track all of the planning, research, and other processes now underway for restoration of the Great Lakes. Keeping track of the activities of Great Lakes agencies is virtually impossible for volunteer members of the advocacy organizations. This may be part of the reason that there has been a strong trend in the latest phase of the Great Lakes Agreement for local action against sources of contamination or for restoration of natural areas, but limited attention to basin-wide issues or policies. The recent situation can be contrasted with Great Lakes United leadership across the border in opposition to diversion of Great Lakes water and toxic contamination in the 1980s, the period when the IJC biennial meetings were major occasions for gathering and communication for the Great Lakes community, and a forum for expression of opinion by citizens.

In Canada, many environmental groups spend much less energy on Great Lakes issues than a decade ago. Some groups remain active on Great Lakes issues, but have their attention continually drawn to other issues such as deregulation and trade.

In the United States, some Great Lakes environmental leaders of the 1980s moved on to new national positions.[61] Many environmental organizations had difficulty sustaining adequate funding, with major staff turnover. In 1996 the board of directors of the Charles Stewart Mott and other foundations considered whether to continue the support that had been essential to expanding the capacity of the regime in the 1980s. Fortunately, the major foundations continued their support, especially the Joyce and Mott foundations. The Joyce Foundation stresses support for activities that affect regional policy, while the Mott Foundation stresses capacity building for environmental groups and support for local restoration projects. The state of the economy in both countries reduced foundation resources, and there has not seemed to be as much support available to assist public education and nongovernmental involvement as there had been earlier, especially in light of the complexity of the issues.

DECREASED EMPHASIS ON SCIENCE

Scientists and others are concerned about the future of the research programs because of funding cuts that interfere not only with current activities but the education of future researchers.[62] In both countries, funding for research and science has continued to decrease. One official noted that funding for the Great Lakes basin is less than for any other basin in Canada.[63] Congressional authorization of funding for the Florida Everglades was a major inspiration for the new legislation proposed in 2003.

WITHDRAWAL OF THE LEAD AGENCIES FROM THE IJC

The challenges facing the Great Lakes also come from within the regime. A major cause in the first half of the 1990s was diminished interaction between the IJC and the lead agencies, and confusion about the roles and mandates of the advisory boards. Both factors seem to have weakened the binational process that has been a major strength of the regime.

Issues that have been raised are whether the lead agencies have sufficient commitment to the IJC processes, whether the IJC is able to get the relevant information from the governments in order to properly assess progress under the agreement, and the lack of attention by the lead agencies to the IJC recommendations and their uncertain willingness to implement them. In any case, the governments are relying less on the IJC generally, as evidenced by the very few references to the IJC in recent years.

Some scientists, government agency personnel, IJC staff, and environmentalists have expressed doubts about whether the emerging new institutions of the parties, such as the BEC and SOLEC, also generally undermine the interaction in the larger community that was an earlier strength of the regime. In effect, there are now two parallel processes within the Great Lakes regime. One process pertains to the traditional IJC functions of assessment of progress under the agreement with the assistance of its advisory boards, while the other process is led by the governments in the BEC and SOLEC processes.

Lack of Communication with Other International Institutions

Another external uncertainty that could affect the regime is the establishment of the Commission for Environmental Cooperation for North America without any consideration of a role for the ijc.[64] Toxic contamination, pollution prevention, and air quality are overlapping issues that concern both agencies. Even though the cec uses Great Lakes experience and information in dealing with toxic contamination, to date there has been little formal coordination between the two agencies.

Another issue is whether and how the Great Lakes region will contribute to implementation of the objectives of the Stockholm Convention for Persistent Organic Pollutants. Virtual elimination of toxic contamination requires action at every level of political jurisdiction; neither the ijc nor the governments to date have considered possible linkage between the binational and global efforts.

Emerging Opportunities for Revitalization of the Regime

In summary, emerging opportunities for revitalization within the regime include:

- Upcoming review of the GLWQA and apparent consensus to consider the need for change;
- The willingness of the governors and premiers to come together around the 2001 Annex to the Great Lakes Charter;
- Inclusion of the NGO community in development of the annex;
- New desire of local governments to participate;
- Revived Congressional interest in the Great Lakes;
- Re-energizing of the Blue Group around the restoration legislation;
- The public-education and information campaign by the Biodiversity Project; and
- High degree of public support for Great Lakes initiatives.

Three Questions for the Future

For continuing future progress, all of these new circumstances must be confronted by the community that is most responsible for past successes.[65] Three major questions confront the Great Lakes community for the future of the Great Lakes Agreement and the Great Lakes themselves:

- How can the community come together to restore the political will of the governments for restoration and protection of the Great Lakes ecosystem?

- Will the integrity of the Great Lakes Agreement be maintained in the review by the governments that began in 2005?
- If the agreement is no longer functional, what changes can be made to restore its vitality or apply the experience it provided in developing a new regime to carry on the task of restoring and protecting the Great Lakes?

Given the finding here that successes under the agreement have depended on the community that has participated in its implementation to date, the answers to these questions seem to depend on the willingness and ability of the community to seek the answers.

CHAPTER 8

A VISION FOR RENEWAL OF THE GREAT LAKES REGIME

NEITHER THE UNITED STATES NOR CANADA CAN SAVE THE GREAT LAKES without the other's help. Since 1972 the Great Lakes Water Quality Agreement has confirmed the special relationship between these neighbors and fostered a powerful binational community committed to its goals. In the review of the Great Lakes Water Quality Agreement (to begin in 2005), the governments of the United States and Canada must decide whether to strengthen or to abandon this foundation for a binational regime that is essential for cleanup and restoration of the world's largest freshwater ecosystem.

A strong agreement will keep the fundamental goal of ecological restoration and bind the governments to achieve objectives agreed to by both sides as necessary for water quality protection. A renewed agreement is needed to expand coordination of scientific research and to monitor both environmental conditions and programs. It can provide the framework for improved exchange of information and the consideration of needed actions by government at all levels, and define the relative roles of federal, state, provincial, and local agencies. Perhaps most importantly, a renewed agreement could revitalize a binational sense of community and mobilize the political will of the governments, which would provide the most hope for a good future for the Great Lakes.

In the end, the past 33 years of the Great Lakes Agreement has taught us one thing—the agreement has been effective and remains the essential foundation for what has been referred to as the Great Lakes community. This is not the time to start from scratch by undertaking a review and assuming there is a need for a *new* agreement. Instead, it is a time to undertake a review and assume that the basic structure, overall goal, governing principles, and essential features of the existing agreement are sound. What is needed is a *renewed* agreement that may include some updating of the wording in the agreement;

updating, revising and adding to the annexes; and most important, a re-affirmation of the political and resource commitment to implement the agreement. A renewed agreement is the key to future preservation of the Great Lakes and the community that seeks to protect it.

The Need for Review

Past experience explains why review of the Great Lakes Agreement is needed. The regime it created succeeded in reversing eutrophication and then turned to reducing the levels of toxic contaminants, following the first review. A binational approach in the new millennium is just as essential for dealing with invasive species, cleanup of contaminated sediments, habitat restoration, potential consequences of climate change, and other likely threats not yet recognized.

In the 1990s the U.S. Environmental Protection Agency and Environment Canada withdrew from the institutional arrangements managed by the International Joint Commission as the lead agencies for the governments. The resulting fragmentation within the regime undermined a binational approach to Great Lakes governance. Yet the governments, the research community, the nongovernmental advocacy organizations, and the business community on both sides appear to remain united behind the agreement's visionary goal of ecological integrity. This unity of purpose provides the basis for evaluation of lessons learned from the regime's history, and improvement of its capacity.

The governments will review the agreement because they are required to do so under Article x. The nature and scope of the review as proposed in early 2005 seems to be properly founded on the desire for the review to be comprehensive and inclusive. What really matters, however, is how the governments intend to approach the agreement's relevance.

The parties also have the option of serving notice of intent to terminate the agreement. Outright abandonment of the agreement is unlikely, but there is danger that the governments could seek changes that would further undermine the agreement's effectiveness as a driver of domestic policy. In other words, complacency and the lack of appreciation for the importance of the agreement can be just as damaging as outright abandonment. The lack of the recognition of the binational character of the Great Lakes in the restoration legislation pending before the U.S. Congress is evidence of this fear.

The shared understanding of the need for restoration of the chemical, physical, and biological integrity that the agreement calls for may be clear, but how to achieve it is not. An open and comprehensive review of the agreement is needed to confirm commitment to the vision of restored integrity, and to consider how to improve the implementation. A review would not assume maintenance of existing institutions and processes, but would provide the opportunity for desirable change.

Criteria for Evaluation

Review, or evaluation, requires criteria for assessing results. There are five key criteria suggested for evaluation, emanating from a review of the history of the agreement.

The fundamental criterion is whether a specific objective, an institution, or a process furthers the key overall objective of the agreement—namely, the goal of *the restoration and protection of the physical, chemical or biological integrity of the Great Lakes.* Implicit in this criterion is evaluation of whether the programs are efficient in use of resources.

As an executive agreement under the Boundary Waters Treaty, the second criterion is that the agreement must be consistent with the original purpose to prevent disputes and to maintain an equal partnership in management of shared water resources. Binationalism is the key feature of the institutional arrangements and the processes called for in the treaty, including the function of the International Joint Commission as an independent agency relied on by the governments for objective expert advice. Binationalism within the IJC is likely the reason that the IJC has never been called on to resolve a dispute concerning waterways that cross the boundary since the treaty was signed in 1909. Evidence that binationalism is faltering within the IJC requires that the review address this important element for the "special relationship" in the institutional function of the IJC.

A third essential criterion is that the agreement should reflect the political will of the governments. The agreement will remain valuable only as long as the governments are committed to achieving its goals. The dependence of governmental commitment on the concerns of citizens underscores the need for a review that is open and inclusive enough not only to test, but possibly reinforce, the political will of both governments.

A fourth important criterion is whether there are sufficient measures of accountability of all actors within the regime to ensure that the mechanisms of the agreement will continue to work long after the completion of the review.

Fifth, there has to be confidence in, and reliance upon, the institutions that serve the agreement. The establishment of parallel institutions outside the agreement process following the 1987 Protocol raises questions about the governments' understanding of, and commitment to the institutions.

What If There Had Been No Great Lakes Agreement?

Without the Great Lakes Water Quality Agreement, the "dead zone" in Lake Erie would likely have continued to expand, and the walleye fishing would not have improved in the 1980s. By now, Lake Michigan and Lake Ontario might also have their own dead zones due to ongoing excessive phosphorus loadings.

Pollution from Saginaw Bay probably would have spread into Lake Huron, and Lake Superior would not have been protected from the eutrophication experienced elsewhere in the system. Farmers both inside and outside the Great Lakes basin might still be spending more for energy to plow their fields, and losing more soil than they do now with the conservation tillage that was first initiated to reduce fertilizer runoff into Lake Erie.

The world would not have learned so much or so quickly about how persistent organic pollutants can destroy ecological integrity and damage human health without the research that the agreement fostered in the Great Lakes. It is unlikely that China or Russia or any country in Africa would have recognized by now on their own the processes of atmospheric deposition and long-range transport of PCBs and their chemical cousins.

Polar bears and the Inuit people in the Arctic would be in even more danger without the understanding in the Great Lakes of how contaminants can be released from sediments and cycled through the water into the air and back again, to be deposited ultimately in the cold north. People in Mexico and Central America would still be using DDT to control malaria mosquitoes

---

Recommendations for the Review Process

The Great Lakes Agreement is clear that the required periodic review must be carried out by the parties to suit their own purposes. It would also be consistent with the spirit and the principles of the Boundary Waters Treaty for the parties to request advice and assistance. Four issues should be considered:

- Whether a third independent party should be requested to review progress under the agreement to date, and to advise whether substantive changes are needed.
- An advisory role for the ɪJC in the review process.
- How to involve the Great Lakes community and the general public.
- Recognition that the review does not mandate renegotiation of goals and objectives.

A Possible Third Party Independent Review

In 1985, the Royal Society of Canada and the National Academy of Sciences of the United States carried out a joint comprehensive review that fed into the

without the alternatives inspired by Great Lakes research. Who knows how many more kids would grow up everywhere with less capacity to learn because the global burden of persistent organic pollutants kept growing and growing and growing? And perhaps bald eagles would be long gone.

How many wetlands are being restored and natural areas preserved because the agreement calls for an ecosystem approach to management?

Would Asian carp already be in the Great Lakes without the intense attention to invasive species made possible by quick exchange of Great Lakes data between scientists and governments?

Would citizens in Canada and the United States be working together to convince their governments to adopt the policies and laws and to spend the money necessary to protect the largest freshwater system on the globe?

Would there be a Great Lakes community of environmentalists, scientists, industry, and governments at every level working together peacefully toward the same goals and objectives? And how would they know what to do?

And ultimately, would the Great Lakes still look as blue from outer space as they do now? It will be better to keep the agreement than to risk finding out.

It could be argued that the failures for Great Lakes cleanup and protection that were stressed in the 2003 General Accounting Office report are evident because of the research, monitoring, and information exchange that occur because of the Great Lakes Agreement. Certainly one of its contributions is the ongoing monitoring that brought quick attention to problems and even some solutions. A renewed and strengthened binational agreement will continue that tradition.

1987 negotiation process. The review focused on progress toward virtual elimination of toxic contaminants but also addressed institutional issues and the challenge of an ecosystem approach to management.

Another independent review would both assist the parties in addressing the complex issues resolved and enhance the credibility of the final outcome. Otherwise, the parties' lead agencies are in the position to, in effect, review their own performance; an awkward position that has caused difficulty in the agreement process in the past.

Conceivably, the Royal Society and National Academy could be requested to facilitate a third party review again. One advantage of this option is consistency with the operating principles of both the Boundary Waters Treaty and the Great Lakes Agreement of seeking advice from a binational panel of experts and reliance on science. Another advantage is that both institutions exist to serve their governments and can mobilize expertise to carry out the independent review for such a process.

Creation of a special panel, rather like a study board for a reference by the governments to the IJC, could be a second option. An equal number of members with appropriate professional capacity and knowledge could be appointed by each side.

In either case, the reviewing agency should be given a definite mandate and clear terms of reference covering the following elements:

- Overall objectives, including the scope of the review.
- The time frame for completion.
- Specific issues to be addressed, with discretion to add additional topics.
- Appropriate resources.
- Consultation with participants in the Great Lakes community and opportunity for public comments.
- Specific reporting requirements.

An Advisory Role for the IJC

The IJC can provide advice to the parties in connection with the review but should not lead the review and cannot serve as an independent third party. The structure, responsibilities, and performance of the agreement institutions, including the IJC, are topics for the review. The reason being that the agency would have as much difficulty as the parties in critically analyzing its own behavior.

The analytical difficulty would be compounded by the lack of confidence in the IJC that the governments have demonstrated by their withdrawal from IJC processes and the diminished stature of the IJC within the Great Lakes community. In any case, any independent reviewers should receive cooperation from the IJC and its staff as well as from the agencies of the parties.

The review process proposed in early 2005 stated that the governments will direct the IJC to solicit public input that "preserves the integrity and independence of the commission and respects the mandate and stature of the IJC." It is not clear at this time if additional responsibilities will be given to the IJC.

Public Participation in the Review

The agreement does not require consultation with the public in the periodic reviews, but making the public part of the review process is consistent with the agreement's recognition of the importance of public understanding and involvement. The definition of "the public" should not be limited to selected stakeholders and environmental leaders. Efforts should be made to inform and engage a larger public, a process that can be assisted both by the governments and by environmental organizations.

It is more feasible to engage the public in identification of broad goals and major issues than in evaluation of specific requirements and precise wording. The growing number of statements of goals for the Great Lakes from within the broad community offer additional sources for the formal reviewers to consider as public values and concerns. They include, for example, the Great Lakes United Green Book, the nine priorities of the Council of Great Lakes Governors, the Great Lakes Commission's seven major goals, the Annex 2001 to the Great Lakes Charter and its aim of ecological improvement, any restoration plans such as the so-called Regional Collaboration being developed in response to a presidential executive order, as well as any state plans that may be developed in response to the proposed restoration legislation of the U.S. Congress.

Issues for the Review

The Great Lakes Agreement is more than 30 years old and has not been significantly changed since 1987. To the credit of its drafters, the agreement requires review approximately every six years, but does not require negotiation of an entirely new agreement with every review. Review and renegotiation should be recognized as separate issues in all review activities. A determination of whether the agreement should be renegotiated or left alone cannot be made until a review has been completed. At that point, there are a number of options.

- The agreement can be left as it is;
- The agreement can be renewed; or
- The agreement can be renegotiated *de novo*.

  Whether renegotiation is needed will depend on results of the formal review. The history, analysis, and observations in this book suggest that there is a good case for the renewal of the Great Lakes Agreement and not a renegotiation. In other words, changes can be made for specific improvements without a fundamental renegotiation of the agreement itself. A *renewed agreement* should not be confused with a *new agreement*. In the former instance, the essential objectives, principles, and features are kept with perhaps some updating and certainly strengthening aspects of the agreement, its annexes, and its institutions.

  With this in mind, the following five recommendations identify critical issues and suggest possible ways to strengthen the process.

- The ecological vision and binational character of the existing agreement should be affirmed.
- The scope of the agreement should remain focused on water quality, although there should be recognition of the new stresses on water quality

including climate change, invasive species, loss of biodiversity, and land use.

- There should be an evaluation of the effectiveness of institutions established by the agreement under the purview of the International Joint Commission as well as specific objectives, programs, and accountability processes.
- The relationship between the processes required by the agreement and the external processes established by the governments should be examined.
- Criteria for evaluating the effectiveness of restoration efforts should be adopted.

Affirmation of the Goal

No serious challenge has been made to the ecological vision for the Great Lakes that is not already articulated in the Great Lakes Agreement itself: "*to restore and maintain the chemical, physical and biological integrity of the waters of the Great Lakes Basin Ecosystem*" Some critics would like to remove the words "of the waters" in hopes of broadening the scope of this vision. With the ecosystem approach, however, the effect is the same; the interconnection between the air, water and land as well as wildlife and humans is acknowledged as the reason that all parts of the environment have to be protected in order to protect the waters properly.

Add New Policy Goals

Continuing commitment to the goals and objectives of the Great Lakes agreement by the parties, by the diverse membership of the Great Lakes community, and with the support of the public at large can provide the foundation for restoring the sense of community that seemed to fade during the 1990s. Restoration of the sense of community, and thereby fostering the political will of the national governments, requires that the common goals of the agreement be reflected in Great Lakes institutions. A key challenge is to ensure development and acceptance of new goals and objectives that provide the ecological guideposts for the regime. The importance of these common goals and objectives in the past is instructive for future discussions.

The 1978 Agreement broke new ground in articulating the goal of "virtual elimination" in an international agreement for the purposes of pursuing chemical integrity of the waters of the Great Lakes. This policy goal should remain since it is now integral to both the domestic law of Canada and the U.S. and international law under the Stockholm Convention.

With the goal of virtual elimination for persistent toxic substances, new objectives should be established for substances that were not known to be concern and are now threats to the Great Lakes. If the agreement is extended to address climate change, air toxics, invasive species, or whatever, innovative and ambitious goals should also be established. The Great Lakes should continue as the region where policy innovation is allowed to flourish and inspire decision-makers both in North America and globally.

It can, however, be foreseen that new innovations can also be incorporated into the agreement. The agreement should reflect policy trends, but also set the foundation for innovation as it has done in the past. Consideration should be given to incorporating such policies as:

- The precautionary principle: This policy would expressly give guidance to decision makers to take precautionary measures where there is uncertainty of science;
- Watershed planning: This approach has already taken hold in many jurisdictions within the basin and there is a need to integrate and expand within the basin;
- Pollution prevention and materials use policy; Although these terms are inherent within the goal of virtual elimination, many jurisdictions have attempted to impose measures to prevent pollution, address the use of existing toxic chemicals and investigate how to deal with toxic substances in everyday products.

SCOPE OF THE AGREEMENT

A threshold issue is how to best achieve existing goals and objectives, and how to address and respond to the onslaught of new and emerging issues. It is this question which has sparked so much debate on the possible scope and content of a new agreement. The many new and emerging issues include:

- Atmospheric deposition of persistent toxic contaminants from within and outside the watershed;
- Combined overflows and nonpoint source pollution;
- Increased urbanization, shoreline development, and wetlands loss;
- Water export, diversion, conservation, and other water quantity issues;
- Exotic and invasive species; and
- The presence of new chemicals not previously identified.

Some are convinced that the new perceptions about the nature of the Great Lakes problems and solutions demand a new agreement altogether. They argue that the Great Lakes Agreement should be transformed into a "sustainability agreement" and broadened to incorporate provisions to respond to the kinds of issues noted above.

The Great Lakes Agreement must continue to focus on water quality and retain its present scope. Some of the new and emerging issues can be encompassed under the goal of an "ecosystem approach" to the management of the existing agreement using the flexibility that requires periodic review and allows changes in specific objectives. The ecosystem approach as a foundation to the agreement recognizes the interconnection between air, water and land as well as wildlife and humans. The agreement, though updated and possibly with new annexes, can both retain the focus on water quality and address many other issues affecting the Great Lakes. Other issues may have to be addressed through the development of new international, binational, and/or domestic legislative and policy initiatives (although they could be recognized and coordinated through the Great Lakes Agreement). The legal vehicle by which commitments are made is not as important as the fact that there are commitments by all levels of government, and that there is coordination of those commitments.

REVIEW OF INSTITUTIONS

A review of the agreement should include attention to the effectiveness of the processes and institutions established by the agreement. The issue includes the purpose, scope, and content of the provisions for joint processes and institutions, whether they help achieve the goals, and the performance of the parties.

The 1987 Protocol called for Remedial Action Plans in local areas of concern to support development of Lakewide Management Plans now underway in accordance with the Protocol. They were intended to achieve "virtual elimination" and thereby restore 14 beneficial uses that the IJC identified as due to the presence of toxic contaminants. While accepted in some communities, the results of the RAPS have been uneven and, in many cases, meager. Meanwhile, the little attention given to virtual elimination in SOLEC and the decline of attention to agreement-related issues in the environmental community means that the relationship between goals of institutions and processes within the regime are not always as clear as in the past.

Frustration with the RAP process and the lack of definitive results is shared by participants at the local areas of concern who are weary of endless meetings without results, and by provincial and state governments who did not continue support when federal funding declined. The 2003 General Accounting Office report cited the seeming lack of success with RAPS as a reason for a new approach to Great Lakes cleanup.

The broad goals of the Great Lakes Agreement should be integrated into Great Lakes restoration plans that the states would develop should Congress approve the pending restoration legislation. Watershed planning initiatives now being widely discussed should be vigorously examined as a key innovation within a renewed agreement. As such, the relationship between RAPS and watershed management planning regimes should be closely studied.

Evaluation should also include whether the states and local governments will accept goals and objectives established in a binational agreement provided they are given adequate funding and participate in developing the goals and objectives. Experience demonstrates greater success when the goals and objectives are accepted than when they are imposed as in the RAP and LAMP process.

CONTINUITY AND COMPETENCE OF THE IJC

The performance of the IJC in carrying out the processes for which it is responsible, including working with the advisory boards and the parties and providing information to the general public, should be reviewed. The importance of attention to the function of the boards and the IJC is underscored by the establishment by USEPA and Environment Canada of separate institutions independent of the IJC with functions that parallel those of the Water Quality and Science Advisory boards.

These actions suggest dissatisfaction with the IJC processes that seems to be a factor in the decline in vitality of the Great Lakes community in the 1990s and current attitudes within and outside government toward the IJC. The IJC should in turn evaluate its own role in maintaining the effectiveness of its institutions.

The IJC must retain its essential role as an overseer to the workings and progress under the agreement. However, mechanisms must be put in place to ensure it can better perform this role. Revamping of its board structure, understanding better the roles of its internal components (such as the regional office) and affirming basic operating principles (such as parity and binationalism) will go a long way to ensuring effectiveness and restoring confidence in this institution.

RELATIONSHIP BETWEEN PARTIES AND IJC

The ostensible purpose of the Binational Executive Committee was to strengthen the relationship between the agencies of the parties and the IJC by facilitating information exchange. The BEC now serves as a policy forum for government agencies. The original stated purpose of State of the Lakes Ecosystem Conference was to facilitate reporting on progress by providing information need by the IJC to make its biennial reports to the governments. SOLEC now seems to function in part as the IJC advisory boards did formerly, although differently and perhaps not as well.

The cost of participation in IJC boards and report preparation was stated as a reason for withdrawal from the IJC processes. The lead agencies for the parties should evaluate whether it is efficient and less costly to operate the BEC, SOLEC and the Binational Toxics Strategy independently of the IJC agreement-related processes.

BEC meetings include ongoing complaints and discussion about the reporting requirements of the agreement. Meanwhile, the U.S. Congress requires reporting from the USEPA that overlaps the reporting function of the parties to the IJC. Under the agreement, the original purpose of the reports of the WQB and the SAB on special activities including workshops and conferences was to inform the general public as well as regime participants about results of programs. Congress intended to increase accountability for results in the required reports, but the documents have largely consisted of lists of actions taken rather than results.

The growing multiplicity of reports has not demonstrably increased understanding of Great Lakes problems by the general public. It seems doubtful that very many environmental leaders actually read all of them. Clarification is needed of the relationship of the reports between the BEC and the WQB, between SOLEC and the SAB, and between the biennial reports to Congress and other reports, such as those required by Congress under the Clean Air and Clean Waters acts.

The governments should evaluate the consequences of their withdrawal from the processes managed by the IJC and the establishment of new separate joint institutions in the 1990s by considering the following criteria:

- Will the governments rely on the agreement institutions as being credible and effective?
- Will these institutions have the mandate and terms of reference to assess both the conditions of the Great Lakes and the programs of the governments?
- Will the public view the institutions as credible and effective and will representatives of the public have a meaningful role in them?
- Does a given institution duplicate or compete with existing institutions and is it truly needed?
- Is the institutional arrangement efficient? Does this arrangement improve communication between the lead federal agencies and state, provincial and local governments?

The governments must also ask themselves whether their policies, such as withdrawal of funding to the states, contributed to the disappointments of the Remedial Action Plan process and the slowness in development of the Lakewide Management Plans. If they were to conclude, however, that local watershed management plans are a better way to serve the Great Lakes, the review offers an opportunity to eliminate the RAP process.

The failure to provide adequate information to enable the IJC to carry out its responsibilities for evaluation of programs is still another example of friction and failure of communication between the parties and the independent agency. The result is a lack of evaluation in recent years that would assist the governments or the public in understanding the results of the programs.

Improving the Capacity of the IJC to Acquire and Use Information

Experience in slowing eutrophication and later in understanding the consequences of the presence of toxic contaminants confirmed the value of the joint fact-finding principle that was first adopted in the 1909 Boundary Waters Treaty. It remains essential for avoiding conflicts, identifying problems, and finding mutually acceptable and doable solutions for the more complex environmental problems that exist across the Canada–U.S. boundary today, especially the virtual elimination of toxic contaminants.

Since the WQB is no longer charged with evaluation of the adequacy of agency programs, the IJC now depends on information provided directly by the lead agencies to the federal governments. As a result, the IJC does not receive enough information to fulfill its function of regularly providing independent reporting on progress and the adequacy of programs for achieving the objectives of the agreement.

Lack of information developed jointly through the IJC may also be undermining coherence of the regime due to lack of coordination in identifying issues and priorities. The IJC should inform the parties about the information it needs and be able to obtain it.

A special annex that identifies the information, data, and monitoring required by the IJC and its boards, how it should be collected, and on what timelines, would help meet this need. It would provide a more coherent framework for SOLEC and add certainty and clarity which would allow all interests to work toward the same ends. If the review determines that IJC is not to retain its evaluative role, then alternative means of evaluation and accountability must be determined.

Assuring Continuity and Competence for the IJC

Politicization of the appointment of commissioners is an institutional problem for the IJC. During most of its history, including the time since the adoption of the agreement in 1972, commissioners have been appointed as needed. There were seldom more than one or two vacancies at a time. Although some appointments were made as rewards for political service, the practice was also to consider relevant professional competence and knowledge.

The consequence of the practice that began in 1980, on both sides, of replacing the entire membership with each change of administration of the federal governments has resulted in long gaps in membership that have contributed to lack of leadership and continuity. As in any other institution, the absence of leadership at the policy level leaves staff without direction and with a loss of institutional memory. This situation at the IJC has compounded uncertainty about how the IJC staff could or should respond to changes in relationship between the IJC and the lead government agencies following the adoption of the 1987 Protocol.

The practice has also increased the agencies' lack of confidence in the competence of the IJC. Using appointments as patronage awards has undermined the tradition of independence by the IJC and decision making by consensus by the members in their personal and professional capacity without regard to national concerns. Setting terms for membership that do not coincide with national elections would not alone strengthen the stature of the IJC, but this measure should be considered along with other measures to strengthen the role of the IJC in the regime. At a minimum, the governments should stagger appointments to the IJC in order to assure continuity, stability, and leadership by the commissioners.

Benefits of Binationalism, Equality, and Parity

Its binational character is a major strength of the Great Lakes regime, and with the joint fact-finding approach to problems, a major source of its credibility. Whether intended or not, the establishment of new parallel institutions outside the IJC has undermined its binationalism and led to regression to bilateralism. Furthermore, the language added to Article X in the 1987 Protocol does not require the transfer of functions from the Water Quality Board to the Binational Executive Committee that has occurred.

Since policy is now considered in the BEC rather than the WQB, the interaction between the USEPA and Environment Canada seems to consist more of negotiation between representatives of national interests, with less involvement of states as well as senior level federal officials. Without the information exchange and participation in policy debate that the WQB formerly provided, the 2002 Great Lakes Strategy and the Regional Collaboration Strategy that succeeded it and the separate Canadian Great Lakes Program Plan do not have the binational perspective that led, for example, to the effort to reduce phosphorus levels. The overall effort was curiously and successfully unified even while occurring in many different ways. At present, the sense of a common, binational purpose is lacking in the U.S. and Canadian actions for virtual elimination of toxic contaminants even with the Binational Toxics Strategy.

Binationalism is critical in setting and accepting goals, but as with reducing phosphorus levels, less critical in exactly how they are achieved. It does not mean that both sides must take the same actions, as long as there is understanding and agreement on the common objective.

In the Great Lakes Agreement, Canada and the United States have agreed to participate in an institution in which the collective interests of the Great Lakes Region are considered greater than the separate national interests. Their joint as well as their separate capacities will likely be undermined if withdrawal from the process causes further regression to bilateral action by unequal partners. While the IJC must ensure binationalism in its own operations in order to maintain its ability to collect, analyze, and verify information and data through joint institutions such as the WQB, the lead agencies of the parties also have responsibility to maintain the spirit of binationalism in their direct interactions with each other.

The challenge of maintaining parity and equality with mutual respect and equivalent responsibilities grows as the regime grows. The spirit of binationalism has caused the Council of Great Lakes Governors, the Great Lakes Commission and the new Great Lakes Cities Initiative to reach out to the provinces and Canadian cities.

The roles of the provinces and the states are growing more important as they are given increasing authority for environmental management and programs. One aim of the RAPS and LAMPS was to involve local governments, who are now becoming more involved through watershed management planning. Likewise, binationalism can assist in providing equality and parity for Tribal and First Nation/aboriginal interests as they become increasingly involved in the regime.

Clarification of the Relationship between the IJC and Other International Agencies

The agreements' broad ecosystem management goal means that the jurisdiction of the IJC increasingly overlaps with the responsibilities of other international institutions, especially the Great Lakes Fishery Commission and the Commission for Environmental Cooperation for North America. Now new international actions are being developed under the Stockholm Convention on Persistent Organic Chemicals, and the objectives of the Kyoto Treaty on Climate change are being increasingly acknowledged in Canada and in the United States even without formal ratification.

Expansion of the Great Lakes Fishery Commission's concerns beyond lamprey control to include healthy fish communities overlaps with the agreement's mandate for ecological integrity. Fishery agencies participate in RAPS and LAMPS and share concerns about toxic contamination, preventing introduction of invasive species, and restoration of habitat and biodiversity.

The CEC is only ten years old, but has already undertaken initiatives for control of toxic chemicals that could assist in achievement of the goals of the Great Lakes Agreement, especially for long range transport through the atmosphere. The binational Air Quality Accord between Canada and the United States also overlaps with CEC jurisdiction. Although the CEC relies on Great Lakes information, and its assistance to Mexico in developing alternatives to DDT for malarial control eliminated a source of DDT to the Great Lakes, the CEC and the IJC have no working relationship beyond limited attendance at some meetings. Nor does the IJC have any involvement in planning for implementation of the Stockholm Convention.

The upcoming review of the Great Lakes Agreement offers opportunity to consider clarification of the relationship between the new goals of the Fishery Commission and the IJC as well as whether the IJC should take a more active role in relevant international forums outside the Great Lakes basin.

The IJC could either host or coordinate an annual meeting with each of the key institutions where there are issues of mutual interest for the Great Lakes. Alternatively, consideration could be given to the suggestion in the NRC/RSC report in the 1980s for a periodic summit of all institutions with Great Lakes concerns to share information, consider common purposes, and incidentally build a sense of community.

Maintaining a Strong Great Lakes Community and Public Involvement

The success of the Great Lakes regime depends on the shared commitment to the goals of a community that includes governments, the scientific community, and nongovernmental participants. To revitalize the Great Lakes community, the agencies that represent the parties, the IJC as overseer for implementation, and the nongovernmental players must all consider how they can contribute to maintaining the strength of the community, not just their own interests.

No exact formula can be prescribed for building community, but the first requirements are for its members to appreciate their roles and the value of their contributions, and to respect the contributions of others. To repair any damage caused by mistrust and lack of respect, the jurisdictions, institutions and persons who believe in the goals of the Great Lakes Agreement must consciously work together to maintain and expand the sense of community on which continuing progress in protecting the Great Lakes depends.

While actions that seem to reflect decline in a sense of common purpose have seemed to undermine the sense of community in recent years, paradoxically there are signs that stakeholders in the Great Lakes community are united in accepting that the ultimate goal must be ecological integrity. The Great Lakes Fishery Commission in its most recent strategic plan, the Council of Great Lakes Governors in its Annex 2001 to the Great Lakes Charter, industry in its growing acceptance of pollution prevention in preference to pollution control, and the call by federal, provincial, and state agencies for habitat restoration in solec 96 and new local watershed management plans throughout the basin are all consistent with the ecosystem approach to management that has been the goal of the Great Lakes Agreement since 1978.

A sense of community assumes working partnerships. A further paradox is that the sense of partnership between the ijc as the agency charged with oversight for implementation, and the lead agencies for the governments that are parties to the agreement, has been lost even with growing acceptance of the common goal. Establishment outside the ijc process of the bec and solec as separate institutions for policy consideration and information exchange creates a sense of separation and competition, rather than partnership. A sense of conflict is enhanced when ijc commissioners and staff seek to control the agenda for joint action, instead of working to gain consensus internally in its own operations and externally with the parties.

The ijc further sets itself apart from the community by limiting its interaction with the nongovernmental community, as well as with other international agencies with overlapping concerns. Separate meetings with selected interest groups and allocation of only the final hour of the 2003 biennial ijc meeting for comments from the public do not convey a sense of concern for the views of citizens, whose support is vital to maintaining the commitment of the governments.

Ten years after the cec was established to deal with continental environmental concerns, the ijc still has no substantive working partnership with the tripartite cec for the management of toxic contaminants that is a major concern for both agencies. It seems appropriate for the ijc to lead interaction at the international level on behalf of the Great Lakes community. Industry participation in regime institutions increased in the 1990s, but participation by environmental leaders decreased in the same period. There is widespread agreement that neither the ijc biennial meetings nor other joint institutional activities should be devoted to debate between industry and environmental interests. Yet a mechanism is needed to involve representatives of nongovernmental constituencies, and, through their membership, to reach more of the general public who are essential for maintaining the commitment of governments.

Public concern and growth of nongovernmental participation in the regime through the 1970s and 1980s contributed to the strength of the Great

---

Can the Great Lakes Be Saved?

The Great Lakes can be saved if the political decision-makers and the public understand the plight of the lakes and are willing to respond to the challenges in a timely way. In practice this means:

- Both national governments endorse and support the Great Lakes Water Quality Agreement, whether it is renewed in its existing form or renegotiated.
- Significant (at least several billion dollars) of funding and priority are given to scientific research, ongoing monitoring of the conditions of the Great Lakes ecosystem and gathering information and data on future threats.
- Resources and priority of attention are allocated to immediate remediation of outstanding consequences of the pollution legacy of the Great Lakes, such as contaminated sediments and restoration of damaged habitats.
- The institutional capacity of each level of government for dealing with Great Lakes issues is strengthened. States and provinces must be re-energized and engaged, with a revamping of the Canada–Ontario Agreement to make results more accountable, and development of a new instrument to define relative responsibilities of federal, state, and local governments as well as First Nationals and tribes in the Great Lakes regime.

The Great Lakes can be saved, not just by governments but by the thousands of persons — from all sectors and walks of life — that have worked together as a community over the past half century to further the integrity of the Great Lakes. The Great Lakes Water Quality Agreement is the reminder of our obligation as joint stewards of the lakes and the legacy we owe to future generations.

Lakes regime and were critical to maintaining the will of the governments. Nongovernmental representation in the WQB was proposed in the 1985 report of the Royal Society and the National Academy, and in the 1986 Great Lakes United *Unfulfilled Promises* report. The issue was raised in the 1987 negotiations and may be even more relevant in 2005 because of minimal nongovernmental oversight in the BEC, limited attendance at the SOLEC meetings, and decreased participation in the IJC biennial meetings.

The issue is whether a citizens advisory board should be created to provide a forum for debate and information exchange that would produce recommendations from nongovernmental constituencies to the IJC and/or the parties to the agreement. Alternatively, the issue is whether the IJC and the parties should actively consider how to increase nongovernmental participation in their separate and joint institutions.

The Benefits of a Renewed Agreement

The result of a careful and comprehensive review could determine whether the agreement survives to foster confidence in its institutions and a healthier Great Lakes. The Great Lakes demonstrate the interdependence of the United States and Canada and the Great Lakes Agreement is the embodiment of the special relationship that can exist only between neighbors committed to peace and equitable responsibility and enjoyment of shared resources. A strong agreement to join in their restoration and protection is the best hope for the future of the Great Lakes. A Great Lakes Water Quality Agreement is as needed today as in 1972, but perhaps for different reasons. The boundary and transboundary waters are the shared resource that represents the ties that bind the two countries.

PERSONS INTERVIEWED OR CONSULTED, OR WHO PARTICIPATED IN THE WINGSPREAD CONFERENCE

Valdus Adamkus, George Alexander, Jim Barnes, Elaine Kaplan Beck, Elise Beam, Alfred Beeton, Tim Bendig, Paul Bertram, Pat Bonner, Lori Boughton, Peter Boyer, Marty Bratzel, James Bredin, Irene Brooks, Murray Brooksbank, James Bruce, Dale Bryson, Tim Brown, Kelly Burch, Tanya Cabala, Lynton K. Caldwell, Allegra Cangelosi, Jim Chandler, Edith Chase, Jan Ciborowski, Milton Clark, Hilary Cleveland, Peter Christich, Mike Coffin, Theodora E. Colborn, Sally Cole-Misch, William Cooper, Terry Davies, Bill Davis, Cameron Davis, David Dempsey, Michael Donahue, Gordon Durnil, Jane Dustin, Tom Dustin, Tim Eder, Jane Elder, Mark Elster, Rick Findlay, Eric Firstenberg, George Francis, Kent Fuller, Marc Gaden, John Gannon, Michael Gilbertson, Walter Giles, Ed Glatfelter, Mike Goffin, Emily Green, Chris Grundler, Gary Gulezian, David Hales, Andrew Hamilton, Jim Hanlon, Jean Hennessey, Pat Hill, Paul Horvatin, Ava Hottman, Adele Hurley, John Jackson, Thomas Jorling, Conrad Kleveno, Gail Krantzberg, Eleanor Kulin, George Kuper, Jean LaGorge, David LaRoche, Sheila Leahy, Henry Lickers, Richard Liroff, Orie Loucks, Stephen Lozano, Jim Ludwig, Rees Madsen, Jack Manno, Tom Martin, Gerald Miko, Jan S. Miller, John Mills, Jennifer Moore, Shawn Morton, Don Mount, Don Munton, Thomas J. Murphy, Margaret O'Dell, Patty O'Donnell, Ken Ogilvie, Allen Olson, Jim Park, Dale Phenicie, Kathy Prosser, Mike Quigley, Del Rector, Jay Reed, Eric Reeves, Henry Regier, William Reilly, Mark Reshkin, Ken Richards, David Rockwell, Charles Ross, William Rustem, William Steggles, Judith Stockdale, Vacys Saulys, Wayne Schmidt, Dennis Schornack, Duane Schuepelz, Rick Spencer, Wayland Swain, Nelson Thomas, Rich Thomas, Robert Tolpa, Sheila Tooze, David Ullrich, Jack Vallentyne, Mark van Putten, Martin Visnosky, Jack Weinberg, Lyman Wible, Peter Wise, Charles Wooley, Margaret Wooster.

RECOMMENDATIONS FROM REPORTS ON THE GREAT LAKES REGIME

The following excerpts are some recommendations from selected nongovernmental groups with respect to the Great Lakes Water Quality Agreement and the International Joint Commission. There are various other recommendations found in the reports of the International Joint Commission, accessible at *www.ijc.org*.

Environmental Law Institute, An Evaluation of the Effectiveness of the International Joint Commission (Washington, D.C., 1995)

CHAPTER 4 (RECOMMENDATIONS DIRECTED TO THE IJC)

- The IJC should re-evaluate its role and develop a more meaningful approach to its responsibilities through a strategic planning process which involves the public.
- Strengthen the technical capacity of IJC staff and Boards.
- The IJC should endeavor to strengthen its binational character.
- The IJC should emphasize its monitoring function and use the Water Quality Board to monitor and evaluate the Parties' progress toward achieving the objectives of GLWQA.
- The IJC should devote more effort to working with the Parties, Provinces and States on implementing its recommendations.
- The IJC's staff should continue to provide technical assistance and guidelines for public participation in the RAP process.
- The IJC should add public members to represent all stakeholders on the Water Quality Board, Science Advisory Board, Board of Control and Pollution Advisory Board.
- The IJC should structure its biennial meetings to provide more technical content and more meaningful public participation in IJC activities; greater integration is also required with the SOLEC Conference.

- The IJC should convene multi-stakeholder meetings to review the Parties' progress in implementing water quality goals.
- The IJC should use GLWQA's standards-setting authority to recommend ways to reduce air-borne toxics.
- The IJC should devote greater efforts to influencing the Parties to implement its recommendations for better land use planning, floodplain mapping and forecasting, and set-back requirements for construction along shorelines.
- The IJC should delegate studies of lake levels and flows to existing Board of Control and should devote more time and effort to promoting sound land use planning by the Parties.
- The IJC should use its application authorities under the Treaty to achieve sustainability of water uses in other boundary water ecosystems.

CHAPTER 5 (RECOMMENDATIONS DIRECTED TO THE PARTIES)

- The Parties should authorize the IJC to accept and review public petitions for IJC action on boundary water issues.
- The Parties should authorize the IJC to create standing Boards responsible for recommending standards and monitoring water quality for all boundary watersheds.
- The Parties should establish a fixed number of years for terms of IJC Commissioners, and should stagger the dates of their appointments to prevent wholesale turnover of Commissioners.
- The Parties should allow the public to participate in the process of selecting Commissioners.
- The Parties should form a single IJC Secretariat located in the Great Lakes region.

Michigan Environmental Council, Restoring Greatness to Government: Protecting the Great Lakes in the Twenty-first Century—A Review of Great Lakes Institutions in the Context of Global and Ecosystem Change (April 2004), pp. 23–30 (excerpts).

- International Joint Commission. *(1) The Parties should establish a fixed number of years for the terms of IJC Commissioners and should stagger the dates of their appointments to prevent wholesale turnover of Commissioners. (2) The Parties should authorize the IJC to accept and review public petitions for IJC action on boundary water issues.*
- Create state-level environmental ombudsman positions. *Each Great Lakes state should create, by statute, and fully fund an independent environmental ombudsman within state government with the mandate to examine, analyze and candidly report on the progress of the state in complying, among other things, with the goals of the Clean Water Act and the Great Lakes Water Quality Agreement in restoring the physical, chemical and biological integrity of the Great Lakes ecosystem.*

- Create a standing Great Lakes citizen board, independent of governments. *A region-wide, future oriented Great Lakes citizens' commission could perhaps at times slip the bonds of politics. It could examine, analyze and report on the effects of looming global and local changes and make credible, uncompromising recommendations about actions needed to protect and restore the ecosystem, including its human inhabitants.*

- Convene a binational Conference on the Great Lakes every five to ten years to assemble government officials and key stakeholders, with an emphasis on broad public participation, to assure visibility of Great Lakes trends and monitoring of progress toward ecosystem integrity. *The conference should trace recent trends in Great Lakes ecosystem health, feature the results of current peer-reviewed scientific research on Great Lakes phenomena, include discussions on emerging or anticipated threats to that health and attempt to build consensus for both government and private initiatives to enhance the ecosystem. Staged every five to ten years (or, if organized on a lake-by-lake basis, annually), the conference would not significantly interfere with the continuing work of participants but would serve as a high-visibility reminder of the importance that all participants place on developing common answers to the needs of a globally unique freshwater ecosystem.*

- Establish statutory mechanisms and processes to assure public participation in decisions about the spending and monitoring of any new federal restoration funds allocated to the Great Lakes as part of legislation now before the U.S. Congress

    It is critical for any Great Lakes restoration legislation enacted by Congress to embrace the principle of public participation. We recommend, in general, that the legislation:

    - Assure that the public's view on appropriate restoration priorities be solicited at public meetings and through the Internet before the first round of grants;
    - Assure meaningful citizen membership on any advisory body or oversight board created to assist with recommending grants;
    - Establish an independent auditing board consisting of citizens not affiliated with government institutions to review the effectiveness of the restoration grants and the legislation on an annual or biennial basis.

- Provide clear, legal mechanisms in a proposed new Great Lakes compact and implement state legislation in all eight Great Lakes states, to assure public participation in decisions about water diversions and exports

- Enact legislation to assure monitoring and public reporting on the health of the Great Lakes. *A clear and continuing commitment to basic monitoring of Great Lakes ecosystem health and regular reporting to the public on conditions identified by such monitoring are essential parts of Great Lakes restoration.*

- Establish a Great Lakes Internet "Capitol." *Regional institutions—or the new Great Lakes Citizens Board proposed in this document—could establish a virtual Capitol that provides a central location that explains the role of the various governments in Great*

Lakes decision-making, provides updates on the actions of the many governments affecting Great Lakes ecosystem health, and provides for both formal and informal means of assessing public knowledge and attitudes about Basin-wide issues.

- Create a Great Lakes Sentinel System. *Perhaps in conjunction with the virtual Capitol, a regional institution or the citizens' board could create by e-mail a Great Lakes Sentinel System. The system would provide e-mail and/or paper mail alerts to interested citizens perhaps ten times a year, with basic information about a pending decision or issue and how and when to respond effectively.*

- Create a Great Lakes Congress. *Several commenters have suggested the creation of a Basin-wide assembly, reflecting the relative population and geographic share of the Great Lakes in various jurisdictions, to enhance the citizen voice in decision-making. . . . Recommendations would be transmitted to the appropriate levels of government for review and action.*

- Convene a periodic Great Lakes Summit. *The International Joint Commission, the Great Lakes Fisheries Commission, the Great Lakes Commission, and perhaps other regional bodies, should consider an annual public meeting at which the full range of ecosystem concern can be aired and public preferences assessed.*

- Enhance information available through Great Lakes Media. *Regional institutions should consider an initiative to work with television stations across the Basin to assure frequent delivery of information to citizens, in usable format, about Great Lakes conditions and/or issues.*

- Establish a Great Lakes Leadership Institute. *A Great Lakes Leadership Institute could have a similar, but broader purpose: to enroll and train individuals from across the Basin to become knowledgeable advocates, ecosystem-conscious business leaders, or local, state or federal elected officials devoted to decision-making that take into account the needs of the Great Lakes ecosystem now and in the future.*

- Enhance the participation of municipal governments and their public in Great Lakes protection

1972 GREAT LAKES WATER QUALITY AGREEMENT

UNITED STATES AND CANADA
Great Lakes Water Quality

Agreement, with annexes and texts and terms of reference, signed at Ottawa April 15, 1972;
Entered into force April 15, 1972.

International Joint Commission
United States and Canada
1974

AGREEMENT BETWEEN
THE UNITED STATES OF AMERICA AND CANADA
ON GREAT LAKES WATER QUALITY[1]

The Government of the United States of America and the Government of Canada,

Determined to restore and enhance water quality in the Great Lakes System;

Seriously concerned about the grave deterioration of water quality on each side of the boundary to an extent that is causing injury to health and property on the other side, as described in the 1970 report of the International Joint Commission on Pollution of Lake Erie, Lake Ontario and the International Section of the St. Lawrence River;

Intent upon preventing further pollution of the Great Lakes System owing to continuing population growth, resource development and increasing use of water;

Reaffirming in a spirit of friendship and cooperation the rights and obligations of both countries under the Boundary Waters Treaty signed on January 11, 1909[2] and in particular their obligation not to pollute boundary waters;

Recognizing the rights of each country in the use of its Great Lakes waters;

Satisfied that the 1970 report of the International Joint Commission provides a sound basis for new and more effective cooperative actions to restore and enhance water quality in the Great Lakes System;

Convinced that the best means to achieve improved water quality in the Great Lakes System is through the adoption of common objectives, the development and implementation of cooperative programs and other measures, and the assignment of special responsibilities and functions to the International Joint Commission;

Have agreed as follows:

ARTICLE I

DEFINITIONS

As used in this Agreement:

(a) "Boundary waters of the Great Lakes System" or "boundary waters" means boundary waters, as defined in the Boundary Waters Treaty, that are within the Great Lakes System;

(b) "Boundary Waters Treaty" means the treaty between the United States and Great Britain relating to boundary waters, and questions arising between the United States and Canada, signed at Washington on January 11, 1909;

(c) "Compatible regulations" means regulations no less restrictive than agreed principles;

(d) "Great Lakes System" means all of the streams, rivers, lakes and other bodies of water that are within the drainage basin of the St. Lawrence River at or upstream from the point at which this river becomes the international boundary between Canada and the United States;

(e) "Harmful quantity" means any quantity of a substance that if discharged into receiving waters would be inconsistent with the achievement of the water quality objectives;

(f) "Hazardous polluting substance" means any element or compound identified by the Parties which, when discharged in any quantity into or upon receiving waters or adjoining shorelines, presents an imminent and substantial danger to public health or welfare; for this purpose, "public health or welfare" encompasses all factors affecting the health and welfare of man including but not limited to human health, and the conservation and protection of fish, shellfish, wildlife, public and private property, shorelines and beaches;

(g) "International Joint Commission" or "Commission" means the International Joint Commission established by the Boundary Waters Treaty;

(h) "Phosphorus" means the element phosphorus present as a constituent of various organic and inorganic complexes and compounds;

(i) "Specific water quality objective" means the level of a substance or physical effect that the Parties agree, after investigation, to recognize as a maximum or minimum desired limit for a defined body of water or portion thereof, taking into account the beneficial uses of the water that the Parties desire to secure and protect;

(j) "State and Provincial Governments" means the Governments of the States of Illinois, Indiana, Michigan, Minnesota, New York, Ohio, Pennsylvania, and Wisconsin, and the Government of the Province of Ontario;

(k) "Tributary waters of the Great Lakes System" or "tributary waters" means all the waters of the Great Lakes System that are not boundary waters;

(l) "Water quality objectives" means the general water quality objectives adopted pursuant to Article II of this Agreement and the specific water quality objectives adopted pursuant to Article III of this Agreement.

ARTICLE II

GENERAL WATER QUALITY OBJECTIVES

The following general water quality objectives for the boundary waters of the Great Lakes System are adopted. These waters should be:

(a) Free from substances that enter the waters as a result of human activity and that will settle to form putrescent or otherwise objectionable sludge deposits, or that will adversely affect aquatic life or waterfowl;

(b) Free from floating debris, oil, scum and other floating materials entering the waters as a result of human activity in amounts sufficient to be unsightly or deleterious;

(c) Free from materials entering the waters as a result of human activity producing colour, odour or other conditions in such a degree as to create a nuisance;

(d) Free from substances entering the waters as a result of human activity in concentrations that are toxic or harmful to human, animal or aquatic life;

(e) Free from nutrients entering the waters as a result of human activity in concentrations that create nuisance growths of aquatic weeds and algae.

ARTICLE III

SPECIFIC WATER QUALITY OBJECTIVES

1. The specific water quality objectives for the boundary waters of the Great Lakes System set forth in Annex 1 are adopted.

2. The specific water quality objectives may be modified and additional specific water quality objectives for the boundary waters of the Great Lakes System or for particular sections thereof may be adopted by the Parties in accordance with the provisions of Articles IX and XII of this Agreement.

3. The specific water quality objectives adopted pursuant to this Article represent the minimum desired levels of water quality in the boundary waters of the Great Lakes System and are not intended to preclude the establishment of more stringent requirements. Notwithstanding the adoption of specific water quality objectives, all reasonable and practicable measures shall be taken to maintain the levels of water quality existing at the date of entry into force of this Agreement in those areas of the boundary waters of the Great Lakes System where such levels exceed the specific water quality objectives.

ARTICLE IV

STANDARDS AND OTHER REGULATORY REQUIREMENTS

Water quality standards and other regulatory requirements of the Parties shall be consistent with the achievement of the water quality objectives. The Parties shall use their best efforts to ensure that water quality standards and other regulatory requirements of the State and Provincial Governments shall similarly be consistent with the achievement of the water quality objectives.

ARTICLE V

PROGRAMS AND OTHER MEASURES

1. Programs and other measures directed toward the achievement of the water quality objectives shall be developed and implemented as soon as practicable in accordance with legislation in the two countries. Unless otherwise agreed, such programs and other measures shall be either completed or in process of implementation by December 31, 1975. They shall include the following:

    (a) <u>Pollution from Municipal Sources</u>. Programs for the abatement and control of discharges of municipal sewage into the Great Lakes System including:

    (i) construction and operation in all municipalities having sewer systems of waste treatment facilities providing levels of treatment consistent with the achievement of the water quality objectives, taking into account the effects of waste from other sources;

    (ii) provision of financial resources to assist prompt construction of needed facilities;

    (iii) establishment of requirements for construction and operating standards for facilities;

    (iv) measures to find practical solutions for reducing pollution from overflows of combined storm and sanitary sewers;

    (v) monitoring, surveillance and enforcement activities necessary to ensure compliance with the foregoing programs and measures.

    (b) <u>Pollution from Industrial Sources</u>. Programs for the abatement and control of pollution from industrial sources, including:

    (i) establishment of waste treatment or control requirements for all industrial plants discharging waste into the Great Lakes System, to provide levels of treatment or reduction of inputs of substances and effects consistent with the achievement of the water quality objectives, taking into account the effects of waste from other sources;

    (ii) requirements for the substantial elimination of discharges into the Great Lakes System of mercury and other toxic heavy metals;

    (iii) requirements for the substantial elimination of discharges into the Great Lakes System of toxic persistent organic contaminants;

    (iv) requirements for the control of thermal discharges;

(v) measures to control the discharge of radioactive materials into the Great Lakes System;

(vi) monitoring, surveillance and enforcement activities necessary to ensure compliance with the foregoing requirements and measures.

(c) Eutrophication. Measures for the control of inputs of phosphorus and other nutrients including programs to reduce phosphorus inputs, in accordance with the provisions of Annex 2.

(d) Pollution from Agricultural, Forestry and Other Land Use Activities. Measures for the abatement and control of pollution from agricultural, forestry and other land use activities, including:

(i) measures for the control of pest control products with a view to limiting inputs into the Great Lakes System, including regulations to ensure that pest control products judged to have long term deleterious effects on the quality of water or its biotic components shall be used only as authorized by the responsible regulatory agencies, and that pest control products shall not be applied directly to water except in accordance with the requirements of the responsible regulatory agencies;

(ii) measures for the abatement and control of pollution from animal husbandry operations, including encouragement to appropriate regulatory agencies to adopt regulations governing site selection and disposal of liquid and solid wastes in order to minimize the loss of pollutants to receiving waters;

(iii) measures governing the disposal of solid wastes and contributing to the achievement of the water quality objectives, including encouragement to appropriate regulatory agencies to ensure proper location of land fill and land dumping sites and regulations governing the disposal on land of hazardous polluting substances;

(iv) advisory programs and measures that serve to abate and control inputs of nutrients and sediments into receiving waters from agricultural, forestry and other land use activities.

(e) Pollution from Shipping Activities. Measures for the abatement and control of pollution from shipping sources, including:

(i) programs and compatible regulations for vessel design, construction and operation, to prevent discharges of harmful quantities of oil and hazardous polluting substances, in accordance with the principles set forth in Annex 3;

(ii) compatible regulations for the control of vessel waste discharges in accordance with the principles set forth in Annex 4;

(iii) such compatible regulations to abate and control pollution from shipping sources as may be deemed desirable in the light of studies to be undertaken in accordance with the terms of references set forth in Annex 5;

(iv) programs for the safe and efficient handling of shipboard generated wastes, including oil, hazardous polluting substances, garbage, waste water and sewage, and their subsequent disposal, including any necessary compatible regulations relating to the type, quantity and capacity of shore reception facilities;

(v) establishment of a coordinated system for the surveillance and enforcement of regulations dealing with the abatement and control of pollution from shipping activities.

(f) Pollution from Dredging Activities. Measures for the abatement and control of pollution from dredging activities, including the development of criteria for the identification of polluted dredged spoil and compatible programs for disposal of polluted dredged spoil, which shall be considered in the light of the review provided for in Annex 6; pending the development of compatible criteria and programs, dredging operations shall be conducted in a manner that will minimize adverse effects on the environment.

(g) Pollution from Onshore and Offshore Facilities. Measures for the abatement and control of pollution from onshore and offshore facilities, including programs and compatible regulations for the prevention of discharges of harmful quantities of oil and hazardous polluting substances, in accordance with the principles set forth in Annex 7.

(h) Contingency Plan. Maintenance of a joint contingency plan for use in the event of a discharge or the imminent threat of a discharge of oil or hazardous polluting substances, in accordance with the provisions of Annex 8.

(i) Hazardous Polluting Substances. Consultation within one year from the date of entry into force of this Agreement for the purpose of developing an Annex identifying hazardous polluting substances; the Parties shall further consult from time to time for the purpose of identifying harmful quantities of these substances and of reviewing the definition of "harmful quantity of oil" set forth in Annexes 3 and 7.

2. The Parties shall develop and implement such additional programs as they jointly decide are necessary and desirable for the achievement of the water quality objectives.

3. The programs and other measures provided for in this Article shall be designed to abate and control pollution of tributary waters where necessary or desirable for the achievement of the water quality objectives for the boundary waters of the Great Lakes System.

ARTICLE VI

POWERS, RESPONSIBILITIES AND FUNCTIONS OF THE INTERNATIONAL JOINT COMMISSION

1. The International Joint Commission shall assist in the implementation of this Agreement. Accordingly, the Commission is hereby given, pursuant to Article IX of the Boundary Waters Treaty, the following responsibilities:

(a) Collation, analysis and dissemination of data and information supplied by the Parties and State and Provincial Governments relating to the quality of the boundary waters of the Great Lakes System and to pollution that enters the boundary waters from tributary waters;

(b) Collection, analysis and dissemination of data and information concerning the water quality objectives and the operation and effectiveness of the programs and other measures established pursuant to this Agreement;

(c) Tendering of advice and recommendations to the Parties and to the State and Provincial Governments on problems of the quality of the boundary waters of the Great Lakes System, including specific recommendations concerning the water quality objectives, legislation, standards and other regulatory requirements, programs and other measures, and intergovernmental agreements relating to the quality of these waters;

(d) Provision of assistance in the coordination of the joint activities envisaged by this Agreement, including such matters as contingency planning and consultation on special situations;

(e) Provision of assistance in the coordination of Great Lakes water quality research, including identification of objectives for research activities, tendering of advice and recommendations concerning research to the Parties and to the State and Provincial Governments and dissemination of information concerning research to interested persons and agencies;

(f) Investigations of such subjects related to Great Lakes water qualities as the Parties may from time to time refer to it. At the time of signature of this Agreement, the Parties are requesting the Commission to enquire into and report to them upon:

(i) pollution of the boundary waters of the Great Lakes System from agricultural, forestry and other land use activities, in accordance with the terms of reference attached to this Agreement;

(ii) actions needed to preserve and enhance the quality of the waters of Lake Huron and Lake Superior in accordance with the terms of reference attached to this Agreement.

2. In the discharge of its responsibilities under this Agreement, the Commission may exercise all of the powers conferred upon it by the Boundary Waters Treaty and by any legislation passed pursuant thereto, including the power to conduct public hearings and to compel the testimony of witnesses and the production of documents.

3. The Commission shall make a report to the Parties and to the State and Provincial Governments no less frequently than annually concerning progress toward the achievement of the water quality objectives. This report shall include an assessment of the effectiveness of the programs and other measures undertaken pursuant to this Agreement, and advice and recommendations. The Commission may at any time make special reports to the Parties, to the State and Provincial Governments and to the public concerning any problem of water quality in the Great Lakes System.

4. The Commission may in its discretion publish any report, statement or other document prepared by it in the discharge of its functions under this Agreement.

5. The Commission shall have authority to verify independently the data and other information submitted by the Parties and by the State and provincial Governments through such tests or other means as appear appropriate to it, consistent with the Boundary Waters Treaty and with applicable legislation.

ARTICLE VII

JOINT INSTITUTIONS

1. The International Joint Commission shall establish a Great Lakes Water Quality Board to assist it in the exercise of the powers and responsibilities assigned to it under this Agreement. Such Board shall be composed of an equal number of members from Canada and the United States, including representation from the Parties and from each of the State and Provincial Governments. The Commission shall also establish a Research Advisory Board in accordance with the terms of reference attached to this Agreement. The members of the Great Lakes Water Quality Board and the Research Advisory Board shall be appointed by the Commission after consultation with the appropriate government or governments concerned. In addition, the Commission shall have the authority to establish as it may deem appropriate such subordinate bodies as may be required to undertake specific tasks, as well as a regional office, which may be located in the basin of the Great Lakes System, to assist it in the discharge of its functions under this Agreement. The Commission shall also consult the Parties about the site and staffing of any regional office that might be established.

2. The Commission shall submit an annual budget of anticipated expenses to be incurred in carrying out its responsibilities under this Agreement to the Parties for approval. Each Party shall seek funds to pay one-half of the annual budget so approved, but neither Party shall be under an obligation to pay a larger amount than the other toward this budget.

ARTICLE VIII

SUBMISSION AND EXCHANGE OF INFORMATION

1. The International Joint Commission shall be given at its request any data or other information relating to the quality of the boundary waters of the Great Lakes System in accordance with procedures to be established, within three months of the entry into force of this Agreement or as soon thereafter as possible, by the Commission in consultation with the Parties and with the State and Provincial Governments.

2. The Commission shall make available to the Parties and to the State and Provincial Governments upon request all data or other information furnished to it in accordance with this Article.

3. Each Party shall make available to the other at its request any data or other information in its control relating to the quality of the waters of the Great Lakes System.

4. Notwithstanding any other provision of this Agreement, the Commission shall not release without the consent of the owner any information identified as proprietary information under the law of the place where such information has been acquired.

ARTICLE IX
CONSULTATION AND REVIEW

1. Following the receipt of each report submitted to the Parties by the International Joint Commission in accordance with paragraph 3 of Article VI of this Agreement, the Parties shall consult on the recommendations contained in such report and shall consider such action as may be appropriate, including:
   (a) The modification of existing water quality objectives and the adoption of new objectives;
   (b) The modification or improvement of programs and joint measures;
   (c) The amendment of this Agreement or any annex thereto.
   Additional consultations may be held at the request of either Party on any matter arising out of the implementation of this Agreement.

2. When a Party becomes aware of a special pollution problem that is of joint concern and requires an immediate response, it shall notify and consult the other Party forthwith about appropriate remedial action.

3. The Parties shall conduct a comprehensive review of the operation and effectiveness of this Agreement during the fifth year after its coming into force. Thereafter, further comprehensive reviews shall be conducted upon the request of either Party.

ARTICLE X
IMPLEMENTATION

1. The obligations undertaken in this Agreement shall be subject to the appropriation of funds in accordance with the constitutional procedures of the Parties.

2. The Parties commit themselves to seek:
   (a) The appropriation of the funds required to implement this Agreement, including the funds needed to develop and implement the programs and other measures provided for in Article V, and the funds required by the International Joint Commission to carry out its responsibilities effectively;
   (b) The enactment of any additional legislation that may be necessary in order to implement the programs and other measures provided for in Article V;
   (c) The cooperation of the State and Provincial Governments in all matters relating to this Agreement.

ARTICLE XI
EXISTING RIGHTS AND OBLIGATIONS

Nothing in this Agreement shall be deemed to diminish the rights and obligations of the Parties as set forth in the Boundary Waters Treaty.

ARTICLE XII

AMENDMENT

This Agreement and the Annexes thereto may be amended by agreement of the Parties. The Annexes may also be amended as provided therein, subject to the requirement that such amendments shall be within the scope of this Agreement.

ARTICLE XIII

ENTRY INTO FORCE AND TERMINATION

This Agreement shall enter into force upon signature by the duly authorized representatives of the Parties, and shall remain in force for a period of five years and thereafter until terminated upon twelve months' notice given in writing by one of the Parties to the other.

IN WITNESS WHEREOF the Representatives of the two Governments have signed this Agreement.

DONE in two copies at Ottawa this fifteenth day of April 1972 in English and French, each version being equally authentic.

For the Government of the United States of America

For the Government of Canada

NOTES

1. As found at TIAS 7312.

2. TS 548;36 Stat. 2448.

GREAT LAKES WATER QUALITY AGREEMENT OF 1978 (REVISED)

Agreement, with Annexes and Terms of Reference, between the United States and Canada signed at Ottawa November 22, 1978 and Phosphorus Load Reduction Supplement signed October 16, 1983

as amended by Protocol signed November 18, 1987
Office Consolidation

INTERNATIONAL JOINT COMMISSION UNITED STATES AND CANADA

September, 1989

PROTOCOL AMENDING THE 1978 AGREEMENT BETWEEN THE UNITED STATES OF AMERICA AND CANADA ON GREAT LAKES WATER QUALITY, AS AMENDED ON OCTOBER 16, 1983

AGREEMENT BETWEEN CANADA AND THE UNITED STATES OF AMERICA ON GREAT LAKES QUALITY, 1978

PROTOCOL AMENDING THE 1978 AGREEMENT BETWEEN THE UNITED STATES OF AMERICA AND CANADA ON GREAT LAKES WATER QUALITY, AS AMENDED ON OCTOBER 16, 1983

The Government of the United States of America and the Government of Canada,

REAFFIRMING their commitment to achieving the purpose and objectives of the 1978

Agreement between the United States of America and Canada on Great Lakes Water Quality, as amended on October 16, 1983;

HAVING developed and implemented cooperative programs and measures to achieve such purpose and objectives;

RECOGNIZING the need for strengthened efforts to address the continuing contamination of the Great Lakes Basin Ecosystem, particularly by persistent toxic substances;

ACKNOWLEDGING that many of these toxic substances enter the Great Lakes System from air, from ground water infiltration, from sediments in the Lakes and from the runoff of non-point sources;

AWARE that further research and program development is now required to enable effective actions to be taken to address the continuing contamination of the Great Lakes;

DETERMINED to improve management processes for achieving Agreement objectives and to demonstrate firm leadership in the implementation of control measures;

Have agreed as follows:

AGREEMENT BETWEEN CANADA AND THE UNITED STATES OF AMERICA ON GREAT LAKES QUALITY, 1978

The Government of Canada and the Government of the United States of America,

HAVING in 1972 and 1978 entered into Agreements on Great Lakes Water Quality;

REAFFIRMING their determination to restore and enhance water quality in the Great Lakes System;

CONTINUING to be concerned about the impairment of water quality on each side of the boundary to an extent that is causing injury to health and property on the other side, as described by the International Joint Commission;

REAFFIRMING their intent to prevent further pollution of the Great Lakes Basin Ecosystem owing to continuing population growth, resource development and increasing use of water;

REAFFIRMING in a spirit of friendship and cooperation the rights and obligations of both countries under the Boundary Waters Treaty, signed on January 11, 1909, and in particular their obligation not to pollute boundary waters;

CONTINUING to recognize that right of each country in the use of the Great Lakes waters;

HAVING decided that the Great Lakes Water Quality Agreements of 1972 and 1978 and subsequent reports of the International Joint Commission provide a sound basis for new and more effective cooperative actions to restore and enhance water quality in the Great Lakes Basin Ecosystem;

RECOGNIZING that restoration and enhancement of the boundary waters cannot be achieved independently of other parts of the Great Lakes Basin Ecosystem with which these waters interact;

CONCLUDING that the best means to preserve the aquatic ecosystem and achieve improved water quality throughout the Great Lakes System is by adopting common objectives, developing and implementing cooperative programs and other measures, and assigning special responsibilities and functions to the International Joint Commission;

Have agreed as follows:

ARTICLE 1

DEFINITIONS

As used in this Agreement:

(a) "Agreement" means the present Agreement as distinguished from the Great Lakes Water Quality Agreement of April 15, 1972;

(b) "Annex" means any of the Annexes to this Agreement, each of which is attached to and forms and integral part of this Agreement;

(c) "Boundary waters of the Great Lakes System" or "boundary waters" means boundary waters, as defined in the Boundary Waters Treaty, that are within the Great Lakes System;

(d) "Boundary Waters Treaty" means the Treaty between the United States and Great Britain Relating to Boundary Waters, and Questions Arising Between the United States and Canada, signed at Washington on January 11, 1909;

(e) "Compatible regulations" means regulations no less restrictive than the agreed principles set out in this Agreement;

(f) "General Objectives" are broad descriptions of water quality conditions consistent with the protection of the beneficial uses and the level of environmental quality which the Parties desire to secure and which will provide overall water management guidance;

(g) "Great Lakes Basin Ecosystem" means the interacting components of air, land, water and living organisms, including humans, within the drainage basin of the St. Lawrence River at or upstream from the point at which this river becomes the international boundary between Canada and the United States;

(h) "Great Lakes System" means all of the streams river, lakes and other bodies of water that are within the drainage basin on the St. Lawrence River at or upstream from the point at which this river becomes the international boundary between Canada and the United States;

(i) "Harmful quantity" means any quantity of a substance that if discharged into receiving water would be inconsistent with the achievement of the General and Specific Objectives;

(j) "Hazardous polluting substance" means any element or compound identified by the Parties which, if discharged in any quantity into or upon receiving waters or adjoining shorelines, would present an imminent and substantial danger to public health or welfare; for this purpose, "public health or welfare" encompasses all factors affecting the health and welfare of humans including but not limited to human health, and conservation and protection of flora and fauna, public and private property, shorelines and beaches;

(k) "International Joint Commission" or "Commission" means the International Joint Commission established by the Boundary Waters Treaty;

(l) "Monitoring" means a scientifically designed system of continuing standardized measurements and observations and the evaluation thereof;

(m) "Objectives" means the General Objectives adopted pursuant to Article III and the Specific Objectives adopted pursuant to Article IV of this Agreement;

(n) "Parties" means the Government of Canada and the Government of the United States of America;

(o) "Phosphorus" means the element phosphorus present as a constituent of various organic and inorganic complexes and compounds;

(p) "Research" means development, interpretation and demonstration of advanced scientific knowledge for the resolution of issues but does not include monitoring and surveillance of water or air quality;

(q) "Science Advisory Board" means the Great Lakes Science Advisory Board of the International Joint Commission established pursuant to Article VIII of this Agreement;

(r) "Specific Objectives" means the concentration or quantity of a substance or level of effect that the Parties agree, after investigation, to recognize as a maximum or minimum desired limit for a defined body of water or portion thereof, taking into account the beneficial uses or level of environmental quality which the Parties desire to secure and protect;

(s) "State and Provincial Governments" means the Governments of the States of Illinois, Indiana, Michigan, Minnesota, New York, Ohio, Wisconsin, and the Commonwealth of Pennsylvania, and the Government of the Province of Ontario;

(t) "Surveillance" means specific observations and measurements relative to control or management;

(u) "Terms of Reference" means the Terms of Reference for the Joint Institutions and the Great Lakes Regional Office established pursuant to this Agreement, which are attached to and form an integral part of this Agreement;

(v) "Toxic substance" means a substance which can cause death, disease, behavioural abnormalities, cancer, genetic mutations, physiological or reproductive malfunctions or physical deformities in any organism or its offspring, or which can become poisonous after concentration in the food chain or in combination with other substances;

(w) "Tributary waters of the Great Lakes System" or "tributary waters" means all the waters within the Great Lakes System that are not boundary waters;

(x) "Water Quality Board" means the Great Lakes Water Quality Board of the International Joint Commission established pursuant to Article VIII of this Agreement.

ARTICLE II

PURPOSE

The purpose of the Parties is to restore and maintain the chemical, physical, and biological integrity of the waters of the Great Lakes Basin Ecosystem. In order to achieve this purpose, the Parties agree to make a maximum effort to develop programs, practices and technology necessary for a better understanding of the Great Lakes Basin Ecosystem and to eliminate or reduce to the maximum extent practicable the discharge of pollutants into the Great Lakes System.

Consistent with the provisions of this Agreement, it is the policy of the Parties that:

(a) The discharge of toxic substances in toxic amounts be prohibited and the discharge of any or all persistent toxic substances be virtually eliminated;

(b) Financial assistance to construct publicly owned waste treatment works be provided by a combination of local, state, provincial, and federal participation; and

(c) Coordinated planning processes and best management practices be developed and implemented by the respective jurisdictions to ensure adequate control of all sources of pollutants.

ARTICLE III

GENERAL OBJECTIVES

The Parties adopt the following General Objectives for the Great Lakes System. These waters should be:

(a) Free from substances that directly or indirectly enter the waters as a result of human activity and that will settle to form putrescent or otherwise objectionable sludge deposits, or that will adversely affect aquatic life or waterfowl;

(b) Free from floating materials such as debris, oil, scum, and other immiscible substances resulting from human activities in amounts that are unsightly or deleterious;

(c) Free from materials and heat directly or indirectly entering the water as a result of human activity that alone, or in combination with other materials, will produce colour, odour, taste, or other conditions in such a degree as to interfere with beneficial uses;

(d) Free from materials and heat directly or indirectly entering the water as a result of human activity that alone, or in combination with other materials, will produce conditions that are toxic or harmful to human, animal, or aquatic life; and

(e) Free from nutrients directly or indirectly entering the waters as a result of human activity in amounts that create growths of aquatic life that interfere with beneficial uses.

ARTICLE IV

SPECIFIC OBJECTIVES

1. The Parties adopt the Specific Objectives for the boundary waters of the Great Lakes System as set forth in Annex 1, subject to the following:

(a) The Specific Objectives adopted pursuant to this Article represent the minimum levels of water quality desired in the boundary waters of the Great Lakes System and are not intended to preclude the establishment of more stringent requirements.

(b) The determination of the achievement of Specific Objectives shall be based on statistically valid sampling data.

(c) Notwithstanding the adoption of Specific Objectives, all reasonable and practicable measures shall be taken to maintain or improve the existing water quality in those areas of the boundary waters of the Great Lakes System where such water quality is better than that prescribed by the Specific Objectives, and in those areas having outstanding natural resource value.

(d) The responsible regulatory agencies shall not consider flow augmentation as a substitute for adequate treatment to meet the Specific Objectives.

(e) The Parties recognize that in certain areas of inshore waters natural phenomena exist which, despite the best efforts of the Parties, will prevent the achievement of some of the Specific Objectives. As early as possible, these areas should be identified explicitly by the appropriate jurisdictions and reported to the International Joint Commission.

(f) The Parties recognize that there are areas in the boundary waters of the Great Lakes System where, due to human activity, one or more of the General or Specific Objectives of the Agreement are not being met. Pending virtual elimination of the persistent toxic substances in the Great Lakes System, the Parties, in cooperation with the State and Provincial Governments and the Commission, shall identify and work toward the elimination of:

    (i)   Areas of Concern pursuant to Annex 2;

    (ii) Critical Pollutants pursuant to Annex 2; and

    (iii) Point Source Impact Zones pursuant to Annex 2.

2. The Specific Objectives for the boundary waters of the Great Lakes System or for particular portions thereof shall be kept under review by the Parties and the International Joint Commission, which shall make appropriate recommendations.

3. The Parties shall consult on:

(a) The establishment of Specific Objectives to protect beneficial uses from the combined effects of pollutants; and

(b) The control of pollutant loading rates for each lake basin to protect the integrity of the ecosystem over the long term.

ARTICLE V

STANDARDS, OTHER REGULATORY REQUIREMENTS, AND RESEARCH

1. Water quality standards and other regulatory requirements of the Parties shall be consistent with the achievement of the General and Specific Objectives. The Parties shall use their best efforts to ensure that water quality standards and other regula-

tory requirements of the State and Provincial Government shall similarly be consistent with the achievement of these Objectives. Flow augmentation shall not be considered as a substitute for adequate treatment to meet water quality standards or other regulatory requirements.

2. The Parties shall use their best efforts to ensure that:

(a) The principal research funding agencies in both countries orient the research programs of their organizations in response to research priorities identified by the Science Advisory Board and recommended by the Commission;

(b) Mechanisms be developed for appropriate cost-effective international cooperation; and

(c) Research priorities are undertaken in accordance with Annex 17.

ARTICLE VI

PROGRAMS AND OTHER MEASURES

1. The Parties, *in cooperation with State and Provincial Governments,* shall continue to develop and implement programs and other measures to fulfil the purpose of this Agreement and to meet the General and Specific Objectives. Where present treatment is inadequate to meet the General and Specific Objectives, additional treatment shall be required. The programs and measures shall include the following:

(a) **Pollution from Municipal Sources.** Programs for the abatement, control and prevention of municipal discharges and urban drainage into the Great Lakes System. These programs shall be completed and in operation as soon as practicable, and in the case of municipal sewage treatment facilities no later than December 31, 1982. These programs shall include:

(i) Construction and operation of waste treatment facilities in all municipalities having sewer systems to provide levels of treatment consistent with the achievement of phosphorus requirements and the General and Specific Objectives, taking into account the effects of waste from other sources;

(ii) Provision of financial resources to ensure prompt construction of needed facilities;

(iii) Establishment of requirements for construction and operating standards for facilities;

(iv) Establishment of pre-treatment requirements for all industrial plants discharging waste into publicly owned treatment works where such industrial wastes are not amenable to adequate treatment or removal using conventional municipal treatment processes;

(v) Development and implementation of practical programs for reducing pollution from storm, sanitary, and combined sewer discharges; and

(vi) Establishment of effective enforcement programs to ensure that the above pollution abatement requirements are fully met;

(b) **Pollution from Industrial Sources.** Programs for the abatement, control and prevention of pollution from industrial sources entering the Great Lakes System. These programs shall be completed and in operation as soon as practicable and in any case no later than December 31, 1983, and shall include:

(i) Establishment of water treatment or control requirements expressed as effluent limitations (concentrations and/or loading limits for specific pollutants where possible) for all industrial plants, including power generating facilities, to provide levels of treatment or reduction or elimination of inputs of substances and effects consistent with the achievement of the General and Specific Objectives and other control requirements, taking into account the effects of waste from other sources;

(ii) Requirements for the substantial elimination of discharges into the Great Lakes System of persistent toxic substances;

(iii) Requirements for control of thermal discharges;

(iv) Measures to control the discharges of radioactive materials into the Great Lakes System;

(v) Requirements to minimize adverse environmental impacts of water intakes;

(vi) Development and implementation of programs to meet industrial pretreatment requirements as specified under sub-paragraph (a) (iv) above; and

(vii) Establishment of effective enforcement programs to ensure the above pollution abatement requirements are fully met;

(c) **Inventory of Pollution Abatement Requirements.** Preparation of an inventory of pollution abatement requirements for all municipal and industrial facilities discharging into the Great Lakes System in order to gauge progress toward the earliest practicable completion and operation of the programs listed in sub-paragraphs (a) and (b) above. This inventory, prepared and revised annually, shall include compliance schedules and status of compliance with monitoring and effluent restrictions, and shall be made available to the International Joint Commission and to the public. In the initial preparation of this inventory, priority shall be given to the problem areas previously identified by the Water Quality Board;

(d) **Eutrophication.** Programs and measures for the reduction and control of inputs of phosphorus and other nutrients, in accordance with the provisions of Annex 3

(e) **Pollution from Agriculture, Forestry, and Other Land Use Activities.** Measures for the abatement and control of pollution from agriculture, forestry and other land use activities including:

(i) Measures for the control of pest control products used in the Great Lakes Basin to ensure that pest control products likely to have long term deleterious effects on the quality of water or its biota be used only as authorized by the responsible regulatory agencies; that inventories of pest control products used in the Great Lakes Basin be established and maintained by appropriate agencies; and that research and educational programs be strengthened to facilitate integration of cultural, biological and chemical pest control techniques;

(ii) Measures for the abatement and control of pollution from animal husbandry operations, including encouragement to appropriate agencies to adopt policies and regulations regarding utilization of animal wastes, and site selection and disposal of liquid and solid wastes, and to strengthen educational and technical assistance programs to enable farmers to establish waste utilization, handling and disposal systems;

(iii) Measures governing the hauling and disposal of liquid and solid wastes, including encouragement to appropriate regulatory agencies to ensure proper location, design and regulation governing land disposal, and to ensure sufficient, adequately trained technical and administrative capability to review plans and to supervise and monitor systems for application of wastes on land;

(iv) Measures to review and supervise road salting practices and salt storage to ensure optimum use of salt and all-weather protection of salt stores in consideration of long-term environmental impact;

(v) Measures to control soil losses from urban and suburban as well as rural areas;

(vi) Measures to encourage and facilitate improvements in land use planning and management programs to take account of impacts on Great Lakes water quality;

(vii) Other advisory programs and measures to abate and control inputs of nutrients, toxic substances and sediments from agricultural, forestry and other land use activities;

(viii) Consideration of future recommendations from the International Joint Commission based on the Pollution from Land Use Activities Reference; and

(ix) Conduct further non-point source programs in accordance with Annex 13;

(f) **Pollution from Shipping Activities.** Measures for the abatement and control of pollution from shipping sources, including:

(i) Programs and compatible regulations to prevent discharges of harmful quantities of oil and hazardous polluting substances, in accordance with Annex 4;

(ii) Compatible regulations for the control of discharges of vessel wastes, in accordance with Annex 5;

(iii) Such compatible regulations to abate and control pollution from shipping sources as may be deemed desirable in the light of continuing reviews and studies to be undertaken in accordance with Annex 6;

(iv) Programs and any necessary compatible regulations in accordance with Annexes 4 and 5, for the safe and efficient handling of shipboard generated wastes, including oil, hazardous polluting substances, garbage, waste water and sewage, and for their subsequent disposal, including the type and quantity of reception facilities and, if applicable, treatment standards; and

(v) Establishment by the Canadian Coast Guard and the United States Coast Guard of a coordinated system for aerial and surface surveillance for the purpose of enforcement of regulations and the early identification, abatement and clean-up of spills of oil, hazardous polluting substances, or other pollution;

(g) **Pollution from Dredging Activities.** Measures for the abatement and control of pollution from all dredging activities, including the development of criteria for the identification of polluted sediments and compatible programs for disposal of polluted dredged material, in accordance with Annex 7. Pending the development of compatible criteria and programs, dredging operations shall be conducted in a manner that will minimize adverse effects on the environment;

(h) **Pollution from Onshore and Offshore Facilities.** Measures for the abatement and control of pollution from onshore and offshore facilities, including programs and compatible regulations for the prevention of discharges of harmful quantities of oil and hazardous polluting substances, in accordance with Annex 8;

(i) **Contingency Plan.** Maintenance of a joint contingency plan for use in the event of a discharge or the imminent threat of a discharge of oil or hazardous polluting substances, in accordance with Annex 9;

(j) **Hazardous Polluting Substances.** Implementation of Annex 10 concerning hazardous polluting substances. The Parties shall further consult from time to time for the purpose of revising the list of hazardous polluting substances and of identifying harmful quantities of these substances;

(k) **Persistent Toxic Substances.** Measures for the control of inputs of persistent toxic substances including control programs for their production, use, distribution and disposal, in accordance with Annex 12;

(l) **Airborne Toxic Substances.** Programs to identify pollutant sources and relative source contribution, including the more accurate definition of wet and dry deposition rates, for those substances which may have significant adverse effects on environmental quality including the indirect effects of impairment of tributary water quality through atmospheric deposition in drainage basins. In cases where significant contributions to Great Lakes pollution from atmospheric sources are identified, the Parties agree to consult on appropriate remedial programs. *The Parties shall conduct such programs in accordance with Annex 15;*

(m) **Surveillance and Monitoring.** Implementation of a coordinated surveillance and monitoring program in the Great Lakes System, in accordance with Annex 11, to assess compliance with pollution control requirements and achievement of the Objectives, to provide information for measuring local and whole lake response to control measures, and to identify emerging problems.

(n) **Remedial Action Plans.** *Measures to ensure the development and implementation of Remedial Action Plans for Areas of Concern pursuant to Annex 2;*

(o) **Lakewide Management Plans.** *Measures to ensure the development and implementation of Lakewide Management Plans to address Critical Pollutants pursuant to Annex 2.*

(p) **Pollution from Contaminated Sediments.** *Measures for the abatement and control of pollution from all contaminated sediments, including the development of chemical and biological criteria for assessing the significance of the relative contamination arising from the sediments and compatible programs for remedial action for polluted sediments in accordance with Annex 14; and*

(q) **Pollution from Contaminated Groundwater and Subsurface Sources.** *Programs for the assessment and control of contaminated groundwater and subsurface sources entering the boundary waters of the Great Lakes System pursuant to Annex 16.*

1. The Parties shall develop and implement such additional programs as they jointly decide are necessary and desirable to fulfil the purpose of this Agreement and to meet the General and Specific Objectives.The Parties shall develop and implement such additional programs as they jointly decide are necessary and desirable to fulfil the purpose of this Agreement and to meet the General and Specific Objectives.

ARTICLE VII

POWERS, RESPONSIBILITIES AND FUNCTIONS OF THE INTERNATIONAL JOINT COMMISSION

1. The International Joint Commission shall assist in the implementation of this Agreement. Accordingly, the Commission is hereby given, by a Reference pursuant to Article IX of the Boundary Waters Treaty, the following responsibilities:

(a) Collation, analysis and dissemination of data and information supplied by the Parties and State and Provincial Governments relating to the quality of the boundary waters of the Great Lakes System and to pollution that enters the boundary waters from tributary waters and other sources;

(b) Collection, analysis and dissemination of data and information concerning the General and Specific Objectives and the operation and effectiveness of the programs and other measures established pursuant to this Agreement;

(c) Tendering of advice and recommendations to the Parties and to the State and Provincial Governments on problems of and matters related to the quality of the boundary waters of the Great Lakes System including specific recommendations concerning the General and Specific Objectives, legislation, standards and other regulatory requirements, programs and other measures, and intergovernmental agreements relating to the quality of these waters;

(d) Tendering of advice and recommendations to the Parties in connection with matters covered under the Annexes to this Agreement;

(e) Provision of assistance in the coordination of the joint activities envisaged by this Agreement;

(f) Provision of assistance in and advice on matters related to research in the Great Lakes Basin Ecosystem, including identification of objectives for research activities, tendering of advice and recommendations concerning research to the Parties and to the State and Provincial Governments, and dissemination of information concerning research to interested persons and agencies;

(g) Investigations of such subjects related to the Great Lakes Basin Ecosystem as the Parties may from time to time refer to it.

2. In the discharge of its responsibilities under this Reference, the Commission may exercise all of the powers conferred upon it by the Boundary Waters Treaty and by any legislation passed pursuant thereto including the power to conduct public hearings and to compel the testimony of witnesses and the production of documents.

3. The Commission shall make a full report to the Parties and to the State and Provincial Governments no less frequently than biennially concerning progress toward the achievement of the General and Specific Objectives including, as appropriate, matters related to Annexes to this Agreement. This report shall include an assessment of the effectiveness of the programs and other measures undertaken pursuant to this Agreement, and advice and recommendations. In alternate years, the Commission may submit a summary report. The Commission may at any time make special reports to the Parties, to the State and Provincial Governments and to the public concerning any problem of water quality in the Great Lakes System.

4. The Commission may in its discretion publish any report, statement or other document prepared by it in the discharge of its functions under this Reference.

5. The Commission shall have authority to verify independently the data and other information submitted by the Parties and by the State and Provincial Governments through such tests or other means as appear appropriate to it, consistent with the Boundary Waters Treaty and with applicable legislation.

6. The Commission shall carry out its responsibilities under the Reference utilizing principally the services of the Water Quality Board and the Science Advisory Board established under Article VIII of this Agreement. The Commission shall also ensure liaison and coordination between the institutions established under this Agreement and other institutions which may address concerns relevant to the Great Lakes Basin Ecosystem, including both those within its purview, such as those Boards related to the Great Lakes levels and air pollution matters, and other international bodies as appropriate.

ARTICLE VIII

JOINT INSTITUTIONS AND REGIONAL OFFICE

1. To assist the International Joint Commission in the exercise of the powers and responsibilities assigned to it under this Agreement, there shall be two Boards:

    (a) A Great Lakes Water Quality Board which shall be the principal advisor to the Commission. The Board shall be composed of an equal number of members from Canada and the United States, including representatives from the Parties and each of the State and Provincial Governments; and

    (b) A Great Lakes Science Advisory Board shall provide advice on research to the Commission and to the Water Quality Board. The Board shall further provide advice on scientific matters referred to it by the Commission, or by the Water Quality Board in consultation with the Commission. The Science Advisory Board shall consist of managers of Great Lakes research programs and recognized experts on Great Lakes water quality problems and related fields.

2. The members of the Water Quality Board and the Science Advisory Board shall be appointed by the Commission after consultation with the appropriate government or governments concerned. The functions of the Boards shall be as specified in the terms of Reference appended to this Agreement.

3. To provide administrative support and technical assistance to the two Boards, and to provide information service for the programs, including public hearings, undertaken by the International Joint Commission and by the Boards, there shall be a Great Lakes Regional Office of the International Joint Commission. Specific duties and organization of the Office shall be as specified in the Terms of Reference appended to this Agreement.

4. The Commission shall submit an annual budget of anticipated expenses to be incurred in carrying out its responsibilities under this Agreement to the Parties for approval. Each Party shall seek funds to pay one-half of the annual budget so approved, but neither Party shall be under an obligation to pay a larger amount than the other toward this budget.

ARTICLE IX

SUBMISSION AND EXCHANGE OF INFORMATION

1. The International Joint Commission shall be given at its request any data or other information relating to water quality in the Great Lakes System in accordance with procedures established by the Commission.

2. The Commission shall make available to the Parties and to the State and Provincial Governments upon request all data or other information furnished to it in accordance with the Article.

3. Each Party shall make available to the other at its request any data or other information in its control relating to water quality in the Great Lakes System.

4. Notwithstanding any other provision of this Agreement, the Commission shall not release without the consent of the owner any information identified as proprietary information under the law of the place where such information has been acquired.

ARTICLE X

CONSULTATION AND REVIEW

1. Following the receipt of each report submitted to the Parties by the International Joint Commission in accordance with paragraph 3 of Article VII of this Agreement, the Parties shall consult on the recommendations contained in such report and shall consider such action as may be appropriate, including:
   (a) The modification of existing Objectives and the adoption of new Objectives;
   (b) The modification or improvement of programs and joint measures; and
   (c) The amendment of this Agreement or any Annex thereto.
   Additional consultations may be held at the request of either Party on any matter arising out of the implementation of this Agreement.
2. When a Party becomes aware of a special pollution problem that is of joint concern and requires an immediate response, it shall notify and consult the other Party forthwith about appropriate remedial action.
3. *The Parties, in cooperation with State and Provincial Governments, shall meet twice a year to coordinate their respective work plans with regard to the implementation of this Agreement and to evaluate progress made.*
4. The Parties shall conduct a comprehensive review of the operation and effectiveness of this Agreement following every third biennial report of the Commission required under Article VII of this Agreement.

ARTICLE XI

IMPLEMENTATION

1. The obligations undertaken in this Agreement shall be subject to the appropriation of funds in accordance with the constitutional procedures of the Parties.
2. The Parties commit themselves to seek:
   (a) The appropriation of funds required to implement this Agreement, including the funds needed to develop and implement the programs and other measures provided for in Article VI of this Agreement, and the funds required by the International Joint Commission to carry out its responsibilities effectively;
   (b) The enactment of any additional legislation that may be necessary in order to implement the programs and other measures provided for in Article VI of this Agreement; and
   (c) The cooperation of the State and Provincial Governments in all matters relating to this Agreement.

ARTICLE XII

EXISTING RIGHTS AND OBLIGATIONS

Nothing in this Agreement shall be deemed to diminish the rights and obligations of the Parties as set forth in the Boundary Waters Treaty.

ARTICLE XIII

AMENDMENT

1. This Agreement, the Annexes, and the Terms of Reference may be amended by agreement of the Parties. The Annexes may also be amended as provided therein, subject to the requirement that such amendments shall be within the scope of this Agreement. All such amendments to the Annexes shall be confirmed by an exchange of notes or letters between the Parties through diplomatic channels which shall specify the effective date or dates of such amendments.

2. All amendments to this Agreement, the Annexes, and the Terms of Reference shall be communicated promptly to the International Joint Commission.

ARTICLE XIV

ENTRY INTO FORCE AND TERMINATION

This Agreement shall enter into force upon signature by the duly authorized representatives of the Parties, and shall remain in force for a period of five years and thereafter until terminated upon twelve months' notice given in writing by one of the Parties to the other.

ARTICLE XV

SUPERSESSION

This Agreement supersedes the Great Lakes Water Quality Agreement of April 15, 1972, and shall be referred to as the "Great Lakes Water Quality Agreement of 1978."

IN WITNESS WHEREOF the undersigned representatives, duly authorized by their respective Governments, have signed this Agreement.

DONE in duplicate at Ottawa in the English and French languages, both versions being equally authentic, this 22nd day of November 1978.

EN FOI DE QUOI, les représentants soussignées, dûment autorisés par leur Gouvernement respectif, ont signé le présent Accord.

FAIT en double exemplaire à Ottawa en français et en anglais, chaque version faisant également foi, ce 22e jour de novembre 1978.

ANNEX 1

SPECIFIC OBJECTIVES

These Objectives are based on available information on cause/effect relationships between pollutants and receptors to protect the recognized most sensitive use in all waters. These Objectives may be amended, or new Objectives may be added, by mutual consent of the Parties.

I. CHEMICAL

A. **Persistent Toxic Substances**

1. Organic

   (a) Pesticide

Aldrin/Dieldrin The sum of the concentrations of aldrin and dieldrin in water should not exceed 0.001 microgram per litre. The sum of concentrations of aldrin and dieldrin in the edible portion of fish should not exceed 0.3 microgram per gram (wet weight basis) for the protection of human consumers of fish

Chlordane The concentration of chlordane in water should not exceed 0.06 micrograms per litre for the protection of aquatic life.

DDT and Metabolites The sum of the concentrations of DDT and its metabolites in water should not exceed 0.003 micrograms per litre. The sum of the concentrations of DDT and its metabolites in whole fish should not exceed 1.0 microgram per gram (wet weight basis) for the protection of fish-consuming aquatic birds.

Endrin The concentration of endrin in water should not exceed 0.002 micrograms per litre. The concentration of endrin in the edible portion of fish should not exceed 0.3 micrograms per gram (wet weight basis) for the protection of human consumers of fish.

Heptachlor/Heptachlor Epoxide The sum of the concentrations of heptachlor and heptachlor epoxide in water should not exceed 0.001 micrograms per litre. The sum of concentrations of heptachlor and heptachlor epoxide in edible portions of fish should not exceed 0.3 micrograms per gram (wet weight basis) for the protection of human consumers of fish.

Lindane The concentration of lindane in water should not exceed 0.01 micrograms per litre for the protection of aquatic life. The concentration of lindane in edible portions of fish should not exceed 0.3 micrograms per gram (wet weight basis) for the protection of human consumers of fish.

Methoxychlor The concentration of methoxychlor in water should not exceed 0.04 micrograms per litre for the protection of aquatic life.

Mirex For the protection of aquatic organisms and fish-consuming birds and animals, mirex and its degradation products should be substantially absent from water and aquatic organisms. Substantially absent here means less than detection levels as determined by the best scientific methodology available.

Toxaphene The concentration of toxaphene in water should not exceed 0.008 micrograms per litre for the protection of aquatic life.

   (b) Other Compounds

Phthalic Acid Esters The concentration of dibutyl phthalate and di (2-ethylhexyl) phthalate in water should not exceed 4.0 micrograms per litre and

0.6 micrograms per litre, respectively, for the protection of aquatic life. Other phthalic acid esters should not exceed 0.2 micrograms per litre in waters for the protection of aquatic life.

Polychlorinated Biphenyls (PCBs) The concentration of total polychlorinated biphenyls in fish tissues (whole fish, calculated on a wet weight basis), should not exceed 0.1 micrograms per gram for the protection of birds and animals which consume fish.

Unspecific Organic Compounds For other organic contaminants, for which Specific Objectives have not been defined, but which can be demonstrated to be persistent and are likely to be toxic, the concentrations of such compounds in water or aquatic organisms should be substantially absent, i.e., less than detection levels as determined by the best scientific methodology available.

2. Inorganic

    (a) Metals

    Arsenic The concentrations of total arsenic in an unfiltered water sample should not exceed 50 micrograms per litre to protect raw waters for public water supplies.

    Cadmium The concentration of total cadmium in an unfiltered water sample should not exceed 0.2 micrograms per litre to protect aquatic life.

    Chromium The concentration of total chromium in an unfiltered water sample should not exceed 50 micrograms per litre to protect raw waters of public water supplies.

    Copper The concentration of total copper in an unfiltered water sample should not exceed 5 micrograms per litre to protect aquatic life.

    Iron The concentration of total iron in an unfiltered water sample should not exceed 300 micrograms per litre to protect aquatic life.

    Lead The concentration of total lead in an unfiltered water sample should not exceed 10 micrograms per litre in Lake Superior, 20 micrograms per litre in Lake Huron and 25 micrograms per litre in all remaining Great Lakes to protect aquatic life.

    Mercury The concentration of total mercury in a filtered water sample should not exceed 0.2 micrograms per litre nor should the concentration of total mercury in whole fish exceed 0.5 micrograms per gram (wet weight basis) to protect aquatic life and fish-consuming birds.

    Nickel The concentration of total nickel in an unfiltered water sample should not exceed 25 micrograms per litre to protect aquatic life.

    Selenium The concentration of total selenium in an unfiltered water sample should not exceed 10 micrograms per litre to protect the raw water for public water supplies.

    Zinc The concentration of total zinc in an unfiltered water sample should not exceed 30 micrograms per litre to protect aquatic life.

(b) Other Inorganic Substances

Fluoride The concentration of total fluoride in an unfiltered water sample should not exceed 1200 micrograms per litre to protect raw water for public water supplies.

Total Dissolved Solids In Lake Erie, Lake Ontario and the International Section of the St. Lawrence River, the level of total dissolved solids should not exceed 200 milligrams per litre. In the St. Clair River, Lake St. Clair, the Detroit River and the Niagara River, the level should be consistent with maintaining the levels of total dissolved solids in Lake Erie and Lake Ontario not to exceed 200 milligrams per litre. In the remaining boundary waters, pending further study, the level of total dissolved solids should not exceed present levels.

B. **Non-Persistent Toxic Substances**

1. Organic Substances

    (a) Pesticides

    Diazinon The concentration of diazinon in an unfiltered water sample should not exceed 0.08 micrograms per litre for the protection of aquatic life.

    Guthion The concentration of guthion in an unfiltered water sample should not exceed 0.005 micrograms per litre for the protection of aquatic life.

    Parathion The concentration of parathion in an unfiltered water sample should not exceed 0.008 micrograms per litre for the protection of aquatic life.

    Other Pesticides The concentration of unspecified, non-persistent pesticides should not exceed 0.05 of the median lethal concentration on a 96-hour test for any sensitive local species.

    (b) Other substances

    Unspecified Non-Persistent Toxic Substances and Complex Effluents Unspecified non-persistent toxic substances and complex effluents of municipal, industrial or other origin should not be present in concentrations which exceed 0.05 of the median lethal concentration in a 96-hour test for any sensitive local species to protect aquatic life.

    Oil and Petrochemicals Oil and petrochemicals should not be present in concentrations that:

    (i)   can be detected as visible film, sheen or discoloration on the surface;

    (ii) can be detected by odour;

    (iii) can cause tainting of edible aquatic organisms; and

    (iv) can form deposits on shorelines and bottom sediments that are detectable by sight or odour, or are deleterious to resident aquatic organisms.

2. Inorganic Substances

    Ammonia The concentration of un-ionized ammonia (NH_3) should not exceed 20 micrograms per litre for the protection of aquatic life. Concentrations of total ammonia should not exceed 500 micrograms per litre for the protection of public water supplies.

Hydrogen Sulfide The concentration of undissociated hydrogen sulfide should not exceed 2.0 micrograms per litre to protect aquatic life.

C. **Other Substances**

1. Dissolved oxygen In the connecting channels and in the upper waters of the Lakes, the dissolved oxygen level should not be less than 6.0 milligrams per litre at any time; in hypolimnetic waters, it should be not less than necessary for the support of fishlife, particularly cold water species.

2. pH Values of pH should not be outside the range of 6.5 to 9.0, nor should discharge change the pH at the boundary of a limited use zone more than 0.5 units from that of the ambient waters.

3. Nutrients

   Phosphorus The concentration should be limited to the extend necessary to prevent nuisance growths of algae, weeds and slimes that are or may become injurious to any beneficial water use. (Specific phosphorus control requirements are set out in Annex 3.)

4. Tainting Substances

   (a) Raw public water supply sources should be essentially free from objectionable taste and odour for aesthetic reasons.

   (b) Levels of phenolic compounds should not exceed 1.0 microgram per litre in public water supplies to protect against taste and odour in domestic water.

   (c) Substances entering the water as the result of human activity that cause tainting of edible aquatic organisms should not be present in concentrations which will lower the acceptability of these organisms as determined by organoleptic tests.

II. PHYSICAL

A. **Asbestos** Asbestos should be kept at the lowest practical level and in any event should be controlled to the extent necessary to prevent harmful effects on human health.

B. **Temperature** There should be no change in temperature that would adversely affect any local or general use of the waters.

C. **Settleable and Suspended Solids, and Light Transmission** For the protection of aquatic life, waters should be free from substances attributable to municipal, industrial or other discharges resulting from human activity that will settle to form putrescent or otherwise objectionable sludge deposits or that will alter the value of Secchi disc depth by more than 10 per cent.

III. MICROBIOLOGICAL

Waters used for body contact recreation activities should be substantially free from bacteria, fungi, or viruses that may produce enteric disorders or eye, ear, nose, throat and skin infections or other human diseases and infections.

IV. RADIOLOGICAL

The level of radioactivity in waters outside of any defined source control area should not result in a TED50 (total equivalent dose integrated over 50 years as calculated in accordance with the methodology established by the International Commission on Radiological Protection) greater than 1 millirem to the whole body from a daily ingestion of 2.2 litres of lake water for one year. For dose commitments between 1 and 5 millirem at the periphery of the source control area, source investigation and corrective action are recommended if releases are not as low as reasonably achievable. For dose commitments greater than 5 millirem, the responsible regulatory authorities shall determine appropriate corrective action.

SPECIFIC OBJECTIVES – SUPPLEMENT TO ANNEX 1

1. **General Principles**

   (a) <u>Interim Objectives for Persistent Toxic Substances</u> Consistent with the policy stated in paragraph (a) of Article II and Paragraph 2 of Annex 12 that the discharge of any or all persistent toxic substances be virtually eliminated, the Specific Objectives set out in Annex 1 for such substances are adopted as interim objectives.

   (b) <u>Detection Levels</u> As used in this Annex, "absent" means that the substances are not detectable when analyzed using the best available technology, which may include biological indicators. Detection levels will be subject to change as technology improves and new levels are adopted.

2. **Specific Objectives Review Process**

   (a) The Parties, in consultation with State and Provincial Governments, shall consult on or before July 1, 1988, and at least once every two years thereafter for the purpose of considering the adoption of proposals by the Parties, State and Provincial Governments or recommendations of the Commission to:

      (i) establish or modify Specific Objectives under Annex 1; and

      (ii) establish action levels under Annex 12.

      The Parties, in cooperation with State and Provincial Governments, shall ensure that the public is consulted in the development and adoption of the Specific Objectives.

   (b) In proposing a substance for a new Specific Objective, the Parties, State and Provincial Governments or the Commission shall be guided by, but not limited to, the lists prepared by the Parties under paragraph (c), below, identifying substances that are present or potentially present within the water, sediment or aquatic biota of the Great Lakes System and are believed, singly or in synergistic or additive combination with another substance, to have acute or chronic toxic effects on aquatic, animal or human life.

   (c) The Parties, on or before December 31, 1988, shall compile and maintain three lists of substances as follows:

(i) List No. 1 shall consist of all substances (1) believed to be present within the water, sediment or aquatic biota of the Great Lakes System and (2) believed, singly or in synergistic or additive combination with another substance, to have acute or chronic toxic effects on aquatic, animal or human life.

(ii) List No. 2 shall consist of all substances (1) believed to be present within the water, sediment or aquatic biota of the Great Lakes System and (2) believed, singly, or in synergistic or additive combination with another substance to have the potential to cause acute or chronic toxic effects on aquatic, animal or human life.

(iii) List No. 3 shall consist of all substances (1) believed to have the potential of being discharged into the Great Lakes System and (2) believed, singly or in synergistic or additive combination with another substance, to have acute or chronic toxic effects on aquatic, animal or human life.

In compiling such lists, the Parties shall employ all data available, including that resulting from activities undertaken pursuant to Annex 12.

(c) Determinations regarding whether a substance, singly or in synergistic or additive combinations with another substance, has actual or potential acute or chronic effects or whether a substance has the potential of being discharged into the Great Lakes System according to paragraph (c) above, shall be made using standard methods agreed to by the Parties in consultation with State and Provincial Governments by April 1988.

3. **Lake Ecosystem Objectives.** Consistent with the purpose of this Agreement to maintain the chemical, physical and biological integrity of the waters of the Great Lakes Basin Ecosystem, the Parties, in consultation with State and Provincial Governments, agree to develop the following ecosystem objectives for the boundary waters of the Great Lakes System, or portions thereof, and for Lake Michigan:

(a) <u>Lake Superior</u> The Lake should be maintained as a balanced and stable oligotrophic ecosystem with lake trout as the top aquatic predator of a cold-water community and the Pontoporeia hoyi as a key organism in a food chain; and

(b) <u>Other Great Lakes</u> Ecosystem Objectives shall be developed as the state of knowledge permits for the rest of the boundary of the Great Lakes System, or portions thereof, and for Lake Michigan.

ANNEX 2 – REMEDIAL ACTION PLANS AND LAKEWIDE MANAGEMENT PLANS

1. **Definitions.** As used in this Annex:

(a) "Area of Concern" means a geographic area that fails to meet the General or Specific Objectives of the Agreement where such failure has caused or is likely to cause impairment of beneficial use or of the area's ability to support aquatic life.

(b) "Critical Pollutants" means substances that persist at levels that, singly or in synergistic or additive combination, are causing, or are likely to cause, impairment of beneficial uses despite past application of regulatory controls due to their:

    (i) presence in open lake waters;

    (ii) ability to cause or contribute to a failure to meet Agreement objectives through their recognized threat to human health and aquatic life; or

    (iii) ability to bioaccumulate.

(c) "Impairment of beneficial use(s)" means a change in the chemical, physical or biological integrity of the Great Lakes System sufficient to cause any of the following:

    (i) restrictions on fish and wildlife consumption;

    (ii) tainting of fish and wildlife flavour;

    (iii) degradation of fish wildlife populations;

    (iv) fish tumors or other deformities;

    (v) bird or animal deformities or reproduction problems;

    (vi) degradation of benthos;

    (vii) restrictions on dredging activities;

    (viii) eutrophication or undesirable algae;

    (ix) restrictions on drinking water consumption, or taste and odour problems

    (x) beach closings;

    (xi) degradation of aesthetics;

    (xii) added costs to agriculture or industry;

    (xiii) degradation of phytoplankton and zooplankton populations; and

    (xiv) loss of fish and wildlife habitat.

(d) "Point Source Impact Zone" is defined as an area of water contiguous to a point source where the water quality does not comply with the General and Specific Objectives of this Agreement.

2. **General Principles**

(a) Remedial Action Plans and Lakewide Management Plans shall embody a systematic and comprehensive ecosystem approach to restoring and protecting beneficial uses in Areas of Concern or in open lake waters.

(b) Such Plans shall provide a continuing historical record of the assessment of Areas of Concern or Critical Pollutants, proposed remedial actions and their method of implementation, as well as changes in environmental conditions that result from such actions, including significant milestones in restoring beneficial uses to Areas of Concern or open lake waters. They are to serve as an important step toward virtual elimination of persistent toxic substances and toward restoring and maintaining the chemical, physical and biological integrity of the Great Lakes Basin Ecosystem.

(c) The Parties, State and Provincial Governments, and the Commission have identified Areas of Concern and the development of the of Remedial Action Plans for them has begun. Furthermore, the Parties and State   and Provincial Governments have begun developing lakewide strategies for Lakes Ontario and Michigan. By incorporating an Annex for Remedial Action Plans and Lakewide Management Plans in this Agreement, the Parties intend to endorse and build upon these existing efforts.

(d) Point source impact zones exist in the vicinity of some point source discharges. Pending the achievement of the virtual elimination of persistent toxic substances, the size of such zones shall be reduced to the maximum extent possible by the best available technology so as to limit the effects of toxic substances in the vicinity of these discharges. These zones shall not be acutely toxic to aquatic species, nor shall their recognition be considered a substitute for adequate treatment or control of discharges at their sources.

(e) The Parties, in cooperation with State and Provincial Governments, shall ensure that the public is consulted in all actions undertaken pursuant to this Annex.

3. **Designation of Areas of Concern**. The Parties, in cooperation with State and Provincial Governments and the Commission, shall designate geographic Areas of Concern. The Commission, in its evaluation role, shall review progress in addressing Areas of Concern, and recommend additional Areas of Concern for designation by each Party.

4. **Remedial Action Plans for Areas of Concern**

(a) The Parties shall cooperate with State and Provincial Governments to ensure that Remedial Action Plans are developed and implemented for Areas of Concern. Each plan shall include:

(i) a definition and detailed description of the environmental problem in the Areas of Concern, including a definition of the beneficial uses that are impaired, the degree of impairment and the geographic extent of such impairment;

(ii) a definition of the causes of the use impairment, including a description of all known sources of pollutants involved and an evaluation of other possible sources;

(iii) an evaluation of remedial measures in place;

(iv) an evaluation of alternative additional measures to restore beneficial uses;

(v) a selection of additional remedial measures to restore beneficial uses and a schedule for their implementation;

(vi) an identification of the persons or agencies responsible for implementation of remedial measures;

(vii) a process for evaluating remedial measure implementation and effectiveness; and

(viii) a description of surveillance and monitoring processes to track the effectiveness of remedial measures and the eventual confirmation of the restoration of uses.

(b) The Parties, in cooperation with State and Provincial Governments, shall ensure that affected State and Provincial Governments not now covered by this Agreement will be involved in the development of such plans and consulted on their implementation.

(c) The Parties shall cooperate with State and Provincial Governments to classify Areas of Concern by their stage of restoration progressing from the definition of the problems and causes, through the selection of remedial measures, to the implementation of remedial programs, the monitoring of recovery, and, when identified beneficial uses are no longer impaired and the area restored, the removal of its designation as an Area of Concern.

(d) The Remedial Action Plans shall be submitted to the Commission for review and comment at three stages:

(i) when a definition of the problem has been completed under sub-paragraphs 4 (a) (i) and (ii);

(ii) when remedial and regulatory measures are selected under sub-paragraphs 4 (a)(iii), (iv),(v) and (vi); and

(iii) when monitoring indicates that identified beneficial uses have been restored under sub-paragraphs 4(a) (vii) and (viii).

5. **Designation of Critical Pollutants for the Development of Lakewide Management Plans**. The Parties, in cooperation with State and Provincial Governments and the Commission, shall designate Critical Pollutants for the boundary waters of the Great Lakes System or for a portion thereof. The Commission, in its evaluative role, shall review progress in addressing Critical Pollutants and recommend additional Critical Pollutants for designation by the Parties. Substances on List No. 1 under Annex 1 Supplement shall be considered for designation as Critical Pollutants.

6. **Lakewide Management Plans for Critical Pollutants**

(a) The Parties, in consultation with State and Provincial Governments, shall develop and implement Lakewide Management Plans for open lake waters, except for Lake Michigan where the Government of the United States of America shall have that responsibility. Such Plans shall be designed to reduce loadings of Critical Pollutants in order to restore beneficial uses, Lakewide Management Plans shall not allow increases in pollutant loadings. in areas where Specific Objectives are not exceeded.

Such Plans shall include:

(i) a definition of the threat to human health or aquatic life posed by Critical Pollutants, singly or in synergistic or additive combinations with another substance, including their contribution to the impairment of beneficial uses;

(ii) an evaluation of information available on concentration, sources, and pathways of the Critical Pollutants in the Great Lakes System, including all information on loadings of the Critical Pollutants from all sources, and an estimation of total loadings of the Critical Pollutants by modelling or other identified methods;

(iii) steps to be taken pursuant to Article VI of this Agreement to develop the information necessary to determine the schedule of load reduction of Critical Pollutants that would result in meeting Agreement Objectives, including steps to develop the necessary standard approached and agreed procedures;

(iv) a determination of load reduction of Critical Pollutants necessary to meet Agreement Objectives;

(v) an evaluation of remedial measures presently in place, and alternative additional measures that could be applied to decrease loadings of Critical Pollutants;

(vi) identification of the additional remedial measures that are needed to achieve the reduction of loadings and to eliminate the contribution to impairment of beneficial uses from Critical Pollutants, including an implementation schedule;

(vii) identification of the persons or agencies responsible for implementation of the remedial measures in question;

(viii) a process for evaluating remedial measure implementation and effectiveness;

(ix) a description of surveillance and monitoring to track the effectiveness of the remedial measures and the eventual elimination of the contribution to impairments of beneficial uses from the Critical Pollutants;

(x) a process for recognizing the absence of a Critical Pollutant in open lake waters.

(b) The Parties shall classify efforts to reduce Critical Pollutants by their stages of elimination progressing from the definition of the problem, through the selection of remedial measures, to the implementation of remedial programs, the monitoring of recovery, and the removal of designation as a Critical Pollutant when it is no longer likely to cause, singly or in synergistic or additive combination with another substance, impairment of identified beneficial uses.

(c) Lakewide Management Plans shall be submitted to the Commission for review and comment at four stages;

(i) When a definition of the problem has been completed under sub-paragraphs 6 (a)(i), (ii) and (iii);

   (ii) When the schedule of load reductions is determined under paragraph 6(a) (i), (ii) and (iii);

  (iii) When remedial measures are selected under sub-paragraph 6 (a)(v), (vi) and (vii); and

  (iv) When monitoring indicates that the contribution of the Critical Pollutants to impairment of identified beneficial uses has been eliminated under sub-paragraphs 6(a)(viii) and (ix)

7. **Reporting Progress**

  (a) Point Source Impact Zones that are associated with direct significant discharges of industrial and municipal wastes shall be identified delineated and reported to the Commission beginning September 30, 1989. They shall be reviewed biennially and their limits revised to achieve the maximum possible reduction in size and effect in accordance with improvements in waste treatment technology and consistent with the policy of virtual elimination of persistent toxic substances.

  (b) The Parties shall report, by December 31, 1988, and biennially thereafter, to the Commission on the progress in developing and implementing the Remedial Action Plans and Lakewide Management Plans and in restoring beneficial uses. Information from these reports shall be included in the Commission's biennial report under paragraph 3 of Article VII.

ANNEX 3 – CONTROL OF PHOSPHORUS

1. The purpose of the following programs is to minimize eutrophication problems and to prevent degradation with regard to phosphorus in the boundary waters of the Great Lakes System. The Goals of phosphorus control are:

  (a) Restoration of year-round aerobic conditions in the bottom waters of the Central Basin of Lake Erie;

  (b) Substantial reduction in the present levels of algal biomass to a level below that of a nuisance condition in Lake Erie;

  (c) Reduction in present levels of algal biomass to below that of a nuisance condition in Lake Ontario unleading the International Section of the St. Lawrence River;

  (d) Maintenance of the oligotrophic state and relative algal biomass of Lakes Superior and Huron;

  (e) Substantial elimination of algal nuisance growths in Lake Michigan to restore it to oligotrophic state; and

  (f) The elimination of algal nuisance in bays and in other areas wherever they occur.

2. The following programs shall be developed and implemented to reduce input of phosphorus to the Great Lakes:

  (a) Construction and operation of municipal waste treatment facilities in all plants discharging more than one million gallons per day to achieve, where necessary to meet the loading allocation be developed pursuant to paragraph 3 below, or to meet local conditions, whichever are more stringent, effluent concentration of 1.0 milligram per litre total phosphorus maximum for plants in the basins of Lakes Superior, Michigan, and Huron, and of 0.5 milligram per litre total phosphorus maximum for plants in the basins of Lakes Ontario and Erie.

(b) Regulation of phosphorus introduction from industrial discharges to the maximum practicable extent.

(c) Reduction to the maximum extent practicable of phosphorus introduced from diffuse sources into Lakes Superior, Michigan, and Huron; and the reduction by 30 per cent of phosphorus introduced from diffuse sources into Lakes Ontario and Erie, where necessary to meet the loading allocations to be developed pursuant to paragraph 3 below, or to meet local conditions, whichever is more stringent.

(d) Reduction of phosphorus in household detergents to 0.5 per cent by weight where necessary to meet the loading allocation to be developed pursuant to paragraph 3 below, or to meet local conditions, whichever are more stringent.

(e) Maintenance of a viable research program to seek maximum efficiency and effectiveness in the control of phosphorus introductions into the Great Lakes.

3. The following table establishes phosphorus loads for the base year (1976) and future phosphorus loads. The Parties, in cooperation with the State and Provincial Governments, shall within eighteen months after the date of entry into force of this Agreement confirm the future phosphorus loads, and based on these establish load allocations and compliance schedules, taking into account the recommendations of the International Joint Commission arising from the Pollution from Land Use Activities Reference. Until such loading allocations and compliance schedules are established, the Parties agree to maintain the programs and other measures specified in Annex 2 of the Great Lakes Water Quality Agreement of 1972.

BASIN	1976 PHOSPHORUS LOAD IN METRIC TONNES PER YEAR	FUTURE PHOSPHORUS LOAD IN METRIC TONNES PER YEAR
Lake Superior	3,600	3,400*
Lake Michigan	6,700	5,600*
Main Lake Huron	3,000	2,800
Georgian Bay	630	600*
North Channel	550	520*

Saginaw Bay	870	440*
Lake Erie	20,000	11,000**
Lake Ontario	11,000	7,000**

* These loadings would result if all municipal plants over one million gallons per day achieved an effluent of 1 milligram per litre of phosphorus.

** These loadings are required to meet the goals stated in paragraph 1 above.

PHOSPHORUS LOAD REDUCTION SUPPLEMENT TO ANNEX 3 OF THE 1978 AGREEMENT BETWEEN THE UNITED STATES OF AMERICA AND CANADA ON GREAT LAKES WATER QUALITY

1. The purpose of this Supplement is to outline measures to fulfill the commitments undertaken pursuant to paragraph 3 of Annex 3 of the 1978 Great Lakes Water Quality Agreement which requires that:

> ". . . .The Parties, in cooperation with the State and Provincial Governments, shall within eighteen months after the date of entry into force of this Agreement confirm the future phosphorus loads, and based on these establish load allocations and compliance schedules, taking into account the recommendations of the International Joint Commission arising from the Pollution from Land Use Activities Reference . . ."

2. Table 1 establishes the recommended phosphorus target loads which represent planning guides for the Parties. Table 1 replaces the table contained in paragraph 3 of Annex 3 of the 1978 Great Lakes Water Quality Agreement (GLWQA).

TABLE 1 – PHOSPHORUS TARGET LOADS, METRIC TONNES PER YEAR

BASIN	PHOSPHORUS TARGET LOADS
Lake Superior	*See Section 3(b)*
Lake Michigan	"
Main Lake Huron	"
Georgian Bay	"
North Channel	"
Saginaw Bay	440*
Lake Erie	11,000**
Lake Ontario	7,000**

*Target load designed to alleviate drinking water taste and odour problems.

**Target loads proposed to meet ecosystem objectives in Annex 3. The allocation of the phosphorus target loads between the two countries shall be consistent with the equal rights of both Parties in the use of their boundary waters.

3. **Phosphorus Load Reductions**

    (a) Lower Lakes: Table 2 summarizes the estimated phosphorus loading that will be discharged to the Lower Lakes basins when all municipal waste treatment facilities over one million gallons per day achieve compliance with the one milligram per litre (1 mg/l) effluent concentration (on a monthly average basis) as required by Article VI, 1(a) of the 1978 GLWQA. The table also shows the further reductions required to meet the Phosphorus Target Loads.

    TABLE 2 – PHOSPHORUS LOAD REDUCTION TARGETS, METRIC TONNES PER YEAR

BASIN	ESTIMATED LOADINGS AT 1 MG/L*	PHOSPHORUS TARGET LOAD	ESTIMATES OF FURTHER REDUCTIONS REQUIRED
Lake Erie	13,000	11,000	2,000
Lake Ontario	7,430	7,000	430

    *Estimated loading when all municipal waste treatment facilities over one million gallons/day achieve 1 mg/1 phosphorus effluent target levels.

    (b) Upper Lakes: Load reductions for the Upper Lakes will be accomplished by achieving the 1 mg/l phosphorus effluent concentration (on a monthly average) at municipal waste treatment facilities discharging more than one million gallons per day. The Parties further agree to maintain the present oligotrophic state of the open waters and relative algal biomass of Lakes Superior and Huron. In addition, the United States agrees to undertake efforts to achieve the substantial elimination of algal nuisance growths in Lake Michigan. Further measures will be implemented as required for Saginaw Bay, various localized nearshore problem areas and Green Bay.

    (c) Table 3 presents the distribution of further reductions in phosphorus loading required for Lake Erie (in metric tonnes/year) in order to achieve the estimated target loads. These figures will be used by the Parties in the development of detailed plans for achieving further phosphorus reductions as described in 4(a) and (b) below.

    TABLE 3 – ALLOCATION OF REDUCTIONS TO MEET TARGET LOADS FOR LAKE ERIE AS SHOWN IN TABLE 1

CANADA	U.S.	TOTAL
300	1,700	2,000

    (d) For Lake Ontario, the Parties, in cooperation and full consultation with State and Provincial Governments, agree to review the measures to achieve further phosphorus reductions in this Basin and will, within one year, meet to allocate the further phosphorus reductions between the parties. Plans to achieve the required reductions set out in Table 2 will be developed using these figures in accordance with procedures described in 4(a) and (b) below.

4. **Phosphorus Load Reduction Plans**

    (a) Phosphorus load reduction plans will be developed and implemented by the Parties in cooperation and full consultation with State and Provincial governments to achieve the phosphorus reductions for Lake Erie and Ontario described in Table 2. The plans will include phosphorus control programs and other measures as outlined in Section 5 and will describe any additional measures which will be undertaken to evaluate and review progress in achieving the phosphorus load reductions. A staged approach, incorporating target dates for achieving further reductions, will be included in the plans to provide the Parties and State and Provincial governments with a framework for implementing and evaluating the effectiveness of controls.

    (b) These detailed plans shall be tabled by the Parties with the International Joint Commission 18 months after agreement on this Supplement to Annex 3. The Parties will provide the Commission with progress reports and annual updates of these plans.

5. **Programs and Other Measures.** The following phosphorus control programs and measures will be developed and implemented by the Parties in cooperation and full consultation with State and Provincial governments to achieve the required reductions in accordance with the plans developed pursuant to Section 4. The Parties recognize that the responsibility for the control on nonpoint sources is shared between the Parties and the State and Provincial governments.

    (a) <u>Municipal Waste Treatment Facilities</u>

        (i) Priority will be given to the continuation and intensification of efforts to ensure that municipal waste treatment facilities discharging more that one million gallons per day achieve an effluent concentration of 1 mg/1 total phosphorus on a monthly average.

        (ii) Where necessary, consideration will be given to operating facilities capable of greater phosphorus reduction at higher level of phosphorus removal than that required in 5(a)(i).

        (iii) Where necessary, municipal waste treatment facilities designed, built, expanded or modified after October 1, 1983 should allow for later modification to provide for greater removal of phosphorus than that required under 5 (a)(i).

    (b) <u>Detergent Phosphorus Limitation</u>. Priority will be given to continuing efforts to limit phosphorus in household detergents.

    (c) <u>Industrial Discharges</u>. Reasonable and practical measures will be undertaken to control industrial sources of phosphorus.

(d) <u>Nonpoint Source Programs and Measures</u>. Priority management areas will be identified and designated for application of urban and agricultural programs and measures which include:

(i)   Urban drainage management control programs where feasible consisting of level 1 measures throughout the Great Lakes Basin; and level 2 measures where necessary to achieve reductions or where local environmental conditions dictate (Note 1); and

(ii) Agricultural nonpoint source management programs where feasible consisting of level 1 measures throughout the Basin and level 2 measures where necessary to achieve reductions of where local environmental conditions dictate (Note 1).

NOTE 1: *Level 1 nonpoint source control options include:* <u>Agricultural:</u> adoption of management practices such as: animal husbandry control measures, crop residue management, conservation tillage, no-till, winter cover-crops, crop rotation, strip cropping, vegetated buffer strips along stream and ditch banks, and improved fertilizer management practices. <u>Urban:</u> adoption of management practices such as: erosion controls, use of natural storage capacities and street cleaning. *Level 2 nonpoint source controls include Level 1 plus:* <u>Agricultural</u>: adoption of intensive practices such as: contour plowing, contour strip cropping, contour diversions, tile outlet-terraces, flow control structures, grassed waterways, sedimentation basins and livestock manure storage facilities. <u>Urban</u>: adoption of practices such as: artificial detention and sedimentation of stormwater and runoff and reduction of phosphorus in combined sewer overflows.

(e) <u>Research.</u> Pursuant to the provisions of paragraph 2(e) of Annex 3, the Parties will make special efforts to assure that their research activities will be responsive to the Programs and Other Measures described herein.

(f) <u>Monitoring and Surveillance.</u> The Parties will develop and implement surveillance and monitoring measures to determine the progress of Phosphorus Load Reduction Plans for the Lower Lakes as called for under Section 4 above, and to evaluate efforts taken by the Parties to reduce phosphorus in the Great Lakes Basin. These measures will include an inventory of areas treated, watershed modelling and improved measurement of tributary loadings to the Lower Lakes for the purpose of providing improved nonpoint source loading estimates and the monitoring of mass loadings to the Upper Lakes to maintain or improve the environmental conditions described in Section 3(b).

ANNEX 4 – DISCHARGES OF OIL AND HAZARDOUS POLLUTING SUB-STANCES FROM VESSELS

1. **Definition**. As used in this Annex:

    (a) "Discharge" includes, but is not limited to, any spilling, leaking, pumping, pouring, emitting or dumping; it does not include unavoidable direct discharges of oil from a properly functioning vessel engine;

    (b) "Harmful quantity of oil" means any quantity of oil that, if discharged from a ship that is stationary into clear calm water on a clear day, would produce a film or a sheen upon, or discolouration of, the surface of the water or adjoining shoreline, or that would cause a sludge or emission to be deposited beneath the surface of the water or upon the adjoining shoreline;

    (c) "Oil" means oil of any kind or in any form, including, but not limited to, petroleum, fuel oil, oil sludge, oil refuse, oil mixed with ballast or bilge water and oil mixed with wastes other than dredged material;

    (d) "Tanker" means any vessel designed for the carriage of liquid cargo in bulk; and

    (e) "Vessel" means any ship, barge or other floating craft, where or not self-propelled.

2. **General Principles**. Compatible regulation shall be adopted for the prevention of discharges into the Great Lakes System of harmful quantities of oil and hazardous polluting substances from vessels in accordance with the following principles;

    (a) The discharge of a harmful quantity of oil or hazardous polluting substance, including any such quantities as may be contained in ballast water, shall be prohibited and made subject to appropriate penalties; and

    (b) As soon as any person in charge has knowledge of any discharge, or probable discharge, of harmful quantities of oil or hazardous polluting substances, immediate notice of such discharge shall be given to the appropriate agency in the jurisdiction where the discharge occurs; failure to give this notice shall be made subject to appropriate penalties.

3. **Oil.** The programs and measures to be adopted for the prevention of discharges of harmful quantities of oil shall include;

    (a) Compatible regulations for design, construction, and operation of vessels based on the following principles.

    (i) Each vessel shall have a suitable means of containing on board cargo oil spills caused by loading or unloading operations;

    (ii) Each vessel shall have a suitable means of containing on board fuel oils spills caused by loading or unloading operations, including those from tank vents and overflow pipes;

    (iii) Each vessel shall have the capability of retaining on board oily wastes accumulated during vessel operation;

(iv) Each vessel shall be capable of off-loading retained oily wastes to a reception facility;

(v) Each vessel shall be provided with a means for rapidly and safely stopping the flow of cargo or fuel oil during loading, unloading or bunkering operations in the event of an emergency;

(vi) Each vessel shall be provided with suitable lighting to adequately illuminate all cargo and fuel oil handling areas if the loading, unloading or bunkering operations occur at night;

(vii) Hose assemblies used on board vessels for oil loading, unloading, or bunkering shall be suitably designed, identified, and inspected to minimize the possibility of failure; and

(viii) Oil loading, unloading, and bunkering systems shall be suitably designed, identified, and inspected to minimize the possibility of failure; and

(b) Programs to ensure that merchant vessel personnel are trained in all functions involved in the use, handling, and stowage of oil and in procedures for abatement of oil pollution.

4. **Hazardous Polluting Substances.** The programs and measures to be adopted for the prevention of discharges of harmful quantities of hazardous polluting substances carried as cargo shall include:

(a) Compatible regulations for the design, construction, and operation of vessels using as a guide the standards developed by the International Maritime Organizations (IMO), including the following additional requirements:

(i) Each vessel shall have a suitable means of containing on board spills caused by loading or unloading operations;

(ii) Each vessel shall have a capability of retaining on board wastes accumulated during vessel operation;

(iii) Each vessel shall be capable of off-loading wastes retained to a reception facility;

(iv) Each vessel shall be provided with a means for rapidly and safely stopping the flow during loading or unloading operations in the event of an emergency; and

(v) Each vessel shall be provided with suitable lighting to adequately illuminate all cargo handling areas if the loading or unloading operations occur at night;

(b) Identification of vessels carrying cargoes of hazardous polluting substances in bulk, containers, and package form, and of all such cargoes;

(c) Identification in vessel manifests of all hazardous polluting substances;

(d) Carriage and storage arrangements of all hazardous polluting substances in packaged form using as a guide the International Maritime Dangerous Goods Code; and

(e) Programs to ensure that merchant vessel personnel are trained in all functions involving the use, handling, and stowage of hazardous polluting substances; the abatement of pollution from such substances; and the hazards associated with the handling of such substances.

5. **Additional Measures**. Both Parties, in cooperation with State and Provincial Governments shall take, as appropriate, action to ensure the provision of adequate facilities for the reception, treatment, and subsequent disposal of oil and hazardous polluting substances wastes from all vessels.

ANNEX 5 – DISCHARGES OF VESSEL WASTES

1. **Definitions**. As used in this Annex:

    (a) "Discharge" includes, but is not limited to, any spilling, leaking, pumping, emitting, and dumping;

    (b) "Garbage" means all kinds of victual, domestic, and operational wastes, excluding fresh fish and parts thereof generated during the normal operation of the ship and liable to be disposed of continually or periodically;

    (c) "Sewage" means human or animal waste generated on board ship and includes wastes from water closets, urinals, or a hospital facility;

    (d) "Vessel" means any ship, barge or other floating craft, whether or not self-propelled; and

    (e) "Waste water" means water in combination with other substances, including ballast water and water used for washing cargo holds, but excluding water in combination with oil, hazardous polluting substances, or sewage.

2. **General Principles.** Compatible regulations shall be adopted governing the discharge into the Great Lakes System of garbage, sewage, and waste water from vessels in accordance with the following principles:

    (a) The discharge of garbage shall be prohibited and made subject to appropriate penalties;

    (b) The discharge of waste water in harmful amounts or concentrations shall be prohibited and made subject to appropriate penalties; and

    (c) Every vessel operating in these waters that is provided with toilet facilities shall be equipped with a device or devices to contain, incinerate, or treat sewage to an adequate degree; appropriate penalties shall be provided for failure to comply with the regulation.

3. **Critical Use Areas**. Critical use areas of the Great Lakes System may be designate where the discharge of waste water or sewage shall be limited or prohibited.

4. *The Parties, in cooperation with State and Provincial Governments, shall establish regulation to control the discharge of sewage from* pleasure craft of other classes of vessels operating in the Great Lakes System or designated areas thereof.

5. **Additional Measures**. The Parties shall take, as appropriate, action to ensure the provision of adequate facilities for the reception, treatment, and subsequent disposal of garbage, waste water, and sewage from all vessels.

ANNEX 6 – REVIEW OF POLLUTION FROM SHIPPING SOURCES

1. **Review**. The Canadian Coast Guard and the United States Coast Guard shall continue to review services, systems, programs, recommendations, standards and regulations relating to shipping activities for the purpose of maintaining or improving Great Lakes water quality. The reviews shall include:

   (a) Review of vessel equipment, vessel manning, and navigation practices or procedures, and of aids to navigation and vessel traffic management, for the purpose of precluding casualties which may be deleterious to water quality;

   (b) Review of practices and procedures regarding waste water and their deleterious effect on water quality, including, as required, studies to determine if live fish or invertebrates in ballast water discharges into the Great Lakes System constitute a threat to the System;

   (c) Review of practices and procedures, as well as current technology for the treatment of vessel sewage;

   (d) Review of current practices and procedures regarding the prevention of pollution from the loading, or unloading, or on board transfer of cargo; and

   (e) Review of international ship safety, pollution prevention and civil liability conventions and standards developed by the International Maritime Organization to determine their applicability in the boundary waters of the Great Lakes System

2. **Consultation**. Representatives of the Canadian Coast Guard and the United States Coast Guard, and other interested agencies, shall meet at least annually to consider Annexes 4, 5, 6, 8 and 9 of this Agreement. A report of this annual consultation shall be furnished to the International Joint Commission prior to its annual meeting on Great Lakes water quality. The purpose of the consultation shall be to:

   (a) Provide an interchange of information with respect to continuing reviews, ongoing studies, and areas of concern;

   (b) Identify and determine the relative importance of problems requiring further study; and

   (c) Apportion responsibility, as between the Canadian Coast Guard and the United States Coast Guard, for the studies, or portions thereof, which were identified in subparagraph 2(b) above.

3. **Studies**. Where a review identifies additional areas for improvement, the Canadian Coast Guard and the United States Coast Guard, and other interested agencies, will undertake a study to establish improved procedures for the abatement and control of pollution from shipping sources, and will:

   (a) Develop a brief study description which will include the nature of the perceived problem, procedures to quantify the problem, alternative solutions to the problem, procedures to determine the best alternative, and an estimated completion date;

(b) Transmit study descriptions to the International Joint Commission and other interested agencies:

(c) Transmit the study, or a brief summary of its conclusions, to the International Joint Commission and other interested agencies; and

(d) Transmit a brief status report to the International Joint Commission and other interested agencies if the study is not completed by the estimated completion date.

4. **Responsibility**. Responsibility for the coordination of the review, consultation, and studies is assigned to the Canadian Coast Guard and the United States Coast Guard.

ANNEX 7 – DREDGING

1. There shall be established, under the auspices of the Water Quality Board, a Subcommittee on Dredging. The Subcommittee shall:

(a) Review the existing practices in both countries relating to dredging activities, as well as the previous work done by the International Working Group on Dredging, with the objective of developing, within one year of the date of entry into force of this Agreement, compatible guidelines and criteria for dredging activities in the boundary waters of the Great Lakes System;

(b) Maintain a register of significant dredging projects being undertaken in the Great Lakes System with information to allow for the assessment of the environmental effects of the projects. The register shall include pertinent statistics to allow for the assessment of pollution loadings from dredged materials to the Great Lakes System;

(c) Encourage the exchange of information relating to developments of dredging technology and environmental research.

2. The Subcommittee shall identify specific criteria for the classification of polluted sediments of designated areas of intensive and continuing dredging activities within the Great Lakes System. Pending development of criteria and guidelines by the Subcommittee, and their acceptance of the Parties, the Parties shall continue to apply the criteria now in use by the regulatory authorities; however, neither party shall be precluded from applying standards more stringent than those now in use.

3. The Parties shall continue to direct particular attention to the identification and preservation of significant wetland areas in the Great Lakes Basin Ecosystem which are threatened by dredging and disposal activities.

4. The Parties shall encourage research and investigate advances in dredging technology and the pathways, fate and effects of nutrients and contaminants of dredged materials.

5. The Subcommittee shall undertake any other activities as the Water Quality Board may direct.

ANNEX 8 – DISCHARGES FROM ONSHORE AND OFFSHORE FACILITIES

1. **Definitions**. As used in this Annex:

   (a) "Discharge" means the introduction of polluting substances into receiving waters and includes, but is not limited to, any spilling, leaking, pumping, pouring, emitting or dumping; it does not include continuous effluent discharges from municipal or industrial treatment facilities;

   (b) "Harmful quantity of oil" means any quantity of oil that, if discharged into clear calm waters on a clear day, would produce a film or sheen upon, or discoloration of the surface of the water or adjoining shoreline, or that would cause a sludge or emulsion to be deposited beneath the surface of the water or upon the adjoining shoreline;

   (c) "Facility" includes motor vehicles, rolling stock, pipelines, and any other facility that is used or capable of being used for the purpose of processing, producing, storing, disposing, transferring or transporting oil or hazardous polluting substances, but excludes vessels;

   (d) "Offshore facility" means any facility of any kind located in, on or under any water;

   (e) "Onshore facility" means any facility of any kind located in, on or under, any land other than submerged land;

   (f) "Oil" means oil of any kind or in any form, include, but not limited to petroleum, fuel oil, oil sludge, oil refuse, and oil mixed with wastes, but does not include constituents of dredged spoil.

2. **Principles**. Regulations shall be adopted for the prevention of discharges into the Great Lakes System of harmful quantities of oil and hazardous polluting substances from onshore and offshore facilities in accordance with the following principles:

   (a) Discharges of harmful quantities of oil or hazardous polluting substances shall be prohibited and made subject to appropriate penalties;

   (b) As soon as any person in charge has knowledge of any discharge of harmful quantities of oil or hazardous polluting substances, immediate notice of such discharge shall be given to the appropriate agency in the jurisdiction where the discharge occurs; failure to give this notice shall be made subject to appropriate penalties.

3. **Programs and Measures**. The programs and measures to be adopted shall include the following:

   (a) Review of the design, construction, and location of both existing and new facilities for their adequacy to prevent the discharge of oil or hazardous polluting substances;

   (b) Review of the operation, maintenance and inspection procedures of facilities for their adequacy to prevent the discharge of oil or hazardous polluting substances;

(c) Development and implementation of regulations and personnel training programs to ensure the safe use and handling of oil or hazardous polluting substances;

(d) Programs to ensure that at each facility plans and provisions are made and equipment provided to stop rapidly and safely, contain, and clean up discharges of oil or hazardous polluting substances; and

(e) Compatible regulations and other programs for the identification and placarding of containers, vehicles and other facilities containing, carrying, or handling oil or hazardous polluting substances; and where appropriate notification to appropriate agencies of vehicle movements, maintenance of a registry, and identification in manifests of such substances to be carried.

4. **Implementation**.

(a) Each Party shall submit a report to the International Joint Commission outlining its programs and measures, existing or proposed, for the implementation of this Annex within six months of the date of entry into force of this Agreement.

(b) The report shall outline programs and measures, existing or proposed, for each of the following types of onshore and offshore facilities:

(i) land transportation including rail and road modes;

(ii) pipelines on land and submerged under water;

(iii) offshore drilling rigs and wells;

(iv) storage facilities both onshore and offshore; and

(v) wharves and terminals with trestle or underwater pipeway connections to land and offshore island type structures and buoys used for the handling of oil and hazardous polluting substances.

(c) The report shall outline programs and measures, existing or proposed, for any other type of onshore or offshore facility.

(d) Upon receipt of the reports, the Commission , in consultation with the Parties, shall review the programs and measures outlined for adequacy and compatibility and, if necessary, make recommendation to rectify any such inadequacy or incompatibility it finds.

ANNEX 9 – JOINT CONTINGENCY PLAN

1. **The Plan**. *Annex one (CANUSLAK) of the Canada-United States Joint Marine Contingency Plan, as amended or reviewed, shall be maintained in force for the Great Lakes.* The Canadian Coast Guard and the United States Coast Guard shall, in cooperation with other affected parties, identify and provide detailed Supplements for areas of high risk and of particular concern in augmentation of CANUSLAK. It shall be the responsibility of the United States Coast Guard and the Canadian Coast Guard to coordinate and to maintain the Plan and the Supplements appended thereto.

2. **Purpose**. The purpose of the Plan is to provide for coordinated and integrated response to pollution incidents in the Great Lakes System by responsible federal, state, provincial and local agencies. the Plan supplements the national, provincial and regional plans of the Parties.

3. **Pollution Incidents**.

    (a) A pollution incident is a discharge, or an imminent threat of discharge of oil, hazardous polluting substance or other substance or other substance of such magnitude or significance as to require immediate response to contain, clean up, and dispose of the material

    (b) The objectives of the Plan in pollution incidents are:

        (i) To develop appropriate preparedness measures and effective systems for discovery and reporting the existence of a pollution incident within the area covered by the Plan;

        (ii) To institute prompt measures to restrict the further spread of the pollutant; and

        (iii) To provide adequate cleanup response to pollution incidents.

4. **Funding**. The costs of operations of both Parties under the Plan shall be borne by the Party in whose waters the pollution incident occurred, unless otherwise agreed.

5. **Amendment**. The Canadian Coast Guard and the United States Coast Guard are empowered to amend the Plan subject to the requirement that such amendments shall be consistent with the purpose and objectives of this Annex.

ANNEX 10 – HAZARDOUS POLLUTING SUBSTANCES

1. The Parties shall:

    (a) Maintain a list, to be known as Appendix 1 of this Annex (hereinafter referred to as Appendix 1), of the substances known to have toxic effects on aquatic and animal life and a risk of being discharged to the Great Lakes System;

    (b) Maintain a list, to be known as Appendix 2 of this Annex (hereinafter referred to as Appendix 2), of substances potentially having such effects and such a risk of discharge, and to give priority to the examination of these substances for possible transfer to Appendix 1;

    (c) Ensure that these lists are continually revised in the light of growing scientific knowledge; and

    (d) Develop and implement programs and measures to minimize or eliminate the risk of release of hazardous polluting substances to the Great Lakes System.

2. Hazardous polluting substances to be listed in Appendix 1 shall be determined in accordance with the following procedures:

    (a) Selection of all hazardous substances for listing in Appendix 1 shall be based upon documented toxicological and discharge potential data which have been evaluated by the Parties and deemed to be mutually acceptable.

(b) Revisions to Appendix 1 may be made by mutual consent of the Parties and shall be treated as amendments to this Annex for the purposes of Article XIII of this Agreement.

(c) Using the agreed selection criteria, either Party may recommend at any time a substance to be added to the list in Appendix 1. Such substance need not previously have been listed in Appendix 2. The Party receiving the recommendation will have 60 days to review the associated documentation and either reject the proposed substance or accept the substance pending completion of appropriate procedural or domestic regulatory requirements. Cause for rejection must be documented and submitted to the initiating Party and may be the basis for any further negotiations.

3. The criteria to be applied to the selection of substances as candidates for listing in Appendix 1 are:

(a) Acute toxicological effects, as determined by whether the substance is lethal to:

(i) One-half of a test population of aquatic animals in 96 hours or less at a concentration of 500 milligrams per litre or less; or

(ii) One-half of a test population of animals in 14 days or less when administered in a single oral dose equal to or less than 50 milligrams per kilogram of body weight; or

(iii) One-half of a test population of animals in 14 days or less when dermally exposed to an amount equal to or less that 200 milligrams per kilogram body weight for 24 hours; or

(iv) One-half of a test population of animals in 14 days or less when exposed to a vapour concentration equal to or less than 20 cubic centimetres per cubic meter in air for one hour; or

(v) Aquatic flora as measured by a maximum specific growth rate or total yield of biomass which is 50 per cent lower than a control culture over 14 days in medium at concentrations equal to or less than 100 milligrams per litre.

(b) Risk of discharge into the Great Lakes System, as determined by:

(i) Gathering information on the history of discharges or accidents;

(ii) Assessing the modal risks during transport and determining the use and distribution patterns;

(iii) Identifying quantities manufactured or imported.

4. Potentially hazardous polluting substances to be listed in Appendix 2 of this Annex shall be determined in accordance with the following procedures:

(a) Either Party may add new substances to Appendix 2 by notifying the other in writing that the substance is considered to be a potential hazard because of documented information concerning aquatic toxicity mammalian and other vertebrate toxicity, phytotoxicity, persistence, bio-accumulation, muta-genicity, teratogenicity, carcinogenicity, environmental translocation or because of documented information on risk of discharge to the environ-ment. The documentation of the potential hazard and the selected criteria upon which it is based will also be submitted.

(b) Removal of substances from Appendix 2 shall be by mutual consent of the Parties.

(c) The Parties shall give priority to the examination of substances listed in Appendix 2 for possible transfer to Appendix 1.

5. Programs and measures to control the risk of pollution from transport, storage, handling and disposal of hazardous polluting substances are contained in Annexes 4 and 8; and

6. In addition to the lists of hazardous polluting substances described in Appen-dices 1 and 2 to this Annex, practice and procedures consistent with the general principles of this Agreement shall be applied to those substances categorized as marine pollutants by the International Maritime Organization.

APPENDIX 1 – HAZARDOUS POLLUTING SUBSTANCES

Acetaldehyde	Acetic Acid	Acetic Anhydride
Acetone Cyanohydrin	Acetyl Bromide	Acetyl Chloride
Acrolein	Acrylonitrile	Aldrin
Allyl Alcohol	Allyl Chloride	Aluminum Sulfate
Ammonia	Ammonium Acetate	Ammonium Benzoate
Ammonium Bicarbonate	Ammonium Bichromate	Ammonium Bifluoride
Ammonium Bisulfite	Ammonium Carbamate	Ammonium Carbonate
Ammonium Chloride	Ammonium Chromate	Ammonium Citrate, Dibasic
Ammonium Fluoborate	Ammonium Fluoride	Ammonium Hydroxide
Ammonium Oxalate	Ammonium Silicofluoride	Ammonium Sulfamate
Ammonium Sulfide	Ammonium Sulfite	Ammonium Tartrate
Ammonium Thicoyanate	Ammonium Thiosulfate	Amyl Acetate
Aniline	Antimony Pentachloride	Antimony Potassium Tartrate
Antimony Tribromide	Antimony Trichloride	Antimony Trifluoride
Antimony Trioxide	Arsenic Disulfide	Arsenic Pentoxide
Arsenic Trichloride	Arsenic Trioxide	Arsenic Trisulphide
Barium Cyanide	Benzene	Benzoic Acid
Benzonitrile	Benzoyl Chloride	Benzyl Chloride
Beryllium Chloride	Beryllium Fluoride	Beryllium Nitrate
Butyl Acetate	Butylamine	Butyric Acid
Cadmium Acetate	Cadmium Bromide	Cadmium Chloride
Calcium Arsenate	Calcium Arsenite	Calcium Carbide

Calcium Chromate	Calcium Cyanide	Calcium Dodecylbenzenesulfonate
Calcium Hydroxide	Calcium Hypochlorite	Calcium Oxide
Captan	Carbaryl	Carbon Disulfide
Chlordane	Chlorine	Chlorobenzene
Chloroform	Chlorosulfonic Acid	Chlorpyrifos
Chromic Acetate	Chromic Acid	Chromic Sulfate
Chromous Chloride	Cobaltous Bromide	Cobaltous Foremate
Cobaltous Sulfamate	Coumaphos	Cresol
Cupric Acetate	Cupric Acetoarsenite	Cupric Chloride
Cupric Nitrate	Cupric Oxalate	Cupric Sulfate
Cupric Sulfate, Ammoniated	Cupric Tartrate	Cyanogen Chloride
Cyclohexane	2, 4-D Acid	2, 4-D Esters
Dalapon	DDT	Diazinon
Dicamba	Dichlobenil	Dichlone
Dichlorvos	Dieldrin	Diethylamine
Dimethylamine	Dinitrobenzene (mixed)	Dinitrophenol
Diquat	Disulfoton	Diuron
Dedocylbenzenesulfonic Acid	Endosulfan	Endrin
Ethion	Ethylbenzene	Ethylenediamine
EDTA	Ferric Ammonium Citrate	Ferric Ammonium Oxalate
Ferric Chloride	Ferric Fluoride	Ferric Nitrate
Ferric Sulfate	Ferrous Ammonium Sulfate	Ferrous Chloride
Ferrous Sulfate	Formaldehyde	Formic Acid
Fumaric Acid	Furfural	Guthion
Heptachlor	Hydrochloric Acid	Hydrofluoric Acid
Hydrogen Cyanide	Isoprene	Isopropanolamine
		Dodecylbenzenesulfonate
Kelthane	Lead Acetate	Lead Arsenate
Lead Chloride	Lead Fluoborate	Lead Fluoride
Lead Iodide	Lead Nitrate	Lead Stearate
Lead Sulfate	Lead Sulfide	Lead Thiocyanate
Lindane	Lithium Chromate	Malathion
Maleic Acid	Maleic Anhydride	Mercuric Cyanide
Mercuric Nitrate	Mercuric Sulfate	Mercuric Thiocyanate
Mercurous Nitrate	Methoxychlor	Methyl Mercaptan
Methyl Methacrylate	Methyl Parathion	Mevinphos
Mexacarbate	Monoethylamine	Monomethylamine
Naled	Naphthalene	Naphtenic Acid
Nickel Ammonium Sulfate	Nickel Chloride	Nickel Hydroxide
Nickel Nitrate	Nickel Sulfate	Nitric Acid
Nitrobenzene	Nitrogen Dioxide	Nitrophenol (mixed)

Paraformaldehyde	Parathion	Pentachlorophenol
Phenol	Phosgene	Phosphoric Acid
Phosphorous	Phosphorus Oxychloride	Phosphorus Pentasulfide
Phosphorus Trichloride	Polychlorinated Biphenyls	Potassium Arsenate
Potassium Arsenite	Potassium Bichromate	Potassium Chromate
Potassium Cyanide	Potassium Hydroxide	Potassium Permanganate
Propionic Acid	Propionic Anhydride	Pyrethrins
Quinoline	Resorcinol	Selenium Oxide
Sodium	Sodium Arsenate	Sodium Arsenite
Sodium Bichromate	Sodium Bifluoride	Sodium Bisulfite
Sodium Chromate	Sodium Cyanide	Sodium Dodecylbenzenesulfonate
Sodium Fluoride	Sodium Hydrosulfide	Sodium Hydroxide
Sodium Hypochlorite	Sodium Methylate	Sodium Nitrite
Sodium Phosphate, Dibasic	Sodium Phosphate, Tribasic	Sodium Selenite
Strontium Chromate	Strychnine	Styrene
Sulfuric Acid	Sulfur Monochloride	2,4,5-T Acid
2,4,5-7 Esters	TDE	Tetraethyl Lead
Tetraethyl Pyrophosphate	Toluene	Toxaphene
Trichlorfon	Trichlorophenol	Triethanolamine Dodecylbenzenesulfonate
Triethylamine	Thrimethylamine	Uranyl Acetate
Uranyl Nitrate	Vanadium Pentoxide	Vanadyl Sulfate
Vinyl Acetate	Xylene (mixed)	Xylenol
Zinc Acetate	Zinc Ammonium Chloride	Zinc Borate
Zinc Bromide	Zinc Charbonate	Zinc Chloride
Zinc Cyanide	Zinc Fluoride	Zinc Formate
Zinc Hydrosulfite	Zinc Nitrate	Zinc Phenolsulfonate
Zinc Phosphide	Zinc Silicofluoride	Zinc Sulfate
Zirconium Nitrate	Zirconium Potassium Fluoride	Zirconium Sulfate
Zirconium Tetrachloride		

APPENDIX 2 – POTENTIAL HAZARDOUS POLLUTING SUBSTANCES

Acridine	Allethrin	Aluminum Fluoride
Aluminum Nitrate	Ammonium Bromide	Ammonium Hypophosphite
Ammonium Iodide	Ammonium Pentaborate	Ammonium Persulfate
Antimony Pentafluoride	Antimycin A	Arsenic Acid
Barhan	Benfluralin	Bensulide
Benzene Hexachloride	Beryllium Sulfate	Butifos
Cadmium	Cadmium Cyanide	Cadmium Nitrate
Captafol	Carbophenothion	Chlorflurazole
Chlorothion	Chlorpropham	Chromic Chloride

Chromium	Chromyl Chloride	Cobaltous Fluoride
Copper	Crotoxyphos	Cupric Carbonate
Cupric Citrate	Cupric Formate	Cupric Glycinate
Cupric Lactate	Cupric Paraamino Benzoate	Cupric Salicylate
Cupric Subacetate	Cuprous Bromide	Demeton
Dibutyl Phthalate	Dicapthon	2,4-Dinitrochlorobenzene
p-Dinitrocresol	Dinocap	Dinoseb
Dioxathion	Dodine	EPN
Gold Trichloride	Hexachlorophene	Hydrogen Sulfide
m-Hydroxybenzoic Acid	p-Hydroxybenzoic	Acid Hydroxylamine
2-Hydroxyphenazine-1-		
Carboxylic Acid	Lactonitrile	Lead Tetraacetate
Lead Thiosulfate	Lead Tungstate	Lithium Bichromate
Malachite Green	Manganese Chloride, Anhydrous	MCPA
Mercuric Acetate	Mercuric Chloride	Mercury
Metam-Sodium	p-Methylamino-Phenol	2-Methyl-Napthoquinone
Neburon	Nickel Formate	Phenylmercuric Acetate
Phenyl Naphthylamine	Phorate	Phosphamidon
Picloram	Potassium Azide	Potassium Cuprocyanide
Potassium Ferricyanide	Propyl Alcohol	Pyridyl Mercuric Acetate
Rotenone	Silver	Silver Nitrate
Silver Sulfate	Sodium Azide	Sodium 2-Chlorotoluene-5-Sulfonate
Sodium Pentachlorophenate	Sodium Phosphate, Monobasic	Sodium Sulfide
Stannous Fluoride	Strontium Nitrate	Sulfoxide
Temephos	Thallium	Thionazin
1,2,4-Trichlorobenzene	Uranium Peroxide	Uranyl Sulfate
Zinc Bichromate	Zinc Potassium Chromate	Zirconium Acetate
Zirconium Oxychloride		

ANNEX 11 – SURVEILLANCE AND MONITORING

1. Surveillance and monitoring activities shall be undertaken for the following purposes:

   (a) **Compliance**. To assess the degree to which jurisdictional control requirements are being met.

   (b) **Achievement of General and Specific Objectives**. To provide definitive information on the location, severity, areal or volume extent, frequency and duration of non-achievement of the Objectives, as a basis for determining the need for more stringent control requirements.

   (c) **Evaluation of Water Quality Trends.** To provide information for measuring local and whole lake response to control measures using trend analysis and cause/effect relationships, and to provide information which will assist in the development and application of predictive techniques for assessing impact of new developments and pollution sources. The results of water quality evaluations will be used for:

(i) assessing the effectiveness of remedial and preventative measures and identifying the need for the improved pollution control;

(ii) assessing enforcement and management strategies; and

(iii) identifying the need for further technology development and research activities.

(d) **Identification of Emerging Problems**. To determine the presence of new or hitherto detected problems in the Great Lakes Basin Ecosystem, leading to the development and implementation of appropriate pollution control measures.

(e) **Annex 2 Programs**. To support the development of Remedial Action Plans for Areas of Concern and Lakewide Management Plans for Critical Pollutants pursuant to Annex 2.

2. A joint surveillance and monitoring program necessary to ensure the attainment of the foregoing purposes shall be developed and implemented among the Parties and the State and Provincial Governments. The Great Lakes International Surveillance Plan contained in the Water Quality Board Annual Report of 1975 and revised in subsequent reports shall serve as a model for the development of the joint surveillance and monitoring program.

3. The program shall include baseline data collection, sample analysis, evaluation and quality assurance programs (including standard sampling and analytical methodology, inter-laboratory comparisons, and compatible data management) to allow assessment of the following:

(a) Inputs from tributaries, point source discharges, atmosphere, and connecting channels;

(b) Whole lake data including that for nearshore areas (such as harbours and embayments, general shoreline and cladophora growth areas), open waters of the Lakes, fish contaminants, and wildlife contaminants;

(c) Overflows including connecting channels, water intakes and outlets;

(d) Total pollutant loadings to, storage and transformation within, and export from the Great Lakes System;

(e) The adequacy of proposed load reductions and schedules contained in Lakewide Management Plans; and

(f) Contributions of various exposure media to the overall human intake of toxic substances in the Great Lakes Basin Ecosystem.

4. **Development of Ecosystem Health Indicators for the Great Lakes.** The Parties agree to develop ecosystem health indicators to assist in evaluating the achievement of the specific objectives for the ecosystem pursuant to Annex 1:

(a) with respect to Lake Superior, lake trout and the crustacean *Pontoporeia hoyi* shall be used as indicators:

Lake Trout

– productivity greater than 0.38 kilograms/hectare;

– stable, self-producing stocks;

– free from contaminants at concentrations that adversely affect the trout themselves or the quality of the harvested products.

Pontoporeia hoyi

– the abundance of the crustacean, Pontoporeia hoyi, maintained through-out the entire lake at present levels of 220–320/(metres)^2 (depths less than 100 metres) and 30–160/(metres)^2 (depths greater than 100 metres); and

(b) with respect to the rest of the boundary waters of the Great Lakes System or portions thereof, and for Lake Michigan, the indicators are to be developed.

ANNEX 12 – PERSISTENT TOXIC SUBSTANCES

1. **Definitions**. As used in this Annex:

   (a) "Persistent toxic substance" means any toxic substance with a half-life in water of greater than eight weeks;

   (b) "Half-life" means the time required for the concentration of a substance to diminish to one-half of its original value in a lake or water body;

   (c) "Early warning system" means a procedure to anticipate future environmental contaminants (i.e., substances having an adverse effect on human health or the environment) and to set priorities for environmental research, monitoring and regulatory action.

2. **General Principles.**

   (a) Regulatory strategies for controlling or preventing the input of persistent toxic substances to the Great Lakes System shall be adopted in accordance with the following principles:

      (i) The intent of programs specified in this Annex is to virtually eliminate the input of persistent toxic substances in order to protect human health and to ensure the continued health and productivity of living aquatic resources and human use thereof;

      (ii) The philosophy adopted for control of inputs of persistent toxic sub-stances shall be zero discharge; and

      (iii) The reduction in the generation of contaminants, particularly persist-ent toxic substances, either through the reduction of the total volume or quantity of waste or through the reduction of the toxicity of waste, or both, shall, wherever possible, be encouraged.

   (b) The Parties shall take all reasonable and practical measures to rehabilitate those portions of the Great Lakes System adversely affected by persistent toxic substances.

3. **Programs**. The Parties in cooperation with the State and Provincial Governments, shall develop and adopt the following programs and measures for the elimination of discharges of persistent toxic substances:

   (a) Identification of raw materials, processes, products, by-products, waste sources and emissions involving persistent toxic substances, and quantitative data on the substances, together with recommendations on handling, use and disposition. Every effort shall be made to complete this inventory by January, 1982;

   (b) Establishment of close coordination between air, water and solid waste programs in order to assess the total input of toxic substances to the Great Lakes System and to define comprehensive, integrated controls;

   (c) Joint programs for disposal of hazardous materials to ensure that these materials such as pesticides, contaminated petroleum products, contaminated sludge and dredge spoils and industrial wastes are properly transported and disposed of. Every effort shall be made to implement these programs by 1980.

4. **Monitoring**. Monitoring and research programs in support of the Great Lakes International Surveillance Plan should be established at a level sufficient to identify:

   (a) Temporal and spatial trends in concentration of persistent toxic substances such as PCB, mirex, DDT, mercury and dieldrin, and of there substances known to be present in biota and sediment of the Great Lakes System;

   (b) The impact of persistent toxic substances on the health of humans and the quality and health of living aquatic systems;

   (c) The sources of input of persistent toxic substances; and

   (d) The presence of previously unidentified persistent toxic substances.

5. **Early Warning System**. An early warning system consisting of, but not restricted to, the following elements shall be established to anticipate future toxic substances problems:

   (a) Development and use of structure-activity correlations to predict environmental characteristics of chemicals;

   (b) Compilation and review of trends in the production, import, and use of chemicals;

   (c) Review of the results of environmental testing on new chemicals;

   (d) Toxicological research on chemicals, and review of research conducted in other countries;

   (e) Maintenance of a biological tissue bank and sediment to permit retroactive analysis to establish trends over time;

   (f) Monitoring to characterize the presence and significance of chemical residues in the environment;

   (g) Development and use of mathematical models to predict consequences of various loading rates of different chemicals;

(h) Development of a data bank for storage of information on physical/chemi-cal properties, toxicology, use and quantities in commerce of known and suspected persistent toxic substances;

(i) Development of data necessary to evaluate the loadings of critical pollutants or other polluting substances identified in the boundary waters of the Great Lakes System; and

(j) Further development and use of reproduction, physiological and biochemical measures in wildlife, fish and humans as health effects indicators and the establishment of a data base for storage, retrieval and interpretation of the data.

6. **Human Health**. The Parties shall establish action levels to protect human health based on multimedia exposure and the interactive effects of toxic sub-stances.

7. **Research**. Research should be intensified to determine the pathways, fate and effects of toxic substances aimed at the protection of human health, fishery resources and wildlife of the Great Lakes Basin Ecosystem. In particular, research should be conducted to determine:

(a) The significance of effects of persistent toxic substances on human health and aquatic life;

(b) Interactive effects of residues of toxic substances on aquatic life, wildlife, and human health; and

(c) Approaches to calculation of acceptable loading rates for persistent toxic substances, especially those which,in part, are naturally occurring.

8. **Reporting**. The Parties shall report, by December 31, 1988 and biennially there-after, on the progress of programs and measures to reduce the generation of contaminants in accordance with the principle in sub-paragraph 2 (a) (iii) above.

ANNEX 13 - POLLUTION FROM NON-POINT SOURCES

1. **Purpose**. This Annex further delineates programs and measures for the abate-ment and reduction on non-point sources of pollution from land-use activities. These include efforts to further reduce non-point source inputs of phosphorus, sediments, toxic substances and microbiological contaminants contained in drainage from urban and rural land, including waste disposal sites, in the Great Lakes System.

2. **Implementation**. The Parties, in conjunction with State and Provincial Govern-ments, shall:

(a) identify land-based activities contribution to water quality problems described in Remedial Action Plans for Areas of Concern, or in Lakewide Management Plans including, but not limited to, phosphorus and Critical Pollutants; and

(b) develop and implement watershed management plans, consistent with the objectives and schedules for individual Remedial Action Plans or Lakewide Management Plans, on priority hydrologic units to reduce non-point source inputs. Such watershed plans shall include a description of priority areas, intergovernmental agreements, implementation schedules, and programs and other measures to fulfill the purpose of this Annex and the General and Specific Objectives of this Agreement. Such measures shall include provisions for regulation of non-point sources of pollution.

3. **Wetlands and their Preservation**. Significant wetland areas in the Great Lakes System that are threatened by urban and agricultural development and waste disposal activities should be identified, preserved and, where necessary, rehabilitated.

4. **Surveillance, Surveys and Demonstration Projects**. Programs and projects shall be implemented in order to determine:

    (a) non-point source pollutants inputs to and outputs from rivers and shoreline areas sufficient to estimate loadings to the boundary waters of the Great Lakes System; and

    (b) the extent of change in land-use and land management practices that significantly affect water quality for the purpose of tracking implementation of remedial measures and estimating associated changes in loadings to the Lakes.

    (c) Demonstration projects of remedial programs on pilot urban and rural watersheds shall be encouraged to advance knowledge and enhance information and education services, including extension services, where applicable.

5. The Parties shall report by December 31, 1988 and biennially thereafter, to the Commission on progress in developing specific watershed management plans and implementing programs and measures to control non-point sources of pollution.

ANNEX 14 - CONTAMINATED SEDIMENT

1. **Objectives**. The Parties shall, in cooperation with State and Provincial Governments, identify the nature and extent of sediment pollution of the Great Lakes System. Based on these findings, they shall develop methods to evaluate both the impact of polluted sediments on the Great Lakes System, and the technological capabilities of programs to remedy such pollution. Information obtained through research and studies pursuant to this Annex shall be used to guide the development of Remedial Action Plans and Lakewide Management Plans pursuant to Annex 2, but shall not be used to forestall the implementation of remedial measures already under way. Dredging for the purpose of navigation is addressed in Annex 7.

2. **Research and Studies**.

    (a) **General**. The Parties, in cooperation with State and Provincial Governments, shall exchange information relating to the mapping, assessment and management of contaminated sediments in the Great Lakes System.

(b) **Surveillance Programs**. The Parties, in cooperation with State and Provincial Governments shall:

(i) evaluate, on or before December 31, 1988 and biennially thereafter, existing methods for quantifying the transfer of contaminants and nutrients to and from bottom sediments for use in determining the impact of polluted sediments on the Great Lakes Basin Ecosystem;

(ii) review practices in both countries regarding the classification of contaminated sediments and establish compatible criteria for the classification of sediment quality;

(iii) develop common methods to quantify the transfer of contaminants and nutrients to and from bottom sediments. Such methods shall be used to determine the impact of polluted sediment of the Great Lakes System. As a first step, biological indicators shall be developed to determine accumulation rates in biota from polluted bottom sediments; and

(iv) develop a standard approach and agreed procedures for the management of contaminated sediments by December 31, 1988.

(c) **Technology Programs**

(i) The Parties shall, on or before December 31, 1988 and biennially thereafter, in cooperation with State and Provincial Governments, evaluate existing technologies for the management of contaminated sediments such as isolation, capping, in-place decontamination and removal of polluted bottom sediment.

(ii) The Parties, in cooperation with State and Provincial Governments shall design and implement demonstration projects for the management of polluted bottom sediment at selected Areas of Concern identified pursuant to Annex 2. The design shall be based on the evaluation(s) made pursuant to sub-paragraph (i) above, the Parties shall meet by June 20, 1988 and jointly design a demonstration program and implementation schedule and report progress biennially thereafter.

3. **Long-Term Measures**. The Parties, in cooperation with State and Provincial Governments, shall also ensure that measures are adopted for the management of contaminated sediment respecting:

(a) the construction and the long-term maintenance of disposal facilities; and

(b) the use of contaminated sediment in the creation of land.

4. **Reporting**. The Parties shall report their progress in implementing this Annex to the Commission biennially, commencing with a report no later than December 31, 1988.

ANNEX 15 – AIRBORNE TOXIC SUBSTANCES

1. **Purpose**. The Parties, in cooperation with State and Provincial Governments, shall conduct research, surveillance and monitoring and implement pollution control measures for the purpose of reducing atmospheric deposition of toxic

substances, particularly persistent toxic substances, to the Great Lakes Basin Ecosystem.

2. **Research**. Research activities shall be conducted to determine pathways, fate and effects of such toxic substances for the protection of the Great Lakes System. In particular, research shall be conducted to:

    (a) understand the processes of wet and dry deposition and those associated with the vapor exchange of toxic substances;

    (b) understand the effects of persistent toxic substances, singly or in synergistic or additive combination with other substances, through aquatic exposure routes on the health of humans and the quality and health of aquatic life where a significant source of these substances is the atmosphere, in accordance with sub-paragraph 4(b) of Annex 12; and

    (c) develop models of the intermediate and long-range movement and transformation of toxic substances to determine;

    (i) the significance of atmospheric loadings to the Great Lakes System relative to other pathways; and

    (ii) the sources of such substances from outside the Great Lakes System.

3. **Surveillance and Monitoring**. The Parties shall:

    (a) establish, as part of the Great Lakes International Surveillance Plan (GLISP) instituted under Annex 11, an Integrated Atmospheric Deposition Network in accordance with paragraph 4 below;

    (b) identify, by means of this Network, toxic substances and, in particular, persistent toxic substances, appearing on List No. 1 described in Annex 1, of those designated as Critical Pollutants pursuant to Annex 2 and their significant sources in accordance with sub-paragraph 4(c) of Annex 12, and to track their movements; and

    (c) utilize this Network in order to:

    (i) determine atmospheric loadings of toxic substances to the Great Lakes System by quantifying the total and net atmospheric input of these same contaminants, pursuant to sub-paragraph 3(a) of Annex 11;

    (ii) define the temporal and spatial trends in the atmospheric deposition of such toxic substances in accordance with sub-paragraph 4(a) of Annex 12; and

    (iii) develop Remedial Action Plans and Lakewide Management Plans pursuant to Annex 2.

4. **Components of the Integrated Atmospheric Deposition Network**. The Parties shall confer on or before October 1, 1988, regarding;

    (a) the identity of the toxic substances to be monitored;

    (b) the number of monitoring and surveillance stations;

    (c) the locations of such stations;

    (d) the equipment at such stations;

(e) quality control and quality assurance procedures; and

(f) a schedule for the construction and commencement of the operation of the stations.

5. **Pollution Control Measures**.

(a) The Parties, in cooperation with State and Provincial Governments, shall develop, adopt and implement measures for the control of the `sources of emissions of toxic substances and the elimination of the sources of emissions of persistent toxic substances in cases where atmospheric deposition of these substances, singly or in synergistic or additive combination with other substances, significantly contributes to pollution of the Great Lakes System. Where such contributions arise from sources beyond the jurisdiction of the Parties, the Parties shall notify the responsible jurisdiction and the Commission of the problem and seek a suitable response.

(b) The Parties shall also assess and encourage the development of pollution control technologies and alternative products to reduce the effect of airborne toxic substances on the Great Lakes System.

6. **Reporting**. The Parties shall report their progress in implementing this Annex to the Commission biennially, commencing with a report no later than December 31, 1988.

ANNEX 16 – POLLUTION FROM CONTAMINATED GROUNDWATER

The Parties, in cooperation with State and Provincial Governments, shall coordinate existing programs to control contaminated groundwater affecting the boundary waters of the Great Lakes System. For this purpose, the Parties shall;

(i) identify existing and potential sources of contaminated groundwater affecting the Great Lakes;

(ii) map hydrogeological conditions in the vicinity of existing and potential sources of contaminated groundwater;

(iii) develop a standard approach and agreed procedures for sampling and analysis of contaminants in groundwater in order to: (1) assess and characterize the degree and extent of contamination; and (2) estimate the loadings of contaminants from groundwater to the Lakes to support the development of Remedial Action Plans and Lakewide Management Plans pursuant to Annex 2;

(iv) control the sources of contamination of groundwater and the contaminated groundwater itself, when the problem has been identified; and

(v) report progress on implementing this Annex to the Commission biennially, commencing with a report no later than December 31, 1988.

ANNEX 17 – RESEARCH AND DEVELOPMENT

1. **Purpose**. This Annex delineates research need to support the achievement of the goals of this Agreement.

2. **Implementation**. The Parties, in cooperation with State and Provincial Governments, shall conduct research in order to:

(a) determine the mass transfer of pollutants between the Great Lakes Basin Ecosystem components of water, sediments, air, land and biota, and the processes controlling the transfer of pollutants across the interfaces between these components in accordance with Annexes 13, 14, 15 and 16;

(b) develop load reduction models for pollutants in the Great Lakes System in accordance with the research requirements of Annexes 2, 11, 12 and 13;

(c) determine the physical and transformational processes affecting the delivery of pollutants by tributaries to the Great Lakes in accordance with Annexes 2, 11, 12 and 13;

(d) determine cause-effect inter-relationships of productivity and ecotoxicity, and identify future research needs in accordance with Annexes 11, 12, 13 and 15;

(e) determine the relationship of contaminated sediments on ecosystem health, in accordance with the research needs of Annexes 2, 12 and 14;

(f) determine pollutant exchanges between the Areas of Concern and the open lakes including cause-effect inter-relationships among nutrients, productivity, sediments, pollutants, biota and ecosystem health, and to develop in-situ chemical, physical and biological remedial options in accordance with Annexes 2, 12, 14 and sub-paragraph 1(f) of Annex 3;

(g) determine the aquatic effects of varying lake levels in relation to pollution sources, particularly respecting the conservation of wetlands and the fate and effects of pollutants in the Great Lakes Basin Ecosystem in accordance with Annexes 2, 11, 12, 13, 15 and 16;

(h) determine the ecotoxicity and toxicity effects of pollutants in the development of water quality objectives in accordance with Annex 1;

(i) determine the impact of water quality and the introduction of non-native species on fish and wildlife populations and habitats in order to develop feasible options for their recovery, restoration or enhancement in accordance with sub-paragraph 1(a) of Article IV and Annexes 1, 2, 11 and 12;

(j) encourage the development of control technologies for treatment of municipal and industrial effluents, atmospheric emissions and the disposal of wastes, including wastes deposited in landfills;

(k) develop action levels for contamination that incorporate multi-media exposures and the interactive effects of chemicals; and

(l) develop approaches to population-based studies to determine the long-term, low-level effects of toxic substances on human health.

**TERMS OF REFERENCE FOR THE JOINT INSTITUTIONS
AND THE GREAT LAKES REGIONAL OFFICE**

1. **Great Lakes Water Quality Board**

   (a) This Board shall be the principal advisor to the International Joint Commission with regard to the exercise of all the function, powers and responsibilities (other than those functions and responsibilities of the Science Advisory Board pursuant to paragraph 2 of these Terms of Reference) assigned to the Commission under this Agreement. In addition, the Board shall carry out such other functions, related to the water quality of the boundary waters of the Great Lakes System, as the Commission may request from time to time.

   (b) The Water Quality Board, at the direction of the Commission, shall:

       (i) Make recommendations on the development and implementation of programs to achieve the purpose of this Agreement;

       (ii) Assemble and evaluate information evolving from such programs;

       (iii) Identify deficiencies in the scope and funding of such programs and evaluate the adequacy and compatibility of results;

       (iv) Examine the appropriateness of such programs in light of present and future socio-economic imperatives; and

       (v) Advise the Commission on the progress and effectiveness of such programs and submit appropriate recommendations.

   (c) The Water Quality Board, on behalf of the Commission, shall undertake liaison and coordination between the institutions established under this Agreement and other institutions and jurisdictions which may address concerns relevant to the Great Lakes Basin Ecosystem so as to ensure a comprehensive and coordinated approach to planning and to the resolution of problems, both current and anticipated.

   (d) The Water Quality Board shall report to the Commission periodically as appropriate, or as required by the Commission, on all aspects relating to the operation and effectiveness of this Agreement.

2. **Great Lakes Science Advisory Board**

   (a) This Board shall be the scientific advisor to the Commission and the Water Quality Board.

   (b) The Science Advisory Board shall be responsible for developing recommendations on all matters related to research and the development of scientific knowledge pertinent to the identification, evaluation and resolution of current and anticipated problems related to Great Lakes water quality.

   (c) To effect these responsibilities the Science Advisory Board shall;

       (i) Review scientific information in order to:

           a. examine the impact and adequacy of research and the reliability of research results, and ensure the dissemination of such results;

           b. identify additional research requirements;

      c.   identify specific research programs for which international coop-
eration is desirable; and

    (ii) Advise jurisdictions of relevant research needs, solicit their involve-
ment and promote coordination.

(d) The Science Advisory Board shall seek analyses, assessments and recommendations from other scientific, professional, academic, governmental or
intergovernmental relevant to Great Lakes Basin Ecosystem research.

(e) The Science Advisory Board shall report to the Commission and the Water
Quality Board periodically as appropriate, or as required by the Commission, on all matters of a scientific or research nature relating to the operation and effectiveness of this Agreement.

3. **The Great Lakes Regional Office**

(a) This Office, located in Windsor, Ontario, shall assist the Commission and the
two Boards in the discharge of the functions specified in subparagraph (b)
below.

(b) The Office shall perform the following functions:

    (i)   Provide administrative support and technical assistance for the Water
Quality Board and the Science Advisory Board and their sub-organiza-
tions, to assist the Boards in discharging effectively the responsibilities,
duties and functions assigned to them.

    (ii) Provide a public information service for the programs, including pub-
lic hearings, undertaken by the Commission and its Boards.

(c) The Office shall be headed by a Director who shall be appointed by the
Commission in consultation with the Parties and with the Co-Chairmen of
the Boards. The position of Director shall alternate between a Canadian citizen and a United States citizen. The term of office for the Director shall be
determined in the review referred to in subparagraph (d) below.

(d) The Parties, mindful of the need to staff the Great Lakes Regional Office to
carry out the functions assigned the Commission by this Agreement, shall,
within six months from the date of entry into force of this Agreement, complete a review of the staffing of the Office. This review shall be conducted by
the Parties based upon recommendations of the Commission after consultation with the Co-Chairmen of the Boards. Subsequent review may be
requested by either Party, or recommended by the Commission, in order to
ensure that the staffing of the Regional Office is maintained at a level and
character commensurate with its assigned functions.

(e) Consistent with the responsibilities assigned to the Commission, and under
the general supervision of the Water Quality Board, the Director shall be
responsible for the management of the Regional Office and its staff in carrying out the functions described herein.

(f) The Co-Chairmen of the Boards, in consultation with the Director, will determine the activities which they wish the Office to carry out on behalf of, or in support of the Boards, within the current capability of the Office and its staff. The Director is responsible to the Co-Chairmen of each Board for activities carried out on behalf of, or in support of such Board, by the Office or individual staff members.

(g) The Commission, in consultation with the Director, will determine the public information activities to be carried out on behalf of the Commission by the Regional Office.

(h) The Director shall be responsible for preparing an annual budget to carry out the functions of the Boards and the Regional Office for submission jointly by the two Boards to the Commission for approval and procurement of resources.

NOTES

Chapter 1. The Canada/United States Partnership for the Great Lakes

1. Havighurst, Walter, ed., *The Great Lakes Reader* (New York and London: Macmillan, 1967).

2. International Joint Commission, *The Great Lakes Water Quality Agreement of 1972* (Ottawa and Washington, D.C.).

3. U.S. Environmental Protection Agency and Government of Canada, *The Great Lakes: An Environmental Atlas and Resource Book* (1995).

4. Preliminary report, U.S. Commission on Ocean Policy, Washington, D.C.

5. International Air Quality Board, *Special Report on Transboundary Air Quality Issues* (Ottawa and Washington, D.C.: International Joint Commission, 1998).

Chapter 2. Origin of the Great Lakes Water Quality Agreement

1. N. F. Dreiziger, "Dreams and Disappointments," in *The International Joint Commission Seventy Years On*, ed. Robert Spencer, John Kirton, and Kim Richard Nossal (Toronto: Centre for International Studies, University of Toronto, 1981).

2. See L. M. Bloomfield and Gerald F. Fitzgerald, *Boundary Waters Problems of Canada and the United States* (Toronto: Carswell, 1958), 2–10.

3. U.S. Environmental Protection Agency, with U.S. Department of Agriculture, U.S. Department of Health, Education, and Welfare, and Department of Interior, *National Conference on Polychlorinated Biphenyls (PCBs)* (Chicago, March 1976), EPA 560/6-75004.

4. Phil Weller, *Fresh Water Seas: Saving the Great Lakes* (Toronto: Between the Lines, 1990), 69–70.

5. L. M. Bloomfield and Gerald F. Fitzgerald, *Boundary Waters Problems of Canada and the United States* (Toronto: Carswell, 1958), 10.

6. John W. Holmes, "Introduction," in Spencer, Kirton, and Nossal, *Seventy Years On*, 6.

7. William R. Willoughby, "Expectations and Experience, 1909–1979," in Spencer,

Kirton, and Nossal, *Seventy Years On*, 24–42.

8. See generally Maxwell Cohen, "The Regime of Boundary Waters: the Canadian–U.S. Experience," *Recueil des Cours* 146 (1975).

9. Former Canadian IJC chair Maxwell Cohen, as quoted in *The Standing Senate Committee on Foreign Affairs, Canada–United States Relations*, vol. 1, *The Institutional Framework for the Relationship* (Ottawa: Queen's Printer, 1975), 41.

10. Appendix 3, "IJC References and Applications, 1912–1977," in Spencer, Kirton, and Nossal, *Seventy Years On*, 142–51.

11. International Joint Commission of Canada and the United States, *Pollution of Lake Erie, Lake Ontario and the International Portion of the St. Lawrence River* (Ottawa and Washington, D.C.: IJC, 1970).

12. Maxwell Cohen, "The Commission from the Inside," in Spencer, Kirton, and Nossal, *Seventy Years On*, 106–23.

13. International Joint Commission, Levels Reference Study Board, *Levels Reference Study: The Great Lakes and St. Lawrence River Basin* (report submitted to the IJC, Ottawa and Washington, D.C., March 1993). The study board recommended that "the governments give no further consideration to five-lakes regulation" (39), and instead, that "prevention and land use management measures . . . be applied" (61).

14. Maxwell Cohen, in "Canada, Senate Committee on Foreign Affairs, Minutes of Proceedings, 18 February 1979," 6, cited in William R. Willoughby, "Expectations and Experience: 1909–1979." See also Cohen, "The Regime of Boundary Waters: The Canadian–U.S. Experience."

15. International Joint Commission of United States and Canada, *Rules of Procedure and Text of Treaty*, part 1 (Ottawa and Washington, D.C.: IJC, 1965), 8.

16. International Joint Commission, *An Annotated Digest of Materials Relating to the Establishment and Development of the International Joint Commission* (prepared for the Canadian Section, Ottawa, 1967).

17. Charles Ross, "Water Pollution Control under the Boundary Waters Treaty of 1909" (presented to the International Association for Great Lakes Research, 19 May 1980).

18. Ibid.

19. Interview, IJC commissioner.

20. Standing Senate Committee on Foreign Affairs, "Canada–United States Relations: The Institutional Framework for the Relationship" (Ottawa: Canadian Senate, December 1975), 42.

21. David LeMarquand and Anthony Scott, "Canada's Environment Relations," in *Resources and the Environment: Perspectives for Canada*, ed. O. P. Dwivedi (Toronto: McLelland and Stewart, 1980), 87.

22. Ibid., 2.

23. Don Munton, "Great Lakes Water Quality: A Study in Environmental Politics and Diplomacy," in *Resources and the Environment*, ed. O. P. Dwivedi, 169–71.

24. International Great Lakes Levels Board, International Joint Commission, *Regulation of Great Lakes Water Levels* (report to the International Joint Commission, 1973).

25. Text of identical letters sent by the Secretary of State for External Affairs, Canada, and Secretary of State, United States, for their respective governments to the respective secretariat offices of the International Joint Commission, 7 October 1964, in International Joint Commission of Canada and the United States, *Pollution of Lake Erie, Lake Ontario and the International Section of the St. Lawrence River*, appendix, 1970.

26. R. A. Vollenweider, *The Scientific Basis of Lake and Stream Eutrophication with Particular Reference to Phosphorus and Nitrogen as Factors in Eutrophication*, DAS/CSI/67-27 (Paris: Organization for Economic Cooperation and Development, 1968); A. M. Beeton, "Eutrophication of the St. Lawrence Lakes," *Limnology and Oceanography* 10 (1965): 240–54.

27. Joseph DePinto and Thomas C. Young, "Great Lakes Water Quality Improvement," *Environmental Science and Technology* 20, no. 8 (1986).

28. Paul Bertram, "Reversing Eutrophication in Lake Erie: Management, Monitoring and Money" (presentation to the 25th International Congress of the Societas Internationalis Limnologae [International Society of Limnologists], Barcelona, Spain, 21 August 1992).

29. For a further discussion, see Phil Weller, *Fresh Water Seas: Saving the Great Lakes* (Toronto: Between the Lines, 1990), 89–93.

30. Peter J. Colby, "Alewife Dieoffs: Why Do They Occur?" *Limnos, the Magazine of the Great Lakes Foundation* 4, no. 2 (Summer 1971): 18–27.

31. Many label the recent problems of Lake Erie pertaining to massive fish kills from the loss of oxygen as the "second battle" for Lake Erie, with the first being in the late 1960s and early 1970s. See Jenni Laidman, "Loss of Oxygen in Central Lake Erie Confounding Researchers: 'Second Battle' Looms for the Center of the Lake," *Toledo Blade*, 18 June 2002.

32. Denis Hayes, *The Official Earth Day Guide to Planet Repair* (Washington, D.C.: Island Press, 2000).

33. International Joint Commission of Canada and the United States, *Pollution of Lake Erie, Lake Ontario, and the International Sections of the St. Lawrence River* (1970).

34. John E. Carroll, *Environmental Diplomacy: An Examination and a Prospective of Canadian–U.S. Transboundary Relations* (Ann Arbor: University of Michigan Press, 1983), 130–31.

35. Interview, participating scientist.

36. Jon McDonagh-Dumler, *Toxic Substances and Federal Water Policy: Application of Kinsdon's Model of Agent Change to the Great Lakes Water Quality Agreement of 1972* (dissertation submitted to the Department of Natural Resources, Michigan State University, East Lansing, Michigan, 2000).

37. See Munton, "Great Lakes Water Quality," 159–62; Carroll, *Environmental Diplomacy*, 130–31.

38. Carroll, *Environmental Diplomacy*, 130–31.

39. Ibid., 131.

40. 1972 Amendments to the Federal Water Pollution Control Act, PL 92-500.

41. C. B. Bourne, "Canada and the Law of International Drainage Basins," in *Canadian Perspectives on International Law and Organizations,* ed. R. St. J. MacDonald, Gerald L. Morris, and Douglas M. Johnston (Toronto: University of Toronto Press, 1974), 488.

42. Comments by Joel Fisher in "Science Advisory Board, Review of Annex 1 of the Great Lakes Water Quality Agreement," a workshop sponsored by the Parties' Implementation Work Group of the Science Advisory Board of the International Joint Commission in collaboration with the Great Lakes Commission, held at the Michigan League, Ann Arbor, Michigan, 21 March 2001. Available at , p. 5.

43. See docket 95 in *Bibliography of Reports* (Washington, Ottawa, Windsor: International Joint Commission, February 1996), 21–28.

44. Ibid., docket 94, 20–21.

45. Article VI on Programs and Measures specifically states that "The Parties, in cooperation with State and Provincial Governments, shall continue to develop and implement programs . . ."

46. Interview, IJC staff.

47. Botts and Krushelnicki, *The Great Lakes: An Environmental Atlas and Resource Book*, 3rd ed. (Chicago: Great Lakes National Program Office, U.S. Environmental Protection Agency, 1995).

48. The dependence of the IJC on voluntary actions by the governments is extensively considered in the literature. One source that compares the powers of the IJC with those of other Great Lakes institutions is Michael Donahue, "Institutional Arrangements for Great Lakes Management: Past Practices and Future Alternatives" (Ph.D. diss., University of Michigan, 1986).

49. Jack Manno, "Advocacy and Diplomacy: NGOs and the Great Lakes Water Quality Agreement," in *Environmental NGOs in World Politics: Linking the Local and the Global*, ed. Thomas Princen and Matthias Finger (London and New York: Routledge, 1994), 99–105.

50. Great Lakes Water Quality Agreement of 1972, Article VI, no. 3. Also, Terms of Reference for the Joint Institutions and the Great Lakes Regional Office, 3(b)(ii).

51. Interview, Regional Office staff.

52. Glenda Daniel, "The Great Lakes Water Quality Agreement: A State Perspective" (prepared for the Great Lakes Governance Project of Dartmouth College, December 1995).

53. National Research Council of the United States and the Royal Society of Canada (NRC/RSC), *The Great Lakes Water Quality Agreement: An Evolving Instrument for*

Ecosystem Management (Washington, D.C.: National Academy Press, 1985), 10–13.

54. In 1979 and 1980, Richard Robbins, executive director of the Lake Michigan Federation, objected to the membership of Dr. Mitchell R. Zavon, Hooker Chemical medical director, on the Science Advisory Board because of the growing controversy over the company's operations near Niagara Falls. See correspondence in Lee Botts Collection, Calumet Archives, Indiana University Northwest.

55. Interview, IJC commissioner.

56. The Third Biennial Report was delayed until 1986, when a fourth report should have been due.

57. Lee Botts, personal observation.

58. Great Lakes United, *Unfulfilled Promises: A Citizen's Review of the International Great Lakes Water Quality Agreement* (Buffalo, N.Y.: GLU, February 1987), 10; *Revised Great Lakes Water Quality Agreement of 1978, As Amended by Protocol Signed November 18, 1987*, Article X, p. 3.

59. For a more extensive review of institutions and agencies in the Great Lakes regime, see Henry A. Regier, "Progress with Remediation Rehabilitation and the Ecosystem Approach," *Alternatives* 13, no. 3 (September/October 1986): 47–54, esp. 51.

Chapter 3. Evolution of the Agreement from 1972 to 1978

1. Joseph DePinto and Thomas C. Young, "Great Lakes Quality Improvement," *Environmental Science and Technology* 20, no. 8 (1986).

2. Interview with Alfred Beeton.

3. "Comeback for the Great Lakes," *Time*, 3 December 1979; Dean Rotbart, "Lake Erie Is Cleaner These Days, or Is It? Some Say Troubles Have Just Started," *Wall Street Journal*, 3 September 1980.

4. Science Advisory Board, International Joint Commission, "A Perspective on the Problem of Hazardous Substances in the Great Lakes Basin Ecosystem," Science Advisory Board Annual Report to the IJC (Windsor, Ontario: IJC, 13 November 1980).

5. What is now known as the U.S. Clean Water Act was first passed in 1972 as PL 92-500, or Amendments to the Federal Water Pollution Control Act. After reauthorization with amendments in 1977, it became known as the Clean Water Act. Further amendments were made in 1987 and 1990 (33 U.S.C. Section 1251-1987).

6. National Environmental Policy Act, 32 U.S.C. 4321 et seq.

7. The federal environmental-assessment regime was initiated with the Environmental Assessment Review Process in 1973, followed by the Environmental Assessment and Review Process Guidelines in 1984 and the Canadian Environmental Assessment Act in 1992 (S.C. 1992, c. 37). For a history, see R. Northey, *The Canadian Environmental Assessment Act and the Environmental Assessment Review Process Guidelines Order* (Toronto: Carswell, 1994). Pollution prevention

was declared to be a national policy of Canada. See Canadian Environmental Protection Act S.C. 1999, c. 33, Declaration.

8. Interviews, headquarters and regional USEPA officials.

9. Interview, USEPA official. Region 5 includes Minnesota, Wisconsin, Illinois, Indiana, Michigan, and Ohio, or six of the eight Great Lakes states.

10. Interviews, headquarters and regional USEPA officials.

11. Interview, Region 5 official.

12. The following reports related to the Great Lakes have been submitted to Congress by the U.S. General Accounting Office: 1975 *Cleaning Up the Great Lakes: United States and Canada Are Making Progress in Controlling Pollution from Cities and Towns* (RED-75-338); 1978 *How the United States Can and Should Improve Its Funding of International Joint Commission Activities* (ID-78-10); *A More Comprehensive Approach Is Needed to Clean Up the Great Lakes* (CED-82-63); 1982 *International Joint Commission Water Quality Activities Need Greater U.S. Government Support and Involvement* (report to the Secretary of State; CED-82-97); 1989. *State Department: Need to Reassess U.S. Participation in the International Joint Commission* (GAO/NSIAD-89-164); 1990 *Water Pollution: Improved Coordination Needed to Clean Up the Great Lakes* (GAO/RCED-90-197); 1991 *Water Pollution: Observations on EPA's Efforts to Clean Up the Great Lakes* (testimony before the Subcommittee on Oversight of Government Management, Committee on Governmental Affairs, United States Senate; GAO/T-RCED-92-1); *Water Resources: Future Needs for Confining Contaminated Sediment in the Great Lakes Region* (GAO/RCED-92-89); *Concerning Pesticides Used in the Great Lakes Watershed* (GAO/RCED-93-128); *Ecosystem Management: Additional Actions Needed to Adequately Test a Promising Approach* (GAO/RCED-94-111); *Great Lakes: EPA Needs to Define Organizational Responsibilities Better for Effective Oversight and Cleanup of Contaminated Areas* (GAO-02-563); *Invasive Species: Federal Efforts and State Perspectives on Challenges and National Leadership*; 2003 *Great Lakes: An Overall Strategy and Indicators for Measuring Progress Are Needed to Better Achieve Restoration Goals* (GAO-03-515).

13. Interviews, USEPA staff.

14. Interview, USEPA official.

15. Interview, USEPA official and chair of the WQB.

16. Interview, USEPA official.

17. Clean Water Act, section 101(a)(1).

18. Section 105 of the Clean Water Act provides for research grants and demonstration grants for improved waste treatment, etc., to state and local governments. Section 106 provides grants to assist the states with the pollution-control programs required by the federal law.

19. Interview, USEPA official.

20. Fitzhugh Green speech, in Lee Botts Collection, Calumet Archives, Indiana University Northwest.

21. Municipal Abatement Task Force of the Water Quality Programs Committee, *A Review of the Municipal Pollution Abatement Programs in the Great Lakes Basin* (report to the Great Lakes Water Quality Board) (Windsor, Ontario: International Joint Commission, November 1983), 57.

22. Interview, USEPA official.

23. Interview, USEPA official. See also U.S. Environmental Protection Agency, Office of Great Lakes National Programs, *Voluntary and Regulatory Approaches for Non-point Source Control: Proceedings of a Conference, 22–28 May 1978* (Chicago: USEPA, July 1978), EPA/9-78-001.

24. Rose Ann Sullivan, Paul A. Sanders, and William Sonzogni, *Post-PLUARG Evaluation of Great Lakes Water Quality Management Studies and Programs*, (report of the Great Lakes Basin Commission for the USEPA) (Ann Arbor, Mich.: Great Lakes Basin Commission, September 1980), EPA 905/9-80-006-A.

25. Interview, Great Lakes policy expert.

26. Interview, USEPA research scientist.

27. Glenda Daniel, "The Great Lakes Water Quality Agreement: A State Perspective" (prepared for the Great Lakes Governance Project of Dartmouth College, December 1995).

28. Lee Botts, personal observation.

29. Interview, USEPA official.

30. Interview, state official.

31. The "winter-navigation project" was an Army Corps of Engineers study of the feasibility of maintaining year-round navigation by such means as breaking ice in connecting channels between the lakes, and use of various means of preventing ice formation in harbors.

32. Lee Botts, personal observation. See also Thomas Princen and Matthias Finger, eds., *Environmental NGOs in World Politics: Linking the Global to the Local* (London and New York: Routledge, 1994).

33. Interview, state official.

34. John Jackson, "The Provinces and the Great Lakes Water Quality Agreement" (report prepared for the Great Lakes Governance Project of Dartmouth College, December 1995).

35. See Purpose section, Canada-Ontario Agreement, signed 12 July 1982.

36. Ibid.

37. Interview, Great Lakes policy expert.

38. Interview, Great Lakes research scientists.

39. Interview, Great Lakes research scientists.

40. Interview, Great Lakes scientist.

41. Interview, Great Lakes academic researcher.

42. Leonard Dworsky and George Francis, "A Proposal for Improving Management of the Great Lakes of the United States and Canada" (presented at the 1971–1972

Canada–U.S. University Seminar, Washington, D.C., Office of Water Resources Research, United States Department of the Interior, January 1973).

43. Ibid.

44. Leonard Dworsky and George Francis, "The 1973 Floods and Activities of the International Joint Commission, United States and Canada," in *Testimony to the Hearings before the Subcommittee on Foreign Affairs*, part 1 (U.S. House of Representatives, 1 May 1973), 113.

45. Standing Committee on Foreign Affairs, *Canada–United States Relations: The Institutional Framework for the Relationship*, committee print no. 10 (Washington. D.C.: U.S. House of Representatives, 1975).

46. Leonard Dworsky, Albert E. Utton, and David J. Allee, "The Great Lakes: Transboundary Issues for the Mid-Nineties," *University of Toledo Law Journal* 26 (Winter 1995): 347–86.

47. Great Lakes Water Quality Agreement of 1972, Article VII, no. 1.

48. International Joint Commission, "Report on the Regional Office of the International Joint Commission: A Joint Canada–United States Study Group," (internal review paper, 1979).

49. Ibid.

50. International Joint Commission, "Terms of Reference for the Joint Institutions and the Great Lakes Regional Office, Great Lakes Water Quality Agreement of 1978," with annexes and terms of reference between the United States and Canada, signed at Ottawa, 22 November 1978.

51. International Joint Commission, "Report on the Regional Office," 13.

52. Ibid.

53. Research Advisory Board, Standing Committee on Social Sciences, Economic and Legal Aspects, *Proceedings of a Workshop on Public Participation, Ann Arbor, Michigan, June 23–24, 1975* (Windsor, Ontario: IJC, 1975).

54. Carol Y. Swinehart gave a detailed account of the activities of the Great Lakes Regional Office on public participation in an unpublished paper entitled "Public Information and Public Participation Activities under the Great Lakes Water Quality Agreement of 1972" while she held the position of Communicator for the Marine Advisory Service of the Michigan Sea Grant College Program, Lansing, Michigan, 1980. A copy is in the Lee Botts Collection, Calumet Archives, Indiana University Northwest.

55. 1972 Great Lakes Water Quality Agreement, Terms of Reference for the Establishment of a Research Advisory Board, section 4, p. 5.

56. Interview, former Science Advisory Board chair.

57. Great Lakes Water Quality Board, International Joint Commission, *Annual Report to the International Joint Commission* (Windsor, Ontario: IJC, July 1975), 126.

58. National Research Council of the United States and the Royal Society of Canada (NRC/RSC), *The Great Lakes Water Quality Agreement: An Evolving Instrument for*

Ecosystem Management (Washington, D.C.: National Academy Press, 1985), 10–13.

59. Interview, state official.

60. International Joint Commission, *Third Annual Report: Great Lakes Water Quality Board, 1974* (Washington and Ottawa: IJC 1975), 13.

61. The history of concern about this issue is discussed in NRC/RSC, *The Great Lakes Water Quality Agreement*, 87–88.

62. Terms of Reference for the Establishment of a Research Advisory Board, section 4.

63. Interview, Research Advisory Board chair.

64. Research Advisory Board, International Joint Commission, *Annual Report to the International Joint Commission* (Windsor, Ontario: IJC, July 1977).

65. Great Lakes Science Advisory Board, International Joint Commission, *Annual Report of the Science Advisory Board* (Windsor, Ontario: IJC, July 1977).

66. International Joint Commission, *Rules of Procedure and Text of Treaty* (IJC, 1965), part 1, section 11, pp. 3–5.

67. Thomas Princen and Matthias Finger, *Environmental NGOs in World Politics* (London and New York: Routledge, 1994), 71.

68. Research Advisory Board, *Proceedings of a Workshop on Public Participation*, 1975.

69. *Pollution from Land Use Reference Group Public Consultation Panel Reports to the International Joint Commission*, vol. 1, *United States*, and vol. 2, *Canada* (Windsor, Ontario: IJC, March 1977).

70. Interviews, PLUARG panel chairman and participant.

71. Interview, environmental advocate for Section 112, 1990 U.S. Clean Air Act.

72. Great Lakes Tomorrow was a small not-for-profit group that carried out mainly educational activities from its base at Hiram College, Hiram, Ohio, until it ceased operation in the mid 1980s.

73. The Swinehart paper describes how a question period was allowed in the 1980, 1981, and 1982 annual meetings (Public Information and Participation Activities).

74. Interview, IJC staff. The Swinehart paper also says that by 1978, a total of 5,000 copies of the Water Quality Board and Science Advisory Board reports were being distributed, and that many of the 10,000 annual queries to the Great Lakes Regional Office were from the news media.

75. Interview, IJC public-information staff.

76. The Swinehart paper also says that by 1978, the mailing list for *Focus* had 10,000 names and addresses, and that 2,000 requests for specific information were being received annually in writing and by telephone.

77. The sense of being part of a large community was expressed by most of the persons interviewed for this project who had participated during the 1970s and 1980s.

78. U.S. Water Resources Planning Act (89th Congress, 22 July 1965), 89–80.

79. Personal observation from Lee Botts in her capacity as chairman of the Great

Lakes Basin Commission from 1978 to 1981.

80. Thomas Heidtke, William Sonzogni, and Lee Botts, *Great Lakes Environmental Planning Study: Summary Report* (Ann Arbor, Mich.: Great Lakes Basin Commission, 1981).

81. Rose Ann Sullivan, Paul A. Sanders, and William Sonzogni, *Post-PLUARG Evaluation of Great Lakes Water Quality Management Studies and Programs* (report of the Great Lakes Basin Commission for the USEPA) (Ann Arbor: Great Lakes Basin Commission, September 1980), EPA 905/9-80-006-A.

82. Great Lakes Basin Commission, Fisheries and Environment Canada, and Army Corps of Engineers, North Central Division, *The Role of Vegetation in Shoreline Management: A Guide for Great Lakes Shoreline Property Owners* (Ann Arbor, Mich.: Great Lakes Basin Commission, 1980).

83. Lee Botts, personal observation.

84. Michael Donahue, "Institutional Arrangements for Great Lakes Management: Past Practices and Future Alternatives" (Ph.D. diss., University of Michigan, 1986), 105–7.

85. Great Lakes Fishery Commission, *A Joint Strategic Plan for Management of Great Lakes Fisheries* (Ann Arbor, Mich.: Great Lakes Fishery Commission, December 1980).

86. Lee Botts, personal observation.

87. Interview, Ohio environmental leader.

88. Interview, Indiana environmental leader.

89. Interview, regional staff of national environmental organization.

90. Interview, regional staff of national environmental organization.

91. Great Lakes Tomorrow and Purdue University-Calumet, *Great Lakes Decisions: Decisions for the Great Lakes* (Hammond, Ind.: Great Lakes Tomorrow and Purdue University-Calumet, 1982).

92. Paul Muldoon, personal observation. See John E. Carroll, *Environmental Diplomacy: An Examination of Prospective Canadian–U.S. Transboundary Relations* (Ann Arbor, Mich.: University of Michigan Press, 1983), 18–19.

93. Interview, academic researcher.

94. Paul Muldoon, personal observation.

95. Lee Botts, personal observation.

96. International Joint Commission, Great Lakes Water Quality Board, *Great Lakes Water Quality, 1974*, appendix B, "Annual Report of the Surveillance Subcommittee to the Implementation Committee, Great Lakes Water Quality Board" (Windsor, Ontario: IJC, June 1975).

97. The Water Quality Board reports in the early 1970s tracked how Canada initially had a larger proportion of its population served by "adequate" sewage treatment, but how U.S. efforts to assist local communities to upgrade sewage treatment expanded rapidly under the construction-grant program of section 201 of the

1972 version of the Clean Water Act.

98. Conflict persisted into the 1990s over the differences in the approach of the two countries to control of industrial discharges. The 1976 Water Quality Board report described the differences as follows: "In the United States, the approach to implementing pollution control consists of a relatively structured, legal, regulatory enforcement system. . . . In Canada, existing legislation provides pollution control agencies with administrative discretion" (114).

99. Great Lakes Water Quality Board, International Joint Commission, *Great Lakes Water Quality, 1975* (Windsor, Ontario: IJC), 51.

100. U.S. Environmental Protection Agency, Office of the Regional Administrator, Region 5, "Detergent Phosphate Ban" (position paper prepared by the Region 5 Phosphorus Committee) (Chicago: USEPA, June 1977).

101. Lee Botts, personal observation,.

102. Interview, USEPA research scientist.

103. The Region 5 position paper on phosphate bans estimated a total savings of $41.5 million per year in sewage treatment in the Great Lakes basin, based on experience of the Metropolitan Sanitary District of Greater Chicago after Chicago adopted the first such ban.

104. Inability to remove contaminated sediments because of the high treatment costs and lack of disposal sites remained a major problem in the mid 1990s. Nevertheless, the Water Quality Agreement, as well as the need to protect Lake Michigan as a drinking-water source, was being cited in 1996 as justification for proceeding with a novel approach to removing an estimated more than 1 million cubic yards of sediments from the Indiana Harbor and Ship Canal in East Chicago, Indiana, the largest known accumulation of contaminated sediments in the Great Lakes basin.

105. Great Lakes Water Quality Board, International Joint Commission, *Great Lakes Water Quality, 1977* (Windsor, Ontario: IJC, July 1978), 6–7.

106. Ibid., 13–29.

107. Great Lakes Research Advisory Board, International Joint Commission, *Great Lakes Water Quality Research Needs* (Windsor, Ontario: IJC, July 1976).

108. Research Advisory Board, International Joint Commission, "Structure-Activity Correlations in Studies of Toxicity and Bioconcentration with Aquatic Organisms," published in the proceedings of a symposium sponsored by the Standing Committee on the Scientific Basis for Water Quality Criteria, Burlington, Ontario, 11–13 March 1975, ed. G. D. Veith and D. E. Konasewich (Windsor, Ontario: IJC, 1975).

109. See chapter 3 in Michael R. Reich, *Toxic Politics: Responding to Chemical Disasters* (Ithaca, N.Y., and London: Cornell University Press, 1991).

110. Lee Botts, personal observation.

111. Lee Botts, personal observation.

112. W. R. Swain, "Chlorinated Residues in Fish, Water, and Precipitation from the Vicinity of Isle Royale, Lake Superior," *Journal for Great Lakes Research* 4, nos. 3–4 (1978): 398–407.

113. Research Advisory Board, International Joint Commission, "Structure-Activity Correlations in Studies of Toxicity and Bioconcentration with Aquatic Organisms."

114. Revised Great Lakes Water Quality Agreement of 1978, section 3.

115. International Joint Commission, *Report on Great Lakes Water Quality for 1972* (Ottawa and Washington, D.C.: IJC, July 1973).

116. International Joint Commission, *Second Annual Report on Great Lakes Water Quality* (Ottawa and Washington, D.C.: IJC, 1974), 1.

117. International Joint Commission, *1974 Annual Report on Great Lakes Water Quality* (Ottawa and Washington, D.C.: IJC, December 1975), 15–17.

118. International Joint Commission, *Fifth Annual Report, Great Lakes Water Quality* (Windsor, Ontario: IJC, 1976), 1–2.

119. International Joint Commission, *Annual Report: 1977* (Ottawa and Washington, D.C.: IJC, 1977), 18–19.

120. Ibid., 30–31.

121. Ibid., 38; General Accounting Office, *How the U.S. Should Improve Its Funding of IJC Activities* (Washington, D.C.: General Accounting Office, 8 February 1978), ID-78-10.

122. The 1978 agreement changed the schedule for periodic review to following every third biennial report, or approximately every six years.

123. Interview, USEPA official.

124. Great Lakes Water Quality Board, International Joint Commission, *Sixth Annual Report to the International Joint Commission* (Windsor, Ontario: IJC, July 1978). In this report, the first two recommendations and five of the six highlights concerned toxic contaminants. It was noted that Canada had essentially met the target loading for phosphorus for Lake Erie, and while the inputs still exceeded the limits set in the 1972 agreement for the lower lakes in general, substantial progress was noted.

125. The dependence of the IJC on voluntary actions by the governments is extensively considered in the literature. One source that compares the powers of the IJC with those of other Great Lakes institutions is Michael Donahue, "Institutional Arrangements for Great Lakes Management: Past Practices and Future Alternatives" (Ph.D. diss., University of Michigan, 1986).

Chapter 4. Negotiation of the 1978 Great Lakes Agreement and Its Evolution

1. The terms of the new agreement were explained in an undated brochure titled "Great Lakes Water Quality Agreement 1978," issued by the International Joint Commission, United States and Canada.

2. Revised Great Lakes Water Quality Agreement of 1978, Article 1(v).

3. Interviews, scientist and IJC staff.

4. Great Lakes Water Quality Agreement of 1972, Article 9, section 3.

5. Great Lakes Water Quality Board, International Joint Commission, *Sixth Annual Report to the International Joint Commission* (Windsor, Ontario; IJC, July 1978). In this report, the first two recommendations and five of the six highlights concerned toxic contaminants. It was noted that Canada had essentially met the target loading set for phosphorus for Lake Erie and, while the inputs still exceeded the limits set in the 1972 agreement for the lower lakes in general, substantial progress had been made.

6. Task Group 3, Fifth Year Review of the Canada–United States Great Lakes Water Quality Agreement, co-chairs J. R. Vallentyne, Senior Scientist, Canada Centre for Inland Waters, and N. S. Thomas, Chief, Large Lakes Research Station, U.S. Environmental Protection Agency, Grosse Ile, Michigan, February 1978.

7. PLUARG Public Consultation Panel Reports, vol. 1 for the U.S., and vol. 2 for Canada.

8. Interview, Environment Canada official.

9. Interviews, participating Environment Canada and USEPA officials.

10. The IJC's *Third Annual Report on Progress* for 1974, dated December 1975, discussed the then recent discoveries that low reproductive rates and birth deformities in wildlife were linked to the presence of PCBs and other chlorinated hydrocarbons, and referred to a recent resolution to alert the governments to the implications of the new findings.

11. K. L. E. Kaiser, "Mirex: An Unrecognized Contaminant of Fishes from Lake Ontario," *Science* 185 (1974): 523–25.

12. International Joint Commission, Great Lakes Water Quality Board, *Great Lakes Water Quality Status Report on Organic and Heavy Metal Contaminants in the Lakes Erie, Michigan, Huron, and Superior Basins* (Windsor, Ontario: IJC, 1978), appendix E.

13. See Jack Manno, "Advocacy and Diplomacy in the Great Lakes: A Case History of Nongovernmental Organization Participation in Negotiating the Great Lakes Water Quality Agreement, *Buffalo Law Journal* 1, no. 1 (1993): 16–17; Robert J. Mason, "Public Concerns and PLUARG: Selected Findings and Discussion," *Journal of Great Lakes Research* 6 (1980): 210–22; and A. P. Grima and Robert J. Mason, "Apples and Oranges: Toward a Critique of Public Participation in Great Lakes Decisions," *Canada Water Resources Journal* (1983): 22.

14. The complete list is contained in the Bibliography of Reports issued under the Great Lakes Water Quality Agreements of 1972 and 1978, and 1987 Protocol Amending the 1978 Agreement, International Joint Commission, Great Lakes Regional Office, Windsor, Ontario.

15. R. L. Thomas, J. R. Vallentyne, K. Ogilvie, and J. K. Kingham, "The Ecosystems Approach: A Strategy for the Management of Renewable Resources in the Great

Lakes Basin," in *Perspectives on Ecosystem Management for the Great Lakes: A Reader*, ed. Lynton K. Caldwell (Albany: State University of New York Press, 1988), 31.

16. Manno, "Advocacy and Diplomacy in the Great Lakes," 17.

17. International Joint Commission, International Reference Group on Great Lakes Pollution From Land Use Activities, *Atmospheric Loadings of the Lower Great Lakes and the Great Lakes Drainage Basin* (Windsor, Ontario, March 1977).

18. G. E. Burdick, E. J. Harris, T. M. Dean, J. H. Walker, J. Skea, and C. Colby, "The Accumulation of DDT in Lake Trout and the Effect on Reproduction," *Trans American Fisheries Society* 93 (1964): 127–36.

19. M. Gilbertson, "Pollutants in Breeding Herring Gulls in the Lower Great Lakes," *Canadian Field-Naturalist* 88 (1974): 273–80.

20. W. R. Swain, "Chlorinated Residues in Fish, Water and Precipitation from the Vicinity of Isle Royale, Lake Superior," *Journal of Great Lakes Research* 4, nos. 3–4 (1978): 398–407.

21. Author Lee Botts had many experiences in debating the issue with organized sport-fishing groups, such as the Lake County (Indiana) Fish and Game Preservation Association in 1975.

22. See Citizens' Clearinghouse for Hazardous Wastes, *Love Canal: A Chronology of Events that Shaped a Movement* (Falls Church, Va.: Citizens' Clearinghouse for Hazardous Wastes, 1984).

23. H. Sievering and C. A. Williams, *Potential Loading of Southern Lake Michigan by Dry Depositions: Proceedings of a Workshop on Atmospheric Transport and Removal Processes, Second ICMSE Conference on the Great Lakes* (Lemont, Ill.: Argonne National Laboratory, 1975).

24. What is now called the U.S. Clean Water Act was originally enacted as Amendments to the Federal Water Pollution Control Act of 1965, or Public Law 92-500.

25. The U.S. Congress passed the National Environmental Policy Act and a comprehensive new Clean Air Act in the same year that the USEPA was created. In a race to keep up with the Congress, President Nixon also issued an Executive Order that led to the first permit system for discharge of waste effluents by industries and publicly owned sewage-treatment plants under the 1899 Refuse Act. Interview with Environment Canada official.

26. In her capacity as assistant to the administrator for Congressional and Intergovernmental Affairs at Region 5 from 1975 to 1978, author Lee Botts was directly involved in budget politics within the USEPA.

27. Interviews, state officials.

28. Interviews, USEPA officials.

29. Don Munton provided insight on this issue in "Great Lakes Water Quality: A Study in Environmental Politics and Diplomacy," in *Resources and the Environment: Policy Perspectives for Canada*.

30. Interview, IJC commissioner.

31. Interview, USEPA headquarters official.

32. The negotiating team for Environment Canada included James Bruce, assistant deputy minister; Robert Slater, director general Ontario Region; and Ron Shimizu. Russell McKinney was from External Affairs. For the USEPA, the team included George Alexander, Region 5 administrator; Tudor Davies, headquarters Water Division; and Conrad Kleveno, Office of International Activities. William Marks, Michigan Department of Natural Resources, represented the states.

33. Casey Bukro, "Bureaucrats Note: That Blue Stuff Is the Great Lakes," *Chicago Tribune*, 14 September 1978.

34. Interviews, USEPA and Environment Canada officials.

35. Interview, USEPA official.

36. Most of the correspondence raising issues about the regional office and other issues in preparation for the negotiation was signed by Jorling.

37. United States Senior Review Group on Review of the Great Lakes Water Quality Agreement, *Report of Sub-Group A* (Washington, D.C.: Environmental Protection Agency, Office of International Activities, 29 April 1977).

38. Ibid., 6–7.

39. Munton, "Great Lakes Water Quality," 170. (See note 29)

40. Interestingly, the Citizens Right to Sue provision of the U.S. Clean Water Act had been introduced by Michigan senator Philip Hart and was based on a Michigan law that environmental activists had sought in the early 1970s.

41. Munton, "Great Lakes Water Quality," 171.

42. United States Senior Review Group on Review of the Great Lakes Water Quality Agreement, *Report of Sub-Group A.*

43. Munton, "Great Lakes Water Quality," 171.

44. Interviews, USEPA and Canadian officials.

45. Interview, USEPA official.

46. In 1979 author Lee Botts, in her capacity as chair of the Great Lakes Basin Commission, argued with Jorling that the USEPA should address the problem of atmospheric deposition of toxic contaminants because of the ecosystem goal of the Great Lakes Agreement. He replied that the "no-discharge" goal of the U.S. Clean Water Act was a much stronger ecological goal than the virtual-elimination goal of the Great Lakes Agreement.

47. Memo from Alice Brandeis Popkin, deputy assistant administrator for Resources Management, USEPA in Washington, D.C.; Letter from Richard D. Vine, deputy assistant secretary for Canadian Affairs, to Barbara Blum, deputy administrator USEPA, 1979.

48. "Carter Urged to Seek Funds for Accord on Great Lakes," *Toledo Blade*, 28 November 1978.

49. The Congressional appropriation for the Great Lakes National Program Office

has ranged between $13.1 and $15.5 million per year from 1990 to 2004, and the number of staff positions has likewise remained static at about 40.

50. Interview, nongovernmental participant in 1987 review.

51. United States Senior Review Group on Review of the Great Lakes Water Quality Agreement, *Report of Sub-Group A.*

52. According to Munton, these meetings were attended by some 240 persons, with the presentation of some 40 statements; Munton, "Great Lakes Water Quality," 169.

53. Other issues were also considered, including new standards for radionuclides; Munton, "Great Lakes Water Quality," 171.

54. On 14 September 1978, a *Milwaukee Journal* editorial, under the title "Soiling the Great Lakes Cleanup," protested a reported attempt by the U.S. Office of Management and Budget to get Article 2 deleted from the agreement because of the estimated $5 million expenditure that would be required to meet agreement obligations.

55. Personal observation of author Lee Botts, based on protests from the states to her in her capacity as chairman of the Great Lakes Basin Commission from 1978 to 1981.

56. Great Lakes Water Quality Agreement, signed 14 April 1972, International Joint Commission, Ottawa and Washington, D.C., Article II.

57. 1978 Great Lakes Water Quality Agreement, Article II introduction.

58. Ibid., Article I(g).

59. Ibid, p. 1.

60. Ibid, Article II.

61. Ibid, Article I(h).

62. Great Lakes Science Advisory Board, *The Ecosystem Approach: Scope and Implications of an Ecosystem Approach to the Transboundary Problems in the Great Lakes Basin* (special report to the International Joint Commission) (Windsor, Ontario: IJC, 1978), 1.

63. Research Advisory Board, International Joint Commission, *1978 Annual Report* (Windsor, Ontario: IJC, 1978), 1.

64. The International Joint Commission, *Fifth Annual Report.*

65. Ibid., appendix.

66. Great Lakes Science Advisory Board, *The Ecosystem Approach.*

67. Interview, scientist member of the SAB.

68. Revised Great Lakes Water Quality Agreement of 1978, Article II(a).

69. Ibid, Article I(v).

70. Author Lee Botts, personal observation.

71. Interviews, USEPA and Environment Canada officials.

72. Paul Muldoon and John Jackson, "Keeping Zero in Zero Discharge: Phasing Out Persistent Toxic Substances in the Great Lakes Basin," *Alternatives* 20, no. 4 (September/October 1994): 14–20.

73. The Phosphorus Load Reduction Supplement to Annex 3 was signed on 7 October 1983. It allocated target loads between the two countries for Lake Erie and Lake Ontario and pledged both sides to maintain the "present oligotrophic state" of Lake Superior and Lake Huron. The U.S. also agreed to substantial elimination of algal nuisance in Lake Michigan, with additional efforts to be made in Saginaw Bay, Green Bay, and other localized nearshore problem areas.

74. 1978 agreement, Article VI(1).

75. Interview, negotiator.

76. International Joint Commission, *Seventh Annual Report, Great Lakes Water Quality* (Ottawa and Washington, D.C.: IJC, 1980), 61.

77. International Joint Commission, *IJC Directive No. 1 to the Great Lakes Water Quality Board Pursuant to the 1978 Great Lakes Water Quality Agreement*, dated 14 March 1980. According to the directive, selective key functions are as follows:

    5. The Board shall keep currently informed regarding the matters assigned to the Commission under Article 7 of the Agreement. The Board shall also keep informed regarding programs and other measures taken with respect to, or relevant to, implementation of the Agreement and shall assess the adequacy and effectiveness of such programs, in particular those specified under the Agreement under Article 6(1) and the Annexes referenced therein.

    6. The Board shall be responsible for the collation, assessment, and analysis of data and information relevant to paragraph 5. The Board shall review, as appropriate, procedures for the submission of such data from the various jurisdictions and recommend changes to the Commission as appropriate.

    7. The Board shall tender timely advice on all matters concerning the Agreement and further shall submit a full report to the Commission biennially, beginning in 1981, upon all aspects relating to the operations and effectiveness of the Agreement, and on the Board's activities. In alternate years, the Board shall submit a summary report updating all or part of the previous report to the extent that information is available.

    12. With respect to the programs and other measures upon which the Board shall report to the Commission, the Board shall:

        (a) make recommendations on the development and implementation of programs to achieve the purpose of the Agreement as set forth in Article 2 thereof;

        (b) assemble and evaluate information evolving from such programs;

        (c) identify deficiencies in the scope and funding of such programs and evaluate the adequacy and compatibility of the results;

        (d) examine the appropriateness of such programs in the light of current and future socio-economic imperatives; and

        (e) advise the Commission on the progress and effectiveness of such programs and submit appropriate recommendations.

78. Role Structure and Operation of the Great Lakes Water Quality Board, Final Proposal, 26 February 1980, approved at the Forty-Second Meeting of the Great

Lakes Water Quality Board, 15 July 1980.

79. In interviews in 2003, former members reiterated their earlier comments about how participation in the Water Quality Board had helped them to advocate for policies needed for the Great Lakes in their home agencies.

80. C. Ian Jackson, "Editorial: Mixed Signals from the International Joint Commission," *Journal of Great Lakes Research* 18, no. 3 (1992): 355.

81. Interviews, WQB members, IJC and agency staff.

82. NRC/RSC, *The Great Lakes Water Quality Agreement*, 87. Concerns identified in this report included the data-collection process. The NRC/RSC was critical of the fact that there was little effective interagency coordination among state, federal, and provincial governments (84). Complete data sets were provided only for some jurisdictions, and some of the most obvious questions about total loadings of toxic substances, specific chemicals, and the relative contribution of sources were left with only partial or even no response from a basin-wide perspective.

    There was also the issue of the "completeness" of the data being collected and transmitted by the WQB to the commission. The report noted that "the Board is composed of senior officials who represent these governments. While these representatives may be willing to share sensitive information among themselves, they may be less willing to share it with the Commission or to release it publicly." (85)

83. For example, the Third Biennial Report in 1986 emphasized the need for greater interagency coordination between the parties for monitoring and surveillance as well as research.

84. See NRC/RSC, *The Great Lakes Water Quality Agreement*, 90–91, where the IJC's Second Biennial Report is quoted and discussed.

85. Ibid.

86. International Joint Commission, IJC Directive to the Great Lakes Science Advisory Board. In carrying out this responsibility, the SAB is to:

    (a) Keep informed on scientific and research matters encompassed within the scope of the 1978 Great Lakes Water Quality Agreement and as it deems appropriate shall seek analyses, assessments, and recommendations from other scientific, professional, academic, governmental and inter-governmental groups relevant to the Great Lakes Basin Ecosystem research and scientific knowledge. . . . Further the SAB shall:

    (i) assess the impact and the adequacy of research efforts;

    (ii) assess the reliability and potential applicability of research results;

    (iii) identify research priorities and additional research requirements; and

    (iv) identify specific research programs for which international cooperation is desirable.

87. NRC/RSC, *The Great Lakes Water Quality Agreement*, 89.

88. Personal observation by author Lee Botts in her capacity as chairman of the Great Lakes Basin Commission from 1978 to 1981.

89. Interview, SAB member.

90. Interview, IJC staff.

91. NRC/RSC, *The Great Lakes Water Quality Agreement*, 89. The issue was also addressed by the IJC in its First Biennial Report in 1981, p. 29.

92. Keith Bulen, Indiana; Don Totten, Illinois; and Robert C. McEwen of New York.

93. Interview, USEPA official.

94. Interview, WQB member.

95. Most of the information in this section is derived from a report prepared by John Jackson, *The Provinces and the Great Lakes Water Quality Agreement*.

    The COA that was renegotiated in 1986 was retroactive to 1 April 1985, and with few changes was a word-for-word continuation of previous versions. Surveillance provisions continued, but the federal government's support for sewage treatment was phased out and two elements were added:

    1. A commitment for the federal government and Environment Canada and Ontario to work together and share costs of the "Phosphorus Load Reduction Program" that had been added to the GLWQA in 1983; and

    2. A commitment for them to work together to assess and classify the Areas of Concern that the Water Quality Board had identified in 1985 and to develop Remedial Action Plans for the Areas of Concern.

    See Canada-Ontario Agreement Respecting Great Lakes Water Quality, appendix 1 of schedule B, April 1985.

96. *Annual Report, Canada-Ontario Agreement Respecting Great Lakes Water Quality* (October 1984), 18.

97. Toby Vigod, "The Law and the Toxic Blob," *Alternatives* 13, no. 3 (September/October 1986): 24–28.

98. Ontario Ministry of the Environment, *A Policy and Program Statement of the Government of Ontario on Controlling Municipal and Industrial Discharges into Surface Waters* (1986).

99. Quebec is included in certain Great Lakes activities because of the obvious impact. There is always a representative of the Province of Quebec on the Water Quality Board, usually the "Chef du Service des Pesticides and des Eaux Souterraines." A Quebec representative is also included in the negotiating team when the agreement is reviewed or renegotiated. Quebec plays the role of watchdog, to make certain that pollution control in the Great Lakes will reduce the contamination of the St. Lawrence River flowing through Quebec. Inclusion of Quebec is also important because of the ongoing tension regarding the threat of Quebec withdrawal from the Canadian confederation.

100. Notes for Remarks by the Honourable Tom McMillan, Federal Minister of the Environment (speech given at the signing of the Canada-Quebec Convention on the St. Lawrence River, Montreal, Quebec, 3 June 1988).

101. Interview, state official.

102. Interview, Indiana environmental advocate.

103. Interview, Wisconsin environmental-agency official.

104. The charter and background material to it can be found in "Final Report and Recommendations: Great Lakes Governors' Task Force on Water Diversion and Great Lakes Institutions," a report to the governors and premiers of the Great Lakes states and provinces prepared at the request of the Council of Great Lakes Governors, January 1985.

105. The Great Lakes Toxic Substances Control Agreement, signed 21 May 1986 by the governors of the eight Great Lakes states.

106. Interview, official in charge of a state Great Lakes program.

107. Katherine Davies, "Human Exposure Routes to Persistent Toxic Chemicals in the Great Lakes Basin: A Case Study," in *Toxic Contamination in Large Lakes*, vol. 1 (NW Schmidtke, 1988), 195–222.

108. Interview, National Wildlife Federation staff advocate for the Water Quality Initiative.

109. U.S. Environmental Protection Agency, the Indiana Board of Health, and the Lake Michigan Federation, *A Master Plan for Improving Water Quality in the Grand Calumet River and the Indiana Harbor and Ship Canal* (Chicago: USEPA, 1983).

110. Great Lakes Water Quality Board, International Joint Commission, *1985 Report on Great Lakes Water Quality* (Windsor, Ontario: IJC, June 1985).

111. Interview, USEPA official.

112. International Joint Commission, Standing Committee on Public Information, "Terms of Reference" as approved 2 September 1980.

113. International Joint Commission, "Public Participation Policy," 7 November 1980.

114. Ibid.

115. Interview, staff of major environmental organization.

116. Interviews, staff members of several regional and national organizations.

117. Final Report and Recommendations: Great Lakes Governors' Task Force on Water Diversion and Great Lakes Institutions.

118. Adele Hurley, who later was named Canadian chair of the IJC in 1995, was the executive director that Ontario set up in Washington, D.C., to seek acid-rain controls in the U.S. Clean Air Act.

119. The consequences of the increase in local opposition to hazardous-waste landfills are considered in Robert Gottlieb, *Forcing the Spring: The Transformation of the American Environmental Movement* (Washington, D.C., and Covelo, Calif.: Island Press, 1994).

120. For more in-depth information, see Paul Muldoon, *Cross Border Litigation: Environmental Rights in the Great Lakes Ecosystem* (Toronto: Carswell, 1986), appendix C.

121. David Israelson, "'Storm Warning' Returns—More or Less Unchanged," *Sunday Star*, 16 November 1986.

122. Dana Robbins, "The Environment Keeps Him Talking," *Burlington Spectator*, 6 Octo-

ber 1986, and "Federal Government Downplays Great Lakes Pollution Risks," *Ottawa Citizen*, 15 March 1991. In another example, two Environment Canada researchers in Burlington, Tom Muir and Anne Sudar, completed their compilation of the results of scientific studies on the effects of contamination in the Great Lakes in 1986. Their report concluded that there is reason to suspect a link between contaminants in the Great Lakes and human health problems. Finally in late 1987, after repeated public calls for the results of their work, their report, *Toxic Chemicals in the Great Lakes Ecosystem*, was released. But Environment Canada left its logo off the report to ensure that people would not see it as a government-endorsed document. See Doug Draper, "Niagara Cancer Rate Higher: Feds Keep Report under Wraps for More than a Year," *St. Catharine's Standard*, 14 November 1987.

A decade later, a similar government hesitation about releasing scientific materials occurred. Health Canada's Great Lakes Health Effects Program compiled detailed health statistics for each of the areas of concern in Canada. They buried the reports until an NGO member made the Windsor media aware of the presence of these reports and released one of the reports that had been brown-bagged to him. This occurred at the IJC's biennial meeting in Milwaukee in 1999. As a result of the considerable resultant media attention, Health Canada released all of the reports a month later.

123. Manno discusses how Great Lakes groups formed alliances to oppose winter navigation ("Advocacy and Diplomacy in the Great Lakes," 28).

124. International Joint Commission, "Public Participation Policy," 1980.

125. The Sierra Club has more freedom to lobby on legislation because it lost its tax-exempt status under Section 501(3) of the U.S. Internal Revenue Tax Code in the 1960s. Organizations eligible to receive contributions that are tax exempt cannot devote more than a small fraction of their resources to partisan political activity or direct lobbying on legislation. In Great Lakes Week, the Sierra Club taught volunteer members of tax-exempt organizations how to lobby as private citizens.

126. Interview, Sierra Club staff members.

127. Author Lee Botts, personal observation.

128. Interviews, staff of Lake Michigan Federation and Coast Alliance.

129. U.S. Clean Water Act, Section 118(a)(2).

130. Interviews, staff of participating organizations.

131. Interviews, Lake Michigan Federation staff and members of the board of directors.

132. Author Lee Botts, personal observation as a member of an advisory group to the Joyce Foundation.

133. One of the most significant Wingspread events was the meeting of experts in the fields of anthropology, immunology, medicine, law, toxicology, wildlife management, zoology, and others on 26–28 July 1991. The result was a consensus statement signed by 21 scientists concerning the role of chemically induced alterations

in sexual development, and the implications for human health of exposure of wildlife to toxic chemicals in the Great Lakes and elsewhere.

134. Interviews, staff of Center for the Great Lakes.

135. Ibid. Also interviews, staff of Great Lakes Protection Fund.

136. Interview, Northeast-Midwest Institute staff.

137. See Caldwell, *Perspectives on Ecosystem Management for the Great Lakes.* This book was based on the concepts that were considered in the series of meetings and workshops that emerged from the series of interuniversity seminars organized in connection with implementation of the Great Lakes Water Quality Agreement.

138. Author Lee Botts served as the U.S. co-chair of the seminar as a research associate at Northwestern University.

139. NRC/RSC, *The Great Lakes Water Quality Agreement,* 58.

140. Theodora E. Colborn, A. Davidson, S. N. Green, R. A. Hodge, C. I. Jackson, and R. A. Liroff, "Foreword," in *Great Lakes, Great Legacy?* (Washington, D.C., and Ottawa: The Conservation Foundation and the Institute for Research on Public Policy, 1990), xiv.

Chapter 5. Evolution of the Great Lakes Regime from 1987 to 1997

1. The context for the U.S.–Canada relationship with respect to the environment is detailed in a series of articles in *International Environmental Affairs.* See M. Valiante and P. Muldoon, "Annual Review of Canada–U.S. Environmental Relations: 1988," *International Environmental Affairs* 1, no. 3 (1989): 294–308; M. Valiante and P. Muldoon, "Annual Review of Canada–U.S. Environmental Relations: 1989," *International Environmental Affairs* 2, no. 3 (1990): 252–64; M. Valiante and P. Muldoon, "Annual Review of Canada–U.S. Environmental Relations: 1990," *International Environmental Affairs* 3, no. 3 (1991): 207–18; M. Valiante and P. Muldoon, "Annual Review of Canada–U.S. Environmental Relations: 1991," *International Environmental Affairs* 4, no. 3 (1992): 254–72; M. Valiante and P. Muldoon, "Annual Review of Canada–U.S. Environmental Relations: 1992," *International Environmental Affairs* 5, no. 3 (1993): 200–18.

2. Interview, nongovernmental participant.

3. The U.S. Great Lakes Critical Programs Act (PL 101-380, 18 August 1990) is an amendment to the Clean Water Act.

4. Section 112(m) of the 1990 Clean Air Act (U.S. PL 101-549, U.S sections 7401 et seq.) required the USEPA to study atmospheric deposition of toxic contaminants into the Great Lakes, Lake Champlain, Chesapeake Bay, and coastal waters. The subsequent "Great Waters Report" relies mainly on data resulting from Great Lakes research. U.S. Environmental Protection Agency, *Deposition of Air Pollutants to the Great Waters: First Report to Congress* (Research Triangle Park, N.C.: USEPA, Office of Air Quality Planning and Standards Research, May 1994), EPA-453/R-93-055.

5. U.S. Great Lakes Fish and Wildlife Restoration Act (PL 101-537). The subsequent report to Congress discusses fishery management issues, including the increasing presence of nonindigenous species. See *Report to Congress: Great Lakes Fishery Resources Restoration Study* (Washington, D.C.: U.S. Fish and Wildlife Service, Department of the Interior, 1995).

6. William K. Reilly, Administrator, U.S. Environmental Protection Agency, "Remarks at the Release of *Great Lakes, Great Legacy*," Chicago, 11 October 1989; "Aiming Before We Shoot: The 'Quiet Revolution' in Environmental Policy" (address to the National Press Club, Washington, D.C., 26 September 1990).

7. Interview, USEPA official.

8. See Lynn Peterson, The Great Lakes Enforcement Strategy: Using Enforcement Resources to Maximize Risk Reduction and Environmental Restoration in the Great Lakes Basin, Third International Conference on Environmental Enforcement, U.S. Environmental Protection Agency.

9. The USEPA programs are described in Bill Clinton and Al Gore, *Reinventing Environmental Regulation* (Washington, D.C.: Executive Office of the President, 16 March 1995).

10. See Council of Great Lakes Governors, *The Great Printers Project: Recommendations to Make Pollution Prevention a Standard Practice in the Printing Industry* (Chicago: Council of Great Lakes Governors, July 1994). This joint project of the Governors Council with the Environmental Defense Fund and the Printing Industries of America included agreements among the states to purchase paper produced by pollution-prevention methods in order to create a market incentive. The program was supported with funding from the Great Lakes Protection Fund.

11. Personal communication.

12. U.S. Environmental Protection Agency, Great Lakes National Program Office, *Mining Ideas: Turning a Grant Assistance Program into a Knowledge Base—A Report on the Ecological Protection and Restoration Program in the Great Lakes Basin*, April 1996.

13. Canadian Environmental Protection Act, 1988.

14. Environment Canada, "New Federal Regulations to Control Pulp and Paper Pollution," news release, 4 December 1991.

15. See Peter Gorrie, "Ottawa Ebbs on Paper-Mill Effluents," *Toronto Star*, 9 November 1991, D6; and Canadian Institute for Environmental Law and Policy, *Response to the Federal Pulp and Paper Regulatory Strategy* (Toronto: Canadian Institute for Environmental Law and Policy, May 1990).

16. This commitment was realized with the establishment of the National Pollutant Release Inventory (NPRI), which is now incorporated into the Canadian Environmental Protection Act, 1999.

17. See Debora L. VanNijnatten, "The ARET Challenge" and "The Day the NGOs Walked Out," in *Voluntary Initiatives: The New Politics of Corporate Greening*, ed.

Robert B. Gibson (Toronto: Broadview Press, 1999), 93–110.

18. The delay in the renegotiation of the COA invoked considerable comment. For a review and commentary, see Royal Commission on the Future of the Toronto Waterfront, *Regeneration: Toronto's Waterfront and the Sustainable City: Final Report* (Toronto: Royal Commission, 1992), 142–43.

19. Ontario estimated that it was putting $145 million each year into Great Lakes programs (letter from Ontario Environment Minister Bud Wildman to Federal Government Minister Jean Charest, 27 May 1993), while the federal government was spending $55 to $60 million.

   The issue of who would pay for infrastructure improvements was similarly controversial. Almost $1.5 billion of the total estimated $2.5 billion expenditures for needs anticipated under a revised COA were to cover costs for upgrading sewage-treatment plants and control combined sewer overflows. See John Jackson, "The Provinces and the Great Lakes Water Quality Agreement."

20. The federal government's refusal to contribute to infrastructure costs was discussed in the letter from Ontario Environment Minister Bud Wildman to Federal Environment Minister Jean Charest, dated 27 May 1993.

21. F. Inscho and M. Durfee, "The Troubled Renewal of the Canada-Ontario Agreement Respecting Great Lakes Water Quality," *Publius: Journal of Federalism* 25, no. 1 (Winter 1995): 59–61.

22. Ibid., 62–63.

23. The differences in the most recent COA include "Inclusion of an Ecosystem Perspective." The new COA was broadened to address "human and ecosystem health," with goals for conservation and protected areas, fish and wildlife conservation, climate change, and land and water-use management. Measurable targets are also set, such as removing nine areas from the AOC list by 2000 and seeking a 90 percent reduction in use, generation, and release of seven priority substances by 2000. One negotiator noted that the new COA "reflects a maturing relationship between the federal and provincial governments because they now bring common resources to the COA" (Interview with Ken Richards, 13 July 1995).

24. Unlike other COAs, the new COA established that both levels of government are responsible for achievement of the GLWQA objectives, with the phrase "Canada and Ontario agree to" throughout the document.

25. The central theme of the federal government's refusal to contribute to infrastructure costs was discussed in the letter from Ontario Environment Minister Bud Wildman to Federal Environment Minister Jean Charest, dated 27 May 1993.

26. Burkhard Mausberg, *Still the B.A.T. for Water Quality? A Four Year Review of the Ministry of the Environment's Municipal/Industrial Strategy for Abatement (MISA)* (Toronto: Pollution Probe and the Canadian Institute for Environmental Law and Policy, 1990).

27. Although the regulations aimed for zero discharge, the actual regulatory limit was

something different. However, the facilities are required to submit plans as to how those facilities would reach zero discharge within a specified time.

28. Province of Ontario, Ministry of the Environment and Energy, "Clean Water Regulation for Ontario's Pulp and Paper Industry Becomes Law," News Release, 25 November 1993.

29. F. Inscho and M. Durfee, "The Troubled Renewal of the Canada-Ontario Agreement Respecting Great Lakes Water Quality," *Publius: Journal of Federalism* 25, no. 1 (Winter 1995): 59–61.

30. See Canadian Council of the Ministers of the Environment, *Environmental Management Framework Agreement*, October 1995. For an in-depth analysis, see report by K. L. Clark and M. S. Winfield, *The Environmental Management Framework Agreement: A Model for Dysfunctional Federalism* (Toronto: Canadian Institute for Environmental Law and Policy, Brief 96/1, February 1996).

31. See K. L. Clark and M. Winfield, "Harmonizing to Protect the Environment? An Analysis of the CCME Environmental Harmonization Process," November 1996.

32. Government of Canada, *CEPA Review: The Government Response Environmental Protection Legislation Designed for the Future, A Renewed CEPA, A Proposal* (Ottawa: The Queen's Printer, 1995).

33. Ontario Ministry of the Environment and Energy, *Responsive Environmental Protection: A Consultation Paper* (Toronto: July 1996). Also see Canadian Environmental Law Association, *Responding to the Roll-Backs* (Toronto: October 1996).

34. Ontario Ministry of the Environment and Energy, *Responsive Environmental Protection*, 52–53.

35. See Debora L. VanNijnatten "The Day the NGOs Walked Out."

36. Canada–United States Air Quality Agreement, signed 13 March 1991 in Ottawa. See Richard J. Smith and Susan Biniaz, "Beyond Dispute: An Air Quality Agreement in the Context of a Consultative Relationship," *Canada–U.S. Law Journal* 17 (1991): 421–29; Agreement between the Government of Canada and the Government of the United States of America on Air Quality, article 9.

37. The Wingspread/Dartmouth Binational Working Conference on Acid Precipitation was held at the Wingspread Conference Center, Racine, Wisconsin, on 1–5 October 1984, to consider the possible relationship between the Great Lakes Agreement and the air-quality agreement.

38. The only role of the IJC is to transmit comments received, without providing its own independent advice, comments, or recommendations. In November 1995, the IJC held hearings on progress under the accord. In addition to a number of written submissions, 14 oral presentations were made in Ottawa and one in Washington, D.C. See the IJC "Summary Response Document," December 1995.

39. See Article 10(2). The powers of the commission include:

   1. Under Article 13, the Secretariat has the ability to prepare a report for the Council on any matter within the scope of the annual programs;

2. Under Article 14, the Secretariat is empowered to receive a submission from any non-governmental organization or person asserting that a Party is failing to effectively enforce its environmental law, and then there is a process to follow upon the filing of the complaint; and

3. Under Article 22, there is a process for any Party to request consultations with any other Party regarding whether there has been a persistent pattern of failure by that other Party to effectively enforce its environmental law.

In 1996 a resolution was under consideration to "limit certain pollutants between the three countries," and a bird die-off at the Silva Creek Reservoir is being investigated ("Update on CEC Activities," October 1995).

40. Commission for Environmental Cooperation, Resolution 5/95. The four substances are mercury, DDT, PCBs, and chlordane.

41. Nevertheless, an IJC influence is present through personnel recruited at the CEC. The first U.S. director was Jean Hennessey, a former IJC commissioner. Janine Ferretti, the first Canadian director, was a former executive director of an environmental organization that had a historical presence in Great Lakes issues. The staff scientist for the CEC was the former staff scientist for the IJC in Ottawa.

42. J. J. Black, "Field and Laboratory Studies of Environmental Carcinogenesis in Niagara River Fish," *Journal of Great Lakes Research* 9 (1983): 326–34.

43. David DeVault, Paul Bertram, D. M. Whittle, and Sarah Rang, *Toxic Contaminants in the Great Lakes* (background paper for 1994 State of the Lakes Ecosystem Conference, Chicago, Environment Canada and USEPA, August 1995, EPA 905-R-95-016).

44. J. Jacobson, S. Jacobson, and P. Schwartz, "Prenatal Exposure to an Environmental Toxin: A Test of the Multiple Effects Model," *Developmental Psychology* 20, no. 4 (1984): 523–32. S. Jacobson, G. Fein, and J. Jacobson, "The Effect of Intrauterine PCB Exposure on Visual Recognition Memory," *Child Development* 56 (1985): 853–60. E. Lobnky, J. Reihman, T. Darvill, J. Mather Sr., and H. Daly, "Neonatal Behavioral Assessment Scale Performance in Humans Influenced by Maternal Consumption of Environmentally Contaminated Lake Ontario Fish, *Journal of Great Lakes Research* 22, no. 2 (1996): 198–212.

45. Peter Montague, "Chemicals and the Brain, Part 1," and "Chemicals and the Brain, Part 2," *Rachel's Environment and Health Weekly* (Environmental Research Foundation, Annapolis, Md.), 20 June 1996 and 4 July 1996.

46. Steven F. Arnold et al., "Synergistic Activation of Estrogen Receptor with Combinations of Environmental Chemicals," *Science* 272 (7 June 1996), 1489–92.

47. IJC, *Fifth Biennial Report*, 15.

48. IJC, *Sixth Biennial Report*, 18.

49. IJC, *Seventh Biennial Report*, 4–5.

50. IJC, *Eighth Biennial Report*, 11.

51. Environment Canada and the U.S. Environmental Protection Agency, *Toxic Contaminants in the Great Lakes.*

52. W. W. Bowerman, V. J. Kramer, and J. P. Giesy, "A Review of Factors Affecting Productivity of Bald Eagles in the Great Lakes Region: Implications for Recovery" (abstract from *Environmentally Induced Alterations in Development: A Focus on Wildlife*, Racine, Wisconsin, 10–12 December 1993).

53. International Joint Commission, *Third Biennial Report* (Windsor, Ontario: IJC, December 1986), 8.

54. This account of the negotiations is based on interviews with both government and NGO participants, and a paper by John Jackson, "The Negotiation of the 1987 Protocol to the Great Lakes Water Quality Agreement" (prepared for the Great Lakes Governance Project of Dartmouth College, February 1996).

55. Interview, IJC staff.

56. Interview, industry representative.

57. Confidential interviews.

58. Interview, IJC staff.

59. A. L. Hamilton, Memorandum to Commissioners, dated 15 March 1988. See also C. Ian Jackson and David Runnalls, *The Great Lakes in the 1990s: An Environmental Scan for a Renewed Canada-Ontario Agreement* (Ottawa: Institute for Research on Public Policy, July 1991), 9. The report was prepared at the request of the Ontario Ministry of the Environment and Environment Canada, 1991.

60. See chapter 2 in Gordon Durnil, "The International Joint Commission," in *The Making of a Conservative Environmentalist* (Bloomington: Indiana University Press, 1995).

61. International Joint Commission, *Task Force Report on the IJC's Roles and Priorities under the Revised Great Lakes Water Quality Agreement* (Windsor, Ontario: IJC, April 1990).

62. The original task force was reconstituted in accordance with the commission's decision at its December 1990 executive meeting, and its directives are contained in the commission's Memorandum of Understanding of 12 December 1990. The *Task Force Report on the IJC's Roles and Priorities under the Revised Great Lakes Water Quality Agreement* was discussed by the boards and council at the IJC semiannual meeting in the spring of 1990, and set the stage for a redefinition of the roles of the commission and its advisory boards. The report was then reviewed and revised by a "Reconstituted Task Force," which delivered its report in March of 1991. The document was accepted in April 1991, at a meeting in Washington, D.C., and hereafter will be referred to as the "Reconstituted Task Force Report" (International Joint Commission, *Reconstituted Task Force on Commission's Role and Priorities under the Great Lakes Water Quality Agreement* [Windsor, Ontario: IJC, 15 March 1991]).

63. IJC, Reconstituted Task Force Report.

64. Ibid., 2.

65. In the minutes to a 1991 SAB meeting, Commissioner Durnil outlined the ration-

ale for the priorities process: "In the first instance, it was the responsibility of the Commission to give direction; and in the second, there is limited funds and so the resources need to be directed and managed to address the most important issues . . . despite the considerable increase in budget over the years, the increase has not been reflected in the programs of the Boards, or used directly to address water quality matters. There was a sense then, that too much was being spent on overhead, to the detriment of program activities under the Agreement" (Minutes of the 84th Science Advisory Board Meeting, held at Burlington, Ontario, 19–21 November 1991, p. 3).

66. The *1979 Annual Report of the Water Quality Board* (Windsor, Ontario: IJC, 1979) refers to the SAB recommendations about the potential effects of acid rain within the Great Lakes ecosystem in recommending attention to this issue (50).

67. Interview, scientist.

68. Interview, former SAB member.

69. International Joint Commission, *1993–1995 Priorities and Progress Under the Great Lakes Water Quality Agreement* (Ottawa and Washington, D.C.: August 1995).

70. Paul Muldoon, personal observation.

71. For example, there was considerable interest by some board members concerning the progress of a cleanup at the General Motors site at Massena, New York. See Minutes of the 99th Meeting of the Science Advisory Board, 22 September 1995, Duluth, Minnesota.

72. IJC, Reconstituted Task Force Report, 3.

73. With new roles and responsibilities being delegated to the parties, the role for the WQB obviously had to change. It is not clear what other options were considered, but the Reconstituted Task Force Report outlined in detail the new terms of reference for the WQB (see appendix A). Appendix A is the full text of the new mandate of the WQB. The important provisions listed on p. 3 are as follows:

1. The Water Quality Board's function is to give advice on broad policy questions, including Commission priorities.

2. To provide the Commission with advice from the perspective of each member's current experience, the membership of the Water Quality Board should continue to be drawn from senior levels of federal, provincial and state government.

3. The existing substructure of the Water Quality Board should be disbanded subject to an orderly transition through October 1991 as envisaged in Section C.3 (Transition Period) below.

4. [The Water Quality Board is] to make assessments of progress on implementation of the Agreement from time to time through the Science Advisory Board, task forces or other mechanisms.

74. Great Lakes Water Quality Board, International Joint Commission, "A Shared Policy Vision for the Great Lakes: A Workshop Report of the Great Lakes Water Quality Board" (17–18 June 1991).

75. Great Lakes Water Quality Board, *Cleaning Up Our Great Lakes: A Report from the Water Quality Board to the International Joint Commission on Toxic Substances in the Great Lakes Basin Ecosystem* (Windsor, Ontario: August 1991).

76. Great Lakes Water Quality Board, International Joint Commission, *1993 Report of the Great Lakes Water Quality Board to the International Joint Commission* (Windsor, Ontario: September 1993).

77. IJC, *1993–95 Priorities and Progress*, chapter 1.

78. Confidential interviews.

79. Interviews of state representatives on WQB by Glenda Daniel.

80. Terms of Reference for the Joint Institutions and the Great Lakes Regional Office, appended to the 1978 Great Lakes Water Quality Agreement, Section 2.

81. Science Advisory Board, International Joint Commission, "The Role of the Science Advisory Board" (Conclusions of a Workshop held on 19 November 1991 at Burlington, Ontario, dated 14 January 1992), 6. Hereafter referred to as the "SAB Workshop Report."

82. James R. Ludwig, "Editorial: Science, Research, and Public Policy in the Great Lakes: Making Science Subservient to Politics on IJC Boards," *Journal of Great Lakes Research* 21, no. 2 (1995): 159. This editorial was responded to by Michael Donahue in "Commentary: The IJC and Its Advisory Boards: Setting the Record Straight," *Journal of Great Lakes Research* 21, no. 30 (1995): 405–7.

83. Interview, EPA official.

84. Interview, SAB member.

85. Minutes of the Science Advisory Board Meeting, 19 November 1992, Burlington, Ontario, 5.

86. Interview, former IJC commissioner.

87. Virtual Elimination Task Force, "Persistent Toxic Substances: Virtually Eliminating Inputs to the Great Lakes Interim Report" (Windsor, Ontario: IJC, July 1991), 6.

88. Virtual Elimination Task Force, *Persistent Toxic Substances: Report of the Virtual Elimination Task Force to the International Joint Commission, A Strategy for Virtual Elimination of Persistent Toxic Substances* (Windsor, Ontario: IJC, August 1993).

89. Terms of Reference for the Joint Institutions and the Great Lakes Regional Office, section 3(f).

90. Confidential interviews.

91. IJC, Reconstituted Task Force Report, 3.

92. Lee Botts, personal observation.

93. Don Lajoie, "IJC Backers Hold Rally To Save Windsor Office," *The Windsor Star*, 24 January 1992, A3.

94. Gary Rennie, "Proposed Changes a Threat to IJC, Ex-Official Claims," *The Windsor Star*, 24 January 1992, A3. See also Paul McKeague, "IJC Stays in Windsor, But Library Has To Go," *The Windsor Star*, 15 February 1992, A1.

95. Interviews, former IJC commissioners.

96. Interview, University of Windsor staff person.

97. Proposal for a Binational Management Framework, an Appendix to the Eighth Meeting of the Parties in Cooperation with State and Provincial Governments under the 1987 Protocol to the 1978 Great Lakes Water Quality Agreement, Summary Record, Chicago, 19 November 1991, p. 1.

98. International Joint Commission, Indicators for Evaluation Task Force, *Indicators to Evaluate Progress under the Great Lakes Water Quality Agreement* (Windsor, Ontario: IJC, April 1996).

99. Washington, D.C., 1991.

100. Lee Botts and Bruce Krushelnicki, produced by Environment Canada, the U.S. Environmental Protection Agency, Brock University, and Northwestern University, 1987.

101. Annual attendance figures provided by Great Lakes Regional Office show that attendance grew slowly in the 1970s, increased in the 1980s, and exploded from 1989 on.

102. Lee Botts, personal observation.

103. Paul Muldoon, personal observation.

104. Interviews, nongovernmental group representatives.

105. The largest national network of such grass-roots groups in the U.S. is maintained by the Citizen's Clearinghouse For Hazardous Wastes, Falls Church, Va. This organization was founded by Lois Gibbs, who had played a lead role in organizing local residents at Love Canal.

106. Confidential interview.

107. Great Lakes United, *Unfulfilled Promises*.

108. Lee Botts, personal observation.

109. Interviews, former IJC commissioners and former EPA official.

110. Interview, former EPA official. .

111. Interview, former IJC official.

112. Interviews, nongovernmental group representatives.

113. 1991 Water Quality Board report to the International Joint Commission. For example, see National Wildlife Federation and the Canadian Institute for Environmental Law and Policy, *A Prescription for Healthy Great Lakes: Report of the Program for Zero Discharge* (Washington, D.C.: National Wildlife Federation, 1991).

114. Interviews, nongovernmental group representatives.

115. Notes for Remarks by the Honorable Jean Charest, Minister of the Environment, at the Biennial Meeting of the International Joint Commission, Traverse City, Michigan, U.S.A., 1 October 1991, pp. 6 ff.

116. "A Citizens' Biennial Review of Canadian and U.S. Government Actions to Protect and Restore the Great Lakes" (prepared for the Biennial Meeting of the International Joint Commission, 21–14 October 1993).

117. Confidential interviews.

118. See "Our Lakes, Our Health, Our Future" (presentation to the International Joint Commission, Eighth Biennial Meeting, 22–25 September 1995, Duluth, Minnesota, coordinated by Great Lakes United, Buffalo, New York).

119. Remarks of T. Baldini (presentation at meeting discussing IJC Consultation Processes, 8 October 1996).

120. A number of commissioners stated this view at the 8 October 1996 consultation on the proposed new IJC's consultation plan, held in Detroit, Michigan.

121. International Joint Commission, "The International Joint Commission and Its Public: Expanding Consultation under the Great Lakes Water Quality Agreement" (discussion Paper, Washington, D.C.: IJC, September 1996), 2.

122. This view was expressed by industry representatives at an 8 October 1996 consultation on the proposed new IJC consultation plan, held in Detroit, Michigan.

123. Paul Muldoon, personal observation.

124. John Jackson, "IJC Cancels Biennial Meeting," in *Great Lakes United* 10, no. 4 (Fall 1996): 1.

125. International Joint Commission, *Fifth Biennial Report*.

126. International Joint Commission, *Eighth Biennial Report*, 13.

127. For instance, the history of the concept is discussed in depth in National Wildlife Federation and the Canadian Institute for Environmental Law and Policy, *A Prescription for Healthy Great Lakes* (1991).

128. Alana M. Fuierer, "The Anti-Chlorine Campaign in the Great Lakes: Should Chlorinated Compounds Be Guilty Until Proven Innocent?" *Buffalo Law Review* 43 (1995): 181–229; Durnil, *The Making of a Conservative Environmentalist*.

129. The contrasting views of the chlorine issue can be discerned from two appendices to the report on the Virtual Elimination Task Force. See G. N. Werezak, "A Report on Chlorine to the Virtual Elimination Task Force"; D. K. Phenecie, "Virtual Elimination in the Pulp and Paper Industry"; and T. Muir, T. Eder, P. Muldoon, and S. Lerner, "Case Study: Application of a Virtual Elimination Strategy to an Industrial Feedstock Chemical—Chlorine," in *Three Background Reports to the Virtual Elimination Task Force on the Subject of Chlorine and Organochlorines* (Windsor, Ontario: IJC, April 1993). See also John R. Ehrenfeld, "Science, Scientists and Chlorine, or It's a Wicked World Out There" (presentation to "The Future Uses of Chlorine: Symposium on the Role of the University," Massachusetts Institute of Technology, Cambridge, Massachusetts, 14–15 November 1994).

130. Interview, former IJC commissioner.

131. Interviews, former SAB chair and former IJC commissioner.

132. For example, see *Report of the Great Lakes Science Advisory Board* (1989), 71; Great Lakes Science Advisory Board, *1991 Report to the International Joint Commission*, 41.

133. International Joint Commission, Virtual Elimination Task Force Report.

134. Craig Waddell, "Saving the Great Lakes: Public Participation in Environmental Policy," in *Green Culture: Environmental Rhetoric in Contemporary America*, ed. Carl G. Herndl and Stuart C. Brown (Madison: University of Wisconsin Press, 1996), 153.

135. The IJC is mentioned in virtually every one of the numerous reports concerning a chlorine ban by industry, in scientific journals or in the general news media. See, for example, Ivan Amato, "Crusade to Ban Chlorine," *Garbage* 6, no. 2 (Summer 1994): 30–39. Gordon Durnil spoke on the subject at the 1992 United Nations Conference on Environment and Development in Rio de Janeiro, Brazil.

136. Great Lakes United, Clean Production Task Force, *Planning for the Sunset: A Case Study for Eliminating Dioxin by Phasing out PVC Plastics* (Buffalo, N.Y.: GLU, May 1995).

137. The reports from the parties began in 1989: *First Report of Canada under the 1987 Protocol on the 1978 Great Lakes Water Quality Agreement* (prepared by the Government of Canada and the Government of the Province of Ontario under the 1986 Canada-Ontario Agreement Respecting the Great Lakes Water Quality Agreement, December 1988, released on 8 February 1989); and *U.S. Progress in Implementing the Great Lakes Water Quality Agreement: Annex Reports to the International Joint Commission* (Chicago: Great Lakes National Program Office, U.S. Environmental Protection Agency, officially transmitted 7 June 1989). For an example of joint assessment, see Canada and the United States, *State of the Great Lakes* (Ottawa and Washington, D.C.: Environment Canada and the U.S. Environmental Protection Agency, 1995).

138. Minutes from the Binational Executive Committee Meeting, at Rosemont, Illinois, 19 May 1994.

139. For example, see "Summary Record of the Eighth Meeting of the Parties in Cooperation with State and Provincial Governments under the 1987 Protocol to the 1978 Great Lakes Water Quality Agreement," 19 November 1991, at Chicago, Illinois.

140. See "Proposal for a Binational Management Framework," Minutes from the Binational Executive Committee Meeting, 19 November 1991, p. 2.

141. See Minutes of the Binational Executive Committee Meeting, 19 May 1994, p. 1.

142. Binational Executive Committee, "Draft Discussion Paper, Great Lakes Binational Executive Committee: Roles and Responsibilities" (Binational Executive Meeting, 9 March 1995).

143. See NRC/RSC, *The Great Lakes Water Quality Agreement*, p. 48, for discussion of the differences between the Canadian and the U.S. approach to regulation of direct municipal and industrial discharges.

144. Interview, former EPA official.

145. Environment Canada and U.S. Environmental Protection Agency, "Canada–United States Strategy for the Virtual Elimination of Persistent Toxic

Substances in the Great Lakes Basin" (Draft for Consultation, August 1995).

146. For example, see the letter from Mark Winfield of the Canadian Institute of Environmental Law and Policy to Ron Shimizu of Environment Canada and Chris Grundler of the U.S. Environmental Protection Agency, dated 25 September 1995.

147. Minutes, Binational Executive Meeting, 19 May 1994, p. 3.

148. Governments of the United States of America and Canada, *State of the Great Lakes 1995* (Burlington/Chicago: USEPA and Environment Canada, 1995).

149. Environment Canada and U.S. Environmental Protection Agency, "Nearshore Waters of the Great Lakes," "Impacts of Changing Land Use," "Integration Paper," and "Information and Information Management" (draft background papers for the State of the Lakes Ecosystem Conference '96, Windsor, Ontario, 6–8 November 1996).

150. International Joint Commission, Indicators for Evaluation Task Force, White Paper, "Indicators to Evaluate Agreement Progress," 4 May 1995.

151. Indicators for Evaluation Task Force, International Joint Commission, *Indicators to Evaluate Progress under the Great Lakes Water Quality Agreement* (Ottawa and Washington, D.C.: IJC, April 1996.

152. Confidential interviews.

153. This section is based on Neely Law and John Jackson, "A Report on the Remedial Action Plan Process in the Great Lakes" (prepared for the Great Lakes Governance Project of Dartmouth College, March 1996).

154. J. H. Hartig, and M. A. Zarull, eds., *Under RAPs: Toward Grassroots Ecological Democracy in the Great Lakes Basin* (Ann Arbor: University of Michigan Press, 1992).

155. J. H. Hartig, *Practical Steps to Implement an Ecosystem Approach in Great Lakes Management*, Proceedings of Workshop in November 1994 (Windsor, Ontario: USEPA and Environment Canada with the IJC and Wayne State University, 1995).

156. Law and Jackson, "A Report on the Remedial Action Plan Process," 16.

157. Tim Brown, Lake Michigan Forum; Martin Visnosky, Lake Erie Forum; Tim Bendig, Lake Ontario Forum, personal communications at SOLEC 96.

158. United States Environmental Protection Agency, Great Lakes National Program Office, "Lake Michigan Forum Lakewide Work Plan, 1996–1998," November 1996.

159. Ibid, 6. Like the earlier Green Bay Mass Balance Study, whose techniques are being used for the larger-scale whole-lake program, the Lake Michigan Mass Balance Study is intended to identify and quantify all sources of toxic contaminants into the lake and how they are cycled within the ecosystem. The purpose is to help set priorities for control measures.

160. Environment Canada and U.S. Environmental Protection Agency, "Information and Information Management," (draft background paper, State of the Lakes Ecosystem Conference '96, Windsor, Ontario, 6–8 November 1996), 46.

161. Letter to Michael Donahue, Executive Director, Great Lakes Commission, signed

by representatives of Great Lakes United, the Lake Michigan Federation, Sierra Club, National Audubon Society, Citizens for a Better Environment, and Northwatch, 10 June 1994.

162. Interviews, IJC staff and commissioner.

Chapter 6. The Continuing Evolution of the Great Lakes Regime from 1997 to 2005

1. House Bill 2720 and Senate Bill 1398, both introduced on 14 July 2003.

2. "Summary Results of Conference on Renegotiation of the Great Lakes Water Quality Agreement," Wingspread Conference Center, Johnson Foundation, Racine, Wisconsin, 21–13 January 2004.

3. All the Great Lakes states and Ontario issue health advisories to the public against consumption of certain fish because of unsafe levels of toxic contaminants, but the advisory statements are not consistent with each other and are publicized in different ways. Agreement on a uniform health advisory has not been reached in spite of widespread agreement about the need and efforts by the USEPA to work with the states and the Great Lakes Fishery Commission for this purpose.

4. U.S. Environmental Protection Agency, "Great Lakes Contaminated Sediments: Realizing Remediation II," available at . In 2002, contaminated sediments had been removed at about half the 41 U.S. sites awaiting cleanup in the Great Lakes basin at a cost of over $300 million.

5. International Association for Great Lakes Research, *Research and Management Priorities for Aquatic Invasive Species*, Great Lakes Science and Management Policy Project, Ann Arbor, Michigan, 15 November 2002.

6. Great Lakes Beach Conference, Beach Public Health Protection and Management Forum, sponsored by the U.S. Environmental Protection Agency, Office of Water and Region 5, and the City of Chicago, 6–8 February 2001, Chicago, Illinois.

7. International Association for Great Lakes Research, *Linking Science and Policy for Urban Nonpoint Source Pollution in the Great Lakes Region*, Great Lakes Science and Policy Project, Ann Arbor, Michigan, November 2002.

8. George Kling et al., *Confronting Climate Change in the Great Lakes Region: Impacts on Our Communities and Ecosystems* (Cambridge, Mass.: Union of Concerned Scientists and Ecological Society of America, April 2003).

9. Belden, Russonello, and Stewart, *Protecting the Great Lakes: Responsibility to Awareness to Action: Analysis of Public Opinion in the Great Lakes States for the Biodiversity Project and the Joyce Foundation* (Washington, D.C.: October 2002).

10. Robert F. Kennedy Jr., "Crimes Against Nature," *Rolling Stone*, 11 December 2003, 1.

11. The "Canada-Wide Accord on Environmental Harmonization" called for a number of subagreements, although only three were signed: the Canada-Wide Agree-

ment on Standard-Setting, the Canada-Wide Agreement on Environmental Assessment, and the Canada-Wide Agreement on Inspections and Enforcement.

12. A Canada-Wide Standard is more analogous to a set of objectives than a regulation. It is up to the jurisdiction how to implement the standard, e.g., as a voluntary measure, an economic instrument, or a regulation. For standard-setting, eight substances were selected to be given priority under the agreement, including dioxins and furans, mercury, etc. For each substance, a federal-provincial process was initiated to identify priority emission categories or uses and then develop "Canada-wide standards" for that substance. Either the provincial or the federal governments would be assigned to further these standards.

13. For a critique of the agreement, see Canadian Environmental Law Association (Brief 332) and the Canadian Institute for Environmental Law and Policy, "Brief to the House of Commons Committee on Environment and Sustainable Development," the CCME Harmonization Initiative, October 1997. The Canadian Environmental Law Association challenged the legality of the agreement. Although unsuccessful, the court did raise a number of concerns about the agreements. See Canadian Environmental Law Association v. Canada (Minister of the Environment) *Canadian Environmental Law Reports* (New Series) 34 (2000), p. 159 (Federal Court of Appeal), confirming the decision that can be found at: *Canadian Environmental Law Reports (New Series)* 30 (1999), p. 59 (Federal Trial Division).

14. Since 1998, it is fair to say that there had been some discernible progress in discrete areas, such as dioxins and furans for incinerators. However, funding for CCME itself had declined over the years, reducing its own capacity; timelines fell by the wayside; and few, if any, new priorities or tasks under the agreements were assigned to the processes under the agreement. Hence, while the harmonization agreements remain, the enthusiasm for them significantly diminished.

15. Department of Foreign Affairs and International Trade, "Canada Announces Coming into Force of Amendments to International Boundary Waters Treaty Act," news release, 10 December 2002.

16. The report was triggered following the release of the International Joint Commission's Sixth Biennial Report (Ottawa and Washington, D.C.: IJC, March 1992).

17. Ibid.; and "Review of the Great Lakes Water Quality Agreement by the Governments of Canada and the United States" (draft scoping paper discussed at the Binational Executive Committee Meeting, 30 July 1998), 1.

18. International Joint Commission, Ninth Biennial Report on Great Lakes Water Quality (Ottawa and Washington, D.C., 1998), 3.

19. Binational Executive Committee, Summary Record, 30 July 1998, p. 2. The scoping paper was attached to the Summary Record. See "Review of the Great Lakes Water Quality Agreement by the Governments of Canada and the United States," (draft scoping paper, 30 July 1998).

20. For those that have argued for a focused agreement, see M. Gilbertson, *Can. J.*

Fish. Aquat. Sci. 54: 483–95 and "Are Causes Knowable? Some Consequences of Successional Versus Toxicological Interpretation of the Great Lakes Water Quality Agreement." For a contrary point of view, see Charles K. Minns and John R. M. Kelso, "Now It is Time for a Great Lakes Ecosystem Management Agreement that Subsumes the Great Lakes Water Quality Agreement," *J. Great Lakes Res.* 26, no. 1 (1999): 1–2; and W. W. Bowerman et al., "Editorial: Is It Time for Great Lakes Ecosystem Management Agreement to Separate from the Great Lakes Water Quality Agreement," *J. Great Lakes Res.* 25, no. 2 (2000): 237–38. The Water Quality Board in 1995 proposed that the agreement should formally recognize the concept of pollution prevention. See Water Quality Board in *1993–1995 Priorities and Progress under the Great Lakes Water Quality Agreement* (International Joint Commission, 1995).

21. 1996–1997 Binational Report on the Protection of the Great Lakes Water Quality to the IJC (October 1997) See also "Review of the Great Lakes Water Quality Agreement by the Governments of Canada and the United States" (draft scoping paper discussed at the Binational Executive Committee Meeting, 30 July 1998), "Attachment No. 2."

22. Binational Executive Committee, Summary Record, 30 July 1998, p. 2.

23. Review of the Great Lakes Water Quality Agreement, 3 February 1999. BEC Annex 1 (specific chemical objectives), Annex 2 (RAPs and LaMPs), Annex 3 (control of phosphorus), and Annex 11 (surveillance and monitoring) were deemed to be high priority for review. Medium priority were Annex 7 (dredging), Annex 10 (hazardous polluting substances), Annex 12 (persistent toxic substances) and Annex 14 (contaminated sediments). The coast guards would be requested to comment on annexes related to their mandates: Annex 4 (discharge of oil/hazardous substances), Annex 5 (discharge of wastes), Annex 8 (discharge from onshore/offshore facilities), Annex 9 (Joint Contingency Plan), and Annex 10 (hazardous polluting substances). Expert groups were assigned to each of the annexes for the purposes of conducting the review.

24. Binational Steering Committee with support from Designated Annex Leads and Their Expert Advisors, *Draft Options Paper to the Binational Executive Committee on the Review of the Canada/U.S. Great Lakes Water Agreement,* July 1999. Binational Executive Committee, Summary Record, 21–22 July 1999, p. 5.

25. Binational Executive Committee, Summary Record, 21–22 July 1999, p. 8.

26. In a 23 March 2000 letter directed to "Great Lakes Colleagues," J. Charles Fox, USEPA Assistant Administrator for the Office of Water, and Francis X. Lyons, National Program Manager, Great Lakes National Program Office, noted that "Under the auspices of the Binational Executive Committee, we expect to continue to review the effectiveness of the Agreement, but [at] a lower priority."

27. Irene Brooks, Chair, Great Lakes Commission, in a letter directed to Hon. Carol Browner and Hon. David Anderson, 31 January 2000, urged an "open, objective

and thorough review," and then serious consideration "of any prospective amendment to the agreement and annexes that may arise from the review."

28. Science Advisory Board, "Review of Annex 1 of the Great Lakes Water Quality Agreement," (a workshop sponsored by the Parties' Implementation Work Group of the Science Advisory Board of the International Joint Commission in collaboration with the Great Lakes Commission, held at the Michigan League, Ann Arbor, Michigan, 21 March 2001). Available at .

29. Interview, nongovernmental observer.

30. Binational Executive Committee, "IJC-Parties Reporting Requirements under the Great Lakes Water Quality Agreement" (2002).

31. Binational Executive Committee, Decision/Action Item Report, 5–6 December 2002, p. 1.

32. The history of the negotiations are outlined in John Buccini, "The Long and Winding Road to Stockholm: The View from the Chair," in *Northern Lights Against POPs: Combatting Toxic Threats in the Arctic*, ed. David Leonard Downie and Terry Fenge (Montreal and Kingston: McGill-Queen's University Press, 2003), 224–55. A chronology is provided in David Downie and Mike Kraft, "Appendix 2: POPs Science and Policy: A Brief Northern Lights Timeline," in Downie and Fenge, 276–83.

33. For example, International Joint Commission, *Seventh Biennial Report on Great Lakes Water Quality* (Ottawa and Washington, D.C., 1994), 13–14.

34. See United Nations Environment Program website at *http://www.chem.unep.ch/pops/* for the following:
    • Stockholm Convention Homepage,
    • Canada POPs Fund,
    • POPs related Global Environmental Facility Projects,
    • Proceedings, Reports and Documents,
    • Information on POPs, their Alternatives and Alternative Approaches, and
    • POPs Global Monitoring Programme.
    See the Stockholm Convention website at for meeting reports, etc. For Convention text, see *http://www.pops.int/documents/context/context_en.pdf.* Also see Peter L. Lallas, "The Role of Process and Participation in the Development of Effective International Environmental Agreements: A Study of the Global Treaty on Persistent Organic Pollutants (POPs)" *J. of Environmental Law* 19 (2000/2001): 83.

35. There is little doubt that the toxic threats in the Arctic were a primary motivation for the push for a global solution to the problem of persistent organic pollutants. A valuable source of information in this regard is David Leonard Downie and Terry Fenge, eds., *Northern Lights Against POPs: Combatting Toxic Threats in the Arctic*, supra. It is interesting to note that John Buccini, who chaired the international negotiations, did not recognize the Great Lakes as a key rationale or a source of influence for the initiation or negotiation of the treaty. See Buccini, "The Long and Winding Road to Stockholm: The View from the Chair," in Downie and

Fenge, supra, although he agreed a strong scientific basis on the problem aided the negotiations (252–53). However, in a chronology of events leading to the negotiation, Great Lakes activities were clearly recognized; see David Downie and Mike Kraft, "Appendix 2: POPs Science and Policy: A Brief Northern Lights Timeline," in Downie and Fenge, supra, 276–83.

36. The seven negotiating sessions were: Montreal, Canada, 1998 (INC1); Nairobi, Kenya, 1999 (INC2); Geneva, Switzerland, 1999 (INC3); Bonn, Germany, 2000 (INC4); Johannesburg, South Africa, 2000 (INC5); Stockholm, Sweden, 2001 (Conference of Plenipotentiaries); Geneva, Switzerland, 2002 (INC6) and Geneva, Switzerland, 2003 (INC7).

37. Lee Botts, personal observation.

38. *Statutes of Canada*, chapter 33.

39. A review of these issues can be found in Canadian Environmental Law Association (Brief 346), Presentation to the House of Commons Standing Committee on Environment and Sustainable Development With Respect to Bill C-32, the Canadian Environmental Protection Act, 2 June 1998.

40. Hon. Dennis R. O'Connor, *Report of the Walkerton Inquiry*, part 1, *The Events of May 2000 and Related Issues* (January 2002); Hon. Dennis R. O'Connor, *Report of the Walkerton Inquiry*, part 2, *A Strategy for Safe Drinking Water* (May 2002).

41. *Report of the Walkerton Inquiry*, part 1, 414–16. These numbers exclude the persons working for the Ontario Clean Water Agency before and after its creation.

42. Safe Drinking Water Act, Statute of Ontario 2002, c. 32. The Safe Drinking Water Act and other regulatory instruments arising from the implementation from the Walkerton inquiry can be found at *www.env.on.ca.gc/water.html*.

43. Advisory Committee on Watershed-based Source Protection, *Final Report: Protecting Ontario's Drinking Water: Toward a Watershed-Based Source Protection Planning Framework*, April 2003.

44. Province of Ontario, *White Paper on Watershed-based Source Protection Planning*, 12 February 2004.

45. *2002 Report of the Commissioner of the Environment and Sustainable Development to the House of Commons, Great Lakes and St. Lawrence Basin*, chapter 1, "A Legacy Worth Protecting: Charting a Sustainable Course in the Great Lakes and St. Lawrence River Basin" (Minister of Public Works and Government Services Canada, 2001).

46. Ibid., 9.

47. Ibid., 17.

48. Ibid., 28, 288.

49. Ibid., 33.

50. Ibid., 30.

51. Ibid., 30.

52. Ibid., 36.

53.   Environment Canada, "Great Lakes Action Plan 2001–2006," found at *www.on.ec.gc.ca/water/greatlakes/action-plan*.

54.   Interview, Environment Canada official.

55.   Background material, "Integrated Water Resource Management and Great Lakes Program Renewal Workshop" (4–5 March 2004, Toronto, Ontario), table 1.

56.   Background material, "Integrated Water Resource Management and Great Lakes Program Renewal Workshop," table 4, pp. 9–11.

57.   Office of Air Quality Planning and Standards, Research Triangle Park, N.C, EPA-453/R-00-005.

58.   U.S. Environmental Protection Agency, Office of Air Quality Planning and Standards, "Deposition of Air Pollutants to the Great Waters: First Report to Congress, May 1994, EPA-453/R-93-055"; "Deposition of Air Pollutants to the Great Waters: Second Report to Congress, June 1997, EPA-453/R-97-011"; and "Deposition of Air Pollutants to the Great Waters: Third Report to Congress, June 2000, EPA-453/R-00-005." The website is *www.epa.gov/oar/oaqps/gr8water/*.

59.   Personal communication to Lee Botts.

60.   "Great Lakes Ecosystem Report 2000," (Chicago: USEPA, Great Lakes National Program Office, January 2001).

61.   Ibid, E1.

62.   This report is available at *www.epa.gov/glnpo/solec/*.

63.   The SOLEC reports are available at *www.epa.gov/glnpo/solec/*.

64.   GAO, "Great Lakes: EPA Needs to Define Organizational Responsibilities Better for Effective Oversight and Cleanup of Contaminated Areas," GAO-02-563, May 2002.

65.   International Joint Commission, *The Status of Restoration Activities in the Great Lakes Areas of Concern* (Windsor, Ontario: IJC, April 2003).

66.   Editorial, *Port Clinton News Herald*, 5 February 2004.

67.   U.S. Policy Committee, *Great Lakes Strategy 2002: A Plan for the New Millennium* (2002), 1.

68.   Ibid., 4.

69.   Ibid., 3.

70.   Interview, USEPA official.

71.   Letter to Ted Smith, GLNPO, "Great Lakes Groups' Comments on the Draft U.S. Great Lakes Strategy," coordinated by the National Wildlife Federation, Great Lakes Natural Resources Center, Ann Arbor, Mich., 31 July 2001.

72.   Ibid., 1–2.

73.   GAO, "Great Lakes: An Overall Strategy and Indicators for Measuring Progress Are Needed to Better Achieve Restoration Goals," GAO-03-515, April 2003.

74.   GAO, "A More Comprehensive Approach Is Needed To Clean Up the Great Lakes," CED-82-83, 21 May 1982.

75.   GAO report, 2002.

76. USEPA, "EPA's Great Lakes Program," EPA/OIG Report 99P00212 (Washington, D.C., 1 September 1999.

77. GAO, "Great Lakes," April 2003, p. 47.

78. Hearing record on CD provided by GLNPO.

79. Comprehensive Everglades Restoration Plan (CERP), Water Resources Development Act of 2000, PL 106-541.

80. Associated Press report, 22 May 2003, dateline Washington, D.C.

81. Lee Botts, personal observation.

82. Lee Botts, personal observation.

83. Council of Great Lakes Governors, "Principles for the Management of Great Lakes Water Resources: A Supplementary Agreement to the Great Lakes Charter" (Chicago: CGLG, 18 June 2001).

84. Letter to Hon. Michael DeWine, United States Senate, on Council of Great Lakes Governors letterhead, signed by the governors of the eight Great Lakes states, expressing appreciation for introduction of the legislation and saying, "We welcome the opportunity to join you in building momentum for this historic advance. . . ." (1 October 2003).

85. "Mayors' Statement: Great Lakes Protection and Restoration Plan," presented at the Great Lakes Mayors' Initiative 2002 workshop on "Great Lakes, Great Ideas," 5 November 2002.

86. Paul Muldoon, personal observation.

87. The Nature Conservancy, Great Lakes Program, "Conservation of Biodiversity in the Great Lakes Basin Ecosystem: Issues and Opportunities," (Chicago, Ill.: January 1994).

88. Great Lakes United, "The Great Lakes Green Book: Summary of a Citizens' Action Agenda for Restoring the Great Lakes–St. Lawrence River Ecosystem (Buffalo, N.Y.: GLU, June 2003).

89. Lee Botts, personal observation.

90. Lee Botts, personal communication.

91. See www.glc.org/restore/.

92. Cangelosi, Allegra, "Great Lakes Restoration," *Economic Review of the Northeast-Midwest Institute* (Fall 2003).

93. Pollution Probe, "Managing Shared Waters Resource Kit," 24 June 2002.

94. Personal communications to Lee Botts and Paul Muldoon.

95. Interviews, USEPA and Environment Canada officials.

96. "Great Lakes Binational Executive Committee: Roles and Responsibilities," 9 March 1995, with Proposed Revisions, July 1998, pp. 1–2.

97. Issue Note, 21–22 July 1999.

98. International Joint Commission, *Fifth Biennial Report on Great Lakes Water Quality*, 7.

99. "Canada–United States Strategy for the Virtual Elimination of Persistent Toxic

Substances in the Great Lakes (1997)," found at *www.glbts.html*.

100. The Level 1 substances include mercury, polychlorinated biphenyls (PCBs), dioxins and furans, hexachlorobenzene (HCB) and benzo(a)pyrene (B(a)P), octachlorostyrene (OCS), alkyl-lead, and five pesticides: chlordane, aldrein/dieldrin, DDT, mirex, and toxaphene.

101. Progress reports with respect to these goals can be found at *www.glbts.html*.

102. As of 1 December 2003, the latest report is U.S. Environmental Protection Agency and Environment Canada, *Great Lakes Binational Toxics Strategy: 2002 Progress Report* (undated). In May 2002, the governments also put out a summary document covering the first five years. See Environment Canada and U.S. Environmental Protection Agency, *The Great Lakes Binational Toxics Strategy: Five Year Perspective* (May 2002).

103. For example, the Canadian Environmental Law Association made a conscious decision not to participate in the processes under the strategy. Also see Great Lakes United, "Eliminating Long-lived Poisons from the Great Lakes: Recommendations for Year Two Under the Binational Toxics Strategy," statement read by Margaret Wooster, Great Lakes United, at the meeting of stakeholders of the Binational Toxics Strategy Meeting, Chicago, 16 November 1998. In recent years, fewer environmental groups have maintained their participation in the processes, questioning whether the program adds value to existing programs of the government. Interview, environmental group representative.

104. "Review of Progress Under the Canada–United States Great Lakes Binational Toxic Strategy," in *A Report to the Great Lakes Water Board by the Progress Review Work Group* (13 November 2001). This report was forwarded to the commission chairs by the co-chairs of the Water Quality Board by way of a letter of transmittal dated 29 November 2001.

105. Ibid., appendix A.

106. The consultant's report is a lengthy, in-depth report that contains 45 recommendations. Thompson, Gow & Associates, "Evaluation of the Canada–United States Great Lakes Binational Toxics Strategy," final report prepared for the Binational Toxics Strategy Progress Review Work Group and the International Joint Commission, 12 July 2001.

107. "Review of Progress Under the Canada–United States Great Lakes Binational Toxic Strategy," in *A Report to the Great Lakes Water Board by the Progress Review Work Group*, 10.

108. Ibid., 12.

109. Ibid., 10.

110. Ibid., 12.

111. Ibid., 11.

112. International Joint Commission, *Eleventh Biennial Report on Great Lakes Water Quality* (September 2002), 58–60.

113. These reports can be found in Environment Canada and USEPA, *State of the Lakes Ecosystem Conference Peer Review Report*, 7–8 October 2003, dated November 2003. For a current review of the SOLEC activities, see *www.epa.gov/glnpo/ solec/solec_2004/index.html*.

114. Mark Winfield and Greg Jenish, *Troubled Waters? A Review of the Performance of the Governments of Canada and Ontario under the 1994 Canada-Ontario Agreement Respecting the Great Lakes Basin Ecosystem*, 1999.

115. Canada-Ontario, *Canada-Ontario Agreement Respecting the Great Lakes Basin Ecosystem*, 22 March 2002.

116. Personal communication with Environment Canada official.

117. Two other appointments include Irene Brooks and Allen Olson.

118. International Joint Commission, *Ninth Biennial Report on Great Lakes Water Quality* (Ottawa and Washington, D.C., 1998.) See the following graphs: "Trends in Phosphorus Loadings" (c. 4), and "Trends in Toxics Loadings" (c. 6).

119. International Joint Commission, *Tenth Biennial Report on Great Lakes Water Quality* (Ottawa and Washington, D.C., 2000).

120. International Joint Commission, *Eleventh Biennial Report on Great Lakes Water Quality* (Ottawa and Washington, D.C., 2002).

121. Interview, Canadian environmental activist.

122. Binational Executive Committee, *Lake Huron Binational Partnership*, 20 June 2002.

123. Binational Executive Committee, *BEC Consensus Position on the Role of LaMPs in the Lake Restoration Process*, 22 July 1999.

124. Ibid., 2.

125. International Joint Commission, *Tenth Biennial Report on Great Lakes Water Quality*, 6.

126. John Jackson, "Summary of Findings on LaMPs," memo to Paul Muldoon and Lee Botts, 28 March 2004, p. 1.

127. "Funding for Cleanup Programs Gets Axed," *St. Catharine's Standard*, 10 February 1997.

128. Statewide Public Advisory Council, *Michigan Areas of Concern News* (Fall 2000), 1.

129. International Joint Commission, *The Status of Restoration Activities in the Great Lakes Areas of Concern*, April 2003, 3.

130. U.S. Policy Committee, *Great Lakes Strategy 2002: A Plan for the New Millennium*, (April 2002), 32.

131. Canada-Ontario, *Canada-Ontario Agreement Respecting the Great Lakes Basin Ecosystem* (March 2002), 11.

132. Canada-Ontario, *Draft: Policy Regarding Change in RAP Status to "Area of Natural Recovery,"* September 1997; USEPA, *Draft: Restoring United States Areas of Concern: Delisting Principles and Guidance*, June 2001.

133. John Jackson, "Summary of Findings on RAPs," memo to Paul Muldoon and Lee Botts, 28 March 2004, p. 2.

134. International Joint Commission, *The Status of Restoration Activities in the Great Lakes Areas of Concern*, 18.

135. International Joint Commission, *Tenth Biennial Report on Great Lakes Water Quality*, ii.

136. Ibid., 2–3. For an example of concerns raised by members of public-advisory committees, see Michigan Statewide Public Advisory Council, *An Action Agenda for Restoring Michigan's Great Lakes Toxic Hot Spots*, March 2003.

137. Lake Superior Binational Program, "Protecting Lake Superior Lakewide Management Plan: Stage 2—Load Reduction Targets for Critical Pollutants," 1999.

138. Lake Superior Binational Program, *Lake Superior Lakewide Management Plan (LaMP) 2000: Summary Edition* (April 2000), 13–14. According to this report, the 60 percent reduction target that was met for mercury was because of the closure of two plants in the Lake Superior basin: the iron-sintering plant in Wawa, Ontario, and the Copper Range smelter in White Pine, Michigan.

139. John Jackson, memo to Paul Muldoon and Lee Botts, "The Lake Superior Zero Discharge Demonstration Project," January 2004, pp. 3–4.

140. See Lake Superior Work Group, "Lake Superior Task Force Issue Paper: Pollutant Load Reductions," 12 September 2000, p. 1; Lake Superior Task Force, "BEC Decision Paper: Great Lakes Mercury Reductions," 20 May 2001; and Chemical Committee of Lake Superior Work Group, "Lake Superior LaMP Zero Discharge Demonstration Program (ZDDP) Discussion Paper," December 2003.

141. Jane Reyer, Senior Counsel, National Wildlife Federation, letter to Robert Browne and Nick Lewis, Co-chairs, Lake Superior Binational Forum, 8 November 2003.

142. Dr. Michael J. Donahue, "The Case for Good Government: Why a Comprehensive Review of the Great Lakes Water Quality Agreement is Needed," *Toledo Journal of Great Lakes' Law* 2, no. 1 (Fall 1999): 1–11.

143. Lee Botts and Paul Muldoon, "A Survey of Stakeholders' Views with Respect to the Review of the Great Lakes Water Quality Agreement," submitted to Environment Canada, March 2003.

144. Lake Michigan Federation and the Canadian Environmental Law Association, *Summary Results of Wingspread Conference on Renegotiation of the Great Lakes Water Quality Agreement*, 21–23 January 2004, p. 2.

145. In February 2003, the Science Advisory Board of the IJC held a workshop on emerging issues. The summary emanating from this workshop can be found in *Priorities Report under the Great Lakes Water Agreement, 2001–2003*, chapter 5, "Emerging Great Lakes Issues in the Twenty-first Century."

146. "Review of the Great Lakes Water Quality Agreement: Background Material for the Great Lakes Binational Executive Committee," 14–15 January 2004, Niagara Falls, Ontario.

147.   Great Lakes Binational Executive Meeting, "Action Item Report," 14–15 January 2004, Niagara Falls, Ontario, pp. 2–3.

148.   Environment Canada/USEPA, *Developing a Proposed Process for the Review of the Great Lakes Water Quality Agreement and Great Lakes Water Quality Agreement Proposed Review Process, 2004.*

149.   See article written by SAB co-chair Dr. Michael J. Donahue, "The Case for Good Government: Why a Comprehensive Review of the Great Lakes Water Quality Agreement is Needed," *Toledo Journal of Great Lakes' Law* 2, no. 1 (Fall 1999), 1–11.

150.   Science Advisory Board, *Priorities Report under the Great Lakes Water Agreement, 2001–2003*, presented at the 2003 Biennial Meeting of the International Joint Commission, 18 September 2003.

151.   International Joint Commission, "Great Lakes Declaration," 2003 Great Lakes Conference and Biennial Meeting, Ann Arbor, Michigan, 20 September 2003.

152.   Presentation to the Standing Committee on Environment and Sustainable Development, by the Right Honourable Herb Gray, Chair, Canadian Section, International Joint Commission, 7 October 2003; available at *www.ijc.org/rel/comm/gray031007-e.htm.*

153.   International Joint Commission, *Focus* 28, no. 2 (Autumn/Winter 2003): 2.

154.   Pollution Probe, *Recommendations on the Review of the 1987 Canada–United States Great Lakes Water Quality Agreement (GLWQA), Phase I Report* (Ottawa, 9 September 2003).

155.   See "Science and the Great Lakes Water Quality Agreement" (workshop held at The Michigan League, Ann Arbor, Michigan, 4–6 February 2004).

156.   Based on observations and notes by Paul Muldoon, participant at the workshop.

Chapter 7. Past Successes and New Challenges

1.   Interviews, IJC and government-agency staffs, environmental leaders.

2.   Environics Research Group, "Great Lakes Public Opinion Survey" (prepared for Environment Canada, March 2004). Nelden, Russonello, and Stewart, "Protection of the Great Lakes: Responsibility to Awareness to Action: Analysis of Public Opinion in Great Lakes States for the Biodiversity Project and the Joyce Foundation," October 2002.

3.   See "Specific Objectives Supplement to Annex 1" (section 2) of the 1987 Protocol of the Great Lakes Water Quality Agreement.

4.   Terms of References for the Joint Institutions and the Great Lakes Regional Office, 3(b)(ii).

5.   On 9 July 2002, the *Windsor Star* carried a story with the headline "Lake Erie 'Dead Zone' Getting Worse: Scientists Confused," quoting Jan Ciborowski, a biologist at the University of Windsor. In 2002, Ciborowski headed a special summer research program funded by the USEPA to assess changing conditions in Lake Erie. See *www.epa.gov/glnpo/lakeerie/eriedeadzone.html.*

6. International Joint Commission, *Phosphorus Management for the Great Lakes*, final report of the Phosphorus Management Strategies Task Force to the International Joint Commission's Great Lakes Water Quality Board and the Great Lakes Science Advisory Board (Windsor, Ontario: IJC, July 1980), 64–66.

7. Lee Botts, personal observation.

8. Gulls, food wastes, and animals were all reported as having been identified as contributors of fecal *E. coli* bacteria on swimming beaches at the 2001 Great Lakes Beach Conference, "A Beach Public Health, Protection, and Management Forum," sponsored by the U.S. Environmental Protection Agency, Office of Water and Region 5, and the City of Chicago, 6–8 February 2001, Chicago, Illinois.

9. Ibid.

10. Phil Weller, *Fresh Water Seas: Saving the Great Lakes* (Toronto, Ontario: Between the Lines, 1990).

11. NRC/RSC, *The Great Lakes Water Quality Agreement*, 105. See also Lynton K. Caldwell, "Implementing an Ecosystem Approach," in *Perspectives on Ecosystem Management*.

12. Revised Great Lakes Water Quality Agreement of 1978.

13. J. Jacobson, S. Jacobson, and P. Schwartz, "Prenatal Exposure to an Environmental Toxin: A Test of the Multiple Effects Model," *Developmental Psychology* 20, no. 4 (1984), A523–32; S. Jacobson, G. Fein, and J. Jacobson, "The Effect of Intrauterine PCB Exposure on Visual Recognition Memory, *Child Development* 56 (1985), pp. 853–60; E. Lobnky, J. Reihman, T. Darvil, J. Mather Sr., and H. Daly, "Neonatal Behavioral Assessment Scale Performance in Humans Influenced by Maternal Consumption of Environmentally Contaminated Lake Ontario Fish, *J. Great Lakes Research* 22, no. 2 (1996), pp 198–212.

14. Theodora E. Colborn, Dianne Dumanoski, and John Peterson Myers, *Our Stolen Future* (New York: Dutton, 1996).

15. See *Atmospheric Deposition of Toxics to the Great Lakes: Integrating Science and Policy* (a report by the Delta Institute, Chicago, Illinois, 2000).

16. Interview, industry spokesman.

17. See *www.pops.int/documents/implementation*.

18. The annual "Taking Stock" reports from the CEC provide the most comprehensive accounting of the use of toxic substances for North America. See Commission for Environmental Cooperation of North America, *Taking Stock 2000: North American Pollutant Releases and Transfers* (Montreal, April 2003). See also *www.cec.org/files/pdf/pollutants/smoc-overviewupdate.2002*.

19. See 1996 SOLEC background papers at *www.epa.gov/glnpo/solec*.

20. William K. Reilly, "Aiming Before We Shoot: The 'Quiet Revolution' in Environmental Policy" (address to the National Press Club, Washington, D.C., 26 September 1990).

21. Jane Elder, "The Big Picture: The Sierra Club's Critical Ecoregions Program,"

Sierra Club Magazine 79, no. 2 (March/April 1994).

22. The first report for a LaMP was the Lake Michigan Lakewide Management Plan, published by the Water Division of Region 5, USEPA, in draft form in January 1992.

23. See *www.glc.org/*.

24. Great Lakes Aquatic Habitat Network and Fund, "Reflections of Success: Stories of Successful Projects from the Field," *Tip of the Mitt Watershed Council*, vol. 3, 2003.

25. Lake Michigan Federation, "Lake Michigan Biodiversity Recovery Support Document," Urban Aquatic Habitat Summit, 3 November 2000.

26. *Great Lakes Aquatic Habitat News* 10, no. 2 (March/April 2002), 12.

27. See *www.epa.gov.glnpo/ecopage/glbd/issues*.

28. See *www.epa.gov/glnpo/ecopage/glbd/cwplan/*.

29. See *www.epa.gov/grtlakes/lakemich/* and *www.epa.glnpo/lakeerie/*.

30. Lake Michigan Watershed Academy, co-sponsored by the Great Lakes Commission, the Lake Michigan Federation, the Lake Michigan Forum, the Lake Michigan LaMP Partners, the Northeastern Illinois Planning Commission, Western Michigan University, and the USEPA, Kalamazoo, Michigan, 12–14 March 2003.

31. *See www.glfc.org/pubs/specialpubs/strategicvision2001*.

32. See *www.nemw.org/gldivert121103_naftzger*.

33. See *www.cgli.org/*.

34. See *www.wildlifehbc.org*.

35. International Joint Commission, *Seventh Biennial Report*, 40.

36. See *www.epa.gov/med/grosseile_chronology.html*.

37. NRC/RSC, *The Great Lakes Water Quality Agreement*.

38. For details about the study, see Thomas J. Murphy, "The U.S. EPA and Science of the Great Lakes," *J. of Great Lakes Research* 22, no. 1 (1996): 1–4.

39. Interview, environmental leader.

40. See *www.iaglr.org*.

41. Thomas Heidtke, William Sonzogni, and Lee Botts, *Great Lakes Environmental Planning Study: Summary Report* (Ann Arbor, Mich.: Great Lakes Basin Commission, September 1981).

42. For a detailed review and case studies, see Paul Muldoon, *Cross Border Litigation: Environmental Rights in the Great Lakes Ecosystem* (Toronto: Carswell, 1986).

43. See *www.state.gov/r/pa/ei/bgn/2089.html*.

44. Interviews, government-agency staffs, IJC staff, and environmental leaders.

45. Lee Botts and Paul Muldoon, personal communication,.

46. Interviews, IJC staff.

47. Policy Solutions Ltd., "Great Lakes Restoration and Protection Priorities: An Overview of Programs, Funding Streams, and Critical Gaps Prepared for the Council of Great Lakes Governors," 5 May 2004.

48. Colborn et al., *Great Lakes, Great Legacy.*

49. See International Joint Commission, Great Lakes Science Advisory Board, *1993 Report to the International Joint Commission* (Windsor, Ontario: IJC, October 1993) for a historical overview of how toxic contamination was addressed to that point.

50. Interviews, IJC staff.

51. Jackson, John, "Improving Interconnections Between Scientists and Citizen Activists" (presentation to Science Advisory Board, IJC 12th Biennial Meeting, Ann Arbor, Michigan, 18 September 2003).

52. Interviews, agency staff and environmentalist participants in RAPs.

53. International Joint Commission, *Eighth Biennial Report*, 3.

54. Mike Quigley, "Editorial: The Best and Worst of Times," *Journal of Great Lakes Research* 21, no. 4 (1995), 409.

55. The position of the Great Lakes Water Quality Coalition against the proposed Great Lakes Water Quality Initiative was spelled out in an undated position paper about 1992 when the organization's headquarters was located in Cleveland, Ohio. This paper is in the files of the Lake Michigan Federation in Chicago, Illinois.

56. K. H. Nicholls and G. J. Hopkins, "Recent Changes in Lake Erie (North Shore) Phytoplankton: Cumulative Impacts of Phosphorus Loading Reductions and the Zebra Mussel Introduction," *Journal of Great Lakes Research* 19, no. 4 (1993): 637–47.

57. Environment Canada, U.S. Environmental Protection Agency, Background Paper on Nearshore Waters of the Great Lakes, State of the Lakes Ecosystem Conference, Windsor, Ontario, 6–8 November 1996, p. 119.

58. Ibid.

59. See *Journal of Great Lakes Research* 21, no. 4 (1995), Special Section on Zebra Mussels in the Saginaw Bay, Lake Huron Ecosystem; contains 11 articles on the history of colonization and effects of zebra mussels.

60. Personal communication at Wingspread conference, January 2004.

61. Mark van Putten, founder and director of the National Wildlife Federation's Great Lakes Resources Center, became president of the National Wildlife Federation in 1996. Jane Elder, founder and director of the Sierra Club's Great Lakes Program, became head of the national Biodiversity Consortium.

62. The role of research is described in a summary of results of A Public Forum on the Future of Great Lakes Science organized by John Gannon and John Hartig at the 1995 Biennial IJC meeting in Duluth, Minnesota. This was published in the *Lakes Letter* 27, no. 1 (April 1996) (Ann Arbor, Mich.: International Association of Great Lakes Research). John Gannon and John Hartig, *A Public Forum on the Future of Great Lakes Science: A Summary*, held at the IJC biennial meeting on 24 September 1995 in Duluth, Minnesota.

63. Personal communication at the January 2004 Wingspread conference.

64. The Commission for Environmental Cooperation is a trilateral agency that

involves Mexico as well as the parties to the Great Lakes Water Quality Agreement, and was established under the environmental side agreement to the North American Free Trade Agreement of 1994.

65. Review is required following every third biennial report of the IJC to the governments. In 1993, the IJC and the governments agreed to continue the Great Lakes Agreement as it was amended by the 1987 Protocol.

GLOSSARY

Advisory board. A panel appointed to provide advice to the IJC as specified in the Boundary Waters Treaty or the Great Lakes Water Quality Agreement.

Annex. A section appended to the Great Lakes Water Quality Agreement on a specific topic.

Area of Concern. An area identified by the IJC where failure to achieve objectives of the Great Lakes Water Quality Agreement has resulted in impairment of one or more of 14 beneficial uses. The agreement outlines the phases for remediation in Annex 2.

Atmospheric deposition. Deposit of pollutants from the atmosphere in rain or snow, through vapor exchanges or deposition of particles.

Bilateral. Separate actions taken by two different parties to achieve common ends.

Binational Executive Committee. A binational committee managed by the U.S. Environmental Protection Agency and Environment Canada, with members representing federal, state, and provincial governments, that meets twice yearly under terms of the 1987 Protocol.

Binational. A institution or activity in which representatives of two countries serve the joint interests, rather than the individual interests, of the separate nations.

Bioaccumulation. Sequestration of metals or chemicals in living tissue, such as PCBs in fatty tissue, that increase over time with continued exposure.

Blue Group. The informal consortium of environmental organizations that consult and strategize with each other on Great Lakes issues.

Canada-Ontario Agreement. An agreement between the Canadian federal government and province of Ontario that pertains to commitments between the two levels of government intended to further the goals of the Great Lakes Agreement.

Connecting channels. The rivers and canal that connect the five Great Lakes, including the St. Marys, St. Clair, Detroit, and Niagara rivers, and the Welland Canal.

Contaminated sediments. Particles of matter on the bottoms of water bodies that contain toxic pollutants.

DDT. Dichloro-diphenyl-trichloroethane, a persistent pesticide whose use for most purposes has been banned in Canada and the United States.

Diversion. Transfer of water from one watershed to another.

Drainage basin. A hydrologic system and the land that drains into it.

Ecological integrity. "When the physical, chemical and biological components of the waters of the Great Lakes Basin Ecosystem are restored and maintained in an unimpaired condition" (IJC, *Eighth Biennial Report*).

Ecosystem. The system of relationships between living organisms and the place, or environment, that they inhabit, including humans.

Ecosystem approach. A management concept that considers effects on the relationship between organisms and their environment in an ecosystem, rather than a single medium such as air, water, or land.

Effluent. Waste water discharged from a source such as industry or a municipal sewage-treatment plant.

Eutrophication. The status of a body of water where increase of minerals and organic nutrients favors growth of plants.

Exotic species. Species that are not native to an ecosystem, but are present because of deliberate or accidental introduction.

Great Lakes Regional Office. The office established under the Great Lakes Water Quality Agreement to assist in implementation.

Great Lakes basin. The geographic area in Canada and the United States that drains into the Great Lakes.

Great Lakes basin ecosystem. The ecosystem within the drainage basin of the Great Lakes and St. Lawrence River, upstream from the international boundary between Canada and the United States.

Invasive species. An exotic or non-native species that competes destructively with native species for food and habitat.

Lakewide Management Plans. Management plans that the Great Lakes Water Quality Agreement requires to be developed for the open waters of each of the five Great Lakes.

Limiting nutrients. The critical nutrient whose presence in excessive amounts triggers algae growth as a sign of accelerated eutrophication, which is phosphorus in the Great Lakes.

Nongovernmental. A person, an organization, or an institution that is not an official part of government.

Nonpoint-source pollution. Pollution from a diffuse source where pollutants reach waterways from a wide area or from many small sources, rather than a single distinct identifiable source.

Parties. The governments that are signatories to the Great Lakes Water Quality Agreement, or the agencies that represent them in the implementation process.

PCBs. A class of persistent organic chemicals that bioaccumulate.

Persistent bioaccumulative contaminants. Toxic contaminants that both do not decompose readily and bioaccumulate in living tissues, and that can affect the health of living organisms. As defined in the Great Lakes Water Quality Agreement, a chemical with a half-life of over eight weeks.

Persistent organic pollutants. Chemicals that persist in the environment for a long period of time and bioaccumulate in the fat cells of living organisms.

Point-source pollution. A distinct identifiable source from which pollution is discharged directly into the environment, such as a discharge pipe.

POPs Treaty. The Stockholm Convention on Persistent Organic Pollutants concluded in May 2001.

Precautionary principle. A principle that is a current or emerging norm of international law that states that governments should not avoid taking measures to prevent harm, even though there is scientific uncertainty.

Regime. The interacting participants and institutions that operate under a mutual agreement in accordance with accepted rules or values to achieve common goals.

Reverse onus. A requirement that the user or discharger of a pollutant be required to demonstrate that the substance does not damage the health or well-being of living organisms.

Sunsetting. A process leading to a phaseout of the generation or use of a persistent toxic substance.

Toxic contaminants. As defined in the Great Lakes Water Quality Agreement, substances that affect the health or well-being of living organisms.

Watershed management planning. A process of developing a management plan for a specific watershed.

Weight of evidence. "A decisionmaking approach that takes into account the cumulative body of evidence, scientific and otherwise, with the extent of the potential consequences, to reach a conclusion on the need for action against environmental contaminants" (IJC, *Eighth Annual Report*).

INDEX